Japan's National Security

Japan's National Security

*Structures, Norms and Policy Responses
in a Changing World*

Peter J. Katzenstein
and
Nobuo Okawara

East Asia Program
Cornell University
Ithaca, New York 14853

The *Cornell East Asia Series* publishes manuscripts on a wide variety of scholarly topics pertaining to East Asia. Manuscripts are published on the basis of camera-ready copy provided by the volume author or editor.

Inquiries should be addressed to Editorial Board, Cornell East Asia Series, East Asia Program, Cornell University, 140 Uris Hall, Ithaca, New York 14853.

Table of Contents

List of Tables and Figures

Tables

Figures

Abbreviations

ABM	Anti-Ballistic Missile
ACDA	Arms Control and Disarmament Agency
ASDF	Air Self-Defense Force
ASEAN	Association of Southeast Asian Nations
ASW	Anti-Submarine Warfare
AWACS	Airborne Warning and Control System
CINCPAC	Commander-in-Chief, Pacific
CIST	Center for Information on Strategic Technology
COCOM	Coordinating Committee on Export Controls
DARPA	Defense Advanced Research Projects Agency
DoD	Department of Defense
DPC	Defense Production Committee
DSP	Democratic Socialist Party
EPA	Economic Planning Agency
FHI	Fuji Heavy Industries
FSX	Fighter Support Experimental
GSDF	Ground Self-Defense Force
IDDN	Integrated Defense Digital Network
IEA	International Energy Agency
IPRA	Industrial Problems Research Association
JAEI	Japan Aviation Electronics Industry
JCP	Japan Communist Party
JDA	Japan Defense Agency
JDIA	Japan Defense Industry Association
JMTC	Joint Military Technology Commission
JNOC	Japan National Oil Corporation
JOA	Japan Ordnance Association
JSC	Joint Staff Council
JSP	Japan Socialist Party

KHI	Kawasaki Heavy Industries
LDP	Liberal Democratic Party
MAAG-J	Military Assistance Advisory Group-Japan
MHI	Mitsubishi Heavy Industries
MITI	Ministry of International Trade and Industry
MLRS	Multiple Launch Rocket System
MOF	Ministry of Finance
MOFA	Ministry of Foreign Affairs
MSA	Maritime Safety Agency
MSDF	Maritime Self-Defense Force
MTDPE	Mid-Term Defense Program Estimate
NATO	North Atlantic Treaty Organization
NDC	National Defense Council
NDPO	National Defense Program Outline
NICs	Newly Industrializing Countries
NORAD	North American Air Defense
NPA	National Police Agency
NPT	Non-Proliferation Treaty
ODA	Official Development Assistance
OTA	Office of Technology Assessment
PARC	Policy Affairs Research Council
PDPC	Petroleum Development Public Corporation
PMO	Prime Minister's Office
RIMPAC	Rim of the Pacific Exercise
SAC	Strategic Air Command
SAM	Surface-to-Air Missiles
SCAP	Supreme Commander for the Allied Powers
SCC	Security Consultative Committee
SDC	Subcommittee for Defense Cooperation
SDF	Self-Defense Forces
SDI	Strategic Defense Initiative
SDIO	Strategic Defense Initiative Organization
SEATO	Southeast Asia Treaty Organization
SOFA	Status of Forces Agreement
SSM	Surface-to-Ship Missile
STA	Science and Technology Agency
SWNCC	State-War-Navy Coordinating Committee
TRDI	Technical Research and Development Institute
WWMCCS	World-wide Military Command and Control System
VTOL	Vertical-Take-Off-and-Landing

Preface

This monograph focuses on a subject that, with the end of the Cold War, will become of growing importance for Asian and international politics. The disintegration of the Soviet Union and the rapid rise of Japan as an economic power raise important questions about the manner in which the Japanese government will define and defend Japan's national security. An analysis of the Japanese military can teach us much about the organization of power in contemporary Japan and the form of democracy that has evolved in Japan since the end of World War II. And a study of the Japanese military should also help us gauge more accurately the character of the Japanese state, a controversial subject among specialists and policymakers alike.

This monograph offers a description of the organizational structures and norms that shape Japan's policy of external security. It traces the institutional and political relations that link various governmental actors within the state, with domestic society, and with a variety of transnational structures; it analyzes the legal and social norms that help actors define the interests that inform policy; and it seeks to explain Japan's economic, military and political security policies during the last two decades.

This monograph is part of a broader set of studies that seek to explain Japan's security policies in recent years. This explanation will be based on two comparisons: with Japan's policy of internal security on the one hand [Katzenstein and Tsujinaka, 1991] and with Germany's policies of internal and external security on the other [Katzenstein, 1989 and 1990]. A comparison with Japan's internal security policy is a useful complement to this monograph's focus on the military and external security. It should help us relate our conclusions about Japan to those reached in numerous studies of Japan's political economy. The comparison with Germany may reveal those elements that are distinctive of Japan's approach to security. And it should tell us something about the two states that, having benefitted from the end of the Cold War, will have a growing influence in world politics.

Our work has been helped immeasurably by a large number of individuals—government officials, scholars, members of the business community and journalists—who were willing to provide us in a large number of interviews with data and insights on the issue of Japan's security. We are particularly grateful for the help and support which Professor Seizaburo Sato has given us throughout the project. We are also much in debt to a number of individuals who read and commented on earlier drafts of this study: Reinhard Drifte, Takashi Inoguchi, Robert Keohane, Shigekatsu Kondo, Mike Mochizuki, Masashi Nishihara, Dan Okimoto, Hideo Otake, T.J. Pempel, Richard Samuels, Takashi Shiraishi, Robert Smith, Akihiko Tanaka, Yutaka Tsujinaka and Keiichi Tsunekawa. Their critical comments and suggestions were extremely helpful even when, at our own risk, we chose to disregard them.

This research was made possible in part by a grant of the German Marshall Fund of the U.S. to Peter Katzenstein.

We are very grateful to the research assistance of Francis Adams, Bronwyn Dylla, Kozo Kato, Marc Lynch, Roy Nelson and Thaveeporn Vasavalkul. And we are also very much in debt to Bronwyn Dylla, Kenna March and Karen Smith who helped us to prepare this manuscript for publication. Finally, we would like to thank Cornell's East Asia Program for its willingness to include this monograph in Cornell's East Asia Series.

Ithaca
August 1992

Peter J. Katzenstein
Nobuo Okawara

I
Introduction

The end of the Cold War in Europe, the crisis in the Mideast over Iraq's annexation of Kuwait, and the disintegration of the Soviet Union as a major pole in world politics signal a momentous change in the structure of the international system. The traditional political coordinates which helped us to understand global politics in the era of bipolarity no longer suffice. A number of potential nuclear threshold states exist inside the former Soviet Union which is confronting serious internal security threats and the prospect of fragmentation. The United States won a decisive military victory in the Gulf War. And it succeeded in extracting the necessary resources from its allies, in part because the United States was not able to fund itself the deployment of American forces in Saudi Arabia in 1991. With the disintegration of the Soviet Union, the United States remains as the only superpower in global politics. But growing economic and social problems at home are limiting its capacities in ways that are not characteristic of traditional conceptions of superpower status.

This change in international politics raises important questions about Japan's future role in the international system. In July 1991 a Japanese public opinion poll reported that, with the end of the Cold War, for the first time since 1945, a larger number of Japanese saw the United States rather than the Soviet Union as the primary threat to Japanese security [Wall Street Journal, 1991]. After the end of the Cold War where is Japan heading? Pessimists believe that Herman Kahn's prediction of 1970 will finally be proven correct; Japan will quickly evolve into a superstate with nuclear weapons [Kahn, 1970]. And to support their worst fears they may point to books such as Edwin Hoyt's grim description of the rise of militarism in Japan in the 1970s and 1980s [Hoyt, 1985]. Even less sensational and alarmist analyses see substantial change as inevitable. In a book called The New Superpowers Jeffrey Bergner discusses Japan and Germany and argues

1

that, at a minimum, "Japan's budgetary capabilities will lead inevitably to a far larger Japanese military role" [Bergner, 1991, p.111].

Optimists, on the other hand, believe that the foundations of an enduring Pacific Community have been laid during the last three decades. In a draft of its first comprehensive assessment of the world after the Cold War the Pentagon argues that the break-up of the Soviet Union has concealed a less visible victory, "the integration of Germany and Japan into a U.S.-led system of collective security and the creation of a democratic 'zone of peace'" [New York Times, 1992, A14. Tyler, 1992]. In that view Japan will continue to aspire to be the Switzerland of Asia, a competitive, noninterventionist trading state that heeds the universal interest of peace and profit rather than narrow aspirations for national power [Bobrow, 1984, p.38]. When he was Director of the Japan Defense Agency in 1970, Yasuhiro Nakasone expressed this view before a presumably receptive American audience. "Japan does not want to hang on to the outdated concept that economic great powers must necessarily become military great powers. Nor do we want to adopt the philosophy that in order to become a great power, we must possess nuclear arms" [Emmerson, 1971, p.2. Mendel, 1970, p.1046]. Americans, under the umbrella of the British Royal Navy, thought before World War I that they were no longer part of the imperialistic politics of the Old World. Similarly "many present-day Japanese would like to think that they have parted with old Imperial ways and with the complications of world power politics, while enjoying peace and security under the Pax Americana" [Okazaki, 1982a, p.192].

Neither of these two visions is intellectually compelling. The case for the inevitability of a nuclear-armed, militarist Japan is just as implausible in the light of all we know about contemporary Japan as is the notion that Japan will be the first and only example in history of a state wielding huge economic and technological power without corresponding military might. This monograph develops a third line of argument instead. The future will be neither a repeat of the past, as the pessimists fear, nor a total break with it, as the optimists would have it.

But how should we think about the future? What will be the evolution of Japan's domestic structure and the subordinate role that the military has played within it? Will the changes that are affecting Japan's position in the international system weaken the relationship with the United States through the intensification of economic, political and eventually perhaps military competition? Or will these changes make the U.S.-Japan relationship more equal and link the two states in a security partnership and in advantageous economic competition in global markets? And how will the norms that help the Japanese define their standards of behavior evolve? To answer these questions we need to study empirically how Japan is organized for the exercise of power, how it defines its security interests and what the consequences of organization and definition are for its political choices.

The analytical perspective we adopt shapes profoundly our answers to these questions. Students of national security often rely on arguments that look to the structure of the international system as the key determinant of national strategy. The conventional wisdom among foreign policy experts on Japan's security policy exemplifies this type of analysis. The consequences of the end of the Cold War, according to this line of argument, are much more consequential in Europe than in Asia. While the Cold War in Europe defined the balance of power along clear lines of division between East and West, in Asia this split was only one among many. The collapse of Communism and the disintegration of the Soviet Union thus has created much less compelling incentives for a change in Japan's security policy than is true for European states such as Germany. Indeed, the outbreak of detente on the central front in Europe is viewed especially by members of the Self-Defense Forces (SDF) as harmful to Japan's security. For it has enabled Russia to redeploy its forces in the Asian theater thus threatening Japan more directly [Takahara, 1992, p.22]. In short, in focusing on the regional balance of power this analysis seeks to account for the conservative and incremental responses of Japan's security policy [Inoguchi, 1991c. Schmiegelow and Schmiegelow, 1990. Rapkin, 1990. Kosaka, 1989. Mochizuki, 1990, 1991a, 1991b].

An alternative formulation of this analytical perspective focuses on a different aspect of the regional balance of power and comes to dramatically different conclusions. George Friedman's and Meredith Lebard's recent book argues that war between the United States and Japan is inevitable [Friedman and Lebard, 1991]. For them geography is destiny: "Japan's politics has been governed by its geography" [Friedman and Lebard, 1991, p.259]. Both the United States and Japan are naval powers. The United States needs to control the sealanes because of its expansive notion of self-defense. Japan needs to control the sealanes because of its dependence on the import of virtually all important raw materials. Japanese vulnerability and American assertiveness will make the break between the two countries inevitable. A showdown is inevitable, since Japan cannot permanently subordinate itself to America's political demands, and since America cannot forego naval supremacy as its most important military asset [Friedman and Lebard, 1991, pp.160-88, 255-56, 259, 269, 290, 300, 324, 400-01]. If it were a question of morality the fault would probably lie more with the United States than with Japan [Friedman and Lebard, 1991, p.xiv]. But this conflict does not involve moral questions. "The struggle between Japan and the United States, punctuated by truces, friendships, and brutality, will shape the Pacific for generations. It will be the endless game about which the philosophers have written, the game of nations—the war of all against all" [Friedman and Lebard, 1991, p.403].

Friedman's and Lebard's prose relies very heavily on the verb "must." In their Hobbesian world a country's security policy is dictated by the international conditions in which it finds itself. Japan and the United States have no meaningful choices to make. Objective forces shape experience and consciousness [Friedman and Lebard, 1991, p.278]. The domestic determinants of foreign policy thus are of little consequence. Applied to Japan this reasoning sees rationality everywhere. The mentality of business, for example, is warlike; and the Liberal Democratic Party (LDP) adopts a finely honed sense of strategic rationality in its approach to national security issues [Friedman and Lebard, 1991, pp.154, 337]. Applied to the United States this analysis uncovers profound irrationalities. The U.S. navy does not exercise its power over the high seas because brute interference with free trade is objectionable to America's moral principles; and relinquishing overseas naval bases, for example in the Philippines, is a catastrophic blunder rooted in the failure of appreciating the future threats in the Pacific [Friedman and Lebard, 1991, pp.255-56, 396]. Why morality and stupidity should be an attribute only of American politics is a question never posed, let alone answered. For a Hobbesian world determines national security policy and thus vitiates the necessity of having to understand domestic politics.

A third and final type of explanation of Japan's security policy seeks to avoid that mistake by highlighting the effect different international regimes have on Japan. These regimes are shaped not only by the distribution of international capabilities, as in the view of the systemic theories just reviewed, but also by international institutions, international processes and transnational politics which help define the normative basis of international order. For the past, this analytical perspective makes a sharp distinction between the unforgiving power politics that characterized Western imperialism before 1945 and the beneficial effects of American hegemony after 1945 [Iriye, 1991]. For the future, this perspective distinguishes between a variety of different international orders, including a reassertion of American leadership, Pax Nipponica, Japan's continued playing the role of supporter state, and a new "bigemony" uniting the United States and Japan in the exercise of joint leadership of an emerging Pacific Community [Inoguchi, 1986. 1991a, pp.155-77]. And a perspective stressing the importance of international regimes offers Japan the prospect of assuming gradually a position of international leadership on particular issues thus smoothing the period of transition in global politics.

This modified realist or institutionalist perspective offers important insights. It is intuitively plausible. Beyond the distribution of capabilities which is so central to systemic perspectives, it incorporates international institutions and processes as well as transnational politics that affect both the interests and norms informing international regimes. Furthermore, this perspective appears to account for a very important difference in Japanese foreign policy before and after 1945. In the era of Western imperialism before 1945, Japanese security policy adopted the norms and rules of the game of power politics which then prevailed. After 1945, by way of contrast, Japan was shielded by the effect of American hegemony and could deemphasize the military component of its security policy. The advantages of modified realism with its focus on international institutions are thus worth the sacrifice in parsimony that systemic theorists value so highly. Modified realism points us in the right direction. We need to analyze the structures and processes which shape the interests and norms that characterize different international regimes.

But applied to the foreign policy of states, modified realism suffers from a potentially serious flaw. A focus on international institutions and processes is often insufficient for explaining foreign policy choices unless the domestic structures and norms that help establish and support international orders are included explicitly in the analysis. Japanese security policy, for example, was relatively peaceful in the 1920s. And it was militarist in the 1930s and 1940s. These dramatically different security policies occurred, however, in the same international order marked by the preeminence of Western imperialism in a multipolar international system. The focus on international regimes thus points in the right direction, toward the study of institutional structures and norms that help shape the interests of actors. But, applied to the analysis of foreign policy choices, it needs to pay close attention to the domestic and transnational structures and norms that inform policy choice.

Analytical perspectives that focus attention exclusively or predominantly at the level of the international system, we can conclude, suffer from serious weaknesses if we wish to understand the security policies of particular states. We are reminded of these limitations by the fact that different variants of systemic explanations yield contradictory predictions about Japan's security policy. Systemic analyses point to the incentives which the international system created for virtually no change in policy (in the analysis of Asia's regional balance of power), dramatic change in policy (in the analysis of the U.S.-Japan relationship), and incoherence in policy (in the swing from a pacifist to a militarist Japanese foreign policy in the 1930s). Closer attention to the domestic and transnational structures and norms may help in circumventing these difficulties.

Although the end of the Cold War in Asia was not as dramatic as in Europe, the disintegration of the Soviet Union and the end of Communism in Russia signals a sharp break in the structure of the international system and initiates a period of transition and change. The Japanese government is not alone in reacting with confusion and uncertainty to these changes. But act it must. Japan's security policy, we argue in this monograph, is influenced not only by international but also by domestic factors: (1) the structure of the state broadly conceived, including its transnational dimension, and the incentives it provides on the one hand, and (2) the context of social and legal norms, most of them domestic, which help define policy interests and the standards of appropriateness for specific policy choices.

The organization of the Japanese state has made it virtually impossible, short of a domestic political revolution, for an autonomous and powerful military establishment to emerge in Japan. Inside the government the military is fenced in by a number of institutional procedures that severely circumscribe the access military professionals have to the centers of political power. The principle of civilian control is so firmly entrenched that the failed attempt by the famous Japanese writer Yukio Mishima in 1970 to get the SDF to rise against the status quo appeared to most Japanese like a personal tragedy of the postwar economic miracle rather than a return to the militarist politics of the 1930s. The structure of state-society relations in Japan isolates the military from a public which, at best, can muster no more than passive tolerance for the armed forces. In Japan's defense economy, however, government-business relations are excellent, and the same is true of the economic sectors that are responsible for supplying the Japanese economy with the raw materials, particularly oil, to keep the wheels of industry turning. Finally, the transnational relations between the Japanese and the American militaries have grown increasingly close during the 1980s and have made the Self-Defense Forces de facto a junior partner in the strategic mission of the U.S. armed forces in East Asia.

The second main determinant of Japan's security policy is the normative context, both social and legal, in which the government develops its security policies. To the Japanese it is self-evident that where possible the country's very substantial economic vulnerability, as shown by its reliance on the import of raw materials, should be reduced. Similarly uncontroversial is the idea that Japan should strive for technological autonomy as an important goal, both for its intrinsic merits and as a useful mechanism for reducing Japan's dependence on raw materials. This consensus on issues of Japan's economic security contrasts starkly with the continued contest over the norms that should inform Japan's military security policy. An anti-militarist public climate continues to mark debates on military issues, reinforced by the provisions of Japan's Peace Constitution. At the same time it is also true that Japan's public has gradually come to accept the necessity of a small national defense and has quietly assented in the 1980s to a substantial build-up of the SDF and an increasingly close defense cooperation with the United States. Finally, issues which touch on Japan's political security—most prominently Japan's relation with the United States in all of its economic, military and diplomatic dimensions—fall between these two extremes. They show neither full consensus nor deep contestation but political disagreements and debate.

The normative context in which policy choices are debated is not only a set of individual predispositions. It reflects also collective learning from the memories of the Pacific War and the experience of postwar reconstruction and prosperity brought about by antimilitarist policies. The lessons of the past have been institutionalized in Japan's political life in the relations betweeen political parties, interest groups, the bureaucracy and the media. The interplay between social and legal norms permits a "flexible" interpretation of the requirements of particular situations that facilitates a redefinition of Japanese interests, often from short-term to long-term interest, which informs its security policy. In sum, norms affecting Japan's security are uncontroversial on issues of economic security, contested on issues of military security and debated on questions of Japan's political security.

Shaped by both structures and norms, Japan's national security policy has two distinctive aspects deserving attention. First, Japan's definition of national security goes far beyond traditional military notions. National security is viewed in "comprehensive" terms. That is, it focuses also on economic and political dimensions. Military security is pursued mainly within the context of the U.S.-Japanese political relationship, and is part and parcel of Japan's quest for the social stability and economic growth that success in international markets has brought. This monograph argues that the structure of the Japanese state explains the comprehensive character of Japan's security policy. The second feature of Japan's security policy worth explanation is the mixture of "flexibility" and "rigidity" which marks the process of policy adaptation to change. In this monograph the terms "flexibility" and "rigidity" are used as analytical devices. They do not reflect any particular policy orientation. On questions of economic security both structures and norms point to flexibility while on military issues they encourage policy rigidity. It is the political issues of security that are analytically most interesting. They show much greater adaptability on military issues, such as the changing mission and deployment of the SDF, than on economic ones, such as the export of militarily relevant technologies to the United States. The apparent contradiction is resolved by the normative context of policy. What matters then is not the economic or military content of policy but its normative context. When norms are consensual on economic or military issues, policy adjustment is quite easy. When norms are contested on military or economic issues, policy adjustment is more difficult.

In contrast to a plethora of writing on Japanese political economy, the existing scholarship written in English on Japan's security policy is quite small. At its best it consists of a small number of monographs and edited volumes [Weinstein, 1971. Emmerson, 1971. Kosaka, 1973. Auer, 1973b. Scalapino, 1977. Okimoto, 1978a. Satoh, 1982. Chapman, Drifte and Gow, 1982. Akao, 1983. Vogel, 1984. Olsen, 1985. Okazaki, 1986. McIntosh, 1986. Holland, 1988. Kosaka, 1989. Makin and Hellmann, 1989. Drifte, 1990a. Maul, 1991. Inoguchi, 1991a], chapters in edited volumes [Buck, 1975. Fukui, 1977. Endicott, 1982a. Sato, 1986. Umemoto, 1988. Rapkin, 1990], and a few excellent articles [Curtis, 1981. Mochizuki, 1983/84. Nishihara, 1983/84. Bobrow, 1984. Johnson, 1986. Bobrow and Kudrle, 1987. Kurth 1989. Tanaka, 1990. Schmiegelow and Schmiegelow, 1990. Samuels, 1991]. The existing literature is both widely scattered and surprisingly uniform. Typical are edited volumes and policy-relevant articles based on current information and, occasionally, interview data. In addition there exist more specialized literatures on changes in Japanese public opinion [Emmerson and Humphreys, 1973. Mendel, 1975. Umemoto, 1985. Hook, 1988. Bobrow, 1989] and the evolution of legal doctrines on defense issues [Haley, 1988. Van de Velde, 1987. Beer, 1989]. And very recently a number of studies have focused on the economic and technological aspects of Japan's national security policy [Samuels and Whipple, 1989. Vogel, 1989. Samuels, 1991. Pempel, 1990a. U.S. Congress, 1990, 1991. Friedman and Samuels, 1992].

Broadly speaking scholarly analyses in Japanese language dealing with Japan's security are also sparse. Because of the abhorrence which the Japanese public felt about all military matters after 1945 and because of the intense partisan conflict over the Security Treaty and the SDF, national security has been a marginal subject for intensive scholarly inquiry in Japan. It is no accident that the term "economic security" found its way easily into public discourse in the 1970s. By contrast "military security" has never been a broadly accepted term. The late 1970s saw a widespread recognition of a growing military threat from the Soviet Union. Yet even then the preferred term was "comprehensive security" rather than "military security" [Umemoto, 1989, pp.128-29]. For some analysts used the term "comprehensive security" to refer primarily to economic security [Sato, 1989, p.167]. This political environment explains why the number of Japanese specialists working on questions of military security remains very small even today. The sparseness of the Japanese literature on military security can also be attributed to the narrow range of Japan's postwar security options [Inoguchi, 1988, p.156]. Furthermore since the prewar military monopolized security studies, there is no tradition of military security studies in universities [Okazaki, 1990a, pp.208-09]. Finally, weak threat perceptions have been reinforced by Japan's relatively sheltered position since 1945, as well as the political consensus that identification of threats itself must factor in the effect of military defense on "Japan's postwar political structure" and "the new basic identity of its postwar political life" [Umegaki, 1988, p.62].

Put briefly, this monograph argues that Japan's national security policy is not simply determined by the structure of the international system. International structures create options and constraints that are affected by their interplay with domestic structures. A conceptualization that focuses on the organization of government, state-society relations and transnational relations as three elements of structure is not able, by itself, to explain fully Japan's national security policy. While it points to the major structural determinants of Japan's comprehensive security policy it does little to account for the mixture of flexibility and rigidity that characterizes the process of policy adaptation. For the interests that we can derive from structures are plastic and can be conceived in different ways, depending on the normative context, both social and legal, in which they are placed. Without an understanding of that context interest-based explanations of Japan's security policy remain incomplete. When international structures change as rapidly as they have in the late 1980s actors will define the objectives and modalities of their political strategies partly in response to the cues that domestic and transnational structures provide. But they also pay attention to the standards of appropriateness that the normative context of thought and action suggests to them. An understanding of the politics by which norms are, and are not, contested is thus particulary important in such situations.

This monograph analyzes both the international and domestic politics of Japan's national security policy. After establishing briefly the historical background of Japan's national security before 1945 in Part 2, it describes the organizational place which the Defense Agency (JDA) occupies inside Japan's government, analyzes the relationship between Japan's military, the public and business, and charts the relations between the military and transnational structures, specifically the United States in Part 3. Part 4 analyzes the context of social and legal norms in which security policy is formulated. Part 5 gives an analysis of the content and change of Japan's economic, military and political security policy during the last two decades. Part 6 offers a brief summary of the major findings.

II

The Japanese Military and National Security before 1945

Between 1868 and 1945 Japan waged four major wars, interspersed with frequent military operations overseas. It was a participant in international power politics based on military capabilities. The state structure in which Japan's prewar military was embedded, the links between the military and civil society, and the social norms these links engendered favored a forceful articulation of military objectives.

The prewar military enjoyed a privileged legal status within the state. Article 11 of the Meiji Constitution of 1889 stipulated that the Emperor had "the supreme command of the Army and Navy." This article was widely interpreted as placing the function of military operations outside of the Cabinet's authority. Article 11 was regarded as enunciating the "principle of the independence of the supreme command" [Hosoya, 1976, p.28]. In the earliest years of the Meiji government the functions of military operations and administration had been integrated in ministry-level organizations. Under the influence of the Prussian model, the General Staff was separated from the Army Ministry in 1878. The newly independent General Staff was given all authority in war, and chief authority in peacetime, over matters pertaining to military operations. After a series of reorganizations in the 1880s, the Navy General Staff was finally separated from the Navy Ministry in 1893 [Yui, Fujiwara, and Yoshida, 1989, pp.488-95]. Thus, as far as military operations were concerned, the two Chiefs of Staff were formally independent from the Cabinet, and even from the Ministers of the Army and Navy. In the 1940s, as Prime Minister and Army Minister, Hideki Tojo faced considerable difficulties in controlling Army operations. Also in the 1940s, the Liaison Conference, composed of key Cabinet members and the Chiefs and Deputy-chiefs of Staff, was unable to function as a cohesive decision making body. In the area of military operations, Chiefs of Staff were directly responsible to the Emperor, while in the area of military

11

administration, they were under the authority of the Ministries of the Army and Navy [Hosoya, 1971, p.97. Maxon, 1957, p.24. Shillony, 1981, p.10].

The original rationale underlying the independence of the supreme command was to insulate the military from politics. Concerned in particular with the growing Popular Rights Movement, early Meiji leaders attempted in a variety of ways to keep the military from being politicized. The "Admonition to the Military" issued by the Army leader Aritomo Yamagata in 1878 and the "Rescript to Soldiers and Sailors" of 1882 warned against the military getting involved in politics. The Army and Navy Penal Laws made political activities by military personnel a criminal offense. The Regulations for Public Meetings and Associations issued in 1880 prohibited military personnel in active service or in the first or second reserves from joining political associations and attending political meetings. The Imperial ordinance of 1890, which granted suffrage to parts of the population, excluded military men, along with priests, religious teachers, and the insane. In a well-known episode, General Tateki Tani, in 1889, spoke out against the government's foreign policy and was forced off the active list. Article 11 of the Constitution thus was one manifestation of the Meiji leaders' determination to have a non-political military [Hackett, 1964, p.344; 1965, p.260. Hosoya, 1976, pp.19-20. Maxon, 1957, pp.21, 24].

But while the line between military administration and operation could in principle be clearly drawn, there inevitably emerged "overlapping spheres of authority" between the Cabinet and the General Staffs [Maxon, 1957, p.34]. From the Cabinet's standpoint, ministers were responsible for matters concerning military operations, to the extent that they closely related to issues under the jurisdiction of the Cabinet [Imai, 1957b, p.119]. The military could claim that involving itself with questions of national security did not constitute meddling in politics [Hosoya, 1976, pp.21-22. Misawa and Ninomiya, 1973, p.325. Nakamura and Tobe, 1988, p.520]. Cabinet-military relations thus tended to be characterized by a "tug of war" [Maxon, 1957, p.34].

At times, the Cabinet was able to assert significant control over the General Staffs. For example, in 1920, the Hara Cabinet and its Army Minister were able to assume control over the operational objectives of the Japanese forces deployed in Siberia. At other times, however, the General Staffs dominated policy making in the area of national security. The controversy over the London Naval Treaty of 1930, for example, significantly enhanced the influence of the Navy's General Staff on national defense issues. In fact, it was during this controversy that the Emperor's right of Supreme Command was interpreted to give the General Staffs veto powers over Cabinet decisions on security matters [Crowley, 1966b, pp.24, 80, 386. Harries and Harries, 1991, pp.128-29]. Ironically, the principle of the independence of supreme command, originally intended as a device to prevent the politicization of the military, came to be used to legitimize the militarization of politics.

Various institutional factors affected the relations between the Cabinet and the General Staffs. First, the Cabinet was not a cohesive decision making body. Article 55 of the Meiji Constitution gave each minister responsibility to advise the Emperor. The Prime Minister was merely a chief among equals, and could neither direct nor dismiss other ministers. Splits inside the Cabinets often led to resignations [Imai, 1973, p.53].

Second, civilians could not head the Army and Navy Ministries. Before 1913 and after 1936 only top officers on active duty could become Army and Navy Ministers. Between 1913 and 1936 the restriction was loosened, but only to permit the appointment of reserve or retired officers. In 1921 Prime Minister Hara temporarily substituted for the Minister of the Navy, but only against the strong opposition of the Army. The fact that the military's cooperation was indispensable for forming and maintaining Cabinets gave it great leverage in Japan's political life [Duus, 1970, p.201. Hackett, 1964, pp.345-46. Hosoya, 1976, p.29. Huntington, 1957, p.131. Imai, 1957a, p.20. Yui, Fujiwara, and Yoshida, 1989, pp.498-99].

Third, military officers were frequently appointed to civilian Cabinet posts. Of the 404 civilian posts in the 43 Cabinets between 1885 and 1945, 115, or about 28 per cent, were held by generals and admirals. Of the 30 Prime Ministers of that 60-year period, 9 were from the Army and 6 were from the Navy, serving for a total of about 30 years. Since the mid-1910s, in contrast to the preceding period, officers assuming the Prime Ministerial post usually left active service. The Home Ministry in 11, and the Foreign Affairs Ministry in 14 of the 43 Cabinets were led by generals and admirals. Only the Finance Ministry was never headed by a military officer [Hackett, 1964, p.346. Imai, 1957a, p.4].

Fourth, the number of senior statesmen who had been the chief creators of the Meiji state (genros) gradually decreased, until, in 1924, there was only one surviving. Until 1901 genros dominated the Prime Ministerial post, and even after withdrawing from government posts, they retained substantial informal influence within the government. Around the turn of the century they were able to exercise considerable control over the staff officers during Japan's wars with China and Russia. For example, during the Russo-Japanese War, genros, some in Cabinet posts, joined the Supreme Command and imposed, to the vexation of professional staff officers, political control over the conduct of the war. The disappearing genros were not replaced by any social or political group planning military operations consistent with political aims [Beckmann, 1957, p.90. Crowley, 1966a, p.284. Hosoya, 1971, pp. 94-95. Imai, 1973, p.54].

The fragmentation of the Cabinet, the exclusion of civilians from the Army and Navy Ministries, the frequent appointment of military officers to civilian Cabinet posts, and the gradual disappearance of the genros were all institutional factors that favored the General Staffs in their "tug of war" with the Cabinet. The principle of the independence of the supreme command could be invoked by the staff officers to support their claim for greater decision making powers. Important components of the prewar state structure thus favored a strong articulation of military security objectives [Krebs, 1991].

The prewar military's institutional links with society were well established. The conscription system originating in 1873 was one such link. For military leaders the conscription system was not merely a means of creating a modern fighting machine; it was "a way of building unity and commitment to national goals through the education of civilians in military values, through the soldier's ethos" [Smethurst, 1974, p.335]. At first there were many categories of exemption from military service, such as heads of household; but by 1889 most of the these had been abolished [Yui, Fujiwara, and Yoshida, 1989, pp.463-69. Hackett, 1964, p.335].

The Imperial Military Reserve Association, created by the Army in 1910, and joined by Navy reserves in 1914, was another important link. Although the Association formally remained private until 1936, it was under the close supervision of the Army Ministry. In 1918, it had 13,000 branches and a membership of 2.3 million. In 1936, it had 14,000 branches and enrolled 2.9 million. In the cities the Army was not as successful as in the rural areas. By the 1920s of those eligible at least 80 per cent joined the rural areas, while less than 40 per cent joined in urban areas. Factory branches numbered only 257 in 1926, and 567 in 1937 [Smethurst, 1974, pp.16-17, 19-20]. The Reserve Association exerted, especially in the 1930s, "a moral and political influence that can hardly be overestimated" [Storry, 1979, p.131]. It was "the most important mass patriotic pressure group in prewar Japan." In the 1930s, reservists and reservists-to-be campaigned against the London Naval Treaty; for withdrawal from the League of Nations; for leniency for the assassins of Prime Minister Inukai; and against the constitutional scholar Tatsukichi Minobe who wrote that the Emperor was an organ of the state [Smethurst, 1974, p.176].

The Reserve Association was joined in its activities by the Greater Japan National Defense Women's Association, created in 1932. By 1937 it had a branch in every city, town, and village of the nation. Like the Reserve Association, it was under the control of the Army. At the grass-roots level reservists were closely involved in the Defense Women's activities that included rifle training, drills, and maneuvers. The Association functioned as the women's arm of the Reserve Association [Smethurst,

1974, pp.xiv, xix, 16-17, 19-20, 23-26, 32-34, 39, 41-46. Fridell, 1970, p.826].

Institutions for educating Japanese youth were also important in linking the military and society. In 1915 a multitude of youth groups were consolidated into the Greater Japan Youth Association. As early as 1908, with social unrest becoming increasingly serious, a rescript appealing for social harmony had been issued. The fear of growing disunity in Japanese society, evidenced by the increasing number of labor and anti-landlord disputes, as well as growing recognition of a new era of total wars that made national cohesion essential for security, prodded the Army into creating this Association. Through it, those too young to join the reserves and those who did not pass the conscription physical examination could be integrated to the Army's national network. Its branches worked closely with the reservists' branches. In a local setting the two branches frequently cooperated in organizing activities such as military drills, disaster relief, and physical training. This was one reason why the Association, although officially under the Home Affairs and Education Ministries' jurisdiction, could be controlled effectively by the Army Ministry [Smethurst, 1974, pp.xiv, 25-26, 32, 34].

Dissatisfied with the lack of uniformity in military education provided by the Youth Association branches, Army leaders soon embarked on another attempt at organizing the young. In 1926 youth training centers were created under the jurisdiction of the Ministry of Education. At these centers young men between the ages of 15 and 20 received, over a four-year period, 800 hours of instruction; 400 hours were allocated to military drills and 100 hours to ethical education. Reservists directed drills, and Army officers inspected the students' military proficiency. In 1934 nearly one million youths, or about 40 per cent of those eligible, were enrolled in 15,000 centers. In 1935, eager to reach an even greater number of youths, the Army created youth schools, in cooperation with the Education Ministry. The youth training centers were merged with one type of vocational schools to form the new schools, where the military education at the centers was provided. Through these schools the Army was able to reach an additional half million young men and half a million young women [Smethurst, 1974, pp.33, 39, 41-43].

Public attitudes toward the military helped assure the prominence of military security objectives in policy. The general public favored the use of military force as a means to enhance national power and prestige. A militaristic spirit was widespread throughout society. At least since Japan's war with China in 1894-95, the inevitability of overseas expansion, supported by military power, was widely supported. In contrast to political parties, for significant parts of the population the military embodied the unselfish pursuit of national objectives [Hosoya, 1976, p.29. Huntington, 1957, p.137. Storry, 1957, p.3].

To be sure, popular support for the military fluctuated. In the years immediately after the Russo-Japanese War, the military enjoyed great prestige and popularity. After World War I, especially in the cities, anti-military sentiment was pervasive. Some officers avoided wearing uniforms on their way to work. And during the Siberian intervention the number of draft evaders reached record heights [Fujiwara, 1957, p.22. Harries and Harries, 1991, pp.127-28. Kato, 1974, p.221. Peattie, 1975, p.6].

Through various institutions the prewar military was able to promote militaristic values. Sometimes men returned to rural communities after military service only to be resented, because of the modernizing effects that military had had on them [Ike, 1968, pp.197-98]. The number of reservists, for example, participating in the rice riots of 1918 was large enough to force the President of the Reserve Association to issue an admonition to its members [Fujiwara, 1957, p.25]. But generally, the activities of the Reserve Association, the military's influence on education, the indoctrination of conscripts, and the memory of military victories over China and Russia created a "reservoir of popular chauvinism that reached even the remotest village" [Duus, 1970, p.205]. Broadly based organizations under the influence of the military and the prevalence of militaristic values, partly brought about through them, provided the Japanese military with a favorable political environment.

At the core of Japan's prewar security policy, embedded in the structures and public attitudes described above, lay three key notions. First, national security required the protection not only of the "line of sovereignty" but also of the "line of interest." This notion was articulated by Prime Minister Yamagata in 1890 in a well known speech before the Diet. The line of interest was understood as consisting primarily of preventing hostile powers from controlling Korea, viewed as a buffer zone assuring the safety of the Japanese islands. Major Meckel, a German officer who arrived in Japan in 1884 at the request of the Japanese government, was instrumental in having the Army internalize the axiom that Japan's security was contingent on Korean independence. The strategic concern with Korea entailed the development of capabilities for overseas deployment of the armed forces. Although a decision had been made in 1870 to use the French, and after the Battle of Sedan, the Prussian model for the Army, and to use the British model for the Navy, the military's original mission had primarily been to maintain internal security. External security became the primary focus after the civil war of 1877. For a while the objective of defending the home islands was dominant. But in response to increasing tensions with China over Korea in the 1880s, the Japanese Army and Navy increasingly developed capabilities for overseas deployment. Between 1885 and 1895 nearly 30 per cent of the annual budgets were spent for a military buildup [Yui, Fujiwara, and Yoshida, 1989, pp.453-60. Crowley, 1966a, pp.276-77. Crowley, 1966b, p.8. Hackett, 1965, p.248. Ike, 1968, p.190. Maxon, 1957, p.21].

Most importantly, the imperative of protecting the interest line of Japan could be interpreted in various ways. Until the 1890s, government leaders spoke of Korean independence as the key to Japan's security. But by the mid-1900s, the General Staff of the Army was advocating the annexation of Korea which took place in 1910. After the Russo-Japanese War, the government became strongly committed to the protection of Japanese interests in Manchuria. In 1912 and 1916 Army officers in the field attempted, without success, to create puppet regimes in Inner Mongolia and Manchuria. In the late 1920s an important item on the agenda of the Army General Staff was how the Army's influence could be enhanced in Inner Mongolia, a region deemed as strategic. The "Fundamentals of National Policy" of 1936 officially called for the promotion of the Mongolian independence movement. Even in negotiations with Chiang Kai-shek in 1944, the government, while proposing major concessions on its part, insisted on maintaining Japanese interests in Manchuria [Berger, 1974, p.218. Crowley, 1966b, pp.9, 111-12; 1974b, p.274. Hosoya, 1976, p.24. Jansen, 1968, pp.182-83. Ogata, 1954, pp.xvi, 176]. Thus the ambiguous notion of protecting the interest line served to legitimize the widening scope of Japan's expansion on the Asian mainland.

Also important in Japan's prewar security policy was the notion that its security depended on controlling the Western Pacific and the sea lines of communication. In the late 1890s Navy leaders argued that the Navy needed to acquire the capability to attack enemy forces far away from the Japanese homeland. At times, they even claimed that Korea was not an essential element in Japan's security strategy [Jansen, 1984, p.68]. They were influenced by Admiral Mahan's doctrine according to which "trade and commerce, backed by the ability to control the seas, provided the keys to national defense" [Crowley, 1966a, p.278]. Influenced by this notion, the Navy began, after the Russo-Japanese War, to focus on the U.S. as the primary, potential enemy. It was determined that Japan should establish superiority over the U.S. Navy in the Western Pacific. In response to the U.S. naval buildup during World War I, Japan's naval budget increased dramatically, from 83.3 million yen in 1914 to 483.6 million yen in 1921. Because of the fear that the arms race with the U.S. would ultimately cause the forming of an Anglo-American alliance against Japan, the Navy was ready to accept arms limitations at the Washington conference of 1921-1922. As it turned out, the agreement reached among the powers in

Washington guaranteed Japan a de facto naval superiority over the U.S. in the Wester Pacific. But at the same time, the U.S. advocacy of a new type of diplomacy resulted in the abrogation of the Anglo-Japanese Alliance which had been formed in 1902. Furthermore, the London Naval Treaty of 1930 adopted a formula which seemed to assure the U.S. of strategic superiority in the near future. This spurred strong domestic opposition to the Treaty which, by the mid-1930s, made Japan remove itself from all international arrangements governing naval armaments. Japan's naval superiority in the Western Pacific was seriously compromised by the U.S. naval buildup of the late 1930s. This was one element in the decision for starting the war with the United States [Crowley, 1966b, pp.25-27; 1970, pp.242-43; 1974a, p.43. Iriye, 1965, pp.15-18; 1971, p.125. Kim, 1978, p.47]. Thus the Navy was steadfast in pursuing its military objective vis-a-vis the United States.

Consistent with the lack of cohesion in the Cabinet, the strategic missions of the two services were not well coordinated. The Imperial National Defense Policy was the "closest thing" to a "long-range and comprehensive defense policy binding on the two services" [Peattie, 1975, p.203]. First created in 1907, it was revised in 1918, 1923, and 1936. In these documents, the Army designated Russia or the Soviet Union, and the Navy designated the U.S., as Japan's major potential adversary. Until the Russo-Japanese War, China or Russia had been perceived to be the primary threats. The new dual mission of the military was originally predicated on the continuance of the Anglo-Japanese Alliance. But the dual mission was maintained also after the abrogation of the Alliance. And in the 1936 version of the policy, Britain was added to the list of potential enemies [Beasley, 1987, p.224. Crowley, 1966b, p.10. Fujiwara, 1973, p.189. Imai, 1957a, p.5. Kim, 1978, p.61].

The Imperial National Defense Policy, in its various versions, never established strategic priorities. It merely registered the rival claims of the Army and the Navy, fighting over the allocation of resources. Such absence of priorities was also notably evident in the "Fundamentals of National Policy" of 1936. It could not coordinate the Army's interest in Manchuria and the Navy's interest in Southeast Asia. In the 1930s Japan was engaged in an arms race with two major powers of the world, and, furthermore, in contrast to them, it was building up both services simultaneously [Asada, 1973, p.245. Barnhart, 1987, p.44. Crowley, 1966a, p.282; 1974b, p.272. Yui, Fujiwara, and Yoshida, 1989, pp.500-01]. Although the military had significant leverage over the Cabinet in the forming of security policy decisions, it was internally divided. Within a structural context giving prominence to military security objectives, the Army-Navy rivalry had particularly serious effects on the conduct of Japan's national security policy.

Finally, since World War I the dual mission of the military was complemented by a third key notion informing Japan's prewar security policy: Japan needed to prepare for total war. For certain segments of the military, one crucial lesson of World War I was that future wars could be won only by mobilizing an economy that coupled massive industrial capabilities with self-sufficiency. Control over resources and markets thus would become essential for strategic purposes; economic vulnerability would constitute strategic weakness; and strategic planning needed to incorporate economic factors. In 1926 a comprehensive plan for mobilizing the nation's economic capabilities was drawn up inside the Army Ministry. The planners had high regard for the first Soviet Five-Years Plan which successfully expanded and modernized the Red Army. By the mid-1930s Manchuria was under Japanese control, and provinces in North China were beginning to be integrated into the Japanese economy. Manchuria and North China came to be viewed both as important strategic barriers against the reemergence of Soviet power in the Far East and as economic bases that enhanced strategic capabilities. Consistent with their strategic focus, officers pushing for the creation of a self-sufficient economic base for the military did not welcome active zaibatsu involvement in the economy of Manchukuo. But the war with China was inhibiting the efforts to achieve self-sufficiency. Fighting in China actually deepened Japan's economic reliance on foreign powers, especially the United States. Achieving self-sufficiency was an important element in Japanese leaders' choice to advance into Indochina and the East Indies in 1940-1941. These areas were to provide raw materials and markets, while North China and Manchukuo were to develop heavy industry [Barnhart, 1987, pp.18-19, 39, 44, 270. Beasley, 1987, pp.224, 225. Berger, 1974, p.210. Crowley, 1970, pp.252-53; 1974b, pp.274, 292. Peattie, 1975, pp.97-98, 186-87. Pelz, 1974, pp.171-73]. The notion of preparing for a total war contributed significantly to the widening of the scope of Japan's military expansion overseas.

The structure of Japan's prewar state provided the Army and Navy General Staffs with important leverage over the Cabinet in national security policy. Through conscription, organizing of reservists and women, and involvement in the education of Japan's youth, the military created a social support base, imbued with militaristic values, that could be mobilized for its purposes. The organization of the government, civil-military relations, and the dominant social norms favored the articulation of a policy that emphasized the need to have strategic buffer zones on the continent, project power in the Wester Pacific, and prepare for total war. The structures and norms shaping Japan's security policy since 1945 have been dramatically different.

III

The Structural Context of Japan's National Security Policy

Japan's security policy is formulated within institutional structures that bias policy strongly against a forceful articulation of military security objectives and accord pride of place instead to a comprehensive definition of security that centers on economic and political dimensions of national security. To the extent that it is purely domestic this institutional structure subordinates military to economic and political security concerns. To this end the Ministries of Foreign Affairs (MOFA), International Trade and Industry (MITI), and Finance (MOF) have penetrated to a substantial degree the Defense Agency. State-society relations reinforce this pattern. Japan's SDF is relatively isolated from the public and government-business relations on questions of weapons procurement and the import of raw materials are close, thus strengthening the economic aspects of Japan's national security policy. The transnational links of Japan's state on the other hand to some extent have counteracted the political incentives that these structures create. They have served as conduits for American pressure for a substantial enlargement in Japan's military defense efforts in the 1980s.

A. Institutional Structures and National Security

The organization of Japan's government puts important ministries such as MOFA, MITI and MOF in charge of the different dimensions of Japan's security policy. This arrangement gives the economic and political perspectives of these ministries their full weight in the formulation and implementation of policy. And it puts the professional military under their direct and indirect supervision inside the JDA.

The JDA consists of the three military services (Ground, Maritime, and Air Self-Defense Forces), the Joint Staff Council (JSC), the internal

21

bureaus (consisting of the Secretariat of the JDA Director and bureaus in charge of defense policy, education and training, personnel, finance, and equipment), the Defense Facilities Administration Agency, and such organizations as the National Defense Academy, the Technical Research and Development Institute, and the Central Procurement Office [Defense Agency, 1990, p.309]. The JSC has one chairman, serving full-time, as well as the chiefs of staff of the three services (Article 27, JDA Establishment Law). The JDA is headed by a minister of state (a Cabinet member) (Article 3, JDA Establishment Law), who is under the control and supervision of the Prime Minister (Article 8, SDF Law). Both the Prime Minister and the JDA Director, as members of the Cabinet, must be civilians (Article 66, Constitution). The SDF is under the Prime Minister's "supreme power of control and supervision" (Article 7, SDF Law). Confronted by an external attack or a threat of attack, the Prime Minister is empowered by the SDF Law to order the SDF to engage in "defense operations" (Article 76). Defense operations require prior, or at least ex post facto, approval by the Diet (Article 76). Also, the Security Council Establishment Law stipulates that the Prime Minister consult the Security Council on the appropriateness of ordering a defense operation (Article 2). The SDF Law also authorizes the Prime Minister to issue an order engaging the SDF in internal security operations when police power is judged to be insufficient for maintaining internal security (Article 78). In a defense operation, "the highest-level commanders of the three services, namely, territorial army commanders of the Ground SDF, the Commander of the Self-Defense Fleet and the district commanders of the Maritime SDF, and the air defense commanders of the Air SDF" receive orders from the Prime Minister via the JDA Director and the chiefs of staff of the three services [Nishihara, 1985a, p.137].

The military services, however, are embedded in an organizational context not apparent from this description of formal power relations. The JDA is one of twelve agencies and commissions that are placed under the supervision of the Prime Minister's Office (PMO). That Office comprises not only the Main Office with the Prime Minister's Secretariat and the Decoration Bureau, but also other organizations such as the JDA, the Economic Planning Agency, the Science and Technology Agency, and the Environment Agency. The head of the Prime Minister's Office and the heads of nine of the external organizations are Cabinet members. In contrast to full-fledged ministries these organizations enjoy only a limited range of freedom. In fact, ministries frequently run interference in the affairs of these organizations. Organizations, such as the JDA, tend to fill a significant number of their senior positions with officials temporarily assigned from other ministries. Compared to the prewar era, the JDA has been a "pale shadow of the former military bureaucracy, in terms of its status, independence and effectiveness" [Stockwin, 1982, p.147. Kato, 1991]. And the JDA's attempts to elevate itself to the status of a ministry have not borne fruit [Fukui, 1970, pp.91-92; Otake, 1990, p.143]. MOFA, MITI, and MOF are the ministries that are of particular importance for the JDA. An understanding of how the SDF's military perspective plays a subordinate role in security policymaking requires an examination of these ministries and how they relate to the JDA.

1. Ministry of Foreign Affairs.

Although MOFA's policymaking capabilities are at times seriously limited, it remains a central actor on questions of security policy. Unlike most other ministries MOFA lacks jurisdiction over a substantial domestic political constituency and thus has no strong links with party politicians. Because Prime Ministers Shigeru Yoshida and Hitoshi Ashida were former MOFA officials in the immediate postwar period, the ministry enjoyed excellent connections at the highest levels of Japan's political leadership. But with the passing of time, both the influence and size of former MOFA officials in the governing party declined, and so did the ministry's political leverage [Okimoto, 1978a, pp.423-424] There are several indications that the ministry has little attraction for party politicians. The post of Parliamentary Vice Minister at MOFA, for example, is "one of the least popular among the government posts at the sub-cabinet level, which an up-and-coming LDP politician would take up with more reluctance than delight" [Fukui, 1981, p.294]. The number of applicants for the LDP post of head of the Foreign Affairs Section in the Policy Affairs Research Council has been decreasing, in sharp contrast to the growing competition for the section chief posts in other policy fields [Nihon Keizai Shimbun-sha, 1983, p.36]. International comparisons of the foreign services of industrial states also indicate the meagerness of the ministry's personnel and budgetary strengths. MOFA's personnel numbers about 4,300, compared to 15,900 for the U.S., 8,200 for the U.K. and about 6,500 for both Germany and France [Taoka and Hanochi, 1991, p.26]. The proportion of the foreign affairs budget in the overall national budget is 1.48% in France, 1.43% in the U.K., 0.82% in the U.S., and only 0.77% in Japan [Kusano, 1989, p.64].

MOFA's resources, however, should not be underestimated. The primary authority to coordinate all aspects of foreign affairs throughout the government is placed in the hands of MOFA [Sato and Matsuzaki, 1986, pp.159-160]. On most important foreign policy issues, MOFA is the "sole coordinator" of conflicting interests [Drifte, 1990a, p.22]. It is the only ministry whose administrative vice-minister briefs the Prime Minister on a regular basis [Nihon Keizai Shimbun-sha, 1983, p.132]. Furthermore, one of the Prime Minister's five secretaries is an official temporarily assigned from MOFA. These five secretaries, four from the bureaucracy and one from outside of government, are members of the Prime Minister's inner circle, together with the Chief Cabinet Secretary, his two deputies (one a Diet member and the other a bureaucrat), and the head of the Cabinet Counsellors' Office. The practice that MOFA provides an aide to the Prime Minister started under Prime Minister Yoshida. The secretary from MOFA was subsequently joined by National Police Agency (NPA) and MOF officials, and, under the Tanaka Cabinet, also by a MITI official [Kataoka, 1982, pp.250, 252; 1990, p.10]. Thus, MOFA has regular access to Japan's top political leadership. And it enjoys the authority to engage in government-wide coordination of foreign policy issues.

It is, therefore, with limited though significant resources that MOFA involves itself in both economic and military security issues. It is in fact the only ministry whose organization permits an involvement in substantive questions touching both areas of security [Kusano, 1989, p.87]. JDA specializes in military security. For MITI economic security issues are of particular importance. The MOF covers both areas, as will be discussed below, but in contrast to the MOFA its approach is quite narrowly confined to the financial aspects of foreign policy issues.

In the MOFA especially relevant to economic security issues are the Office of Economic Security and the International Energy Division, both in the Economic Affairs Bureau. In addition the Economic Cooperation Bureau has been said to be similar to MITI in its outlook on economic security [Otake, 1983a, p.368]. For questions of economic security MOFA's relations with MITI and with the Councillors' Office for Foreign Affairs in the Cabinet Secretariat are very important. The locus of authority to formulate trade policy has been a point of contention between MOFA and MITI. Because trade policy needs to be coordinated with domestic industrial policy MITI insists that it should have the chief role in this area. For MOFA, however, the formulation of trade policy is an integral part of its mission to produce a government-wide consensus on matters involving external relations [Higashi, 1983, pp.49-50]. This rivalry dates back to prewar Japan. It took a dramatic turn in the 1930s when nearly all of MOFA's division heads and deputy division heads threatened to resign in protest against a plan that would have elevated the Trade Bureau in the Ministry of Commerce and Industry (MITI's predecessor) to ministerial status [Fukui, 1981, pp.296-297]. Under Yoshida MOFA was able to penetrate MITI's unit in charge of trade. Reflecting Yoshida's view that trade policy needed to be supervised by MOFA, between 1949 and 1956 its officials served as directors of MITI's International Trade Bureau. The names of MITI's present bureaus handling trade, the International Trade Policy (Tsusho Seisaku) and International Trade Administration (Boeki), still reflect the rivalry. "Tsusho" and "Boeki" were, respectively, names of prewar MOFA and MCI bureaus [Johnson, 1977, pp.264-268].

MOFA's role in military security policymaking focuses on the maintenance of a close and stable political relationship with the United States [Fukui, 1975, p.151]. Forged during the Occupation under the leadership of former diplomats like Ashida and Yoshida, MOFA has always had close relations with the U.S. government. And on questions of military security it has not had to fear serious competition from a Defense Agency that has remained in a subordinate position in government, both politically and bureaucratically. The reversion of Okinawa serves as a good illustration. The roles played by the U.S. and Japanese militaries differed greatly in that case [Hosoya, 1977, p.16]. Until the armed services had agreed to the reversion, U.S officials could not begin serious discussion with the Japanese government. On the Japanese side, the North American Affairs and Security Divisions of the American Affairs Bureau of MOFA, not the JDA, were the principal actors, "even on issues like whether Japan would assert a security stake in Korea and Taiwan" [Destler, 1976, p.85].

MOFA's Security Division in the North American Affairs Bureau plays the central role in military security policymaking. It is in fact responsible for the security relationship with the United States. U.S. requests on matters of security are directed to the North American Affairs Bureau [Van de Velde, 1988a, p.322]. Junior officials with "some background or strong interest" in the field of security are assigned to the division, and they often get reassigned to it in the course of their careers [Van de Velde, 1988a, p.306]. The division maintains close contact with the JDA [Interview No.13, Tokyo, June 14, 1991].

The importance of the Security Division is illustrated by the fact that the JDA proposed its abolition in the 1970s, when the JDA sought to increase its own power in security policy [Lohmann, 1980, p.239]. The Disarmament Division in the United Nations Bureau and the Security Policy Office in the Information and Research Bureau are also involved in military security matters. Since 1973 the JDA has established close personnel ties with MOFA, and its officials, mostly uniformed officers, have been sent to offices in MOFA that deal with security questions [Okimoto, 1978a, pp.421-422]. By 1987 40 JDA officials were serving in MOFA or were assigned to a Japanese embassy [Drifte, 1990a, p.23]. MOFA's involvement in the formulation of military security policy can lead to policy incoherence. For example, a study of the process of drafting the 1976 Defense White Paper shows that JDA's draft, prepared by its Defense Policy Bureau, was sent to MOFA's Security Division and Research and Analysis Bureau (now Information and Research Bureau) for review. As a result of the review the final version of the White Paper retained JDA's "basic standing force" concept, but "without most of the analysis and predictions that made it a logical response to Japan's international environment" [Weinstein, 1979, p.166].

MOFA's analytical and planning capabilities have increased in the 1980s. After the end of the Occupation the unit specializing in research and planning did not have a central place in the ministry's activities [Fukui, 1977, p.16]. However, in the early 1980s the Research Department in the MOFA Secretariat was expanded and became the Research and Planning Department. In 1984 the new department was reorganized once more into an Information and Research Bureau. It is in this bureau that the ministry's Security Policy Office has been placed. These reorganizations have served to upgrade MOFA's policy analysis and planning capabilities. The Security Policy Office has been quite important in analyzing Japan's strategic environment. The Office has complemented the Security Division which deals with the day-to-day management of Japan's security relationship with the United States [Mochizuki, private communication, 1992. Okazaki, 1990a, p.23].

According to MOFA's perspective, it is primarily responsible for Japan's overall security policy, while the JDA has the limited mission of defending Japan against physical attacks. This division of labor is reflected in the relatively low rank given to SDF officers assigned to Japanese embassies as military attaches [Itoh, 1988, p.317]. It has been described in a variety of ways: JDA handles "purely military aspects of defense," and MOFA is in charge of "the broad international aspects of national security" [Okimoto, 1978a, p.357]; JDA is in charge of "narrowly military matters such as weapons procurement and deployment of military forces" [Okimoto, 1978b, p.12]; JDA is merely "the operational arm" of MOFA [Fukui, 1981, p.296]; JDA is "the government office for managing the SDF," rather than "the key organ on security affairs" [Chapman, Drifte, and Gow, 1982, p.73]; MOFA is responsible for "security," and JDA is responsible for "defense" [Ginn, 1982, p.49]; MOFA, along with other major actors, makes "the overall policy," and JDA does "the day-to-day work of organizing for defense" [Kim, 1988, p.104]; and JDA's "defense policies" are "only part of a broader security policy structure for which the Ministry of Foreign Affairs takes primary responsibility" [U.S. Congress, Office for Technology Assessment, 1990, p.102]. Despite slight variations in wordings, these descriptions all point to the importance of the political, organizational and policy distinction between security and defense.

This distinction dates from the 1950s [Fukui, 1975, p.151]. In the prewar era the Ministry of Foreign Affairs fought bitter struggles against the creation, under the military's influence, of organizations such as the Kwantung Agency, the Overseas Affairs Ministry, the Asian Development Agency, and the Greater East Asia Ministry. Because of the disastrous consequences which ensued once the military took over control of foreign policy, MOFA has jealously protected its powers from any possible encroachment by the JDA [Fukui, 1975, p.151; 1981, p.295]. For example, in the late 1970s the JDA seized the initiative in changing the government's policy of funding U.S. forces in Japan. And it criticized MOFA's weak stance toward the Soviet military buildup in the Far East. Some MOFA officials spoke quickly and publicly of the risks inherent in a return to prewar conditions when MOFA had been unable to control Japan's military [Otake, 1983a, pp.224-226, 270-278, 306]. This was an effective strategy for mobilizing allies against the efforts of the JDA to establish a higher political profile.

More importantly, there exist institutional arrangements that provide MOFA with leverage over the JDA. For example, MOFA is deeply involved in military security intelligence. The First and Second Research Divisions of the Defense Policy Bureau of the JDA are in charge of military intelligence. The JDA's Councillor on International Affairs supervises these two divisions. Custom, however, has it that the Councillor is a MOFA official on temporary assignment with the JDA [Inoki, 1991, p.64].

MOFA has two types of bureaus, functional and geographic. Functional bureaus include the Bureaus for Economic Affairs, Economic Cooperation, Treaties, United Nations, and Information and Research. Geographic bureaus deal with Asian Affairs, North American Affairs, Central and South American Affairs, European and Oceanic Affairs, and Middle Eastern and African Affairs. This distinction is very important for the workings of the ministry. Bilateral issues are assigned to geographic bureaus and multilateral issues are assigned to functional ones. Because of its expertise in legal matters the Treaties Bureau, however, although it is functional, also gets involved in bilateral issues. With only one exception, "simultaneous and competitive involvement of a geographic and a functional bureau in the same issue is rare, if not impossible" [Fukui, 1977, p.10]. While they coordinate their activities closely with the administrative vice-minister, the director of a regional or functional bureau and the director of a division within that bureau are at the center of decisionmaking; they can also count on the support of the staff members from other bureaus that are involved on a given issue [Fukui, 1975, p.152]. Bureaus live by the rule of mutual noninterference. Furthermore, MOFA bureaus lack such counterweights as the large staff which assists the American Secretary of

State in his battles with the State Department's bureaus [Destler, 1976, p.74]. MOFA is thus characterized by "subsystem dominance" and "ad hoc decision-making groups formed along bureau-division lines" [Fukui, 1977, p.16]. There are, of course, issues that defy this neat bilateral-multilateral distinction. For example, during the GATT Tokyo Round negotiations the Second North America Division of the North American Affairs Bureau and the First International Organizations Division of the Economic Affairs Bureau reportedly integrated their efforts [Higashi, 1983, p.42]. Furthermore, subsystem dominance in the handling of concrete issues does not preclude close relationships that cut across bureau boundaries. The Economic Affairs Bureau and the Second North American Division in the North American Affairs Bureau, for example, are closely connected [Interview Nos.1 and 6, Tokyo, June 11 and 12, 1991].

In contrast MITI's system differs markedly from the latitude that the individual bureaus enjoy in MOFA. MITI is composed of so-called vertical and horizontal bureaus. Vertical bureaus such as Machinery and Information Industries and Consumer Goods Industries are responsible for industries falling under their jurisdiction; and horizontal bureaus such as International Trade Policy and International Trade Administration are concerned with "functional issues cutting across sectors" [Okimoto, 1989, p.115]. That the two types of bureaus tend to have divergent perspectives is illustrated very clearly by the conflicting stances of the Textile and General Merchandise Bureau (now absorbed into the Consumer Goods Industries Bureau) and the International Trade Bureau towards the textile dispute with the United States in the late 1960s and early 1970s [Destler, Fukui, and Sato, 1979, p.53].

MITI's vertical, or primary, bureaus are in a way analogous to MOFA's geographic bureaus. However, rather than bureau autonomy and the norm of noninterference, ministry-wide, collegial decisionmaking has been the rule in MITI. At the core of this ministry-wide decision-making system are the inter-bureau standing committees—the Bureau Directors' Conference, the General Affairs Division Chiefs' Conference, and the Laws and Ordinances Examination Committee. Although it ranks lowest in status, the last actually is quite influential in shaping the long-term evolution of MITI policy. The committee is composed of deputy directors from the general affairs division of each bureau and the divisions in the Minister's Secretariat. It meets twice a week. While it does not play a significant role in the political decisions that affect how MITI deals with the crisis of the day, week or month, important long-term policy proposals need to be approved by this committee, and, once approved, have a good chance of evolving into official MITI policies. The importance of the committee can be explained by MITI's tradition of encouraging younger officials to play an important decision-making role, and by the fact that deputy division directors occupy a key place in the flow of communication involving units both inside and outside MITI [Interview No.25, Tokyo, December 19, 1991. Fukui, 1978, pp.101-102. Okimoto, 1989, pp.115,118. Omori, 1986, pp.99-100]. Important coordinating committees that examine policy proposals also exist in other ministries such as Labor and Home Affairs; but in this instance they are staffed by division chiefs [Omori, 1986, pp.99-100].

The fact that MOFA's decisionmaking system, unlike MITI's, is characterized by the bureaucratic norm of noninterference between geographic and functional bureaus has important implications for Japan's military security policy. MOFA's central unit for security policy, the Security Division, is part of the North American Affairs Bureau, a geographic bureau. Generally speaking geographic bureaus have the mission of creating and maintaining good political and economic relations with the countries they deal with. The North American Affairs Bureau is no exception. Its First and Second North America Divisions are, respectively, in charge of the political and economic aspects of U.S.-Japan relations. The key unit of MOFA dealing with security policy is thus placed in an organization that happens to have considerable autonomy in policymaking and accords great importance to good relations with the United States. The dominance in MOFA's security thinking of the U.S.-Japan relationship, in all of its political and economic ramifications, thus is deeply embedded in the ministry's organizational arrangements.

The Treaties Bureau, is the one functional unit that plays a regular role in security policy. But the bureau brings to this task a "legalistic mentality" [Fukui, 1977, p.18] and a sensitivity to domestic political demands which is honed by its deep involvement in Diet deliberations, a trait that is typically not shared by the geographic bureaus [Fukui, 1977, p.17-18]. Ideas have circulated inside MOFA that a new Security Bureau ought to be created. MOFA's Security Policy Planning Committee produced an important report in 1980 in which it recommended that Japan should increase its military contributions to the security of the West, and that the SDF should participate in U.N. peacekeeping operations. It also played with the idea of establishing, in the future, a Security Bureau inside MOFA [Otake, 1983a, pp.306-08]. But the idea has not been considered realistic within the ministry. The creation of an independent bureau dealing with security would require abolishing an existing bureau. Furthermore, the North American Affairs Bureau is likely to oppose strongly any move to diminish its powers [Interview No.6, Tokyo, June 12, 1991].

MOFA's wide purview gives it a voice in both economic and military security issues. From its standpoint, Japan's physical security, and to a great extent economic security, derives from smooth Japan-U.S. relations centering on the Security Treaty. Defense is perceived as involving numerous technicalities that are dwarfed by the political salience of maintaining the general framework for Japan's security arrangements with the U.S., a central task for MOFA which articulates frequently and forcefully the political objective of maintaining the viability of that framework.

2. Ministry of International Trade and Industry.

As the ministry in charge of international trade and industry MITI plays a central role on questions of economic security. Ever since the Meiji period the Japanese government has been preoccupied with securing access to raw materials and overseas markets. The crucial importance of international trade for Japan's existence has meant that "the ministry in Japan charged with trade administration occupies a position somewhat analogous to a ministry of defense in other nations" [Johnson, 1977, p.260]. MITI's organizational setup has been briefly described above. In addition, it needs to be noted that energy policy is formed and administered by the Agency for Natural Resources and Energy. In response to the first oil crisis this unit was created as an external bureau of MITI in 1974. It has three departments, in charge of oil, coal, and public utilities. The secretariat of the agency director (a career official) is responsible for overall energy policy [Lesbirel, 1988, p.288]. The relationship between MITI and MOFA's Economic Affairs Bureau used to be quite conflictual. With an evolving division of labor between the two it has, however, improved during the last ten years [Interview No.6, Tokyo, June 12, 1991].

In a variety of ways, furthermore, MITI is involved not only in economic but also in military security issues. First, foreign trade which has security implications is under its jurisdiction. A major clash between MITI and MOFA occurred in 1987-1988, when MOFA insisted, in the wake of the Toshiba incident, on assuming the power to control the export of sensitive goods to Socialist countries [Drifte, 1990a, p.22-23]. This incident of 1987 shed some light on the perspective with which MITI approaches the area of security-related trade. Before this incident Japanese representatives at COCOM meetings had typically opposed, sometimes without good reason, all efforts designed to strengthen export controls. According to a former official who served as administrative vice-minister of MITI during the incident, the intensity of the controversy sharpened MITI's sensitivity to the military significance of a large number of civilian high technologies and the need to impose some export controls [Asahi Shimbun Keizai-bu, 1989, pp.112-114]. A former deputy vice-minister of MITI acknowledged that the Toshiba incident occurred in part because of the traditional avoidance of all discussions of security and defense issues inside MITI [Kuroda, 1989, p.72].

MITI's important role in security-related trade is illustrated also by its extensive involvement in the issue of increasing the flow of militarily relevant technology between Japan and the U.S. [Interview No.14, Tokyo, June 15, 1991]. From the perspective of MITI the flow-back of military technology that results from the improvement of U.S. licenses is unproblematic. Under the terms of the licensing agreement improvements are regularly reported by Japanese firms, and American firms have the right to acquire those technologies as long as certain export procedures are satisfied [Interview No.25, Tokyo, December 19, 1991]. The Export Division in the International Trade Administration Bureau administers Japan's strict arms export ban and the regulations of the Coordinating Committee on Export Controls (COCOM). Attached to the Export Division are the Security Trade Control Office and the Inspector's Office on the Export of Strategic Materials.

The export of dual-use technologies raises particularly thorny issues for MITI. While such export is officially not regulated, firms remain very nervous about it. For both public opinion and the existence of MITI's strict export controls over weapons and weapons technologies impose strict restraints. The International Trade Administration Bureau's extreme caution partially accounts for the small number of defense technologies successfully transferred under an U.S.-Japan agreement of 1983. Officials in the Export Division are responsible for approving technology transfer and will be held accountable should they make any significant political misjudgements, a likely cause of intense political controversy. These officials tend to be sensitive to the concerns of Japanese businessmen over the possible "misapplication" of the transferred technologies. Thus they tend to have a somewhat more cautious attitude towards defense-related technology transfers, if compared, for instance, with officials in the Aircraft and Ordnance Division in MITI's Machinery and Information Industries Bureau [Rubinstein, 1987b, pp. 68-69]. In fact, watching the Diet and public opinion, the Export Division has monitored carefully the export of dual-use technologies, although such export is, as noted in the 1983 agreement, officially free from government regulation. MITI has resorted to administrative guidance to block the export of dual-use technologies, components and products when they were likely to be used for military purposes. Administrative guidance has also been used to prevent Japanese corporations in the U.S. from engaging in the manufacture and sale of dual-use components for military use. MITI, however, does not admit that such administrative guidance takes place, thus seeking to avoid criticism from the

U.S. government [Asahi Shimbun Keizai-bu, 1989, pp.130-136]. Both MITI and American officials insist that the major barrier for accelerating the flow-back of dual-use technologies, spun-off from Japanese production under U.S. military licenses, lies in the fact that private firms own the patents, and that MITI has no statutory authority to make Japanese firms transfer these technologies [Interview Nos. 20 and 25, Tokyo, December 18 and 19, 1991].

The Law for Manufacturing Aircraft (1952) and the Law for Manufacturing Weapons and Munitions (1953) provide the statutory basis for MITI's jurisdiction over the defense industry. The former stipulates that the manufacture and repair of aircraft and supportive equipment requires the permission of the minister in charge of MITI. Similarly, the latter makes such permission a precondition for the manufacture and repair of weapons and munitions. Operational control over defense industry related issues rests with the Aircraft and Ordnance Division. And the director of JDA's Equipment Bureau invariably has served previously as the director of that division [U.S. Congress, Office for Technology Assessment, 1990, p.103].

MITI did not assume responsibility over the defense industry without opposition from other ministries. In preparing for the end of the Occupation, the Ministry of Transport, for example, was drawing up legislation which would have given it, as was true before the war, jurisdiction over the aircraft industry. MITI, however, challenged the Transport Ministry, and each tried to obtain cabinet approval for its proposal. The Transport Ministry based its stand on the need to secure safety in the air. MITI argued that the aircraft industry had strong links to other industries and therefore fell under MITI's overall responsiblity for industrial policy [Otake, 1984a, pp.29-31].

The weapons industry was designated as a major "national policy" industry in September 1952, and MITI was expected to engage in the promotion of the industry's development [Yanaga, 1968, pp.254, 256]. Its jurisdiction was formalized by the 1953 law. Subsequently, the Security Agency, which in 1954 became the JDA, made political moves to wrest jurisdictional control from MITI. The JDA was interested in creating a strong defense industrial base and proposed a nationalization of the weapons industry. MITI, however, was adamantly opposed to nationalization and insisted that a proper balance had to be preserved between the weapons industry and other industries. The agency's attempt was defeated in part because of the opposition of the fiscally conservative Finance Ministry [Otake, 1984a, pp.31-32]. Apparently, even today there still exist some sentiments within the JDA to obtain jurisdiction over Japan's armaments industry [Kim, 1988, p.116]. But its defeat was complete. One important consequence was that, until the mid-1970s, the JDA showed little interest in developing an indigenous defense industry and has remained instead content with a substantial degree of import dependence, especially on the American armaments industry [Otake, 1983a, pp.216-17; 1984a, p.32]. A second consequence was to affirm pride of place to MITI in military procurement decisions. Procurement plans formulated by the JDA are submitted to MITI and MOF for review, and their approval is one requisite step for the formalization of the plans. MITI's views are actually reflected in JDA's draft plan itself, because the plan results from negotiations among the Equipment Bureau, Defense Policy Bureau, and Finance Bureau of the JDA as well as the three staff offices of the SDF [Kataoka and Myers, 1989, pp.65-67].

Despite its links to Japan's defense industry MITI's policy is characterized by the lack of a military perspective. In its review of JDA procurement plans, MITI "pays close attention to the prospective recipients of Defense Agency contracts and carefully reviews each, especially where licensing is involved, to determine its likely impact upon industrial development" [Kataoka and Myers, 1989, p.66]. This effort is helped by the fact that the director of JDA's Equipment Bureau typically comes from MITI. In the early years of the JDA, procurement experts in the Japan National Railways (which was subsequently privatized in 1987) served as the bureau's director. But the post began to be reserved for a MITI official from the late 1950s on. In addition, three or four MITI officials are always placed inside the bureau [Interview No.11, Tokyo, June 14, 1991]. MITI also used to send its officials to JDA's Central Procurement Office; but that practice has ceased [Interview No.11, Tokyo, June 14, 1991]. The reason lies in the sheer increase in the number of JDA officials, a result of the maturation of the agency. But it also came about probably because in the eyes of MITI that post had become expendable. MITI, however, has no intention of relinquishing the post of the Equipment Bureau chief [Interview No.11, Tokyo, June 14, 1991]. The Equipment Bureau's activities are sometimes referred to as "shopping" which is devoid of military security concerns. MITI officials sent to serve in the Bureau rotate back after two years. Typically, they are not interested in defense, and if they develop an interest in security affairs, their career prospects inside MITI will be damaged [Interview No.14, Tokyo, June 15, 1991]. Officials from MITI as well as MOFA do not remain in the JDA until retirement. This contrasts with the career patterns of NPA and MOF officials who do on occasion stay at the JDA after they have been transferred there [Interview No.15, June 17, 1991].

In the first half of the 1950s, MITI was the most enthusiastic proponent within government of the development of Japan's defense industry. Its interest, however, was to develop an export industry which would earn foreign exchange and which would have technological spin-off effects advantageous for civilian industries. The policy instruments that MITI officials planned to use in guiding the armament industry's development were essentially the same as those subsequently used for targeted civilian industries such as steel, automobiles, petrochemicals and computers. But MITI's policy changed when it encountered stiff opposition from the MOF and a change in U.S. policy at the end of the Korean war which aimed at making Japan a market for America's defense industry rather than an arsenal for the United States in Asia. Rather than targeting the defense industry MITI simply shifted its focus to the expansion of other promising industries such as shipbuilding and petrochemicals [Otake, 1984a, pp.33, 40-41,55-56]. The Defense Production Committee (DPC) of the Federation of Economic Organizations thus was still complaining as late as 1985 about the "absence of an arms industry policy" [Drifte, 1986b, p.26].

Although MITI was forced to change its stance towards the defense industry in the mid-1950s, it did not change its view that the defense industry was only one among many industries under its jurisdiction. Some of these industries demand the ministry's close attention; others do not, for reasons that have nothing to do with issues of military security. For example, in its efforts to develop a competitive aerospace industry, MITI is joined by non-military organizations, such as the Science and Technology Agency (STA), the National Space Development Agency, and the Remote-Sensing Technology Center [Eckelmann and Davis, 1983, pp.31-32]. The STA, along with the Ministry of Education, has been in charge of space development [Yoshioka, 1990, pp.129-33]. Officials in the STA are known for their pacifist orientation which partly explains why the STA has very little to do with the JDA [Interview No.15, Tokyo, June 17, 1991]. Even as important an issue as the possible use of satellites by the JDA did not open lines of communication between the two agencies in the mid-1980s [Interviews Nos.15,16,and 21, Tokyo, June 17,17,and 19]. MITI and STA have shared jurisdiction also in the area of R and D for nuclear energy. MITI has been in charge of industrial R and D, while the STA has been responsible for non-industrial R and D [Tsuneishi, 1990, p.109].

The late 1980s has witnessed a growing involvement of MITI in security policy. In response to the Toshiba affair and the Gulf War MITI has enlarged substantially its Export Division. In recent years its staff has more than doubled to about 100. This division is in regular contact with MOFA's Economic Affairs Bureau, specifically the Economic Security Office, which deals with COCOM and the Australia Group as well as with the United Nations Bureau's Disarmament Division and the Nuclear Division. MITI also checks with the JDA, especially on cases of militarily relevant exports. MITI's Export Control Division reviews about one million applications per year [Interview No.24, Tokyo, December 19, 1991].

Furthermore, in April 1989 MITI created the Center for Information on Strategic Technology (CIST). Its mission is to improve the efficiency and effectiveness of Japan's system of export control, particularly in the area of dual-use products and technologies involving weapons of mass destruction. Broadly speaking, it was set up to prevent Japan from finding itself at some future time in a situation similar to that of Germany, Switzerland, France and other suppliers of Iraq after the Gulf War. The Center is sponsored by 24 leading industrial and trade associations, and it is staffed at the top by retired MITI officials who act as president and executive managing president. An active MITI bureaucrat is "on loan" and works in the general coordination division. CIST's top officials meet with MITI officials at least once a month and telephone contact is very regular. CIST has a total staff of 30. It recruits staff members from the private sector, typically from industries such as semiconductors, electronics, manufacturing machineries, and new materials. But it has also systematically recruited staff from the public sector, typically individuals with good connections inside the government. Often they have retired from ministries and agencies such as MITI, JDA, NPA and MOFA as well as peak associations of business such as Keidanren. CIST has a current membership of 180 firms which pay an annual membership fee of about 6,000 dollars each. MITI funds about one half of CIST's total budget. MITI hopes to eventually recruit 800 member firms. But for the time being it must cope with the hostility and skepticism of Japan's business community which in this area opposes the intrusion of government into business affairs [Interview No.24, Tokyo, December 19, 1991. Asahi Shimbun Keizai-bu, 1989, pp.112, 115-117].

The chief purpose of CIST is to create a control list of technologies that should not be exported from Japan. To this end it has formed ten committees and research groups which are reviewing relevant fields of technology such as advanced materials, computers and telecommunications. These committees are in the process of setting up a data bank which codes technologies according to how critical they are for weapons of mass destruction; how available these technologies are abroad; and how controllable their flow will be through government regulation. The hope is that item-by-item reviews, according to these three criteria, will eventually permit intelligent policy choices. In addition, CIST gathers information on the export control regimes of other governments. It is in touch with foreign research organizations. And it disseminates its information monthly through two publications. The creation of a global data bank on technologies is infinitely more complicated than the definition of products that was put on the COCOM list. And considering the bitter conflict over the export of dual-use products, the creation of a technology regime in this area poses a very formidable challenge to which MITI is devoting considerable resources. In the words of one official "modern trade is affected by politics, and we need to educate Japanese firms about this fact of life" [Interview No. 24, Tokyo, December 19, 1991. Asahi Shimbun Keizai-bu, 1989, pp.115-117].

Furthermore, MITI is reportedly planning to create a similar organization, the International High-Tech Center, to increase the information available to U.S. firms which Japanese firms are developing which specific technologies. It thus hopes to facilitate the transfer of Japanese dual-use technologies to U.S. defense firms [Interview No.25, Tokyo, December 19, 1991. Sentaku, 1991, p.96]. MITI is intent on identifying which Japanese corporations possess dual-use technologies important for the U.S., on persuading corporations to cooperate by promising to protect them from domestic criticism, and on shielding Japanese firms from strict controls by the U.S. government [Interview No.3, Tokyo, June 11, 1991]. However, this plan remains controversial inside MITI and cannot count on the support of Japanese firms. But it is possible that the cooperation with the U.S. Department of Defense (DoD) over dual-use technologies may become a means for protecting Japan's high-tech industries from some of the adverse effects emanating from the intensification of U.S.-Japan conflicts over high technologies [Sentaku, 1991, p.99]. For the risk exists that the DoD might try to prevent, through classifying as secret, the creation of the spin-off of technologies from U.S.-Japanese codevelopments that Japanese firms find so attractive. Establishment of a close relationship with DoD thus may give MITI an even larger role than before in security policymaking. While these issues are now actively debated within MITI, with the younger generation advocating a break with MITI's traditional hesitation to get involved in security policy, it is too early to judge confidently how this debate will in the end be resolved [Interview Nos. 24 and 25, Tokyo, December 19, 1991]. But this much we can conclude for sure. Changes in both technology and politics are driving MITI toward a more active role in security policy.

3. Ministry of Finance.

The Finance Ministry is the third major ministry to be involved in security policymaking. The ministry's role has been very prominent in the military security field. Its dedication to the principle of fiscal prudence, its authority to prepare the budget, and its prestige as an organization have made the MOF a very important brake on the unrestrained growth of the SDF and the defense industries. The MOF resisted the strengthening of the Police Reserve under the Occupation; it blocked MITI's plans in the 1950s to embark on the build-up of the defense sector as an export industry; and it restrained the rapid increase in the defense budget during the second Cold War—the pressures from MOFA, JDA, LDP hawks, big business, and the U.S. government to the contrary notwithstanding. Indeed, the ministry has been said to be the strongest force exercising civilian control over the SDF [Otake, 1980, pp.16-18]. Two factors have been important in the MOF's thinking on defense. It feared that a military-industrial complex, once formed, might be impossible to dismantle, and government spending necessary to maintain such a complex might constrain the ministry's discretion in fiscal policy. Furthermore, the ministry's officials remembered all too well that giving in to the pressures of the prewar military for large military spending led first to economic crisis and subsequently to war [Otake, 1984a, pp.42-45, 52-53].

In the ministry's view the "balance defense concept . . . mainly says that any expenditures toward defense should be kept to an absolute minimum because defense does not contribute to capital accumulation for the Japanese nation" [Endicott, 1982b, p.40]. From the standpoint of the MOF, an increase in defense expenditures must be justified "in terms of its positive impact on the domestic economy" [U,S.Congress, Office for Technology Assessment, 1990, p.103]. On the issue of economic policy the MOF has enjoyed an extraordinarily strong position in Japanese politics. Having "either sole or joint jurisdiction over tariff policy, the Export-Import Bank, the Overseas Economic Cooperation Fund, contributions to international organizations, and other similar matters" [Higashi, 1983, p.50], it plays an important role in economic security policymaking. Especially relevant units are its Customs and Tariff Bureau and the International Finance Bureau. Other parts of the Japanese government usually contact organizations such as the U.S. Department of the Treasury or the World Bank only with the consent of the ministry [Asahi Shimbun, November 30, 1991, 13th edition].

But the ministry's influence in the area of national defense is not unlimited. First, its influence extends only over those issues which involve substantial outlays of government funds. The ministry has been largely excluded from other questions of military significance, such as the development of joint operational planning between the United States and the SDF since the mid-1970s [Otake, 1983a, p.142].

Secondly, MOF's control over the limits on defense spending is constrained by the budgetary norm of maintaining "balance" among various ministries. Under such norm, a spending ministry stresses its "budget 'share', or its growth rate in comparison with the budget as a whole" to good effect [Campbell, 1977, p.32]. Notions of balance are especially important for organizations that have a hard time in finding justifications for their expenditures. The JDA is a typical example of such an organization since the SDF have never fought, since its function is limited to the mission of a defensive defense, and since the public's threat perception is weak. At least until the early 1970s, balance notions made possible the growth of defense spending despite an unfavorable domestic political climate for the JDA [Otake, 1981, p.498]. In the 1980s, however, such notions of balance were not important in the planning of the defense budget. Responding to U.S. pressure, the Japanese government exempted defense spending from the general ceiling that the MOF had imposed on the budget increases of ministries [Calder, 1988, p.425. Keddell, 1990, pp.151-57].

Third, the MOF's control has taken the form of placing overall limits on defense expenditure. But the ministry has basically respected the views of the JDA on how the defense budget is to be spent. For instance, the MOF cannot be expected to exercise influence over decisions on force structure [Hirose, 1989, pp.212-213, 241-242; 1990, p.38]. Indeed, it has been suggested that on questions of defense spending the MOF has brought to bear neither any substantive ideas about the means for assuring Japan's security nor any deep interest in Japan's international relations [Otake, 1980, p.18].

The absence of the MOF's substantive intervention in individual programs, however, is not unique to the defense area. First, delegating decisions on specific programs to other ministries is a simple method for avoiding hard choices. Through consultations and routine day-to-day contacts, officials of the ministry learn what are the priorities of spending ministries and the LDP's Policy Affairs Research Council (PARC) sections. Respecting such priorities economizes the ministry's decision-making resources [Campbell, 1977, pp.67-68]. Second, the MOF traditionally considered both macro- and micro-budgeting to be its domain. But the 1955-1970 period saw, among other things, increasing LDP intervention in both areas and even in internal organizational matters of the MOF. Confronting this challenge to its institutional autonomy, "MOF sought to protect its near monopoly over macro-budgeting decisions and its organizational boundaries by allowing control over individual program spending to slip away to the experts in the spending ministries and the LDP politicians" [Campbell, 1975, p.96]. The MOF has thus focused primarily on restraining the overall size and growth of the defense budget. The MOF's emphasis on maintaining undisputed authority over macro-budgeting is compatible with its close examination of JDA's budget requests. Line-item budget forms "reduce expenditures to calculations of quantity and unit price" [Campbell, 1977, p.63], and the appropriateness of JDA's calculations is scrutinized by the ministry. In the procurement of aircraft for example, from the ministry's perspective, cost considerations should basically determine whether or not planes should be produced at home [Campbell, 1977, p.64. Okimoto, 1981, p.281]. The FSX case apparently was no exception [Otsuki and Honda, 1991, p.75].

In sum, the MOF's involvement in defense issues, as in other issue areas, is characterized by a concern with macroeconomic management through macro-budgeting. This orientation lies at the heart of the ministry's budgetary authority. This condition is likely to be an enduring element in Japan's defense decision-making.

4. Mechanisms of Coordination.

Japanese security policy is formulated and implemented largely by these three major ministries as well as the JDA. The three ministries operate along two different dimensions. On questions of economic security MITI, the MOF and the MOFA constitute the core in which Japanese policy is articulated. On questions of military security the central bureaucratic organizations are MOF, MOFA, and the JDA. Because of the prominence of legal issues in the postwar defense debate, the Cabinet Legislation Bureau, an elite unit which oversees all legal aspects of government policy, has also played an important role [Koh, 1989, pp.197-98]. For example, the Bureau has been primarily responsible for the government's interpretation of Article 9 of the Constitution [Kataoka, 1982, p.257].

Both the economic and the military dimensions are integrated in the Cabinet Committee on Comprehensive Security. This committee was created by a decision of the Cabinet in December 1980, following the articulation of the comprehensive security concept by the Ohira government. Its mission is to deliberate on various areas of policy, such as economic and foreign affairs, from the standpoint of security. The committee consists of the Chief Cabinet Secretary, the Ministers of Foreign Affairs, Finance, Agriculture, Forestry and Fisheries, International Trade and Industry, and Transport, and agency heads of Defense, Economic Planning, and Science and Technology. Between 1980 and 1990 the committee met 21 times. The list of items discussed by the committee during that period shows its wide-ranging concerns. It includes energy (12 times); the situation in the Persian Gulf and the Middle East, also related to Japan's energy situation (8 times); science, technology and defense (6 times); Official Development Assistance (ODA) and general economic cooperation (4 times); and 3 meetings each for issues dealing with food and rare metals [Asagumo Shimbun-sha, 1991, pp.134-

136]. But the powers of the Committee have been constricted owing to the efforts of the different ministries to defend their traditional prerogatives [Nishihara, 1983/84, p.202]. Furthermore, the political salience of the notion of comprehensive security diminished sharply after Prime Minister Ohira's death, and the committee has not played an important policymaking role since the early 1980s [Hirose, 1989, p.53]. In fact, the military buildup in the 1980s has worked to the disadvantage of the comprehensive security concept which emphasizes non-military means of enhancing Japan's national security [Interview No.2, Tokyo, June 11, 1991]. The degree of integration between these two dimensions of Japan's security policy making apparatus thus remains tenuous.

At times the two policymaking axes intersect. For example, in the early 1980s it was a matter of contentious debate whether Japan should make an exception for the United States to the ban on exporting arms or military technologies. MOFA and the JDA were proponents of granting such an exception. They argued that basing the export of military technology on the Mutual Defense Assistance Agreement of 1954 would sidestep possible problems with other countries. For in contrast to the U.S. these countries did not have a defensive alliance pact with Japan. Focusing on the possible repercussions of the policy in the Middle East, MITI opposed the change [Gotoda, 1989, pp.30-35].

More typical, however, is the separation of the two dimensions and of economic and military security issues. This separation rests on the premise that the use or threat of military force to ensure Japan's economic security is simply not a viable political option. This premise was not shaken by the Persian Gulf crisis of 1987 when the United States requested Japan's military contribution to the Western effort of ensuring safe passage for Kuwait's tankers in the Gulf. And it was, if anything, reinforced by the Gulf crisis and war of 1990-1991. The Cabinet submitted to the Diet a bill permitting the SDF to assist the multinational forces in the area of logistics and support. But drawing criticisms that it amounted to an authorization of the use of Japanese military force overseas, the bill died quickly in the Diet. SDF minesweepers were sent to the Gulf only after the war had ended. And although the JDA had at times voiced concerns about possible threats posed to Japan's oil shipments, no military precautions were taken [Blair and Summerville, 1983, p.25].

An important coordinating mechanism in the area of economic security is the Councillors' Office for External Affairs. It was created in 1987 as part of an organizational reform to strengthen the coordination functions of the Cabinet, together with the Security Office and the Councillors' Office on Domestic Affairs.

Although its organizational predecessor was in charge of both domestic and foreign affairs, it concerned itself in fact mainly with domestic affairs; nonetheless, MOFA stationed one of its officials in that office [Okina, 1987, p.100]. The mission of the new Councillors' Office on External Affairs is to coordinate the activities of various ministries on matters concerning foreign economic relations. It is staffed by 22 officials from MOFA, the Prime Minister's Office, MOF, MITI, the Economic Planning Agency, and the Ministries of Agriculture, Forestry, and Fisheries, Construction, Transportation, and Posts and Telecommunications [Kusano, 1989, pp.76-78]. MOFA sends four officials to the Office, including its head and his deputy [Interview No.1, Tokyo, June 11, 1991]. The head of the Office enjoys good access to the Prime Minister. The Office thus constitutes one of several channels linking the MOFA with the top political leadership [Interview Nos.6 and 13, Tokyo, June 12 and 14, 1991]. Fearing any intrusion upon its jurisdiction, MOFA had originally opposed the creation of the Office for external affairs. But although that effort failed, MOFA succeeded in securing the directorship of the new Office for one of its own officials thus establishing direct control. MOFA has been quite comfortable with the new coordination of foreign policy at the level of the Cabinet [Interview No.13, Tokyo, June 14, 1991]. Since other ministries were also quite wary of the Office's possible interference in their activities, generally speaking it has not played a significant role in decisionmaking. But the support of the top political leadership can make a difference on specific issues as is illustrated by the prominent role the Councillors' Office for External Affairs has played in the opening of Japanese markets for foreign products [Kusano, 1989, pp.77-78, 86. Interview No.6, June 12, 1991].

While an informal process of interministerial coordination routinely takes place on the various issues of security policy, distinctive institutional arrangements affecting issues of military security assure that political and economic perspectives retain paramount importance in Japan's national security policymaking. First, major defense decisions (involving, for example, weapon systems, defense build-up plans, and annual budgets) which require the approval of the Cabinet need to be cleared first by the Security Council called until 1986 the National Defense Council (NDC). There was some discussion inside the government on whether the new Council should be called "National Security Council" or "Security Council." In seeking to avoid provoking the opposition parties, the government opted in the end for the latter term with its weaker connotation of military security [Angel, 1988-89, p.598]. In setting forth the necessity for setting up the NDC, the government explained before the Diet in the 1950s that 'national defense' was a broad concept which encompassed political, diplomatic, and economic factors, and that it was inappropriate to place matters concerning national defense solely under the JDA's jurisdiction [Kubo, 1978a, p.110; Miyawaki, 1980, p.48]. The NDC, however, met only 50 times between 1946 and 1981. In fact there were seven years when it met only once, and an additional seven years when it did not meet at all [McNelly, 1982, p.359].

The present Security Council has broader responsibilities than did the NDC. In addition to defense issues the Council is responsible for the managing of "serious crises" (Article 2, Security Council Establishment Law). However, because of constant Cabinet reshuffles, ministers often lack a background on security issues. And in the absence of strong administrative support, the Council remains only of subordinate importance in the policy process. For example, it did not play a significant role during the Gulf crisis of 1990-91 [Purrington and K., 1991, pp. 316-17]. The Council advises the Prime Minister and draws on the members of the cabinet and others on an ad hoc basis. Its standing members are the Prime Minister, Vice Prime Minister, Foreign Minister, Finance Minister, Chief Cabinet Secretary, Chairman of the National Public Safety Commission, and the Directors of the Defense Agency and the Economic Planning Agency. MITI was excluded from formal membership when the NDC was originally established in 1956. It was felt then that the inclusion of MITI would necessitate the inclusion of other economic ministries, such as the Ministry of Agriculture and Forestry or the Ministry of Transport [Ishiguro, 1978, p.287]. The MITI minister became a permanent member in 1972 but was again excluded when the Security Council was reconstituted in 1986 [Hirose, 1989, p.54]. While limited to ratifying decisions reached elsewhere, the Council is an institutional expression of the notion that any important defense policy proposal must go through an especially cautious consensus-building process in which virtually all relevant ministries participate.

When the Security Council was created in 1986, the Cabinet Secretariat was also reorganized and a Security Office was set up to replace the NDC Secretariat. The creation of a Security Office for crisis management inside the Cabinet Secretariat had already been proposed by the Comprehensive Security Study Group, an advisory commision convened by Prime Minister Ohira [Sassa, 1991b, p.17]. It serves as the staff for the Council and coordinates government policy on all security issues. For example, all of the important defense proposals that the JDA submits to the Cabinet for approval must first be passed on by the Security Office [Interview No.21, Tokyo, June 19, 1991]. However, the Security Office does not involve itself in questions concerning the U.S.-Japan Security Treaty. Thus it avoids all conflict with MOFA's Security Division [Interview No.13, Tokyo, June 14, 1991]. Officials from various ministries are delegated on temporary assignments to the Security Office. Its core consists of eleven councillors. Six of them serve concurrently in their respective parent ministries—among others, for example, as the Defense Agency's Defense Planning Division Chief, the Finance Ministry's Budget Examiner in charge of defense, and MITI's Aircraft and Ordnance Division Chief [Hirose, 1989, p.56]. The most senior of the councillors is a division-chief level official from the JDA [Interview No.4, Tokyo, December 9, 1991]. There is a division of labor within the Security Office. Officials from the NPA are in charge of non-military crisis management, while officials from JDA, MOFA, MOF, and MITI handle defense issues [Interview No.9, Tokyo, June 13, 1991]. Since they feared to lose some of their prerogatives the MOFA, the JDA, and the MOF were all opposed to the creation of the Security Office inside the Cabinet Secretariat. While proponents of a more forceful coordination of the affairs of government through this Office expected it to be headed by officials of administrative vice-ministerial rank, the ministries have succeeded in institutionalizing the practice of having only a bureau-director level appointment in charge of the Office [Angel, 1988-89, pp.597, 599-600. Kim, 1988, p.104]. Officials on loan from other ministries are mechanically rotated on a two-years basis. This makes it difficult to nurture substantive expertise on security issues at the center of the Japanese government [Sassa, 1991a, p.55]. Evidently, the Security Office is not a cohesive unit of action.

Generally speaking, the different offices in the Cabinet Secretariat have failed to transcend the interests of individual ministries [Kataoka, 1987, p.15; 1990, pp.8, 12; Sato and Matsuzaki, 1986, pp.159-160; Watanabe, 1977a, p.46]. The Security Office has been no exception to this tendency. This has posed a serious problem for those favoring more cohesion in the government while pointing at the same time to the continued importance of interministerial coordination. The predecessor of the present Councillors' Council, the NDC's Counsellors' Council, met 349 times between 1956 and 1986, while the NDC met 69 times during the same period. Negotiations over defense policy involving JDA's Defense Planning Division Chief and MOF's Budget Examiner in charge of defense were an important part of these meetings. Interministerial negotiations continue to be important under the present organizational arrangement of the Cabinet Secretariat. The Security Office is one arena for interministerial coordination which involves the JDA as one participant among several [Hirose, 1989, p.56].

In September 1991 the Secretary General of the LDP proposed the creation of a Cabinet unit, to be directed by a Deputy Chief Cabinet Secretary, that would concentrate on a comprehensive analysis of the information which the MOFA, JDA, NPA, the Cabinet Research Office and other agencies collect. This proposal was a response to criticisms that the

Japanese government lacked sufficient information during the attempted coup in the Soviet Union in August 1991 [Asahi Shimbun, September 7, 1991, 13th edition]. Past experience shows that it is highly probable that such a unit would become yet another arena for the exchange of information and for consultations among independent and relatively powerful ministries.

The Prime Minister has little control over the Cabinet Secretariat. The different offices in the Cabinet Secretariat tend to be arenas for interministerial coordination that impede the exercise of strong Prime Ministerial leadership. In fact the institutional infrastructure for leadership by the Prime Minister is simply inadequate for transcending the interests of strong ministries such as MOF or MITI. A Prime Minister's inner circle is penetrated by the major ministries. In each of the major ministries there are only two posts which can be filled by political appointees, the Minister and the Parliamentary Vice-Minister. And since the latter post has not been important in policymaking, it has been nicknamed "appendix" [Matsuzaki, 1991, p.71]. Appointing loyal supporters to ministerial positions and keeping them in these positions is no easy task for any Prime Minister. Each faction of the LDP is allocated a number of Cabinet posts in proportion to its numerical strength in the party. And each faction submits a list of faction members, compiled on the basis of seniority defined by the number of times a member has been elected to the Diet, from which Prime Ministers make their Cabinet appointments [Stockwin, 1988, p.40]. The large number of Diet members aspiring to serve in the Cabinet has led to the practice of frequent Cabinet reshuffles. Between 1964 and 1987, MOF, MOFA, and MITI ministers on average served, respectively, only 16.4, 15.9, and 13.2 months. All other Cabinet members, excluding Prime Ministers and Chief Cabinet Secretaries, enjoyed an even shorter tenure. The average length of tenure for the JDA director, for example, was only 11.9 months [Stockwin, 1988, p.43].

To improve their influence Prime Ministers have made occasional attempts to create a staff supportive of stronger leadership. For example, in line with the recommendations made by the Provisional Council for Administrative Reform in the mid-1960s, Prime Minister Sato sought to create posts for "Cabinet assistants." They were modelled after the American Presidential assistants. Takeo Fukuda had a plan to set up "Integrated Operations Headquarters", consisting of Diet members and experts outside of government. But neither plan was ever implemented [Kataoka, 1982, pp.253, 285-286].

And Prime Ministers have suffered from the fact that they do not have the option of relying either on groups inside the Liberal Democratic Party, such as the "defense tribe", or on the factions they lead. The "defense tribe", which will be discussed in detail below, is a group of LDP Diet members routinely involved in JDA's decisionmaking. However, like other groups in the LDP it cannot afford to be associated too closely with a Prime Minister, who is usually a faction leader. Tribes act across factional boundaries, and the maintenance of their cohesion necessitates distancing themselves from factional politics [Sato and Matsuzaki, 1986, p.93]. To a certain degree LDP factions are loyal to their leaders. However, party factions are not policy-oriented groups [Sato and Matsuzaki, 1986, pp.54-55, 79]. "Factions as such do not take positions on policy issues, nor do they exhibit any ideological coherence" [Curtis, 1988, p.88]. For example, Prime Minister Miki, a strong supporter of the ratification of the Non-Proliferation Treaty, faced a surprising number of "wait-and-seers" in his own faction [Sigur, 1975, p.186]. There do of course exist policy areas where some factions have a "disproportionate influence" [Curtis, 1988, p.88]. But this is due to the heavy representation of particular factions in particular policy tribes. By itself a faction cannot serve as a staff for a Prime Minister in specific areas of policy. A tribe dominated by the Prime Minister's faction might be able to support the exercise of executive leadership by combining a shared policy orientation with loyalty to the officeholder. But such a political configuration has never existed [Sato and Matsuzaki, 1986, pp.244-245].

In the absence of a secure foundation of political leadership either in government or in the LDP, Prime Ministers have resorted to making use of ad hoc groups. In negotiating the normalization of Japan's relations with the Soviet Union in 1955-1956, Ichiro Hatoyama formed a core decisionmaking group which was composed of LDP influentials and former MOFA officials. MOFA officials were excluded [Watanabe, 1977a, pp.34-35]. Takeo Miki relied on his personal advisors in handling foreign policy, much to the chagrin of the MOFA [Watanabe, 1977a, pp.52-53]. Yasuhiro Nakasone created an advisory commission on security policy, the "Peace Problem Research Council", which recommended in 1984 the dismantling of the one percent ceiling on defense spending [Angel, 1988-89, p.595; Drifte, 1990a, p.17]. Nakasone aspired to being, in his own words, a "presidential-type prime minister." In pursuing this objective, he relied heavily on ad hoc groups such as "advisory commissions", "headquarters," and "promotional groups." The latter two consisted of top members of both the government and the LDP, and were expected to provide for coordination of various interests inside various ministries [Muramatsu, 1987, pp. 311, 320, 322]. This strategy was successful in some cases, and it failed in others [Pyle, 1992, pp. 108-09]. Prime Ministers may even be able to coordinate the ministries directly, on the basis of political leverage gained with much effort during their long careers in the Diet. But such leverage accrues to individuals, not to the position of the Prime Minister itself [Keehn, 1990, pp.1034-35].

On occasion Prime Ministers have been able to lead, even to the point of overriding the interests of important ministries. But the institutional infrastructure for supporting them remains underdeveloped. Significantly, the government's perceived mismanagement of the Gulf Crisis in 1990-1991 has led not to efforts to build such an infrastructure but only to suggestions of how to reorganize the MOFA. In late 1991 the ministry's advisory group proposed the creation of a Comprehensive Policy Bureau and an International Intelligence Bureau. The hope was that the Comprehensive Policy Bureau would formulate foreign policy, including security policy, from a longer-term perspective. In addition it was to coordinate also the work of the functional and geographic bureaus of the ministry [Asahi Shimbun, December 2, 1991, 13th edition]. The new bureau is to absorb the existing United Nations Bureau [Asahi Shimbun, June 14, 1992, 13th edition]. Japan's preparation for participating in U.N. peacekeeping operations has not led either to the creation of a Prime Ministerial staff truly independent from the ministries. In 1991 an Office was created inside the Cabinet's Councillors' Office for External Affairs to prepare for the participation in peacekeeping operations. It consisted of about 30 officials who came from ten ministries and agencies, including MOFA, MITI, MOF, JDA, and the Ministry of Transportation [Asahi Shimbun, July 26, 1991, 13th edition]. What has been institutionalized, however, are arenas of interministerial coordination such as the Offices in the Cabinet Secretariat. These constrict Prime Ministerial leadership. And they shape the policy process dealing with security affairs.

5. Mechanisms of Control.

The embedding of the JDA in interministerial coordination processes is complemented by its lack of institutional autonomy. Important ministries have placed their officials inside the JDA thus colonizing the process of defense policymaking at its inner core. Officials sent on temporary assignment from a number of important ministr 3 constitute a significant part of the agency's personnel. This is not a phenomenon characteristic only of the JDA. Agencies set up since 1945 have often been penetrated politically by more established ministries. Provided the ministries involved agree, the rotation of officials among ministries can be accomplished easily. It is not subject to review or approval by other units of the government [Keehn, 1990, p.1034]. A good example is the Environmental Agency which was created in 1971. The positions of the directors of the Wildlife

Protection Division, the Air Pollution Control Division, the Automobile Pollution Control Division, and the Water Quality Bureau's Planning Division have been reserved, respectively, for officials from the Forestry Agency of the Ministry of Agriculture, Forestry, and Fisheries, MITI, the Transport Ministry and the Construction Ministry [Hatakeyama and Shinkawa, 1984, pp.258-259]. Another example is the Economic Planning Agency (EPA) which evolved from the Economic Stabilization Board that the Occupation authorities had created. The posts of the administrative vice-minister and the director of the minister's secretariat have traditionally been held, respectively, by MITI and MOF officials [Johnson, 1977, p.237]. In 1969 the MOF succeeded in placing its official in the administrative vice-minister post; ever since MITI, MOF, and career EPA officials have been embroiled in bureaucratic battles over the post [Yamauchi, 1991, p.100].

In the case of the JDA, the careers of the directors of the Security Office also illustrate the pervasive influence of other ministries and agencies. Its first director, serving between 1986 and 1989, had entered the NPA in 1954 and was first sent to the JDA in 1977; he became a bureau director in 1980. The second director, serving in 1989-90, entered the NPA in 1957, and was first sent to the JDA in 1986 as a bureau director. The third director assumed the post in 1990. He had entered the Home Affairs Ministry in 1961, was first sent to the JDA in 1986, and became a bureau chief in 1989 [Asahi Shimbun-sha, 1990, p.749, Boei Nenkan Kankokai, 1991, pp.572, 576, 637, 639-40]. Thus the senior officials the JDA sent to head the Security Office in the Cabinet Secretariat have actually spent most of their careers outside the JDA.

Officials sent from other ministries at later stages of their careers to occupy important JDA posts are by no means exceptional. The JDA has eleven top bureaucratic posts: the administrative vice-minister, chief of the secretariat, five bureau chiefs, and four counsellors. (Since the chief of the secretariat and the bureau chiefs serve concurrently as counsellors, the organization chart of the JDA shows ten counsellors). Of these eleven positions, a minimum of four are always reserved for officials from other ministries. One bureau chief position (Equipment) is always held by a MITI official, another one (Finance) is almost always occupied by an official from the MOF. Two counsellor posts (one in charge of international relations, the other in charge of health) are reserved for the Ministries of Foreign Affairs and Health and Welfare. In such cases officials typically have had no prior working experience in the JDA. Thus with only one exception, as of 1987 all of the officials recruited from MITI, MOFA, and the Ministry of Health and Welfare who have occupied the positions, respectively, of Equipment Bureau Chief, Counsellor in charge of International Relations and Counsellor in charge of Health joined the JDA for the first time at this senior stage of their careers. This makes it virtually impossible for them to be inculcated with the perspectives of the professional military [Hirose, 1989, pp.85-89, Appendix 1,2].

The NPA and the MOF have played an especially important role inside the JDA. They have succeeded in placing their officials very frequently in the posts of administrative vice-minister, chief of the secretariat, and bureau chief. For example, between the 1950s and the 1970s, nine of the twelve administrative vice-ministers of the JDA came from the NPA. Five of them first entered the JDA at the bureau chief level and went on to become the top bureaucratic official of the JDA. In the 1980s the balance of power has shifted. Four of the six administrative vice-ministers have come from the MOF. Two of them were first sent to the JDA at the bureau chief level [Hirose, 1989, Appendix 1]. The data on the key post of the Director of the Defense Policy Bureau points to a similar change. The bureau is the JDA's primary link with the DoD [Otsuki and Honda, 1991, pp.75,81]. It plays a predominant policymaking role inside the JDA. It is the place "where nearly all basic policies are analyzed, discussed, and sent on with preliminary recommendations to higher channels for approval" [Okimoto, 1978a, p.390]. The sending of the SDF minesweepers to the Persian Gulf, the co-development of the Fighter Support Experimental (FSX) aircraft with the United States, and Japan's advances in the area of command, control, communication and intelligence (C3I) are all issues in which the bureau has played a major role [Interview No.21, Tokyo, June 19, 1991]. Since 1976 it has had seven directors; while none came from the NPA, as of 1989 three were former MOF officials. Between 1963 and 1976, on the other hand, all five directors had come from the NPA [Hirose, 1989, Appendix 1]. As discussed in Chapter 5 below, the decreasing presence of the NPA inside the JDA coincides with a shift in the SDF's mission from internal to external security.

In the lower echelons of the JDA this pattern of outside penetration recurs. Additional positions are also staffed by officials from other ministries who serve in the JDA for the first time in their careers. Among the about 25 division chiefs, for example, at least four are always recruited from outside the JDA: the Finance Division Chief in the Finance Bureau (Finance Ministry), the Health and Medical Division Chief in the Education and Training Bureau (Ministry of Health and Welfare), the Coordination Division Chief in the Equipment Bureau (MITI), and the First Defense Intelligence Division Chief in the Defense Policy Bureau (National Police Agency) [Hirose, 1989, p.89, Appendix 3]. And some outside appointments are of course also made for some of the remaining 21 division chiefs. MOFA tries to hold on to one division chief post that has been allotted to it; but it does not have any particular one reserved for itself [Interview No.6, Tokyo, June 12, 1991].

Officials who started their careers in the JDA between 1955 and 1968 took 16 to 21 years to reach the position of division chief. The average number of officials entering the JDA upon passing the top-level civil service examination in this period was only 3.4. But because of the gradual increase in the number of officials who entered each year and subsequently rose to senior rank, several ministries and agencies, in addition to the four mentioned above, have had to relinquish division posts that used to be staffed from the outside [Hirose, 1989, pp.89-95, Appendix 3]. In the future to defend their positions outside ministries will have increasing problems, since the number of those entering the JDA annually has risen to about 15 in recent years [Interview No.15, Tokyo, June 17, 1991]. In 1988 for the first time an official who had started his career with the JDA reached its top civil service position [Hirose, 1989, Appendix 1]. But despite this change, in its top- and middle-level appointments the JDA remains deeply penetrated by officials from ministries with a predominantly economic or political orientation.

There exists a great asymmetry in the flow of personnel between the JDA and the major ministries. JDA officials are usually dispatched to other ministries for educational purposes, that is, to experience work in non-military areas and to widen their horizons. They are expected neither to participate in important decisions nor to utilize their military expertise in their host ministries or agencies [Interview Nos.3,15, Tokyo, June 11,17, 1991]. SDF officers, sent to Japanese embassies as military attaches, operate as military experts; they probably consititute the only exception [Interview No.15, Tokyo, June 17, 1991]. In 1990 38 members of the SDF have been stationed around the world at 29 embassies and in Geneva as military attaches, including the United States (6), Soviet Union (3) and many Asian and European countries [Defense Agency, 1990, pp.131-132. Hummel, 1988, p.53]. Working under the authority of the ambassador these assignments clearly are a boost to morale since they permit SDF officers to behave like military professionals. They can, for example, regularly wear their uniforms. But when they return from overseas "they have to learn how to be quiet again" [Interview No. 15, Tokyo, June 17, 1991].

Inside the JDA uniformed officers of the SDF are clearly subordinated to a layer of civilian personnel. The administrative hierarchy for military operation is under the control of the civilian administration which in turn answers to the Director of the JDA, who has consistently been an elected official [Hirose, 1989, pp.60-72. Kataoka and Myers, 1989, p.72. Sase, 1991]. The Occupation introduced a system of strict supervision of the professional military by a civilian bureaucracy that lacks all military ethos and perspective. This arrangement has been endorsed wholeheartedly by Japan's postwar political and economic elite which, on the basis of its prewar experience, retains a profound distrust of the professional military [Otake, 1983a, p.192]. But it should be noted that the civilian-military distinction is a particular instance of the distinction between generalists and specialists that is quite prevalent throughout the Japanese bureaucracy. Generalists are university graduates trained in law or economics, who have passed the top level civil service examination. The supremacy of the generalists over the specialists is entrenched inside various ministries and agencies. The distinction inside the JDA between "civilian bureaucrats" (generalists) and "uniformed personnel" (specialists) has counterparts in organizations such as the NPA, the Maritime Safety Agency, and the Fire Defense Agency [Nishioka, 1988, pp.154-156]. In the eyes of the SDF technical issues easily accessible only to military specialists are sometimes needlessly complicated by powerful generalists who lack the appropriate background training [Interview No.14, Tokyo, June 15, 1991]. A divergence of perspectives between generalists and specialists is not only restricted to the JDA but occurs widely inside Japan's bureaucracy.

A report entitled "On Civilian Control", submitted to the Diet in 1965, describes the division of labor between the internal bureaus and the uniformed officers in the Joint Staff Council and the three staff offices. According to the report, (1) the internal bureaus draft legislative bills as well as the orders of the Cabinet and the Prime Minister's Office; (2) communication and negotiation with the Diet and the various organs of the central government are handled exclusively by the internal bureaus; the staff offices engage in such activities only on minor matters and only with the approval of the Director of the JDA; (3) all plans concerning the SDF's operations and organization are drafted by the JSC and the staff offices, under the Director's general instructions. The internal bureaus draft these instructions and examine the drafts of the plans before sending them to the Director for final approval [Nishioka, 1988, pp.101-102]. This division of labor expresses very clearly the view that the civilian bureaucrats inside the JDA are in charge of the affairs of the SDF.

Civilian bureaucrats are in control of "all promotions beyond colonel (or captain in the MSDF)" [Chapman, Drifte, and Gow, 1982, p.40]. It must be noted though that under the present statutory framework, it is possible to fill high-ranking internal bureau posts with SDF officers. Under the Security Agency Law SDF officers were barred from internal bureau posts above the level of division chief. This provision was dropped from the JDA Establishment Law of 1954 because it was thought that SDF officers would be well qualified to fill posts such as the directorship of the Defense Policy Bureau and the Education Bureau. But the principle of civilian control is very deeply entrenched in the JDA. There is not a single instance of a SDF officer having ever been appointed at the division chief level or higher [Hirose, 1989, pp.66, 70-71].

JDA directors have not counteracted the wide-spread bias against the political articulation of military objectives. Considerations of factional balance and seniority defined by the number of times an individual has been elected to the Diet, rather than of policy expertise, have been dominant in Cabinet appointments. The JDA directorship has been no exception. Furthermore, as will be discussed below, it has been common practice that JDA directors serving in the Cabinet for the first time are not chosen from among those having an interest in security affairs. Between 1972 and 1987, 14 individuals served as the agency's director, seven of whom joined the Cabinet for the first time [Boei Nenkan Kankokai, 1991, pp.635-39. Sato and Matsuzaki, 1986, pp.367-405]. Also, as described above, between 1964 and 1987, the average length of tenure of JDA directors was less than a year [Boei Nenkan Kankokai, 1991, pp.630-39]. Thus, typically, a Diet member with little expertise in the area of security serves as the head of the JDA for a short period of time. This situation has tended to reinforce the political bias against the articulation of military objectives by the JDA.

The distribution of power inside the JDA has been the focus of several well-publicized episodes. For instance, in February 1981 JDA director Omura stated before the Lower House Budget Committee that he would henceforth make certain that high-ranking SDF officers seek approval from civilians higher up in the hierarchy before speaking in public. This was a response to the controversy caused by JSC chairman Takeda. In a magazine interview he had stated that spending only 1 percent of GNP for defense was "meaningless", and that an appropriate figure would be 3 percent. Opposition parties in the Lower House subsequently refused to continue debating a "meaningless" budget. Takeda was forced to resign a day before his scheduled day of retirement [Nishioka, 1988, pp.293-297]. A similar case involved JSC chairman Kurisu in the late 1970s. In June 1978 Kurisu spoke on television about the Soviet military exercises on one of the Kuril Islands. He was subjected to public criticism by JDA's civilian officials who took Kurisu's public pronouncements as a challenge to their position inside the JDA. In their view only the civilians in the JDA have the right to make such public statements on military issues. In the following month Kurisu was forced to resign, after he had ventured to discuss in a press conference what he regarded as defects in the SDF Law and the possibilities of the SDF's extralegal operations in an emergency. For the JDA director Kanemaru and the internal bureaus such public criticism of possible defects in Japan's national defense preparations went beyond acceptable limits [Otake, 1983a, pp.184-189].

In the absence of an effective system of Parliamentary oversight, the tight control which the civilian staff of the JDA exercises over the professional military has sometimes been called "civilian control." But it is not true that the Diet has been a mere rubber-stamping institution. Government statements made in response to Opposition parties' queries and accusations, as well as Diet resolutions, usually adopted unanimously, have constituted important constraints on defense policy. Well known examples are an Upper House resolution banning the overseas deployment of the SDF (1954), the three conditions that the Hatoyama Cabinet imposed on the exercise of the right of self-defense (1956), the Kishi Cabinet's statement opposing the introduction of nuclear weapons by the U.S. military and affirming that, as a matter of policy, the SDF will not be armed with nuclear weapons (1957), the Kishi Cabinet's pronouncement that the SDF will not bomb enemy bases even in self-defense (1959), the Sato Cabinet's ban of arms exports (1967), as well as its announcement of the three non-nuclear principles (1968), and, finally, the Lower House resolution concerning the three non-nuclear principles (1971) [Otake, 1983b, pp. 108-109. Sakanaka, 1991, p.74]. This list could be extended easily. The prohibition of conscription, the definition of the scope of the "Far East" in Article 6 of the Security Treaty, the definition of the substance of the meaning of "prior consultation" with the United States in times of crisis, and the removal of the bombing equipment and the prohibition of midair refueling are other important examples [Endicott, 1982b, p.39. Otake, 1983a, p.174]. Despite the predominance of the LDP in the Diet, the formulation of these constraints on Japan's security policy is due to the party's emphasis on building a broad political consensus.

Furthermore, since the bureaucracy has had little influence over partisan political bargaining in the Diet, leaders of the LDP and of the government have on occasion overridden the opposition of the bureaucracy in favor of compromising with the opposition parties in the Diet [Hirose, 1989, pp.158-61. Otake, 1983a, pp.94-95]. Thus, it is not an overstatement to say that the Diet has been a significant policymaking arena for Japan's security policy. But the above examples of government statements and resolutions illustrate that the Diet has chiefly functioned as an arena where domestic pacifist sentiments are translated into broad policy guidelines, not as an arena where military expertise is brought to bear on discussions of security policy. It is no accident that uniformed officers do not take part in the deliberations of the Diet, and that the Diet set up standing committees dealing with national defense issues as late as 1991 [Hirose, 1989, p.48. Nishihara, 1983/84, p.202]. Several opposition parties opposed the creation of such committees on the ground that such a move would amount to a tacit assent of the constitutionality of the SDF. Parliamentary debates on defense issues have taken place primarily in the Cabinet Committees which have jurisdiction over the laws that established the JDA and SDF, the Budget Committees, and the Foreign Affairs Committees [Hirose, 1989, pp.44-45, 48-49, 248-49. Okimoto, 1978a, p.432]. But defense issues have not dominated the agenda of these committees. "It often works out that security problems are thrust to the fore when sensational events occur. Otherwise, 'routine' questions of national defense can easily pass by the purview of the Diet without being missed" [Okimoto, 1978a, p.432]. In addition to this general tendency, the Budget Committees do not look at ministry and agency budgets individually; the Diet thus does not engage in any meaningful scrutiny of the details of the defense budgets [Hirose, 1989, pp.49-50].

In the early 1970s several proposals recommended the establishment of Diet committees dealing with security affairs. It took a decade to act on these proposals. Reflecting changing public attitudes towards defense, a Special Committee on Security was created in the Lower House in 1980 and in the Upper House in 1981. In 1980 the Upper House set up a Special Committee on Security and Okinawa and Northern Problems [Boeicho, 1991a, p.320. Otake, 1983a, pp.163-64]. Because they were not standing committees, these committees needed to be organized at the beginning of each Diet session. Although the creation of committees specializing in security was a significant indicator of a changing public mood, these committees, it should be added, were not active. Restricted to the gathering of information and research, they were not empowered to examine and vote on legislative bills. The LDP had little interest in research not directly connected to the passing of specific bills. Since there were no bills that could be used as levers to obtain concessions from the LDP in other areas of policy, the opposition parties also did not find the committees to be worth their active involvement [Sakanaka, 1990, p.75]. In September 1991, the Diet Law was amended and standing committees on security were created. To what extent the new standing committees will incorporate military thinking in their activities remains to be seen. According to one prediction, the new committees will simply act like the Cabinet committees which used to have jurisdiction over bills related to, among others, the JDA and SDF. The passing of such bills will be facilitated, however, because the JDA will not be competing with other ministries for the committee's time [Interview No.4, Tokyo, December 9, 1991].

Military professionals have chafed under this system of civilian control, without being able to dislodge or seriously undermine it. In the eyes of the professional military the principle of "civilian control" implies that it should be the exclusive responsibility of the professional military to advise the political leadership on matters requiring professional military expertise [Hirose, 1989, p.5]. Indeed, Article 9 of the Self Defense Forces Law stipulates that the chiefs of the three services are the highest professional advisors to the JDA director on all matters concerning Japan's ground, air and sea forces. The article implies that there are two parallel hierarchies, one civilian and the other military, serving under the director [Hirose, 1989, p.63]. In the late 1970s the chairman of the JSC, General Kurisu, argued in his stormy and brief tenure that the highest ranking uniformed officer was equal in rank to an administrative vice-minister and should, under the correct interpretation of the true meaning of the concept of "civilian control", take his orders from the director but not from civilian bureaucrats [Otake, 1983a, p.185]. In the eyes of the SDF, the time-consuming chain of command from various civilian bodies to the military might nullify Japan's capacity to repel a surprise attack [Tsurutani, 1981, p.100]. Kurisu was in fact advocating a reorganization of the JDA along the lines of the U.S. Department of Defense, where two hierarchies, made up of armed services and civilian administrators, come together in the office of the Secretary of Defense [Kataoka and Myers, 1989, pp.72, 74]. In a recent article, Kurisu has called attention to the fact that one of the Japanese ships sent to the Persian Gulf for minesweeping refueled foreign ships by order of the administrative vice-minister. He asserts that, under Article 9 of the SDF Law, the JDA Director should have been the one giving the order [Kurisu, 1991, p.59]. Another one of Kurisu's proposals aimed at a reorganization of the intelligence service of the SDF. Since the SDF Law puts military intelligence under the purview of the JSC, not the internal bureaus, Kurisu insisted that the chairman of the JSC should be authorized to conduct intelligence briefing for the Director of the JDA [Otake, 1983a, p.190]. This proposal was eventually adopted [Kataoka and Myers, 1989, p.75]. On the other hand, Kurisu's 1977 proposal that the JSC chairman periodically brief the Prime Minister on military matters and that the JSC chairman be attested by the Emperor upon appointment has not been instituted [Otake, 1983a, p.169].

The law establishing the JDA and the "Order concerning the Task Allocation between the Security Agency's Secretariat, Bureaus and Staff Offices", issued during the early 1950s have been the legal basis for the internal bureaus' insistence that they have the authority to exercise control over the staff offices and the JSC. Article 16 of the law grants the chief secretary as well as the bureau directors powers to advise the JDA Director on matters both of military administration and military operation. Still in effect today the order details the task allocation between the internal bureaus and the staff offices. Overall, it may be characterized as placing the internal bureaus above the uniformed personnel in the hierarchy of the JDA. At the time the 1954 law was passed, a proposal was made to replace the order with a new allocation of responsibilities. However, the wide gap which separated the views of the internal bureaus from those of the staff offices on this matter prevented the proposal from being adopted [Hirose, 1989, pp.63, 67-68, 71-72].

It should be noted that the control civilians exercise over the professional military has been facilitated by the rivalry among the three services. One example among several is an episode that relates to the formulation of the Second Defense Buildup Plan. The JSC could not resolve a conflict between the Ground Self-Defense Force (GSDF) and the Air Self-Defense Force (ASDF) over deployment of Surface-to-Air Missiles (SAMs). The JDA Director and the internal bureaus finally intervened to settle the issue. From the standpoint of the internal bureaus, the inability of the services to coordinate among themselves makes the intervention of the civilian bureaucrats simply unavoidable [Hirose, 1989, p.74]. Hoping to create a central command post, the JDA set up a study committee in June 1977 [Nishihara, 1983/84, p.203]. The central command post was set up in 1984 [Sekai Henshu-bu, 1987, p.25]. But as late as 1988 the integration of command and communications systems was still on the political agenda of the JDA [Sato, 1988, p.19]. Formally, the JSC is responsible for the coordination of the three services. It is, however, ill-equipped to perform such a role. First, although he can issue orders on combined operations of two or more services, the JSC chairman does not have the power of command over the service chiefs. In recent years there have been some signs of the strengthening of the JSC. For instance, the JSC has formulated the JDA's mid- and long-term plans since 1977. It also has had an important role in the joint operational planning with the U.S. However, the JSC chairman has remained basically equal in hierarchical status to the service chiefs [Hirose, 1989, p.73]. The JSC does not have powers in the area of procurement. Considering the attention this area has received in defense policymaking, this is a major source of weakness [Interview No.9, Tokyo, June 13, 1991]. It has been repeatedly suggested that the chairman of the JSC be made a member of the National Defense Council, and that he be attested by the Emperor upon appointment by the Prime Minister; but these suggestions have never been acted on [Chapman, Drifte, and Gow, 1982, pp.44-45]. It may be possible for the three services to agree to upgrade the JSC, if a stronger JSC could limit the control exercised by the internal bureaus. But this condition is unlikely to be fulfilled, and none of the services has any incentive to sacrifice a part of its autonomy [Hirose, 1989, pp.73-74].

Secondly, uniformed officers assigned to the secretariat of the JSC tend to act as representatives of each service. It is true that officers trained at the Joint Staff College form an important part of the secretariat. But because its training does not take place at a sufficiently early career stage, the College fails to inculcate in the officers a perspective that transcends the interests of each service [Hirose, 1989, pp.74-75].

The uniformed officers' possession of military expertise and the principle of consensual decisionmaking suggest that it would be a mistake to underestimate military influence in policymaking [Okimoto, 1978a, p.396]. For example, weapons procurement under the National Defense Program Outline (NDPO) of 1976 has largely been consistent with the preferences of the SDF [Hirose, 1989, pp.234-36]. In addition, uniformed officers may provide inputs to the policy process on security issues through their links with the U.S. military. These can influence communications between the two governments and thus help shape the policy process [Chuma, 1985, pp.89-91. Hirose, 1989, pp.227-29. Miyake, Yamaguchi, Muramatsu, and Shindo, 1985, pp.48-49. Otake, 1983a, p.194]. But inherent in the civilian-military arrangements inside the JDA is a strong bias against any military interpretation of Japan's national security requirements. It has frequently been pointed out that JDA's civilian bureaucracy lacks cohesion because it draws its members from various ministries. The heterogeneity of the civilian bureaucracy, however, is closely linked to the prominence of a political and economic definition of security. This bias has been reinforced by embedding the JDA in a variety of interministerial arrangements. Such arrangements are deeply entrenched. One observer pointed out in 1975 that Japan's military defense lacked a mobilization plan, a military court system, emergency legislation, and a civil defense system [Sigur, 1975, p.193]. It still lacks all of these elements today. Even after a decade of rising military tension in the Far East, with the exception of the ASDF, the SDF lacks rules for engaging the enemy [Interview No.3, Tokyo, December 9, 1991. Nishihara, 1983/84, p.200]. It is thus particularly noteworthy that the Second Cold War did not measurably affect the political arrangements either within the JDA or within the government.

B. Civil-Military Relations

This conclusion is reinforced by the system of civil-military relations between state and society. The SDF exists in relative isolation from a Japanese public which, by and large, eschews all military issues. The relative weakness of the representation of military interests inside the LDP reflects this characteristic feature of Japanese politics. Close relations between government and business, furthermore, tend to accentuate the economic dimensions of security, both on questions of weapons procurement and the supply of vital raw materials.

1. The Isolation of the Military from the Public.

Japan's military is remarkably isolated from the Japanese public. Outbursts of public hostility against what used to be called the SDF "tax thieves" have become rare. But in sharp contrast to the police, in the eyes of the public the SDF lacks a convincing political rationale [Interview No.2, Tokyo, December 9, 1991]. Typically the military is greeted with public indifference or thinly veiled hostility. In a survey commissioned by the Prime Minister's Office in 1988, law and order and domestic economic management ranked at the top and national security at the bottom of the public's assessment of important issues [Inoguchi, 1991a. p.157-61].

The SDF has tried energetically to woo the Japanese public. Its public information division employs a staff of about 50 in Tokyo and a total of about 950 at the 250 odd bases that the SDF maintains throughout Japan. Besides a small and little noticed monthly publication the office puts out an annual publication with a circulation of 100,000 that, for lack of a buying public, it purchases itself and then distributes free of charge [Interview No.2, Tokyo, December 9, 1991]. With the exception of the annual defense day celebrations in late October and occasional special events such as a special visitors' day at the American base at Yokosuka after the arrival of the carrier Independent [Interview, No.15, Tokyo, December 14, 1991], the obligatory parades and exhibitions that each service organizes reach only a miniscule portion of the public [Interview No.4, Tokyo, June 11, 1991]. Public relation gimmicks like the opening of the Fuji base of the GSDF to tourists, including a trip to the five lakes of Mount Fuji as an integral part of the tour of the base, have attracted only 1,200 visitors a year [Yomiuri Shimbun, December 28, 1990]. It is thus hardly surprising that the SDF jumped at the chance of cooperating with a Japanese film producer in the production of "Best Guy", a movie that was modelled after Hollywood's successful production of "Top Gun." The movie was shot on location at the ASDF Chitose air-base; and the SDF cooperated in providing ample photo-opportunities in the form of fifty hours of airdrills, saving the movie some 10 millions yen [Kusaoi, 1990].

The relations which the JDA and SDF have with Japan's powerful media are no longer marked by explicit, mutual suspicion. Yet relations are far from comfortable. SDF officials in the public information division watch reporters carefully, especially during their first assignments. And the public information division of the JDA spends a great deal of time and effort in trying to cultivate good relations with individual reporters who normally serve only one-year stints. Occasional conflicts, however, do occur, and serious cases of what the JDA regards as factually wrong reporting may prompt officials to go to the middle management of the newspapers to push for change [Interview No.2, Tokyo, December 9, 1991]. The press pool is assigned to the civilian parts of the JDA rather than to the SDF, a fact that is resented by the professional military. Military secrets interfere to some extent with the informal sharing of information which is the hallmark of Japan's media politics. And the objective pressure for good press coverage is no longer as strong as it was in the late 1960s when the SDF used background briefings in order to create a more favorable opinion climate in anticipation of mass demonstrations against the renewal of the Security Treaty in 1970 [Interview Nos. 2 and 10, Tokyo, June 11 and 13. Interview No. 23, Kyoto, June 24, 1991].

Voluntary associations supporting the SDF exist. In the 1950s they were linked to the modest revival of rightwing nationalism [Morris, 1960, pp.206-68]. Other organized groups supporting the SDF have appeared since, such as the Defense Conference which was formed in 1965 and counts 900 corporations and 500 individuals among its members; ᴣ Friends of the SDF also founded in 1965 with a membership of about 600; and the Merchants' Association for Defense Cooperation, established in 1990 which has a membership of about 1,800 [Asagumo Shimbun-sha, 1991, p.573. Boeicho, Koho-shitsu, 1988, p.5]. Many of these associations are affiliated with conservative politics, are small in size, and lack popular appeal [Interview Nos. 2,7 and 23, Tokyo, June 11 and 13, 1991. Kyoto, June 24, 1991. Interview No.2, Tokyo, December 9, 1991].

The social base of the SDF, however, does not rest with these national associations but with the more than 1,000 local groups that have sprung up around the 250 bases of the SDF that exist throughout Japan. Although it is difficult to estimate the effective membership of these groups, the total number of offical members is about ten million [Interview No.2, Tokyo, December 9, 1991]. Some of these are normal support groups such as SDF veterans, parents of SDF members, groups seeking access to base facilities for sports events, and groups wanting to promote the marriages of eligible daughters living around the base. But others are local lobbies, typically organized by the political elites of the communities surrounding the base, who vie for the public funds that the JDA disburses in compensation for the noise pollution and other harmful side-effects of SDF operations. The bases of the SDF form a local welfare state which generates its own distinctive type of politics [Interview No.22, Tokyo, December 18, 1991]. The Defense Facilities Administration Agency of the JDA spends about 5 percent of Japan's total defense budget on mandatory and discretionary compensations disbursed among the peoples and communities living in the vicinity of military bases [Boeicho, 1991a, p.261. Boeicho, 1991b]. Most of the disbursed funds must be spent on infrastructure investments, thus meeting the regional policy objectives of the government. And the SDF typically pays a per capita fee to communities affected in any substantial way by the presence of the SDF in their vicinity. The whole system is a gigantic exercise in distributive politics through which the JDA, lacking broader social and political supports, generates support among a small and well-organized public.

The weakness of its social base as well as the strength of Japan's economy explain why the SDF has great difficulties in filling its conscription goals; the annual shortfall is about 30,000-40,000 men and is likely to get much larger with the rapid aging of the Japanese population. The rate of enlistment in the GSDF is expected to decline by 50 percent in the 1990s. Furthermore many of the recruits the SDF attract, especially in the GSDF, do not fit the requirements of a high-quality fighting force that the SDF is trying to promote [Interview Nos. 2, 8, 9, 10 and 12, Tokyo, June 11, 13 and 14, 1991. Interview No. 2, Tokyo, December 9, 1991]. In 1989 the National Defense Academy could fill only 438 of its 500 spaces. The drop-out rate after the first year is 10 percent, and about one-third of the graduating class chooses not take up its military commission [Interview No.8, Tokyo, June 13, 1991]. Pay and working conditions are simply not competitive with those in the private sector. However, the effort to recruit women is just beginning. The academy accepted women students for the first time in 1992 [Asahi Shimbun, February 8, 1992, 13th edition].

These problems are reinforced by the lack of tradition with which the SDF must cope [Humphreys, 1975, pp.38-39]. The Imperial Household Agency and the government have seen to it that the emperor has never reviewed any troops of the SDF or even visited their barracks. The suggestion of General Kurisu, Chief of Staff of the GSDF in October 1977, that the Chairman of the JSC should be "attested" by the emperor, was widely criticized by the media as a thinly veiled attempt to revive Japan's military tradition [Nishihara, 1985a, p.136]. However, the absence of traditional norms sustaining the SDF, and in particular the elimination of all links between the military and a transcendental sacred leader, have not been a serious problem. By the standards of other countries morale problems have not been unusual.

At the same time it is also very evident that the SDF has no specific tradition which sustains a new military mission. A 1961 JDA document outlining the moral principles which were to inform the behavior of the SDF does refer to democracy. But there has been no sustained effort to inculcate democratic values in the personnel of the SDF [Japan Defense Agency, 1961. Interview Nos.2, 5, 8, 11, 12 and 13 Tokyo, December 9, 11, 12 and 13, 1991]. Old officers undoubtedly decried the lack of spirit and the materialism of Japan's postwar youth. But with the removal of the emperor from politics the SDF is now simply part and parcel of the norm of popular sovereignty as articulated in Japan's constitution. The ASDF is too young to have a distinct prewar history; and its role model is as much the American airforce as an abstract Japanese military ideal. Only the Maritime Self-Defense Force (MSDF) has shown an awareness of some of the traditions of the Imperial Navy. For better or worse, generational change is pushing relentlessly back the memories of Japan's pre-war military. The tipping point in the officer corp of the SDF was reached in the late 1960s when graduates of the prewar military academies roughly equaled in numbers and proportion those who had attended military academies after 1945. By 1980 the natural process of maturation had removed all prewar officers from the ranks of the SDF [Emmerson, 1971, p.125-27].

This encapsulation of the Japanese military is also evident in the "policy tribes" (zoku) of the LDP. These tribes constitute an important link between state and society in contemporary Japanese politics. Although it had been in use in political circles before, this concept came to be used widely only after the Lockheed scandal of 1976. Investigation into the scandal uncovered some unsavory activities of the "aircraft tribe", itself part of the "transportation tribe" [Itagaki, 1987, p.12].

The long reign of the LDP has made it possible for LDP Diet members to acquire expertise in particular policy areas. They have organized themselves in policy tribes, each specializing in a particular area of policy. The tribes began to appear in the latter half of the 1960s. By the end of the 1970s, they were well established in most of the major public policy issues, including national defense [Sato and Matsuzaki, 1986, pp.92-94]. LDP members acquire expertise in particular policy areas as they climb up career ladders that have become highly institutionalized under the political dominance of the LDP. In the early stages of their careers, LDP politicians typically serve in posts such as a Diet committee director, parliamentary vice-minister, vice-chairman of a section in the LDP's PARC, chairman of an ad hoc committee created inside PARC, or acting chairman of a PARC section. Before they are initiated fully into the informal circles of the policy tribes, aspiring LDP politicians need to operate successfully in such apprenticeship posts [Matsuzaki, 1991, pp.70-75]. Apparently, Diet members are acknowledged as full-fledged tribe members only after they have achieved the position of section chairman of PARC, a post that is thus eagerly sought after [Nihon Keizai Shimbun-sha, 1983, pp. 20-21].

Sato and Matsuzaki define policy tribes as "groups of middle-level members of the Diet that routinely exercise strong influence in policy areas whose boundaries are demarcated basically by reference to ministries and agencies." As middle-level LDP officials, they are distinguished from the "influentials" at the top who exercise influence in a variety of policy areas [Sato and Matsuzaki, 1986, pp.264-66]. Former Prime Minister Kakuei Tanaka, for example, was "a central figure in the telecom wars, in which he participated as a MITI zoku, a finance zoku, and a postal zoku, the only person in the Diet with such varied bases of influence" [Johnson, 1989, p.205].

In contrast to PARC sections the policy tribes are informal groups. The growing influence of the tribes in policymaking has led, to a certain extent, to the ritualization of the deliberations of the PARC sections. One indicator for this is the decreasing number of PARC section meetings held since the late 1970s. Normally section meetings provide no longer a stage for serious discussion of policy issues. And when they do, it is understood by everyone that the section chair can make the final decision [Sato and Matsuzaki, 1986, p.93].

The specialization of policy tribes is defined by the jurisdiction of government ministries and agencies. Tribes are intimately involved in the policymaking of their ministries and agencies. They connect to the bureaucracy on the one hand and to organized social groups on the other. Tribes represent the interests of specific social groups in government policymaking. They engage in what Muramatsu and Krauss call "subgovernment conflict", as they seek to promote the interests of their client groups often together with their counterpart ministries [Muramatsu and Krauss, 1987, p.542]. And the tribes also act to protect their clients' interests from broad policy initiatives, such as administrative reform in the 1980s, that attempt to cut down on vested interests in various policy areas [Nakamura, 1984, pp.60-61]. In return for such activities, social groups provide tribe members with financial contributions and support in electoral mobilization [Matoba, 1986, p.165]. The tribes, however, are not mere agents of social groups. At times they also perform the role of persuading interest groups to make concessions as on the issue of trade liberalization [Kusano, 1989, pp.80-81]. In sum, policy tribes are important in mediating, in various policy areas, between state and society.

In the area of defense, LDP Diet members have formed the "defense tribe." The formal LDP organs that are closely related to this tribe are the Defense Section, the Investigative Commission on Security which deals with long-range defense policy, and the Special Committee on Base Problems. These three organizations are placed under the auspices of PARC. Until standing committees on security were created in 1991 in both Houses of the Diet LDP members serving on Cabinet Committees that dealt with bills touching on the JDA automatically became members of the Defense Section. Those who did not belong to a Cabinet Committee could also choose to join the Defense Section. Each Diet member usually joins three PARC sections

[Nihon Keizai Shimbun-sha, 1983, pp.21, 83]. According to one observer, the members of the defense tribe fall into three sub-groups: (1) those who cultivated an interest in defense while serving in the JDA as Director or Parliamentary Vice-Minister, (2) former civilian or uniformed officials in the JDA, and (3) those representing electoral districts that host military bases [Habara, 1985, pp.82-83]. Significantly, the defense tribe does not include any member of the LDP's top leadership [Interview No.2, Tokyo, June 11, 1991].

The tribe's relations with the defense industry are far from clear. LDP Diet members are generally interested in the industry as a potential source of financial contributions. Eyeing the prospective growth of the industry, a group named the Diet Members' League for the Promotion of National Technology in Defense Equipment was formed in the early 1980s. However, an interminable series of scandals related to procurement and the small number of major new procurement programs have apparently dampened links with industry [Habara, 1985, p.83].

This description of the defense tribe illustrates the lack of well organized social groups that push the tribe to represent their interests in policymaking. In his analysis of the policy process leading to the Fourth Defense Buildup Plan, Hideo Otake notes that the JDA was isolated and virtually left to its own devices in its negotiations with the Finance Ministry. This was in striking contrast to other areas of policy where ministries were strongly supported by Diet members and interest groups in dealing with the powerful Finance Ministry [Otake, 1981, p.491]. Otake notes that "Dietmen never intervene specifically to sponsor a particular procurement project or to back a defense corporation, at least at the budget-making stage. Lobbying efforts are directed exclusively towards the total amount of the defense budget. This contrasts sharply with the 'Highway Construction Tribe' and the 'Education Tribe', which lobby for their electoral districts or for their business sponsors, as well as for increases in the total budget" [Otake, 1982, p.17]. Otake attributes this fact to the weak lobbying effort of the defense industry as well as the small size of the defense industry. Japan's weapons procurement process involves the three military services, JDA's TRDI and civilian bureaus such as Equipment, Finance, and Defense Policy as well as the major military contractors such as Mitsubishi Heavy Industries (MHI). But because politicians interested in defense matters are a step removed, that process is largely shielded from the public's eye [Endicott, 1982a, pp.460-61]. The relatively subordinate position of party politicians has an obvious reason. "Few Dietmen, if any, have an electoral district with a large armament industry. Unlike their American counterparts, Defense Dietmen in Japan are not connected to defense corporations and related unions in their home districts. This is reflected in their 'philosophical approach' to the defense budget" [Otake, 1982, p.18].

Because of their pacifist stand, labor unions, with a few notable exceptions, have refrained from pressuring the JDA on matters of procurement [Otake, 1981, p.492]. It is true that most members of the defense tribe are backed by veterans associations [Otake, 1982, p.15]. But these associations link up with organizations other than the defense tribe. Inside the government their primary channel is the Pension Bureau in the General Management Agency. And inside the LDP Policy Affairs Research Council they are connected with the Cabinet Section and Investigative Commission on Pension and Mutual Aid System [Kanesashi, 1984, p.176. Nihon Keizai Shimbun-sha, 1983, pp.152-154]. It is significant that these associations do not have strong ties with the JDA.

Thus, the defense tribe's efforts to increase the defense budget and to expand the size of five-year plans are not part of the normal political exchange in which tribe members gather both votes and financial contributions in return for policy favors [Otake, 1981, p.491; 1984b, p.290]. Because of the absence of well-organized support groups in society and public reluctance to support the hawkishness of the defense tribe, Diet members interested in national security are considered to be vulnerable in elections. A well-known example is the case of a top leader of the tribe, Zenshiro Hoshina, who failed to get reelected in the 1960s [Otake, 1982, p.20]. Of the seventeen Lower House members whom Inoguchi and Iwai identified as members of the defense tribe [Inoguchi and Iwai, 1987, p.304], five lost their reelection bids in 1990. Another five retired before the election [Takamine, 1991, p.241]. It goes without saying that in some electoral districts where military bases are located, SDF votes may be very important. But members of the SDF generally vote for LDP candidates, whether they belong to the defense tribe or not.

It is therefore hardly surprising that joining the tribe has not been a particularly attractive option for LDP Diet members coming from competitive electoral districts. A present member of the tribe (and former JDA director belonging to the Nakasone faction) recounted in an interview how, at the start of his political career, he asked to be supported as Parliamentary Vice-Minister at MITI, but, over his objection, was virtually ordered by Nakasone to fill the post of Parliamentary Vice-Minister at the JDA. He emphasizes that a "sense of mission" now motivates him in his work as a member of the tribe [Shukan Yomiuri, 1990, p.22]. Assuming the post of parliamentary vice-minister in a ministry with jurisdiction over powerful social groups is an useful stepping stone for joining the tribe associated with that ministry, enjoying access to the votes and the financial support that such groups provide and thus consolidating electoral support.

This is true of the post in MITI. It is not true of the post in the JDA. Electoral pressures keep Diet members away from defense issues unless they "have some reason to take an individual interest" in defense or "feel compelled out of a spirit of public interest" [Okimoto, 1978a, p.436].

Indeed, Defense is considered to be one of the most unpopular tribes, along with Justice, Local Administration, Cabinet and Labor. The defense tribe includes many former JDA directors. Among the seventeen Lower House tribe members mentioned above, seven were former directors of the JDA. Consistent with the small number of Diet members willing to join the tribe is the fact that a Diet member with little or no experience in the defense area may become a JDA director and then, on account of his tenure as director, be recruited into the tribe. This deviates from the standard pattern in which Diet members need to perform effectively in various government, Diet, and LDP posts before being able to join a tribe. The defense tribe is peculiar in that a considerable number of its members join by chance. JDA directors serving in the Cabinet for the first time are often chosen from outside the tribe, because of the perceived hawkishness of the tribe, rather than on the basis of the individual's competence on defense matters [Inoguchi and Iwai, 1987, pp.117-20,131-32,210].

Some data on the membership of PARC sections reinforce the impression that membership in the defense tribe is not very popular. Of the 49 members belonging to the Defense Section in 1978, only 8 (or 16 per cent) remained in 1982. This figure was the lowest among the 17 PARC sections. Similarly low figures were recorded only for the Environment Section (18 per cent) and the Justice Section (19 percent). In sharp contrast the figures were much higher for Health and Welfare (45 percent), Agriculture, Forestry, and Fisheries (42 percent), and Commerce and Industry (42 percent) [Nakamura, 1984, pp.49-50]. A study of the ratio of the number of PARC section members (which is not fixed) and the number of counterpart Lower House committee members (which is fixed) shows that the figure for Defense Section/Cabinet Committee never rose above 2.1 between 1964 and 1987. In 1987, the figures were 7.3 for Construction Section/Construction Committee, 4.9 for Agriculture and Forestry Section/Agriculture, Forestry, and Fisheries Committee, and 4.4 for Commerce and Industry Section/Commerce and Industry Committee, and only 1.9 for Defense Section/Cabinet Committee. The average for all sections/committees was 2.6 [Inoguchi and Iwai, 1987, pp.136-37]. Although the establishment of the Lower House's Special Committee on Security in 1980 was widely interpreted as "a breakthrough in fostering public awareness of national security issues" [Nakada, 1980, p.165], these figures indicate how unpopular national defense issues have remained in the eyes of party politicians.

This is not to argue that defense policy is altogether without a social base in Japanese domestic politics. The Democratic Socialist Party (DSP), for example, enjoys the support of private sector unions and small business. From a position of opposition it has shifted since the mid-1970s to a position that explicitly supports Japan's defense policy [Umemoto, 1985a, pp.155-160]. The strength that this party enjoys among the workers employed in the defense industry, for example, may have been one factor that has contributed to its changing stance. In 1972 labor unions in the aircraft industry apparently constrained the party's opposition to the budget and the Fourth Defense Buildup Plan which had T2 aircrafts as one of its main procurement items [Otake, 1983a, pp.98-99]. In the mid-1970s unions in the shipbuilding and aircraft industries asked the government to increase domestic production of weapons. In the 1980s labor unions in the aircraft industry were deeply concerned about the FSX issue [Otsuki and Honda, 1991, pp.31-33]. Furthermore, the party has enjoyed relatively strong support also among small, self-employed Japanese business. This sector leans towards the conservative end of the political spectrum and thus may have supported the party's changing stance as well [Interview No.14, Tokyo, December 13, 1991]. But the DSP is the exception not the rule. Generally speaking, national defense has no firm social base in Japan.

The system of policy tribes that has emerged in Japan during the postwar decades usually yields a picture of well-organized social groups firmly linked to ministries that have jurisdiction over them. The defense tribe, however, while closely connected to the JDA and influential in areas such as defense budget making, lacks ties to other well organized social groups. It is reasonable to expect that the defense tribe would not lack such ties if the JDA were closely linked to important social groups. The encapsulation of the defense tribe thus reflects the encapsulation of the JDA.

2. The Military and the Civilian Economy.

The Japanese defense economy is built around close links between business and government that reflect a far-reaching subordination of military to political and economic requirements. But to the extent that the civilian economy is complementary with the defense economy, as has been true of Japan's recent advances in high-technology industries, no structural barriers impede the symbiotic relations between the two [Samuels, 1991. Ziegler, 1992, pp.235-43. Kihara, 1977. Bergner, 1991, pp.176-85].

Japan's economy is overwhelmingly civilian and does not feature an American-style military-industrial complex. This, however, does not mean that the defense economy is irrelevant to Japan's civilian economy. The defense economy, understood not as a set of defense contractors producing for a government market, but as a set of technological options pursued as a matter of conscious policy, has been a central, driving force in Japan's push toward technological frontiers. The military significance of this growing national option is easily overlooked. For since 1945 Japanese policy has consistently chosen economic competitiveness over military prowess. Only in recent years has the military implication of the pursuit of economic goals become readily apparent.

Japan's industrial base is geared to commercial products, and its major corporations eschew dependence on military production. Thinking of the military-industrial complex in American rather than Japanese categories Daniel Okimoto concludes that "if ever a major industrial state defied categorization as a military-industrial complex, it would have to be post-war Japan" [Okimoto, 1981, p.288. Auer, 1973b, pp.217-45]. According to different estimates Japan's defense industries accounted for less than 0.5 percent of total industrial output in the 1970s. During the defense build-up of the 1980s it increased very slightly to about 0.6 percent in 1987 [Hopper, 1975a, p.145. U.S. Congress, 1990, p.104 and 1991, p.113. Samuels, 1991, p.53]. In the mid-1980s only 2.0 percent of Japan's total manufacturing capacity was concentrated in the defense sector [McIntosh, 1986, p.51]. And only a little more than one-quarter of Japan's defense budget is spent on weapons procurement. This sum accounted for 0.36 of Japan's total industrial production in 1980 and 0.54 percent in 1989. The corresponding American figure was 14 times larger, or five percent of total industrial production [Okimoto, 1981, pp.285-86. Drifte, 1985a, p.17. Vogel, 1989, p.71. Defense Agency, 1990, p.319. Defense Production Committee, 1991, Table 1].

Furthermore, most Japanese weapon producers are not very dependent on military sales for their profitability. And with a few notable exceptions the dependence on weapons contracts typically declines the bigger the company. Data for the 1970s show that, with one exception (Shin-meiwa Industry), defense contracts for all of Japan's top defense producers accounted for less than 10 percent of total corporate sales. In the United States by way of contrast only one of the leading defense contractors (General Electric) relied on military products for less than 10 percent of its total sales [Hopper, 1975a, pp.142, 147. Okimoto, 1981, p.286. Drifte, 1985a, pp.18-19]. Owing to substantial and steady increases in the Japanese defense budget, by the late 1980s among Japan's largest weapon producers, such as MHI and Kawasaki Heavy Industries (KHI), defense sales as a share of total sales had increased to about 20 percent, still far below corresponding figures for American defense contractors [Vogel, 1989, p.71. U.S. Congress, 1990, p.104 and 1991, p.42. Samuels, 1991, p.57. Todd,

1988, pp.186-88. Chinworth, 1987]. If one thinks of the military-industrial complex only in American terms, that is in terms of the size of the economy servicing the weapons market, David Hopper's conclusion for the 1970s is still apposite two decades later: "the purely defense-oriented perspective is dissipated at the level of the individual weapons-producing company . . . Generally speaking the Japanese business community as a whole has not placed very high priority on the defense production sector" [Hopper, 1975a, pp.143, 116].

But Japan's defense economy should be evaluated not so much in terms of its size, but in terms of the technological options that advances in Japan's civilian economy are creating. The aircraft industry is a case in point. In 1988 about one third of the JDA procurement budget was spent on aircraft [Asagumo Shimbun-sha, 1991, p.262]. The aircraft industry depends not only overwhelmingly on sales to the SDF but embodies the technological advances, especially at the level of components, that have made Japan one of the leading technological powers at the end of the 20th century [Drifte 1985a, p.18]. In this respect the aerospace industry differs from a more traditional industry such as shipbuilding which has looked to the military more conventionally as a way to bolster sagging sales especially in times of economic slow-down. In the aircraft industry contacts between different producers are exceptionally close. And these contacts are reinforced by close communications with government. In this important industry MITI's industrial policy extends not only to prime contractors but includes also subcontracting firms; in contrast the JDA normally is only in close contact with prime contractors [Interview No.1, Tokyo, December 9, 1991]. Each of the major producers "maintains close contact with a special group of suppliers, and each has tight links to the zaibatsu-descended 'keiretsu' business groups. On projects led by Mitsubishi Heavy Industries, for example, avionics may come from Mitsubishi Electric and instrumentation from Mitsubishi Precision" [Noble, 1990, p.21. Gros, 1989. Samuels, 1991, pp.57-58].

The interconnectedness of Japanese business and government is a key ingredient for the creation of a Japanese style civilian-industrial complex that creates a set of military options for the future. Even though they are not significant weapon producers, in some ways virtually "all major manufacturing companies are involved in defence manufacturing" [McIntosh, 1986, p.52]. The top fourteen defense contractors include all of the major civilian manufacturing corporations, with half of the defense business going to Mitsubishi Heavy Industries, Mitsubishi Electric, Kawasaki Heavy Industries, Ishikawajima Harima Heavy Industries and the Toshiba Corporation [McIntosh, 1986, p.54]. In the mid-1970s about 2,000 companies had registered with the Equipment Bureau of the JDA, a figure that had increased by another 15 percent by 1990, although apparently less than half of them are actually awarded contracts. And a well developed system of subcontracting spreads the economic influence of the defense production sector throughout the Japanese economy [Hopper, 1975a, p.117. Interview No. 1, Tokyo, December 9, 1991. Sakai, 1986, p.132]. It is impossible to make reliable estimates of the number of military subcontractors. Specialists in Japan's defense economy use a number of 3,000 as an approximation. Subcontracted work in Japanese programs can run as high as 80 percent of the total value of a contract [Interview No.9, Tokyo, December 11, 1991]. A detailed report concludes that "this diffusion of contracting work contributes to the growth of the domestic defense industrial base in Japan" [U.S. Congress, 1990, p.64]. Since research and development for military equipment rest primarily in the hands of private corporations, the diffusion of military technologies through Japan's elaborate system of subcontractors is also facilitated. According to some recent sources, in a number of Japanese weapon plants defense and civilian production run side-by-side thus accelerating the mutual diffusion of defense and civilian technologies [Interview Nos.1 and 19, Tokyo, December 9 and 17, 1991. U.S. Congress, 1990, pp.64-65].

It is a characteristic feature of Japan's defense industry that major contractors hold a much greater share of the total business than is true of the United States. About 80 percent of domestic procurement is controlled by the top ten contractors compared to only 35 percent in the United States. The leading defense contractor in Japan, Mitsubishi Heavy Industries, manages between one-quarter and one-fifth of the Japanese market compared to General Dynamic's share of less than ten percent of the American market [Drifte, 1985a, pp.18-19]. Since the aircraft industry is more openly cartellized than almost any other in Japan [Gros, 1989, p.35], these tight and stable relations lead to a quick diffusion of whatever technology is being acquired from abroad. Technologies are quickly diffused not only within but also between firms. In the past, when Japan licensed military technologies from the United States, this ensured that technological innovations were put to commercial use as quickly as possible. In the future the reverse process, from civilian to military technologies, will probably be accomplished with similar ease. Since MITI has singled out the aerospace industry as a vital core for industrial growth in the next century, this technological diffusion is obviously very much in the government's interest [Samuels, 1991, pp.55-57. Todd, 1988, pp.258-59].

Japan has chosen limited domestic production under foreign licenses over direct foreign purchase and self-sufficient domestic production. Low barriers between civilian and military technologies have been maintained [Okimoto, 1981, pp.276-78]. Production under foreign license had the big advantage of both requiring and reinforcing a "technological and industrial infrastructure that could be constructed within the framework of civilian programs for economic growth" [Okimoto, 1981, p.279]. Japan leads the world in licensed production of major conventional weapons systems, with virtually all licenses originating from the United States [U.S. Congress, 1991, pp.5,8]. Overall more than four-fifths of Japan's weapons are produced domestically [Okimoto, 1981, p.282. Gros, 1989, p.47. Drifte, 1985a, p.10]. But this general statistic is slightly misleading. Domestic production accounts for only 55 percent for missiles and between 70 and 80 percent for aircraft; this compares to 90 percent or more for naval vessels and the equipment for the GSDF. It is thus not very surprising that despite their smaller dependence on military sales, electronics manufacturers view the defense industry as a promising future growth market. The share of electronics in Japan's defense procurement increased from 11 percent in 1979-82 to 26 percent in 1984-87. Spurred by a major military contract NEC's growth in defense sales in 1987 alone was 25 percent, still less than Fujitsu's 58 percent jump [Vogel, 1989, p.73].

These features of Japan's defense economy must be viewed against the background of a changing relationship between MITI and Japanese business [Okimoto, 1989]. MITI's direct control over Japanese industry has declined during the last two decades. Gone are the days in which MITI could use its leverage over foreign exchange while dealing with relatively small and internationally weak corporations. While the number of MITI's policy instruments has shrunk during the last two decades, the size as well as international strength of Japanese corporations has increased greatly. Dealing with defense contractors who can look for contracts only with the JDA is for government bureaucrats a throwback to an earlier era in the 1950s in which they could shape more directly the intimate relations between business and government.

Business and MITI view the defense industry in economic rather than military terms. The major corporations approach the defense industry in terms of its potential for future growth and technological innovation, while MITI officials values it as an instrument for industrial policy. This convergence of perspectives has led some like Steven Vogel to talk of an "emerging Japanese military-industrial complex" [Vogel, 1989, p.71. Bix, 1970]. But the military part of this complex is not the objective but the instrument for achieving economic and technological aims. "The biggest and most important Japanese companies have a stake in arms production and . . . have excellent access to the political leadership" [Drifte, 1985a, p.28]. Japan's dramatic advances in high-technology industries, Neil Davis argues, thus have given most of Japan's leading corporations enormous market potential in the defense industry. "Warfare beyond the 1980s will be some sort of complex computerized gamesmanship played-out through C3I (Command, Control, Communications and Intelligence). Meanwhile big corporate profits can be generated today by building the C3I infrastructure of tomorrow" [Davis, 1984b, p.11].

Defense is inherently a political business. Since defense contractors have only a few clients to cultivate the incentive to lobby is overwhelming. " 'Defense may only account for three percent of our business,' says Kunio Saito, general manager of NEC's 1st Defense Sales Division, 'but it certainly takes up more than three percent of our energy'" [Vogel, 1989, p.71]. Before the end of the Cold War in Europe, Japan's business leaders viewed the defense industry as having considerable growth potential. "By the year 2000 we are confident that our sales will grow to a level warranting the kind of investment we are making today," declared Yotaro Iida, president of Mitsubishi Heavy Industries in 1987. He expected defense sales at least to double, reaching 600-700 billion yen by the year 2,000 [Vogel, 1989, p.71]. Such optimism appears to have dissipated considerably since 1987. Spending for frontline equipment increased by 7.7 percent in 1986-90, but is projected to shrink by 2.3 percent in 1991-95 [Asahi Shimbun Keizai-bu, 1991, p.128]. This planned cut in defense spending is smaller than in the other major industrial states, thus prompting some critics to predict a further increase in Japan's relative military capabilities. But it does not bode well for a rapid growth in the size of Japan's military-industrial complex. While the technological dynamism that marks both the civilian and military segments of Japan's economy will be left unchanged, by the mid-1990s Japan is likely to confront some very important policy choices about the shape of its defense industry in the twenty-first century. Specifically, will Japan be able to maintain the existing small number of production lines servicing a very small domestic market [Interview No.1, Tokyo, December 9, 1991]?

The concern for maintaining a production line for the building of submarines—one ship delivered to the MSDF each year from two shipyards which produce only in alternate years—forces a decommissioning of one sixteen year-old submarine per year in order to stay within the quantitative ceilings imposed by the NDPO. By American standards this is a great luxury. Similarly, the MSDF has built up a larger anti-submarine air reconnaissance capability in the Pacific than has the United States, even though the geographic area to be covered is much smaller. The reason lies very likely in the requirements of Japan's production line rather than of military strategy or alliance politics. When the MSDF reaches the quantitative ceilings for P3-C's it will probably be forced to decommission perfectly good planes, in the interest of keeping its production lines open [Interview No.23, Tokyo, December 19, 1991]. Commenting on Mitsubishi

Heavy Industries four-year plan starting in 1990, Iida remarked that "on aircraft and tanks, we made a plan that doesn't overstretch ourselves, because JDA's budget for major frontline equipment is unlikely to grow very much." MHI plans in fact to reduce the share of its aircraft and tank division from 20 percent of overall sales in 1989 to 17 percent in 1993 [Asahi Shimbun, June 12, 1990, 13th ed.]. For the same reason MHI, Kawasaki Heavy Industries, and Fuji Heavy Industries (FHI) agreed with Boeing in April 1990 to participate in the B-777 project as program rather than as full partners. Although this was not optimal for these three corporations, KHI and FHI had little choice. Production of P3-C's ends in 1993 and production of the anti-submarine helicopter AH-1 around 1995. In October 1990 KHI announced that it will subcontract for British Airway's civilian aircraft project (A321). The company is also considering reducing its production personnel [Asahi Shimbun, June 12, 1990, 13th ed. Asahi Shimbun Keizai-bu, 1991, p.132. Nakayama, 1991, p.238].

Michael Chinworth's careful case study of business- government relations in the licensed production of the Patriot Missile System underlines the fact that on questions of Japan's national defense there exists a remarkable unity of purpose and a complementary relationship between MITI and business [Chinworth, 1990a, pp.197-98,228-32]. Both business and MITI are viewing Japanese defense in a long-term perspective. This shared perspective does not aim at reestablishing the military in a politically preeminent position. Both are determined to overcome Japan's technological lags in missile technology and aerospace more generally. As in any other industrial sector the commitment to the future expansion of Japan's domestic capability overrides other considerations. In the late 1980s Japan's military aerospace industry, besides arming Japan, serves as a "bellwether for commercial aerospace and provides an important new market for the application of civilian high technology . . . increased defense production has emerged in the 1980s as a new strategy for aerospace industrial development . . . it has emerged because it is a versatile and effective strategy that satisfies the needs and interests of numerous influential groups and . . . has become the basis for a sturdy political coalition" [Samuels and Whipple, 1989, pp.276, 305]. Although the Constitution prohibits strictly the possession of offensive weapons, production for the Japanese navy and airforce, often under American licenses, has already given the "Japanese a springboard, should they wish to use it, from which to leap into export orientated defence manufacturing" [McIntosh, 1986, p.51].

In contrast to the United States, Soviet Union or Britain, in Japan civilian research and development has been the main driving force behind its defense industries. Even though its share in the Japanese defense budget has increased steadily since 1976, in proportional terms military R&D is insignificant compared to expenditures both for American military R&D and Japanese civilian R&D. Despite its growth in the 1980s the defense industry has not encroached on the preeminence of an industry that is producing almost exclusively for commercial markets [Defense Agency, 1990, p.442]. But because of the growing importance of advances in civilian technologies for military applications, the relevance of Japan's commercially oriented business for national security policy has increased greatly. As early as 1981 the head of the JDA acknowledged that "we [the Defence Agency] must depend on the civilian sector. In current technology, there is no distinction between civilian and military technology" [McIntosh 1986, p.56].

A variety of institutions link business and government on issues affecting Japan's defense economy. The Japan Ordnance Association (JOA) (Heiki Kogyo Kai) offers an organizational link that is closely aligned with the GSDF and the JDA. In 1983 it counted 99 corporations among its full members, including all of the leading defense contractors; in addition it had 35 associate members. However, military sales accounted for only 1.23 percent of the total sales of the member companies [Drifte, 1985a, p.29. Vogel, 1989, pp.74-76]. Traditionally the JOA has sought to protect defense contractors because of the risks they face while doing business in a very limited and politically volatile market. It has lobbied the JDA to notify contractors ahead of time of the government's anticipated needs and pushed for higher R&D defense budgets as well as 100 percent domestic content for weapons produced in Japan. The JOA was renamed, reorganized and incorporated in September 1988 and became the Japan Defense Industry Association (JDIA) (Nihon Boei Sobi Kogyokai) [Vogel, 1989, pp.74-76]. It is now an incorporated association which falls under the joint jurisdiction of the JDA and MITI.

In fact, MITI and the JDA both sponsored this reorganization. The JDIA has close ties with the GSDF in particular [Interview No.9, Tokyo, December 11, 1991. Nihon Boei Sobi Kogyokai, n.d., p.1]. For JDA's and MITI's taste the old organization had acted too much like a club of retired officers rather than a lobby for defense producers with an explicit role in policymaking. The mission of the JDIA is to help MITI and the JDA in lobbying members of the Diet, and to provide for some additional informal coordination between firms [Interview No.11, Tokyo, June 14, 1991]. In addition both government and industry favored the creation of the JDIA because they saw a growing need for addressing more systematically and comprehensively issues such as the level of R&D funding and export controls for militarily sensitive technologies, components and products. Another factor in the creation of the association was the growing public acceptance of defense production which derived from a growing perception of the Soviet threat [Interview No.1, Tokyo, January 21, 1992]. The establishment of the Defense Manufacturing Control Association (Boei Seisan Kanri Kyokai) in August 1991, with a membership of 22, including leading defense contractors, under the supervision of the JDA, points in the same direction. It was set up in response to international criticism of Japan when it was discovered in July 1991 that a subsidiary of NEC had shipped illegally missile parts to Iran [Oishi, 1991]. It has a staff of about 30 and is under the jurisdiction of the Prime Minister's Office [Fujishima, 1992, p.217]

The Japanese Aircraft and Space Industry Association (Nihon Koku Uchu Kogyokai) is under the jurisdiction of MITI. It has also close political relations with the ASDF. The Japanese Shipbuilding Industry Association (Nihon Zosen Kogyokai) is under the jurisdiction of the Ministry of Transportation but also enjoys close contacts with the MSDF. Although their contact is not institutionalized, these associations regularly exchange opinions with the JDIA [Interview Nos.1 and 9, Tokyo, December 9 and 11, 1991. Interview No.1, Tokyo, January 21, 1992].

The organizational channels that regulate business-government relations at the peak level center on the Defense Production Committee (DPC) of the Federation of Economic Organizations (Keidanren) [Hopper, 1975a. Vogel, 1989, p.74. Drifte, 1985a, p.29]. Its origin dates back to 1951 when under the name of "Second Committee" of Keidanren's Japan-U.S. Economic Cooperation Council, it dealt with massive U.S. procurements in Japan during the Korean War. It was established as a special committee within Keidanren in 1952. It counted not only top business firms among its members but also, within the advisory staff attached to the committee, former top military officers some of whom had contacts with groups of ex-military men planning an eventual comeback of the Army and Navy [Berger, 1992, p.115. Interview No.17, Tokyo, June 17, 1991. Kurokawa, 1986, pp.213, 219-20]. The DPC is a voice that articulates the demands of Japan's defense corporations. It is an advocate for taking a long-term approach to the specific problems that the defense industry faces in Japan; it favors holding open viable production lines for major weapon systems that are produced domestically; and it speaks for the development of basic technologies by Japanese firms that can be diffused to both the military and civilian economy [Interview No.9, Tokyo, December 11, 1991].

Neither an industrial association nor a national organization of business, the DPC is a hybrid organization in Keidanren. It is one of the "committees with special assignment" that operates under the general administrative auspices of Keidanren, but that is nonetheless relatively autonomous from Keidanren's central organization in terms of membership and financial support [Hopper, 1975a, p.121]. In 1989 for the first time the committee's recommendations on procurement were "invested with the full authority of Keidanren" [Berger, 1992, p.521. Asahi Shimbun Keizai-bu, 1989, p.248]. In contrast to the directors of other units providing administrative support for Keidanren committees, until the 1970s the director of the DPC Secretariat reported directly to the director of the Keidanren Secretariat [Hopper, 1975a, p.128]. In the 1980s the DPC Secretariat became more fully integrated into the organization of Keidanren [Interview No.19, Tokyo, December 17, 1991]. In 1972 membership in the DPC consisted of 71 corporations and 16 industrial associations which had affiliations with Keidanren as well as 12 companies and 4 associations which had no links to Keidanren [Hopper, 1975a, p.121]. With totally civilian companies like Sony joining the DPC in the mid-1980s to prepare their entry into the defense business, by the late 1980s the membership of the DPC had grown slightly to include 81 members [Interview No. 9, Tokyo, December 11, 1991. Vogel, 1989, p.74].

In the late 1960s and early 1970s Japanese business leaders were convinced that, in following the American example, military technologies would very likely lead to advances in civilian technologies and new commercial products [Emmerson, 1971, p.148]. In 1965 the Industrial Problems Research Association (IPRA) had created the Defense Discussion Council (Boei Kondankai). This was "the closest equivalent to an entirely defense-oriented organization within the business community at the level of the zaikai" [Hopper, 1975a, p.120]. It had about 900 members, 300 individuals and 600 corporations, only a small fraction of whom were weapons producers. Its major purpose was to create a better climate of opinion between business and the SDF. Keidanren's top brass thus was acutely interested in the work of the DPC. In 1972-73 the Board of Directors counted among its members the President of Keidanren as well as six of its seven Vice-Presidents [Hopper, 1975a, p.143]. But during the last two decades this interest has waned as the crucial importance of civilian technologies for military technologies became increasingly clear, that is, as "spin-on" became a substitute for the "spin-off" that Japan's business leadership originally had expected to prevail in the 1980s and beyond [Interview Nos.9 and 19, December 11 and 17, 1991]. In 1991 the 18 regular members of the Board of Directors apparently did not include any Vice-Presidents of Keidanren. The committee has been supported by an advisory staff composed of former uniformed officers. But staff size has dwindled from nine in 1970, to 4 in 1980, and only 2 in 1990 [Interview No.1, Tokyo, January 21, 1992]. In addition, in recent years the committee has been served by a secretariat consisting for all intents and purposes, of only two or three officials [Interview No.2, Ithaca, May 29, 1992]. Nonetheless, Keidanren accounts for about 50 percent of the funding of the DPC [Interview No.9, Tokyo, December 11,1991]. The DPC operates under one well-understood rule laid down by Keidanren. It cannot recommend an increase in the government's defense budget [Interview No.17, Tokyo, June 17, 1991]. Japanese big business thus contains the natural political pressure of the defense industry for spending increases. Keidanren's concern with its organizational integrity thus serves to assure politically stable relations with the government and a substantial degree of isolation of Japan's national security policy from interest group pressures.

A fairly elaborate committee structure inside the DPC reflected the prospects for an active armaments industry in the 1950s. But over time most of the special assignments were taken over by industrial associations. By 1974 the DPC had reorganized itself, eliminating in the process a number of "sleeping committees" [Hopper, 1975a, p.126]. In the late 1980s its organization includes the chair, traditionally the CEO of the largest defense contractor, Mitsubishi Heavy Industries, who also serves as Vice Chairman of Keidanren; the Board of Directors which is staffed by the representatives of the eighteen largest defense contractors; a general affairs section; a section for defense contract pricing issues; and a liaison section that keeps the DPC in touch with other organizations interested in Japan's defense economy. In addition it has a small central secretariat [Interview No.9, Tokyo, December 11, 1991]. While the Board of Directors meets only infrequently, the section for general affairs, consisting of corporate representatives at the managing director level, has an important role in DPC decisionmaking [Interview No.2, Ithaca, May 29, 1992]. The DPC makes its views known both through the publication of policy papers as well as through private meetings with LDP Diet members and officials from JDA and MITI [Kurokawa, 1986, 223-24].

In recent years its demands have centered around three issues: increasing the R & D budget of the JDA, raising the domestic content of defense procurement and getting long-term commitments in government contracts [Vogel, 1989, p.74]. Until the mid-1970s the DPC conducted surveys of the defense production sector which it then interpreted and disseminated in an effort to influence government policy. But the changing balance between civilian and military technologies during the last fifteen years has vitiated the need for such studies; and the indigenization of foreign technologies became a less important issue as Japan's technological capabilities increased [Interview No.19, December 17, 1991]. In addition the DPC also collects and publishes data on Japan's defense production as well as on developments abroad that are relevant to Japan's defense industry. The DPC typically tries to influence the terms of political debate only indirectly rather than seeking a high-profile role in lobbying directly the LDP and its committees or the ministries most relevant to the defense industry. For example, it reportedly left public discussion of the one percent ceiling on defense expenditures to the Research Institute for Peace and Security which it was instrumental in creating in 1978 [Kurokawa, 1986, p.223]. Most important are the contacts that the DPC has with the JDA. The main contacts with the JDA are with the Equipment Bureau and not with the Defense Policy Bureau. This reflects a conscious strategy of the DPC to stay away from broader political or military issues as well as the acquiescence of the defense industry more generally in a politically very circumscribed role [Okimoto, 1978a, pp.456-57. Interview No.21, Tokyo, June 19, 1991].

Finally, the organizational links between business and government are reinforced by the informal ties between individual companies and the JDA. After retirement, SDF officers, for whom mandatory retirement ages ranged between 53 and 60 in 1991 [Boeicho, 1991a, p.286], and JDA officials often join the armaments industry (amakudari) thus adding to its political clout in government, including the JDA and the SDF. This pervasive practice of Japanese government-business relations is accepted as perfectly normal for former JDA and SDF officials. Retiring members of the SDF are placed by the staff offices of the three services as well as by the SDF's Prefectural Liaison Offices and a JDA-affiliated national organization which has seven regional offices [Harada, 1991, p.76. Interview No.11, Tokyo, December 12, 1991]. With the increase of corporate interest in defense sales in the 1980s, "military officers . . . now represent the most influential defense lobby of all. A defense contractor, it is said, should have at least one military 'old boy' for every 20 billion yen in annual defense sales" [Vogel, 1989, p.76]. Tables 3.1 and 3.2 illustrate the pattern among top officials. But since many middle-level officials also move after retirement from the SDF into industry, these data illustrate only the proverbial tip of the iceberg. Between 1963 and 1967, 164 of 341 SDF officers leaving the service found employment in registered contractors of the JDA. Between 1964 and 1968, 42 percent of retiring JDA officials joined the defense industry [Bix, 1970, p.40. Roberts, 1969, p.289. Emmerson, 1971, p.150]. Between 1975 and 1980 more than 300 former SDF officers joined the arms industry. Of about 500 top-ranking officers retiring in FY 1988, 57 found employment in the top 20 defense contractors [Drifte, 1985a, p.30. Asahi Shimbun Keizai-bu, 1991, pp.146-47].

The structure of the Japanese defense economy illustrates that military considerations do not dominate over economic ones. At the same time it also shows that the defense economy can serve as an instrument for improving the competitiveness of the civilian economy. Japan has neither a military-industrial complex nor a totally civilian corporate culture. The growing technological preeminence of its high-technology industries have

Table 3-1. Number of Generals in the Arms Industry (1970s)

	GSDF	MSDF	ASDF	Total
Mitsubishi Heavy Industries	4	10	6	20
Ishikawajima Harima Heavy Ind.	0	6	4	10
Kawasaki Heavy Industries	3	6	4	13
Mitsubishi Electric	5	2	3	10
Hitachi Dockyard	0	2	1	3
Nippon Electric	3	3	3	9
Shinmeiwa Industry	0	3	0	3
Fuji Heavy Industries	2	2	2	6
Toshiba	7	6	2	15
Nihon Seikosho	2	1	0	3
Komatsu	2	0	0	2
Hitachi	2	3	2	7
Nihon Kogyo	1	2	0	3
Daikin Kogyo	1	2	1	4
Shimazu Seisakusho	1	2	1	4
Nissan Motors	5	1	0	6
Mitsubishi Precision	0	1	4	5
TOTAL	38	52	33	123

Source: Reinhard Drifte, Japan's Growing Arms Industry (Lausanne: Graduate Institute of International Studies, PSIS Occasional Papers, Number 1/85), p. 31 from Tomiyama Kazuo, Nihon no boei sangyo (Japan's defense industry), Tokyo, 1979, p. 109.

made firms in the civilian sector of the economy directly relevant to the future evolution of Japan's defense industry. Conversely, high-tech firms in the civilian economy are increasingly interested in linking into new developments in weapons technology. Thus they hope to protect themselves against potential competitors who might develop commercial products through advances in defense technology. And the Japanese government wants to eliminate, in this sector as in all others, any vestige of Japan's technological backwardness. Although their motivations differ, both business and government thus act under a strong structural impetus for close cooperation.

Table 3-2. Former Military Officers Of The Rank Of Lieutenant General Or Vice Admiral And Above In Japan's Top Six Defense Contractors (April 1986)

Company	Ground SDF	Maritime SDF	Air SDF	Total
MHI	3	5	5	13
KHI	3	4	3	10
Mitsubishi Electric	2	1	2	5
IHI	1	3	2	6
Toshiba	2	1	1	4
NEC	2	1	2	5

Source: Steve K. Vogel, Japanese High Technology, Politics, and Power (Berkeley Roundtable on the International Economy, University of California, Berkeley, Ca., March 1989), p. 75 from National Security Conference (Anzen hosho konwakai).

3. Government, Business, and the Import of Critical Raw Materials.

As is true of the armaments industry the impetus for a close cooperation between business and government is also very evident on issues dealing with Japan's economic vulnerability. This is true in particular of the import of energy, the most critical of all raw materials on which Japan's industry depends. Japan is very poorly endowed with natural resources. Its economic prosperity depends greatly on a stable supply of raw materials from abroad [Hill, 1986, pp.42-43. Weinstein, 1988, p.27. Chapman, Drifte and Gow, 1982, pp.143-235. Friedman and Lebard, 1991, pp.8-9, 160-88, 278-81, 309-14]. For example, Japan has few domestic sources of minerals. In the case of some minerals such as bauxite, nickel ore, and uranium it is almost completely dependent on foreign supplies. And Japan imports 90 percent of its iron ore, 80 percent of its copper, and about 50 percent of its lead and zinc. Since 85 percent of Japan's land is mountainous or not suitable to farming, Japan is also very dependent on food imports. Highly dependent on foreign supplies of wheat, soya beans, maize and sorghum, Japan has the lowest level of food self-sufficiency in the industrial world; furthermore, that vulnerablitiy has increased during the last decades [McMichael, 1991. Sato, 1991].

The same is true of oil and all other sources of energy. Japan depends almost totally on the import of petroleum, natural gas and fossil fuels and has only very limited capacities to tap domestic coal, geothermal and hydropower. At present Japan imports virtually all of its oil and about 80 percent of its total energy consumption. This vulnerability has been a source of great turmoil and instability in modern Japanese history. Japan's seizure of Manchuria in 1931 initiated a decade in which the government sought to gain a measure of control over the Asian raw materials and oil supplies on which the Japanese economy depended so heavily. That policy paved the way toward Japan's attack on Pearl Harbor and its subsequent defeat in the Pacific War. Apart from the conflict between the two superpowers, since the late 1960s Mideast politics and its effect on oil supply has been the most explosive issue that has affected Japan's security.

Japan's exposed and vulnerable position in a volatile world has left a deep imprint on the relationship between business and government on issues dealing with the import of raw materials, including oil. During the last two decades the bureaucracy has to some extent relaxed its guidance over large exporters. But its relationship with firms importing strategic raw materials such as oil remains very close [Vernon, 1983]. In the words of Ronald Morse "a close but informal consultative mechanism between industry and government that seeks to maximize market forces" is a defining aspect of Japan's energy policymaking system [Morse, 1982, p.255]. As Richard Samuels and Shoko Tanaka, among others, have shown in their studies of energy policy, this relationship is not characterized by the political dictates of government bureaucrats or the economic laws of market forces affecting private firms. Instead it reflects the negotiated outcomes of the relationship between business and government. "State policy never served to transform the market . . . it consistently served to ratify it" [Samuels, 1987, p.196. Tanaka, 1986, pp.41-42, 113].

The reconstruction of the Japanese economy under the protective umbrella of the United States after 1945 occurred in an era of secure, ample and cheap raw materials. Indeed, the growing vulnerability which accompanied Japan's high economic growth may not have been fully recognized in the early years of reconstruction [Vernon, 1983, p.92. Hein, 1990, p.3. Ozawa, 1979, p.191]. But the build-up of Japan's heavy industries, such as shipbuilding, steel, petrochemicals and aluminum, required a massive increase in the import of raw materials, including oil. By the early 1960s foreign oil had surpassed domestic coal as the primary source of energy. Foreign oil corporations such as Shell, Union Oil, Caltex and Stanvac accounted for the bulk of Japan's energy imports. And foreign firms controlled between 50 and 75 percent of Japan's oil refining and distribution system. Energy was one major industry in which foreign firms did extremely well in Japanese markets [Vernon, 1983, p.92. Kaplan, 1975. Tanaka, 1986, pp.32-40]. Japan's dependence on foreign firms was not necessarily an advantage for the Japanese economy, even in times of cheap oil. Dependence on the major oil corporations meant, for example, tied purchases which made it difficult, in a decade of cheap oil, to take advantage of bargains on the international spot market.

The 1962 Petroleum Industry Law was an explicit attempt to return to Japanese nationals some control over domestic energy markets. The law granted MITI a supervisory role over the evolution of the industry, including the licensing of refineries and the approval of production and crude oil acquisition plans [Vernon, 1983, pp.93-95]. By 1970 MITI had implemented a mandatory oil stockpiling plan for all domestic refineries [Fukai, 1988]. The government also sought to diversify Japan's contractual arrangements for importing oil away from the major international oil corporations. For major oil purchases it sought to encourage instead direct deals between domestic energy producers and supplier countries or government-to-government contracts. The intent of this policy was to decrease the risk of a diversion of oil away from Japan in times of oil shortage [Wu, 1977]. Instead of relying on an arms-length relationship with foreign multinationals over whom it had virtually no leverage, the Japanese government sought to develop a close relationship with domestic firms while fashioning an energy policy designed to reduce Japan's economic vulnerability.

The reorganization of existing and the establishment of new public corporations supplemented the new legislative mandate [Johnson, 1978, pp.25-60, 119-140]. The history of Japan's energy-related public corporations stretches back into the 19th century. But in the postwar era there has been a virtual explosion in the number of these corporations, including, among others, the Petroleum Resources Development and the Arabian Oil companies founded in the 1950s, the North Sumatra Petroleum Development and the Kyodo Oil Companies in the 1960s, and the Japan National Oil and the Petroleum Development Corporations in the 1970s. In most cases retired government bureaucrats were placed on the board of these public corporations even if the company was 100 percent privately owned. Thus, in a common endeavor of seeking to reduce the vulnerability of the Japanese economy to disruptions in oil supplies, these companies became the institutional vehicles for the close cooperation between business and government [Wu, 1977. Fukai, 1988]. As Raymond Vernon writes, "if there were unique elements in Japan's program for the acquisition of independent sources of crude oil, however, they were associated with the way in which partnerships, consortium, and trading companies of the country perform to implement the national campaign" [Vernon, 1983, p.97]. In response to the government's initiative of establishing public corporations, Japan's major trading companies created their own petroleum development corporations during the 1970s. And 120 Japanese firms, spanning the full gamut of Japan's industrial structure, joined forces in

October 1973 when they set up the Japan Cooperation Center for the Middle East. This semi-public corporation was intended to facilitate communication with Mideast oil suppliers.

The outcome of this welter of public, private, semi-public and semi-private corporations did not result in an energy industry which was controlled, top-down, by MITI officials. As Samuels notes, in contrast to a "vertically integrated, nationally unified petroleum industry . . . what emerged instead was horizontally fragmented and vertically truncated" [Samuels, 1987, p.225]. Time and again the efforts to organize markets through public corporations which MITI had created were defeated by the strong opposition of Japan's refining industry, industrial consumers, and the MOF [Samuels, 1987, p.204]. Private industry was willing to accept public funds but not public controls. And the MOF was willing, especially in the 1960s, to increase budget allocations but remained adamantly opposed to the growth of MITI's power. For example, only after MITI had scaled back its plans and proposed a public agency limited to a banking rather than commercial role, did it succeed in gaining the approval of all important players for the establishment of the Japan Petroleum Development Corporation in 1967. And while in 1978 the Japanese government managed to overcome opposition from the private sector against the Japan National Oil Corporation (JNOC), a 100 percent state-owned corporation, unlike its Italian or British counterparts this state company was barred from running its own oil exploration or production [Klapp, 1987, pp.174-77].

MITI failed to gain the kind of control in the energy sector that it achieved in the import of metals. Part of the reason for this difference may lie in the fact that in metals the government, not foreign firms, was in full control after 1945 [Samuels, 1987, p.168]. In close cooperation with Japanese business the government moved away from a system in which firms were able to buy metals on the foreign spot market. It established the Metal Mining Agency of Japan in 1963 which provided loans to Japanese firms to promote foreign exploration and development. And by the early 1970s it was lending to Japanese firms 2 billion yen annually [Vernon, 1983, p.99]. The government also organized Japan's principle corporations into buyer groups. Each group had a designated leader in charge of conducting negotiations for the whole group in a given supplier country. Nippon Steel, for example, was responsible for handling all of the steel industry's major iron ore and coal purchases in Australia [Vernon, 1983, p.99]. By the end of the 1960s, imports of metallic ores rested largely on long-term contracts negotiated under this system of coordinated buying. That the government could organize this sector, in contrast to the oil industry, is testimony to the historical legacy of the strong position of foreign firms in the oil industry.

Despite the attempted shift away from foreign oil corporations, in the early 1970s 80 percent of Japan's crude oil imports continued to flow through the vertical channels of foreign firms [Vernon, 1983, p.95]. As long as the price of energy had remained low and the international political system appeared to be stable this was no particular cause of alarm for the Japanese government. But all of that changed with the oil shock of 1973. The psychological effect of the heightened sense of vulnerability was enormous and had a deep effect on the relations between government and business. The Petroleum Supply and Demand Adjustment Law of 1973 expanded the government's ability to control oil imports, granted it the authority to promulgate restrictions on the use of petroleum, to mediate disputes concerning oil allocation, and to impose energy taxation schemes [Morse 1981, 1982]. In addition large refineries and importers were required to submit marketing and import plans for government approval.

The Japan National Oil Company was established to manage an extensive stockpiling program. Japan increased its stored oil reserves from a 36 days supply at the beginning of the 1970s, to a 100 days supply in 1979, and a 140 days supply in 1991 [Chapman et.al., 1982. Sanger, 1990a]. The sharing of power and responsibility between government and business was very evident in this instance. Concerned about the effects which a costly, private stockpiling policy would have for the economic competitiveness of the Japanese energy industry, the government amended the law governing the JNOC in 1978 to launch a supplementary national stockpile policy [Nemetz, Vertinsky and Vertinsky, 1984-85]. Furthermore, the Energy Conservation Law of 1979, adopted in the wake of the second oil shock, required that the 4,500 most energy-intensive firms hire "energy managers" in each of their plants. These mangers went through a rigorous government training program before returning to their companies where they had the right to enforce government standards for energy conservation [McKean, 1983. Shibata, 1983, pp.144-46].

Although MITI enjoys strong statutory authority most of these measures were voluntary and depended on the incentives, financial and otherwise, that the government created in order to coax business along the path of reduced energy vulnerability. The system of administrative guidance of Japan's oil corporations was less important than the informal consultations that provided an opportunity for formulating policy that "was both within the limits set by MITI and consistent with industry consensus" [Upham, 1987, pp.187-88]. MITI's assorted powers, both formal and informal, over the licensing of technology, allocation of raw materials and supervision of commercial operations established the basis for a very close relationship between government and business, intensified by the heightened sense of vulnerability that marked the 1970s [Interview Nos. 6 and 17,

Tokyo, June 12 and 17, 1992. McKean, 1983]. Important court rulings altered the nature of business and government relations in the case of the petroleum industry. Yet compared to the other main industrial states Japan, on questions of energy policy, operates, to use Merrie Klapp's apt terminology, like a sovereign entrepreneur [Klapp, 1987, pp.174-90]. But the relationship between business and government is not shaped by bureaucratic dictates but by the "reciprocal consent" that Richard Samuels has analyzed in his study of Japan's energy sector [Samuels, 1987].

C. Transnational Military Links

The transnational links between the Japanese and American militaries have to some extent loosened the constraints which the organization of the government and state-society relations in Japan have imposed on the military. These links have increased the salience of the military component of Japan's security policy beyond what Japan's domestic politics would otherwise permit. But to date they have not threatened in a serious way the predominance of the political and economic elements in Japan's domestic structure that shape security policy.

Since 1945 Japan's place in the world has been defined largely in terms of its relation to the United States. This was the result of America's postwar diplomacy which succeeded in tying Japan closely to the United States, indeed more strongly than any other major country. Japan's exports are concentrated on the American market to a degree that is unique among all of the major industrial states. And its security policy places Japan outside of any regional defense alliance and makes it fully dependent on the American security guarantee [Tow, 1982. Reed, 1983. Jacob, 1991. Johnson and Packard, 1981. Mochizuki, 1987. Makin and Hellmann, 1989. Murray and Lehner, 1990]. Contacts on security issues occur at all levels—bureaucratic, ministerial and private. They are both routinized and ad hoc [Kohno, 1989, pp.471-72]. Yet despite numerous and increasing contacts in security affairs, the institutionalization of transnational ties between Japan and the United States is surprisingly weak.

On questions of security several institutional links have been created between Japan and the United States: the Security Consultative Committee (SCC), the Subcommittee for Defense Cooperation (SDC), the Security Subcommittee (SSC), the Security Consultative Group (SCG), and the Japan-U.S. Joint Committee (Figure 3-1) [Van de Velde, 1988a, pp.200-06. Lohmann, 1980, p.24]. The SCC and the Joint Committee date from 1960 when the Security Treaty was revised. Other fora were subsequently

Figure 3-1. U.S.-Japanese Consultative Fora   (January 1991)

Japanese side	Legal basis	Consultative forum	Purpose	U.S. side
Minister of Foreign Affairs, Director General of the Defense Agency, and others	Established on the basis of letters exchanged between the Prime Minister of Japan and the U.S. Secretary of State Jan. 19, 1960 in accordance with Article IV of Security Treaty	Security Consultative Committee (18 meetings)	Study of matters promoting understanding between the Japanese and U.S. governments and contributing to the strengthening of cooperative relations in the area of security, that form the basis of security and are related to security	U.S. Ambassador to Japan, Commander-in-Chief of the U.S. Pacific Command, and others
Participants are not specified*	Article IV of Security Treaty	Security Subcommittee (19 meetings)	Exchange of views on security issues of common concern to Japan and the U.S.	Participants are not specified*
Deputy Vice Minister of Foreign Affairs, Director General of North American Affairs Bureau, Ministry of Foreign Affairs, Director General of Defense Facilities Administration Agency, Director General of Bureau of Defense Policy, Defense Agency, Chairman of Joint Staff Council, and others	Established on the basis of the agreement reached between the Minister of Foreign Affairs and the U.S. Ambassador to Japan Jan. 19, 1973 in accordance with Article IV of Security Treaty	Security Consultative Group (24 meetings)	Consultation and coordination concerning operation of Security Treaty and related agreements	Minister and Counsellor at the U.S. Embassy, Commander and Chief of Staff of U.S. Forces, Japan, and others

Japan officials	Basis	Committee	Function	U.S. officials
Director General of North American Affairs Bureau, Ministry of Foreign Affairs, Director General of Defense Facilities Administration Agency, and others	Article XXV of Status of Forces Agreement	Japan-U.S. Joint Committee (Once every 2 weeks in principle)	Consultation concerning implementation of Status of Forces Agreement	Chief of Staff of U.S. Forces, Japan, Counsellor at the U.S. Embassy, and others
Director General of Bureau of Defense Policy, Defense Agency, Chief of JSC Secretariat, and Director General of North American Affairs Bureau, Ministry of Foreign Affairs	Established at the 16th SCC meeting on July 8, 1976 as a substructure of the Committee	Subcommittee on Defense Cooperation (9 meetings)	Study and consultation concerning modes of Japan—U.S. cooperation, which involve among others guidelines necessary to insure coordinated joint action by the SDF and the U.S. military in times of emergency	Minister at the U.S. Embassy, Chief of Staff of U.S. Forces, Japan
Director General of Bureau of Equipment, Defense Agency, and others	Established on the basis of an agreement reached between Administrative Vice-minister, Defense Agency, and U.S. Undersecretary of Defense for Research and Technology	Systems and Technology Forum (12 meetings)	Exchange of views on problems between Japan and U.S. in the area of equipment and technology	Deputy Undersecretary of Defense for International Cooperation and Technology, and others

*Meetings are held from time to time between working level officials of the two governments.

Source: Asagumo Shimbun-sha, *Boei Hando Bukku* (Tokyo: Asagumo Shimbun-sha, 1991), p. 277. *Defense of Japan 1990* (Tokyo: The Japan Times, 1990), p. 294

formed. All seek to facilitate policy coordination across a broad range of security issues involving the U.S.-Japan relationship in general, the Security Treaty, and the Status of Forces Agreement, although some have become inactive.

Set up after an exchange of letters in 1960, the Security Consultative Committee (SCC) had an American and Japanese membership that was deliberately made unequal in rank to facilitate frequent meetings. The Committee attracted an extraordinary amount of attention from the press. Formal briefings were stilted and leaks of informal exchanges were so frequent that one admiral reportedly said that he would include nothing in his report to the Committee which he would hesitate to see published in Time Magazine [Emmerson, 1971, p.140]. The Committee met 17 times between 1960 and 1978, but met for the 18th and last time in 1982 [Boeicho, 1991c]. The Committee stopped meeting largely because the Japanese side wanted to create a greater degree of symmetry in the membership of the group [Van de Velde, 1988a, p.205-06]. This was finally accomplished in 1990 when the United States made the Secretary of State and the Secretary of Defense the official representatives of the United States. This symbolically important step had the consequence that the group will at best work informally and meet only very infrequently—officials talk about a meeting every two or three years under the best of circumstances—ostensibly because of the difficulties of coordinating the schedules of four high-ranking officials [Interview Nos. 20 and 23, Tokyo, December 18 and 19, 1991].

The U.S.-Japan Joint Committee was set up by the Status of Forces Agreement signed simultaneously with the Security Treaty in 1960. It has been slated to meet every two weeks and deals with all issues involving the American bases in Japan. It is, along with the SSC, the most institutionalized of the consultative mechanisms that exist between the two countries in the area of defense and security. Its central members are, on the American side, the Chief of Staff of U.S.F.J. and the Counsellor at the U.S. Embassy, and on the Japanese side, Directors of MOFA's North American Affairs Bureau and JDA's Defense Facilities Administration Agency. It has about two dozen subcommittees, ad hoc working groups, and special panels which deal with the innumerable practical aspects that arise from the operation of the U.S. armed forces stationed on Japanese territory. These units involve officials from MOFA and DFAA, as well as from ministries such as Justice, Finance, Agriculture, Forestry, and Fisheries, Transportation, Construction, Posts and Telecommunications, International Trade and Industry, and agencies such as Meteorology and Environment [Defense Agency, 1990, p.294. Emmerson, 1971, pp.140-41. Interview No.20, Tokyo, December 18, 1991. Nakajo, 1987, pp.432-35].

The Security Subcommittee deals broadly with security issues of concern to the two countries [Asagumo Shimbun-sha, 1991, p.277]. Between 1967, when the first meeting took place, and 1989 it met nineteen times [Boeicho, 1991c]. Its membership is not formally fixed [Asagumo Shimbun-sha, 1991, p.277]. Usually attending on the Japanese side are JDA's Administrative Vice-Minister, Directors of the Defense Policy Bureau, the Defense Facilities Administration Agency and the Defense Policy Division, the Chief of the JSC Secretariat, and MOFA's Deputy Vice-Minister and Director of the North American Affairs Bureau. The U.S. usually sends, among others, an Assistant Secretary of Defense, the Deputy Assistant Secretary for East Asian and Pacific Affairs, the Ambassador to Japan, the Commander-in-Chief, Pacific (CINCPAC) and the Commander U.S.F.J. Overall, about 25 high ranking officials attend [Interview No.9, Tokyo, June 13, 1991. Van de Velde, 1988a, p.206]. It is not clear how effective the Subcommittee is in solving actual problems, especially with the large number of officials attending [Interview Nos.6 and 9, Tokyo, June 12 and 13, 1992]. But the fact that, in contrast to SCC, SCG, and SDC, it has never ceased to meet indicates its usefulness for MOFA and JDA officials as well as their U.S. counterparts.

The SCG was created in 1973 to consult on the implementation of the Security Treaty and agreements related to it. Its most important Japanese participants were MOFA's Deputy Vice-Minister and Director of the North American Affairs Bureau, JDA's Directors of the Defense Facilities Administration Agency and the Defense Policy Bureau, and the Chairman of the JSC. The chief American representatives were the Embassy's Minister and Counsellor, and the Commander and Chief of Staff of the U.S.F.J. [Defense Agency, 1990, p.294]. Apparently the group's main concern was with the consolidation of U.S. bases in Okinawa, an important item on the political agenda after the islands' reversion to Japan in 1972 [Mainichi Shimbun-sha, 1974, p.131]. It met 21 times between 1973 and 1975, three times between 1976 and 1977, and then ceased to meet [Boeicho, 1991c]. The importance of this group in this period is indicated by the fact that between 1973 and 1977, the SSC met only twice [Ministry of Foreign Affairs, 1991c].

The SDC was created in 1976 as a substructure of the SCC. Partly because MOFA wished to protect its authority on matters concerning the Security Treaty from encroachments by the JDA, the SDC was not established as an independent unit [Otake, 1983a, p.143]. It is composed of the Directors of MOFA's North American Affairs Bureau and JDA's Defense Policy Bureau, the head of the JSC's Secretariat, and, on the American side, the Minister in charge of Political Affairs of the U.S. Embassy in Tokyo, and the Chief of Staff of the U.S. Forces, Japan

[Asagumo Shimbun-sha, 1991, p.277. Van de Velde, 1988a, pp.170-71]. After the end of the Vietnam war the SDC aimed at intensifying U.S.-Japanese consultations concerning the scope and modalities of cooperation under the provisions of Articles 5 and 6 of the Security Treaty [Ishiguro, 1987, p.242. Van de Velde, 1988a, pp.165-172]. "The Subcommittee was given joint military planning tasks which were political impossibilities throughout the 1950s and 1960s . . . Coordination of U.S.-Japan command, division of defense roles for air and sea defense and Japanese logistical support for American operations were all taboo subjects in Japan until the loss of Vietnam galvanized an indigenous concern to strengthen the defense relationship . . . Studies concerning the actual division of defense responsibility and service interoperability would become the Subcommittee's initial tasks" [Van de Velde, 1988a, pp.171, 173]. Most importantly, it drafted the 1978 Guidelines for U.S.-Japan Defense Cooperation. Between 1976 and 1978, it met eight times. In contrast, between 1979 and 1990 the SDC met only once. The MOFA apparently hopes to make it a higher level forum involving administrative vice-ministers of MOFA and the JDA, an assistant secretary of DoD, CINCPAC, and the U.S. ambassador to Japan [Interview No.1, Tokyo, June 11, 1991]. But close defense consultation has continued after 1978. A number of major studies have dealt with joint defense planning, sea-lanes defense, the establishment of a Japan-U.S. Defense Coordination Center, the exchange of intelligence, common operational preparations, communications, and the assistance of Japanese facilities to U.S. Forces in crises outside Japan that would have an important impact on Japan [Akaha, n.d. pp.132-33. Asagumo Shimbun-sha, 1991, pp.283-84. Defense Agency, 1990, pp.176-77. Interview Nos.1, 6 and 9, Tokyo, June 11, 12 and 13, 1991. Van de Velde, 1988a, pp.200, 208-09]. According to one report, however, the last item has never been actively studied [Asahi Shimbun, February 17, 1988]. The MOFA is in charge of coordinating the study of this issue [Sakurai, 1990, p.73].

These institutions often offer a useful forum for official statements and replies, rather than a forum for resolving difficult issues. That is left to the myriad of informal contacts, by telephone and in face-to-face meetings at all levels of the bureaucracy, as well as to ad hoc and problem-focused bilateral consultations at the level of the Administrative Vice-Minister or the Bureau Director [Interview No.9, Tokyo, June 13, 1991. Interview Nos. 20 and 23, Tokyo, December 18 and 19, 1991]. But these institutions have facilitated the informal exchange of views and contacts. Equally important, regular consultations create deadlines that force the two bureaucracies, in particular on the Japanese side, to make final decisions [Interview Nos. 2, 5, 6, 11 and 15, Tokyo, June 11, 12, 14 and 17, 1991. Interview No.23, Tokyo, December 19, 1991].

The armed forces of the United States continue to maintain a substantial presence in Japan. Despite the withdrawal of all American ground forces from Japan in 1957, the United States Airforce and Navy, as well as some logistical support staff of the Army, still have about 49,000 men stationed at about a dozen major bases and 120 military installations throughout Japan [Drifte, 1985b, p.155. Satoh, 1982, p.27. Defense Agency, 1990, pp. 184-88, 307-08]. The American base at Okinawa is home to the Third Division of the U.S. Marine Corps, the only amphibious force stationed in the Western Pacific. And a squadron of SAC's tanker planes whose mission it is to refuel B-52 bombers, stationed in Guam, is placed at the Kadena Air Base in Okinawa. The U.S. Army Japan headquarters at Camp Zama and the Seventh Fleet headquarters at Yokosuka are both in the vicinity of Tokyo. The airbases at Misawa, and Kadena are home to the airforce's anti-submarine P-3C Orion airplanes [Defense Agency, 1990, p.307]. Furthermore the U.S. aircraft carrier Midway and its successor, the Independent, have been granted access to Yokosuka since 1973. The U.S. Air Force has deployed F-16s at the Misawa airbase since 1985, with the exception of Okinawa, the first such airforce deployment in Japan since 1971. These military bases are essential for the coordination of operations in the Pacific theater as well as staging areas for potential nuclear strikes against potential enemies of the United States and Japan [Arkin and Chappell, 1985, p.486].

Under the provision of the Status of Forces Agreement (SOFA) more than one-third of the costs of stationing American troops in Japan is paid for by the Japanese defense budget. This figure is much higher per soldier than what is being paid by any NATO member [Sutter, 1982, p.14. Keddell, 1990, p.170. Puckett, 1990, p.11]. In the early 1980s, for example, Japan appropriated about 1 billion dollars for the support of 48,000 American troops while West Germany paid 1.3 billion dollars toward the support of 240,000 American soldiers [Nishihara, 1983/84, p.204]. By 1990 Japan was paying about 2.4 billion or 40 percent of the support costs of U.S. troops, and the percentage was likely to increase further. According to the data made public by the U.S. State Department, by 1995 Japan will pay about three-quarters of the total costs, excluding the salaries of U.S. personnel, of the U.S. military presence in Japan [Kondo, 1991, p.18]. Japanese funds cover construction, environmental abatement, land rentals, local compensations and welfare payments for local workers. The MOFA strongly advocates increased Japanese spending for the stationing of U.S. troops. Fearing its effects on the SDF budget, the JDA is more reluctant [Asahi Shimbun, June 25, 1990, 13th edition].

Some of the transnational security links between Japan and the United States are economic and date back to the early 1950s. After the United

States-Japan Security Treaty became effective at the end of April 1952, the Security Advisory Section replaced a prior organization dealing with the build-up of Japan's National Police Reserve. It was renamed in 1953 and replaced in 1954 by the Military Assistance Advisory Group-Japan (MAAG-J), under the authority of the United States-Japan Mutual Defense Assistance Agreement, signed in March 1954. It became an important pipeline for Japan's rearmament. The Korean war underlined Japan's strategic importance as a forward base of the United States in Asia. That war made Japan into a workshop for supplying American troops. Between 1950 and 1953 special procurement orders of the Department of Defense increased from 191 to 452 million dollars. All told in the 1950s the U.S. placed orders valued at 5.6 billion dollars with Japanese industry, either for U.S. forces deployed in Asia or for those of its Asian allies. The Vietnam war led to a second major boom in the 1960s [Drifte, 1985a, pp.6-7. Bix, 1970, pp.33-34]. In 1966-67, for example, U.S. military contracts with Japanese firms totalled about half a billion dollars, about 50 percent of that year's defense budget [Bix, 1970, p.34]. Direct and indirect procurement reached 63 percent of Japanese exports during the Korean War and between 7 and 8 percent during the Vietnam War [Pharr, 1992, pp.10, 20]. The United States granted Japan military assistance throughout the 1950s and 1960s until Japan's growing economic strength made such assistance unnecessary [Olsen, 1985, pp.76-77]. Between 1950 and 1983, it has been estimated the JDA received about ten billion dollars worth of advanced military technology [Drifte, 1985a, p.9].

Technology transfer mattered from the beginning of the U.S.-Japan security relation. Article 1 of the Mutual Defense Assistance Agreement states that "each Government, consistently with the principle that economic stability is essential to international peace and security, will make available to the other . . . such equipment, materials, services or other assistance as the Government furnishing such assistance may authorize" [Drifte, 1985a, p.8]. But only in the 1980s did the two governments begin to encourage the reverse flow of military technology from Japan to the United States. On the economic issues with relevance for questions of military security affecting Japan and the United States a variety of institutions have been set up [Interview Nos. 6 and 20, Tokyo, June 12 and 19, 1991]. This is true in particular of the economic and technology issues that are beginning to affect deeply the security relations between the two countries. Increasingly aware of the importance of dual-use technologies and its growing dependence on Japanese producers in particular, the U.S. Department of Defense was very eager to cooperate with the JDA in setting up in 1980 the Systems and Technology Forum to facilitate cooperation in military research and development, production and procurement. It met 12 times between 1980 and 1990. Its most important members are the Director of the JDA's Equipment Bureau and DoD's Deputy Undersecretary for International Cooperation and Technology [Asagumo Shimbun-sha, 1991, pp.277, 290]. The MOFA is not a major participant. For example, in 1991 its representative at the forum was only a deputy division director [Interview No.1, Tokyo, June 11, 1991]. Under its auspices a number of technical review groups meet quite regularly dealing with questions affecting joint command, air-defense and the relations between each of the three services and their counterparts. The Forum's activities, however, were immediately undercut by the traditional Japanese policy prohibiting the export of military equipment which the Japanese government has interpreted to include also military technologies [Interview No.3, Tokyo, June 11, 1991. Interview No.20, Tokyo, December 18, 1991. Rubinstein, 1987a, pp.45-46. Kuranari and Mochizuki, 1983. Corning, 1989, pp.278-86].

After the Nakasone government had exempted the export of military technologies to the United States in 1983 from the export ban of armaments, lengthy negotiations between Japan and the United States established in November 1983 a Joint Military Technology Commission (JMTC). It was staffed by State Department and Department of Defense officials in the American Embassy in Tokyo as well as Japanese officials from the JDA, MITI and MOFA [Rubinstein, 1987b. Söderberg, 1986, pp.139-40]. This was followed by detailed arrangements governing the transfer of military technologies in December 1985 [Vogel, 1989, pp.32-36. Okimoto, Rowen and Dahl, 1987, pp.42-46]. The Japanese government disarmed its domestic critics by using the 1954 Agreement with the United States as an umbrella justifying the secrecy deemed necessary for implementation of the agreement [Inoguchi, 1991a, pp.95-96]. However, the JMTC has not met frequently and until the late 1980s only two such transfers had actually occurred, both apparently contrived more for the precedent that they might set for future technology transfers rather than for any important immediate military benefit for the United States [Vogel, 1989, p.36].

Finally, recognizing persisting problems in the field of technology transfer from Japan to the United States, Secretary of Defense Cheney's visit to Tokyo in February 1990 became the occasion for singling out six technology areas of particular interest for the U.S. military [Fujishima, 1992, p.144]. Working groups have been set up since September 1990, when the STF agreed on five technology items for joint study, to lay the groundwork for a broadening flow of dual-use technologies from Japan to the United States [Interview No.3, Tokyo, June 11, 1991. Interview No.1, Tokyo, December 9, 1991]. With technology flow-back quickly becoming "a buzz word for the 1990s" [Interview No.20, Tokyo, December 18, 1991] other organizations of the United States government, such as the Defense

Advanced Research Projects Agency (DARPA) or the Strategic Defense Initiative Organization (SDIO) regularly send delegations to Tokyo on fact finding missions. This leads to contacts with Japanese government agencies and ministries such as TRDI and MITI which help establish the necessary contacts with Japanese firms [Interview No.20, Tokyo, December 18, 1991]. In August 1991 the DoD created, inside the U.S. Embassy in Tokyo, an office for researching and analyzing Japan's technology [Fujishima, 1992, pp.213-14. Saikawa, 1990, p.42]. In September 1991 DoD started a training project for its middle-ranking civilian and military officials which includes training at Japan's research organizations and firms [Fujishima, 1992, pp.214-15].

It is too early to judge the effectiveness of these recent attempts of creating new links in the vital area of technological cooperation between Japan's firms and government agencies and their American counterparts. But their institutionalization appears to be at least as important as corresponding developments in the transnational security links created in the 1960s and 1970s. Institutions specify obligations that the private sector in particular would not readily accept without political pressure [Interview No.20, Tokyo, December 18, 1991]. While close firm-to-firm contacts existed already in the 1950s and 1960s, when Japan began to produce weapons under American license, the curve of Japan's production of conventional weapons systems licensed from American defense contractors moves rapidly upward only after 1976 [U.S. Congress, 1990, p.65, and 1991, p. 108]. Any further institutional integration of the two defense industries, albeit on more equal terms, would continue a trend that has existed for more than a decade.

Transnational links exist also in the absence of formal institutions, especially between the two militaries. Speaking generally, the coordination of SDF operations with the U.S. military has increased greatly during the 1980s. While the SDF is largely in charge of dealing with the United States on technical military issues, such as training and equipment, weapon acquisition issues are handled by the Equipment Bureau of the DA, in cooperation with MITI. MOFA is in charge of the broader security policy questions. On the American side the American Embassy handles the broader political issues and leaves to the U.S. Department of Defense and U.S. Forces Japan strictly military matters and virtually all issues affecting civilian and military intelligence [Interview No.9, Tokyo, June 13, 1991. Interview No.23, Tokyo, December 19, 1991].

Informal links between the two militaries are partly facilitated by their similar structures. For reasons of history Japan's SDF are modelled after the US military. Indeed in their weapons, organization and command structure the SDF are a "mini-size" American force [Emmerson, 1971, p.142]. In the 1950s the curriculum of the three staff colleges of the SDF self-consciously imitated that of the American military. While today changes in the curriculum of the SDF no longer mirror those in the U.S. military, in its broad outlines the curriculum of the SDF officers remains very close to that of the United States military [Interview Nos.5, 13 and 20, Tokyo, December 9, 13 and 18, 1991].

The force structure and mission of the SDF make them an integral component of a more encompassing U.S. security strategy in the Pacific. Relations between the GSDF and the U.S. army are constrained by the small number of U.S. army personnel stationed in Japan as well as intense public scrutiny. But the GSDF's primary mission is not only to defend Hokkaido against a small-scale and limited invasion before a U.S. counterattack reaches Hokkaido. The GSDF's recent adoption of a strategy of seashore defense has given it a larger role in the control over the straits of Japan and thus strengthens its relations with the U.S. navy [Interview Nos. 2, 3, 9 and 10, Tokyo, June 11 and 13, 1991]. The MSDF focuses on antisubmarine surveillance and protection of the straits of Japan and is thus part of the American naval presence in the Western Pacific. Japan's antisubmarine warfare copies that of the United States. Joint training, operation and high levels of interoperability of equipment between the United States and Japan also point to very close relations. Such close contacts are facilitated by the fact that the MSDF and the U.S. navy can exercise together on the open sea, away from the watchful eye of a suspicious public. Language is no barrier between the two services. Since the adoption of an Allied tactical manual in the early 1960s Japanese personnel have used English in their training operations [Interview No.11, Tokyo, December 12, 1991]. In their intensity and strategic significance contacts between the ASDF and the U.S. airforce fall between those of the other two services. In the 1960s the ASDF was the service that kept the closest relations with the U.S. military. When a Japan Air Lines passenger plane was hijacked by members of Japan's Red Army in the early 1970s, a JAL official immediately telephoned not the ASDF but the U.S. Air Force [Emmerson, 1971, p.142]. The ASDF's airdefense system copies that of the U.S. airforce. And its role of protection of the Japanese airspace and regional surveillance and intelligence is auxiliary to the broader mission of the American airforce in Asia.

Increasing transnational links between the three branches of the SDF and the U.S. military are thus of different strength for each of the three services. The links between the two navies are much stronger than those between the two airforces which in turn are stronger than those linking the two armies [Interview No.13, Tokyo, December 13, 1991]. But growing cooperation with the U.S. armed forces has also increased cooperation among the different branches of the SDF. For the U.S. Navy preventing accidental Japanese attacks on U.S. aircraft and ships operating in the vicinity of Japan required, for example, not only close cooperation with the MSDF but also with the ASDF. American pressure in the 1980s thus forced coordination between the MSDF and ASDF that simply had not existed before [Interview No.23, December 19, 1991]. One area where coordination between the MSDF and the ASDF has been absent concerns the training of pilots. Although the MSDF has 200 pilots, the equipment and mission of its aircrafts are so different from those of the ASDF that no overlap in training and exercises exists between the two services [Interview Nos. 10 and 12, Tokyo, June 13 and 14, 1991]. But joint international exercises have led not only to more exercises between the MSDF and the ASDF but have provided also encouragement for staging domestic exercises involving all three branches of the SDF. Between FY 1961 and 1989, the SDF's combined exercises, excluding those held with U.S. forces, numbered fifteen [Defense Agency, 1990, p.139]. Until the late 1970s they were apparently sporadic. But since 1981 these exercises have occurred annually [Interview No.10, Tokyo, June 13, 1991. Sekai Henshu-bu, 1987, p.25]. The SDF were able to hold their first combined joint field training exercises in October 1986. These exercises were preceded by a combined joint command post exercise in February of the same year [Akaha, 1990, p.17]. The experience of foreign joint exercises prompted the SDF to hold domestic combined exercises in earnest [Olsen, 1985, p.95. Interview Nos. 10 and 21, Tokyo, June 13 and 19, 1991]. Transnational military links thus have had a clear effect on Japan's SDF.

American military assistance also has reinforced close links between the two militaries. It has had the dual effect of creating a closer integration between the different branches of the SDF and linking the SDF more closely to the U.S. military. Until the late 1960s the MAAG-J remained the major instrument of the United States to administer the Mutual Defense Assistance Programs in Japan. Compared to the MAAG missions in other countries the Japanese one was unique for the simple reason that Japan never lacked the technical and financial resources necessary for building up modern armed forces. The burden-sharing formula that was built into the security relationship between the two countries meant that from the very beginning U.S. military assistance was granted by the three armed services of the United States. "This method of distribution induced the creation of a counterpart army, navy and airforce . . . Some Americans have lamented this tripartite structure as counterproductive because the Japanese had indicated a desire for a unified service, which might have precluded interservice rivalries . . . One can imagine the difficulties Washington would experience if Japan's armed forces were unitary in structure and not prepared to 'interface' with their U.S. counterparts" [Olsen, 1985, p.76]. In short, the military assistance program of the United States had the effect of replicating, at least to some extent, its own structure, and thus facilitated the functional integration between the two militaries.

Military assistance furthermore creates its own requirements for overseas training of SDF personnel. In the case of Japan the need for overseas training arises in part from the physical limitations of Japan's airspace and military bases. For example, Japan lacks a firing range for artillery and missile training operations which is larger than 20 km. In the late 1980s a total of about 1,400 members of the GSDF who operate the Hawk, Nike and Patriot missile systems travelled for three weeks training sessions to the United States [Interview Nos.3 and 8, Tokyo, December 9 and 11, 1991]. Furthermore the GSDF planned for the fall of 1992 its first ground maneuvers overseas. Three hundred-fifty men, using Japanese tanks, artillery and helicopters shipped by private chartered ships, were to exercise for two weeks in Hawaii [Interview, Nos.3, 8 and 12, Tokyo, December 9, 11 and 12, 1991. Asahi Evening News, May 7, 1991. Mainichi Shimbun, July 24, 1991]. However, due to cuts in the defense budget, the plan was scaled down to involve 130 men using three helicopters [Asahi Shimbun, January 26, 1992, 13th edition]. Two or three advanced pilots are being trained in the United States each year, about ten percent of the Japanese total. And in 1990 a shortage of training aircraft sent another ten pilots to American facilities for the first time in several decades. In addition each service sends about ten officers for advanced training to the United States. The total number of military personnel going to the United States annually for training is about 60 [Interview Nos. 4, 10, 12 and 15, Tokyo, June 11, 13, 14 and 17, 1991. Interview No.5, Tokyo, December 9, 1991]. But this flow of personnel is also strengthened by the growing interoperability of weapon systems which increases the demand for overseas training of SDF personnel [Interview Nos. 3 and 5, December 9, 1991. Defense Agency, 1990, p.135]. Because Japan produces most of its weapons under license, it is closely tied to the American armaments industry. Major SDF purchases of new American equipment (such as the P-3C, the Airborne Warning and Control System (AWACS), the Patriot or the Aegis) will temporarily increase the flow of personnel across the Pacific until Japanese crews have been trained to operate the new equipment. In 1987 about 400 members of the SDF were stationed in New Mexico for training with Nike and Hawk missiles, while another 58 were in Texas as part of the procurement of Patriot missiles [Nakajo, 1987, p.422].

The strength of these transnational links with the U.S. military is illustrated through a comparison with Japan's much weaker security ties with other countries. Every year SDF personnel is sent abroad to study at institutions affiliated with the military. The United States is the most important destination (92 % of 73 persons in 1982, 90 % of 87 in 1983, 85 % of 62 in 1984, 92 % of 48 in 1985, and 90 % of 49 in 1986) [Nakajo, 1987, p.423]. Japan has, however, gradually increased its military training program for foreign officers. Between 1975 and 1986 Japanese military institutions provided training for officers from Thailand (83), Singapore (47), the United States (20), Pakistan (7) and the United Kingdom (2), Malaysia (1) and West Germany (1) [Nakajo, 1987, pp.424-25. Hummel, 1988, p.53. Interview Nos. 10 and 12, Tokyo, June 13 and 14, 1991]. Since language and living costs constitute a very high barrier for expanding these international contacts, the Defense Academy of the JDA offers since 1991 one year of free language instruction followed by a four-years course. However, the total number of foreign officers enrolled in this course is well below ten [Interview No.10, December 12, 1991].

The growing defense links between the two countries are illustrated also by the rising number of joint operational exercises in the 1980s [Olsen, 1985, p.95. Drifte, 1985b, p.156. Van de Velde, 1988a, pp.209-215]. Until the late 1970s such exercises had been restricted largely to the joint exercises of the MSDF with the 7th Fleet which had started in 1955; in addition joint exercises between the ASDF and the 5th Air Force took place in the early 1960s when responsibilities for Japan's air-defense were shifted to the ASDF [Interview Nos. 12 and 16, Tokyo, June 14 and 17, 1991. Matsuo, 1987, p.198]. But since 1980 Japan has participated in an important role in the Rim of the Pacific (RIMPAC) naval exercises, which since 1971 have brought together naval forces from the United States, Canada, Australia and New Zealand [Nakagawa, 1984, p.831]. These are multilateral exercises. Although Japan communicates with other navies during the exercises, its participation remains limited to joint training only with the U.S. Navy. Compared to these joint maneuvers the very brief joint maneuver and communication training exercises held with other navies in the course of the sporadic goodwill port calls of MSDF ships in neighboring countries pale in significance [Interview Nos.11 and 23, Tokyo, December 12 and 19, 1991].

Although much less important for the GSDF, participation of the GSDF in joint operational exercises has also increased during the last decade [Interview Nos.8 and 12, Tokyo, December 11 and 12, 1991]. The 1978 Defense Guidelines have facilitated joint studies of joint operation and, to a lesser extent, joint training. In 1981 the GSDF held for the first time joint maneuvers with the United States in Japan. In May 1983 the GSDF participated for the first time in a joint command-post exercise in the continental United States. Command post exercises with the U.S. army, when held in Japan, last 7-10 days and involve up to 1,500 men. Regiment level field training, conducted without tanks and armored vehicles, but with field artillery and helicopters, last about one week. In the late 1980s about 1,000 U.S. troops were flown to Japan from Hawaii to participate in joint exercises with the GSDF. Company level cold weather training operations typically involve about 200 troops on each side. But despite these developments in joint training, operating under the watchful eye of the Japanese public the GSDF remains much more constrained in cooperating with the U.S. military than do either the MSDF or the ASDF [Interview No.12, Tokyo, December 12, 1991]. The GSDF also has an extensive exchange program with the United States. Each country's personnel is sent to the other's bases to observe training and exercises. Between 1981 and 1986 1,126 Japanese and 1,187 U.S. military personnel participated in these exchanges [Matsuo, 1987, pp.206-212].

The ASDF started a training program with the U.S. Airforce in November 1978 on the same day the SCC approved the Guidelines for Japan-U.S. Defense Cooperation. Joint training focused on aerial combat and rescue operations. Joint command post exercises began in December 1983. Some Japanese pilots receive basic flight training in the United States. And airbattle training involving small numbers of Japansese and American fighters in Japanese airspace have become quite common in the 1980s. These exercises involve an American squadron of fighters that fly to Japan for training purposes a week at a time. Since 1984, the scope of the training has been expanded to include fighter supply, intelligence gathering, battlefield monitoring from the air, and refueling. Furthermore, U.S. planes stationed in Korea have in the 1980s begun to participate in combined joint training operations [Interview Nos.3 and 8, Tokyo, December 9 and 11, 1991. Van de Velde, 1988a, p.211].

Table 3.3 summarizes the data on joint Japan-U.S. military exercises. The data speak for themselves. In FY 1977 there were three exercises, in FY 1982 19, and in FY 1989 24. The first combined field exercises involving the three services of both countries were held in October 1986. In February 1986 the central command post of the JDA, together with the military command posts of American forces stationed in Yokota, Zama and Yokosuka, for the first time carried out joint command exercises. By the time "Keen Edge 87" was staged in October 1987, 13,000 military personnel from both countries participated [Hook, 1988, p.391. Defense Agency, 1990, pp.177-81]. In the eyes of some observers these joint exercises serve also the purpose of strengthening the links between the South Korean and the Japanese military as partners of the United States in an integrated military strategy in Asia [Hook, 1988, pp.391-92]. The end of the Cold War, however, will diminish the number of joint training exercises in the 1990s [Interview No.3, Tokyo, December 9, 1991]. For

Table 3-3. Japan-U.S. Joint Military Exercises (1975-90)

Year**	GSDF	MSDF	ASDF	Unified
1975		1		
1976		2		
1977		3		
1978		3	3	
1979		3*	11	
1980		3	10	
1981	3	6*	12	
1982	4	5	10	
1983	3	5	12	
1984	5	8*	10	
1985	7	7	13	1
1986	7	7*	12	1
1987	7	7	16	1
1988	7	9*	13	2
1989	6	8	9	1
1990	3	7*	8	1

*   includes the RIMPAC exercises
* *   fiscal years

Source: Various editions of Boeicho, <u>Boei Hakusho</u> (<u>Defense White Paper</u>)
(Tokyo: Okurasho Insatsu-Kyoku).

example, between 1991 and 1995, the number of joint combined command post exercises, held annually in recent years, will be reduced to three [Asahi Shimbun, January 18, 1991, 13th edition].

In the foreseeable future Japanese security policy will be focused on the U.S.-Japan relationship. This alliance is of cardinal importance in economic, political and military terms. Noteworthy though is its relatively weak institutionalization, despite undeniable changes in the last decade, especially in comparison with the Atlantic Alliance which is organized around an integrated command structure [Interview Nos.9 and 19, Tokyo, June 13 and 18, 1991]. But this lack of institutionalization is countered by a wide range of informal, transnational ties as well as the depth of Japan's perceived political, economic and military vulnerability which makes high-level meetings between the U.S. President and the Japanese Prime Minister a very important political link between the two countries [Interview Nos.23 and 24, Kyoto and Tokyo, June 24 and 28, 1991]. Alliance management is not so much a matter of institutions as of the informal coordination of the political relations between two different executive branches of governments that seek to harmonize strong domestic political pressures within an evolving diplomatic relationship. This informal coordination is much more pronounced in military security affairs than in economic issues with military relevance such as technology exports. Economic ministries such as MITI and the Department of Commerce operate in a broader political arena and are often involved in a more public type of politics that are less favorable to the forging of informal transnational ties. The foundations of the transnational structures that link the security relations between the two countries thus differ by issue. But the overall effect of the transnational links of the Japanese state has been to push questions of military security higher up on the political agenda than would have been possible in light of the organization of the Japanese government and of Japan's civil-military relations.

IV

The Normative Context of Japan's National Security Policy

National security policy is deeply affected by the social and legal norms that, besides the domestic and transnational structures discussed in Chapter 3, help shape the interests of political actors that inform Japanese security policy. These norms are on questions of economic security largely consensual and on questions of military security deeply contested. Issues of Japan's political security, and in particular its relation to the United States, fall between these two extremes.

Because of political resistance to any constitutional revision, the tension between social and legal norms has led to a system of governing by "constitutional interpretation." The government has tried to influence the evolution of social norms. The opposition has focused on existing legal norms. Both seek to defend or advance their respective political agendas [Hook, 1988, p.386. Peace and Security, 1982]. This political bargaining process began in the crucial decade of the 1950s which defined the political battle lines around the defense issue that separated Right from Left. The buildup of military strength and the government's fluctuating interpretations of the Constitution suggested to many a gradual, unstoppable move towards a remilitarization of Japan. "Desperate to avoid public controversy, the Self Defense Forces continued to grow without . . . public debate about its real needs and goals in a process its critics were to call 'an accumulation of fait accomplis'" [Berger, 1992, pp.108, 480]. "Successive Japanese governments have chosen the way of constitutional interpretation to permit the steady growth of a defense establishment" [Emmerson, 1971, p.114]. At the same time it is also true that even though the LDP government enjoyed a comfortable majority in the Diet in most of the postwar years, on military issues "the voice of public opinion being louder in Japan than in most democracies, the Japanese leadership was never insensitive to the effect on the public of its decisions and actions" [Emmerson, 1971, p.114]. Japan's public opinion has reacted not only to historical memories of the past as interpreted and reinterpreted by existing institutions such as the mass media. With the growing awareness of the Soviet build-up in the Far East since the early 1980s a change in the threat perception of the Japanese public has to some extent modified public opinion [Interview No. 10, Tokyo, December 12, 1991]. On questions of national security Japan's social and legal norms are thus in variable tension with one another: uncontested on issues of economic security, deeply contested on questions of military security, and disputed on issues of political security.

A. Uncontested Norms of Economic Security

For over 100 years economic security has been a powerful idea that has galvanized the Japanese people to collective action. The purpose of action was to "catch up and surpass the West" (oitsuki, oikose). Military industries designed to enhance national security directly were the spearhead of Japan's industrialization after the Meji Restoration. Eventually the normative consensus on the imperative of economic security led a militarist regime down the path to imperialism and war. Since 1945, however, the ideology of economic security has increasingly focused on the development of technology as the most plausible way for reducing Japan's dependence on the import of critical raw materials, such as oil, and as a potent force for gaining growing shares in the markets for commerical products.

The lack of debate about the desirability of reducing Japan's economic vulnerability is not surprising. Japanese policy makers welcomed the free trade of the Pax Americana as the only way for reducing their economic vulnerability, after the failure of military expansion to control foreign markets. "Although the concept of free trade requires globalism, the immediate concern of Japanese economic planners was whether Japan would be allowed access to markets and raw materials in Asia" [Watanabe, 1989b, p.86]. Karel Von Wolferen puts the point more sharply when he writes that the Japanese have a strong fear "of being victimized by circumstances they cannot control. A common Japanese term, higaisha ishiki (victimhood consciousness), reflects a diffuse but fairly strong sense that the world cannot be trusted and that Japan will always be a potential victim of capricious external forces" [Von Wolferen, 1991, p.26]. Susan Pharr agrees when she writes that Japan's foreign policy choices "emerged out of debate, discussion, and the collective mood among successive generations of policymakers faced by pressures inside and outside Japan who shared a perception that the world was a dangerous place" [Pharr, 1992, p.3]. Japan's extreme dependence on foreign sources of energy and other raw materials is one illustration for virtually all Japanese. Indeed the idea of

Japan as a small and isolated island nation, easily held hostage in a hostile international environment, still retains a very powerful hold over Japanese thinking. This is not to say that Japansese elites do not, at times, mobilize this idea to achieve their specific objectives by appealing to the need for the Japanese to counter international vulnerability through collective effort and hard work. Japan's economic vulnerability, it is clear to all, needs to be defended. And characteristically the means for doing so are relatively uncontested.

Japan's commitment to increasing its technological autonomy is similarly uncontroversial. Technology is desirable because it opens up the prospect for sustained, long-term growth. And it may also help to reduce Japan's economic vulnerability by pointing to a future of sustained economic growth less dependent on importing raw materials. As Friedman and Samuels have recently shown, the norm of enhancing Japan's technological autonomy prescribes access to foreign technologies which are appropriated and diffused throughout society and economy. The distinction between military and civilian technology is not essential in the enhancing of such autonomy. What matters instead is that acquired know-how is "diffused aggressively throughout the Japanese economy as a matter of security ideology, national policy and private practice. In the process, defense technology was valued as much for its ability to elevate the fundamental capacities of the economy than as [sic] a means for actually producing military hardware . . . Indigenization, diffusion and nurturing combine the belief that Japan is more secure when it achieves independent scientific and technological capabilities to design, manufacture and innovate. Each is derived from a pervasive sense that Japan must compensate for its special vulnerabilities in a Hobbesian world" [Friedman and Samuels, 1992, pp.4, 6]. Friedman and Samuels argue that this normative consensus about the value of technological autonomy leads to a view of industry totally different from that which can be found in the United States. Industries are valued for the knowledge they generate as much as the products they produce. This national consensus is now so basic that it is virtually unquestioned [Friedman and Samuels, 1992, p.55].

Ideological unanimity on the desirability of defending Japan's economic security through a reduction of its dependence on raw materials and the enhancement of indigeneous technology has not permeated the military security debate. The closely related concern with macro-economic management, however, is to some extent reflected in the economic language in which security issues are at times discussed in Japan. Furthermore, the concept of comprehensive security that informs that discussion is very attuned to economic and political considerations. Talking about national security only in military terms is simply not legitimate for the mainstream of Japanese politics; the conceptual base of public discourse thus does not rest on a narrow notion of military strategy.

The politics of naming is an important part of the battle over the normative foundations of Japan's security policy [Hook, 1990, pp.26, 24-37]. It is thus no accident that the language of Japanese security policy is often non-military. For example, in the official language of the JDA tanks are called "special vehicles", destroyers "escort ships", artillery "special department", and so forth [Asahi Shimbun, September 26, 1991, 13th ed.]. When the SDF sent minesweepers to the Gulf in 1991, they called them "Overseas Minesweeper Force." MOFA preferred the term "Group" or "Unit" instead, arguing that "Force" had connotations of offensive military power [Magami, 1991, pp.187-88]. After 1945 traditional military ranks and titles were replaced with "contrived, artificial terms" [Emmerson, 1971, p.107]. And Japan's political elite and professional military try their best to avoid using the concept of strategy as is illustrated by the White Papers which the JDA issues annually [Okazaki, 1986]. Instead of evoking agressive connotations touching on historical memories of the 1930s and 1940s, and creating political trouble with the opposition in the Diet, the government prefers to talk about "policy" or "guidelines" [Interviews Nos.9 and 16, Tokyo, June 13 and 17, 1991]. Military officers in the GSDF stress the local and reactive, rather than global and active character of Japan's security policy; they use the concept of "forward coping" (zenpo taisho) or "tactics" (senjutsu) [Interview No.7, Tokyo, June 13, 1991]. Similarly, officers in the MSDF contrast the defensive character of Japan's "maritime concept" (kaijo koso) with the offensive, forward deployment of the U.S. "maritime strategy." In their understanding the Japanese navy lacks the combination of independent planning and adequate capability that is required for a military strategy [Interview No.12, Tokyo, June 14, 1991]. This aversion of the SDF to strategic terminology is shared by the Japanese public. It was "economic security" that first found its way into public discourse. "Military security" became an accepted term only subsequently, in the late 1970s, and even then the preferred term was "comprehensive security" [Umemoto, 1989, pp.128-129. Watanabe, 1989, p.7].

"The terms of the Japanese defense debate took place . . . in the arena of economics . . . Consequently, as one representative of Japan's parliament put it, 'We could talk for hours about the level of spending and whether it should be higher or lower. Everyone would be willing to participate in the debate on those terms. But no other issues would ever be allowed to enter into the debate'" [Pempel, 1990a, p.11]. Others have made the same point in referring to Japan's political debate about the appropriate level of defense spending as "the strategy of econometrics" [Cordesman, 1983b]. Although in theory actual defense needs rather than the one percent limit became the criterion, the government never offered a military rationale for this limit [Umemoto, 1985a, p.51]. Japanese security policy thus has frequently been debated in the language of economics, even to the point of eschewing military and strategic considerations.

The use of an economic language for the discussion of national security issues has affected the terms of negotiations with the U.S. Especially until the mid-1970s the defense dialogue—including U.S. criticisms and Japanese rejoinders—pivoted on "fiscal, economic, and statistical arguments, not on issues of military strategy, threat perceptions, or specific military missions" that needed to be carried out. This preoccupation with the economics of security relations was a "curious and striking feature of the U.S.-Japanese defense dialogue" [Okimoto, 1982a, p.234]. To the extent that political attention was focused on marginal budget increases, just below or just above 1 percent of GNP, the government's effort to broaden and deepen its defense relationship with the United States was made easier. Even the United States has relied on economic language to express basic political positions. In September 1988 Secretary of Defense Carlucci stated in public that the United States henceforth would not seek more than 5 percent annual increases in the rate of Japanese defense spending. Further increases in Japan's defense capabilities might move Japan toward developing offensive rather than defensive capabilities, something which was politically not desirable. "The admonition was cast in budgetary terms" [Keddell, 1990, p.232].

In the 1980s Japanese discussions of national security have been cast in terms of the concept of comprehensive security (sogo anzen hosho). In the minds of many people this language provided a plausible political stance that both countered and reinforced some of the arguments of the new military "realists." Predated by systematic thinking about Japan's economic security (resources, energy, etc.) that MITI developed in the 1970s [Interview No. 2, Tokyo, June 11, 1991. Umemoto, 1988, pp.31-32], this language was partly influenced by a study of the Nomura Research Institute that focused on comprehensive security [Interview No. 16, Tokyo, June 17, 1991]. The term "comprehensive" security subsequently appeared in the 1980 report of the Comprehensive National Security Study Group convened by Prime Minister Ohira [Comprehensive National Security Study Group, 1980. Barnett, 1984]. The report was not formally adopted as national policy, but it had a significant impact on the domestic debate on security policy [Chapman, Drifte and Gow, 1982. Bobrow. 1984. Bobrow, Kim and Hill, 1985. International Institute for Strategic Studies, 1987. Tsurutani, 1980. Akao, 1983. Umemoto, 1988. Sato, 1986. Akaha, 1987, pp.4-12, 1990 and 1991. Rix, 1987. L'Estrange, 1990, pp.16-17. Satoh, 1982, p.6. Maswood, 1990, pp.38-39]. The term "comprehensive security" implied that Japan should be concerned about more than the military dimension of security, in terms of both ends and means [Eto and Yamamoto, 1991, pp.72-73]. In contrast to the 1960s and 1970s politics and economics were no longer as "separate" (thus denying the possibility of better relations with the Soviet Union); and Japan was moving into the Western camp rather than following an "omnidirectional" foreign policy.

At the same time the concept of comprehensive security was also useful for those who wanted a rationale to keep defense spending under control, a useful shield, that is, against growing American pressure for increased military spending [Interviews Nos. 2 and 9, Tokyo, June 11 and 13, 1991]. It was, in a way, a concept congenial to politicians who were wary to confront issues of defense viewed with suspicion or hostility by Japanese voters [Interview No. 9, Tokyo, June 13, 1991]. It remains today the guiding idea with which Japan is, for example, trying to further its security arrangements with the United States, seeking to engage Russia in East Asia, and hoping to strengthen its relations with its Asian neighbors as well as the Third World more generally [Interview No. 13, Tokyo, June, 14, 1991. Defense Agency 1990, p. 81]. In short, the doctrine of comprehensive security has become the mechanism by which Japan has partly redefined its posture in the international system in the 1980s. "All Japanese policies with international dimensions—particularly defense, resources, energy, food security, and foreign aid—are placed in a security context. Comprehensive security provides a politically acceptable framework for maintaining a strong emphasis on self-defense capabilities by making security a national concern and not simply a military one" [L'Estrange, 1990, p.17].

The concept of "comprehensive security" conveys a deeper truth about Japan's security policy. National security is embedded deeply in political and economic considerations. "The Japanese notion of 'comprehensive security', with its explicitly economic component and with its postwar de-emphasis on the military component, is the reciprocal of U.S. emphases on military strength and defense technology. It is only a slight exaggeration to say that the Japanese will accept higher factor costs for essentially the same reason that the United States will overpay for its defense systems. It makes each feel more secure . . . The Japanese seem to believe (perhaps correctly) that if consumers are willing or can be convinced to defer consumption or to subsidize production, Japanese industry will contribute over the long run to a more secure, less dependent, and more technologically sophisticated economy that serves the interests of producers and consumers alike" [Samuels, 1989, pp.628,646]. Comprehensive security thus revolves around the social stability and national autonomy that derives from a productive and technologically dynamic national economy. Such an economy is seeking to establish itself firmly in global markets, backed by a diplomacy aimed at strengthening close political relations with the United States. Tsuneo Akaha thus argues that "behind the development of Japan's 'comprehensive security policy' since the late 1970s have been the following favorable factors: (1) the 'greenhouse effect' until the 1970s of the U.S. hegemonic role in East Asia in general and the U.S. security protection for Japan in particular, which had freed Japan from the burden of political commitments and military security responsibilities overseas; (2) the postwar institutionalization of political and legal constraints on defense buildup, including popular opposition to remilitarization; (3) the perennial, deep sense of economic vulnerability in Japan; (4) the widely shared confidence in Tokyo's 'economics first' policy which has brought visible benefits to the nation, including a growing surplus of financial resources . . . Current trends in the East Asian security situation tend to favor further development of the economic dimensions of Japanese comprehensive security policy" [Akaha, 1990, pp.11-12,31].

The consequence of a policy of "comprehensive security" for Japan was spelled out in the 1984 report of the Peace Problem Research Council which Prime Minister Nakasone had appointed. It concluded that Japan's growing international stature required a more active role in international affairs which should fall short of the resumption of a high military profile. "Military power and international stature with far-flung external political commitments lack obvious value in and of themselves. They have merit only as they contribute to governability, the U.S. relationship and economic success. Accordingly, a leading Japanese international affairs analyst can calmly describe the Self-Defense Forces as 'a piece of furniture that any modern house or nation has, a chair for the American visitor to sit on . . . A Japanese defense expert, leaning forward with an air of intense frustration, declared, 'You must understand that we aren't serious about defense'" [Bobrow, 1984, p.37].

Comprehensive security is a symbol that refers not only to the different dimensions of national security but appeals also to a mode of participation in the process of policy formulation. The Japanese word "comprehensive" (sogo), describes a synthetic approach to practical activity. "The idea . . . is to call together everyone who is related to or interested in the project in question and let them participate in it as equally as possible . . . without paying much attention to providing . . . any formal organ for coordination" [Kumon, 1982, p.10. Interview, No. 6, Tokyo, June 12, 1991].

In following commercial rather than territorial objectives and relying on peaceful rather than military means, Japanese policy makers have, perhaps unintentionally, created new national options, as is becoming evident in the area of technology. And this success is drawing Japan inexorably into a world that is making increasing demands on its growing resources and capabilities. Should the American security commitment be withdrawn, a stable international environment, national unity and a prosperous economy would become even more important for Japan to adapt itself to radically new circumstances. In the words of Yukio Satoh, "although the Government has not elaborated fully the concept of 'comprehensive security' in the form of a concrete policy, it stresses the need to perceive Japanese security from a broader perspective than the military. Yet how the concept will be translated into policy remains to be seen" [Satoh, 1982, p.7].

B. Deeply Contested Norms of Military Security

1. Social Norms.

Public attitudes reflect the depth of social learning which came with the disastrous loss of World War II and the American occupation. Many, although by no means all, studies of Japanese foreign policy credit public opinion with a substantial impact on security policy. In the 1950s and 1960s this impact resulted from the combined weight of: the opposition parties in the Diet whose adamant opposition to a return to Japan's militarist past enjoyed broad popular support; the vehement criticism which most of the mass media reserved for any attempt to enhance the status of the military and to develop a more active defense policy; and the possibility of popular demonstrations in the streets. The conservatives who held power in the 1950s, in particular Prime Minister Kishi, chose to advance their political agenda by seeking to contest the pacifist social norms that the Constitution embodied by advocating constitutional reform and, in a broader sense, a partial return to the substance of prewar politics [Otake, 1990]. In the 1970s and 1980s, however, the fronts have been reversed. Increasingly the government has sought to both exploit and mold the gradual change in a public opinion that has come to accept grudgingly the existence of the SDF and the necessity of a modest national defense effort. Without relinquishing its efforts, particularly in the media, to counter the government's policy, the opposition has relied, among other instruments, on a strategy of litigation so as to contest the normative context in which Japan's national security policy is formulated. It did so even when legal redress did not promise a reversal in policy. Litigation itself was a powerful political signal to the public that government policy lacked full legitimacy and thus should not and could not be pursued vigorously.

The anti-militarist climate of opinion was generated by the disastrous outcome of World War II and reinforced by the policies of the American occupation [Emmerson and Humphreys, 1973, pp.93-106. Okimoto, 1978a, pp.63-91]. Nationalistic school teachers were fired. Eliminated from school textbooks were any favorable references to military heroes or victories of the past [Mendel, 1975, pp.154-55]. The teachers union, Nikkyoso, became one of the strongest pacifist forces of the Japanese Left. The Japan Socialist Party (JSP) as well as major newspapers and journals became strong supporters of the new anti-militarist spirit and defended vigorously the postwar Constitution. A concerted effort of the political forces on the Left blocked a revision of the Constitution which conservatives had placed high on the political agenda in the late 1950s. Subsequently, conservative Prime Ministers have persistently sidestepped this volatile issue. Prime Minister Tanaka, for example, argued in the Diet in September 1973 that he had "no intention to revise the Constitution because constitutional revision should be tackled by the government in accordance with public opinion. The present constitution has been firmly established among the people" [Mendel, 1975, p.156]. In the same year the former Director of the Defense Agency and subsequent Prime Minister, Yasuhiro Nakasone, an acknowledged "hawk" by Japanese standards, argued in an interview that "Japan's defense power must have limits and must be operated by the people's intentions" [Mendel, 1975, p.161]. Such rhetoric expresses Japanese common sense, that is, a fundamental social consensus on the fact that the government must take account of strongly held views by the opposition and the general public at large concerning the substance and modality of Japan's security policy.

The preoccupation of the political elite with public opinion has resulted in literally dozens of public opinion polls. The results of these polls have been unambiguous over the years. In a recent article David Bobrow has taken stock of a voluminous literature on Japanese public opinion on international affairs [Bobrow, 1989]. His conclusions are in broad agreement with established findings and assumptions about the views of the Japanese public on security policy. Public attitudes favor a passive over an active stance, alignment with the United States over a policy of equidistance between the United States and the Soviet Union, political dependence over autonomy, and minimal over extensive military spending. Furthermore, generational effects have been relatively small in the last two decades. The overwhelming majority of the Japanese is skeptical about any dramatic departure from the status quo throughout the 1980s [Risse-Kappen, 1991, p.495]. The public favors economic strength, peaceful diplomacy, and a low-key consensus approach; it does not feel seriously threatened by the Soviet Union or Russia; it does not think very highly of the Self-Defense Forces; and it overwhelmingly supports Article 9 of the Constitution. The military is viewed as marginal, and the public shows a marked lack of willingness to resort to armed defense even if Japan should be attacked. "Fewer than one in five respondents would resort to force to resist invasion" [Bobrow, 1989, p.597]. The evidence available suggests that to date the end of the Cold War has not led to great changes in this profile.

The mass public has opposed strongly all attempts to resurrect any of the trappings of militarism [Mendel, 1954, 1959, 1961, 1966, 1967, 1969, 1970, 1971-72, 1975. Watanuki, 1973, 1974. Watanabe, 1977b. Whiting, 1982, pp.1137-41. Getreuer, 1986. Defense Agency, 1990, pp.320-21. Halloran, 1991, pp.12-17. Hatsuse, 1986. Marshall, 1981. Emmerson, 1973]. The importance of public opinion in the shaping of Japan's security policy is unquestioned by Japan's political elite. "Japanese cabinet members have . . . insisted that they must operate within the framework of a domestic consensus, even more than within the limits of the vague Article 9 of the postwar Constitution" [Mendel, 1975, p.150. Satoh, 1982, pp.31-37]. But public opinion does not dictate Japan's security policy. Instead it provides a permissive context in which policy is enacted. "There is a wide discrepancy between Japanese public opinion, as expressed in opinion polls, and the views of the Japanese government, as expressed in Defence White Papers and other government statements" [McIntosh, 1986, p.71]. This helps to explain the substantial changes in Japan's defense policy that have occurred since 1978. Public opinion sets limits that are fairly broad and unspecified and until the 1970s left substantial room for different factions of the LDP to pursue different policies by fighting internal battles and to mobilize public opinion in a struggle for power in the party. Such conflicts were very much in evidence when the Security Treaty was renewed in 1960, and when the Japanese government negotiated with the United States the return of Okinawa in 1969. In the 1980s such conflicts have been less visible.

While Japanese public opinion has accommodated itself to a gradual build-up of national defense, there exists one aspect of public opinion and social norms that is of increasing political relevance as a brake: foreign opinion. Although political elites in neighboring states in both Northeast and Southeast Asia sometimes look at Japan with admiration, suspicion and criticism flare up at regular intervals. The extension of Japan's naval defense perimeter to 1,000 miles in the early 1980s elicited only muted criticism. By contrast Japan's textbook controversy in July 1982, which centered on a relabelling of Japanese "aggression" as Japanese "advance", led to an outcry because it showed Japan to be unrepentant about the evil that it had caused in the 1940s [Interview Nos. 10 and 14, Tokyo, December 12 and 13, 1991. Hook, 1990, pp.25-34]. The strong, adverse reaction of Japan's Asian neighbors to anything that smacks of a revival of

Japanese militarism is an important restraint on Japan's security policy as several episodes in the 1980s illustrate: the protest over the Prime Minister's official visit to the Yasukuni Shrine (September/October 1985), the dismissal of Education Minister Masayuki Fujio after his controversial remarks about Japan's annexation of Korea in 1910 (September 1986), the concern about the decision of the Nakasone government to remove the 1 percent ceiling (January 1987), the protest by the Chinese government over the court decision on the ownership issue of a student dormitory in Kyoto claimed by Taiwan (February/May 1987), the resignation of Vice Minister Kensuke Yanagiya after his undiplomatic remarks about Deng Xiaoping (June 1987), and the dismissal of Minister Seiryo Okuno after his outspoken comments about prewar Japanese policy towards China (May 1988) [Watanabe, A., 1991, pp.10-11]. While mass publics in many Asian countries express a growing level of trust, as shown by opinion surveys, they, too, favor Japan's continued adherence to playing an economic role [Simon, 1986, pp.48-49].

The evolution in the social norms affecting Japan's military security policy is not simply a spontaneous social process. Public opinion has been the target of deliberate policies, by both the SDF and the civilian government. Public officials have tried to stem the powerful influence that the media in particular have had on maintaining or reinforcing public skepticism about all issues dealing with Japan's military security. The SDF have worked very hard trying to win public acceptance. In the early years SDF recruits were occasionally "pelted with stones in the streets, and when they attended movie theaters, people rose from their seats and walked away . . . Graduates of the Defense Academy were refused admission to graduate schools in Japanese universities" [Emmerson, 1971, pp.116-17]. Gradually the SDF developed policies to improve relations, especially with the local communities. "Few details were overlooked . . . All the paraphernalia of public relations were employed" [Emmerson, 1971, p.117]. Disaster relief in particular provided a natural way for winning public confidence. "In the minds of many Japanese, the SDF became not a force created to defend the country but an organization devoted to relief and welfare" [Emmerson, 1971, p.117].

The SDF is evidently a military force "with a high degree of concern for the private or civilian sector" [Endicott, 1982a, p.460]. Without a strong link to the prewar military and untested in its role as a defense force of a democratic Japan, its public image has been a major concern for the SDF. "The Defense Agency and the Self Defense Forces must spend much time and energy in trying to build a favorable public image. Public relations was a principal objective of the 1970 defense white paper" [Emmerson and Humphreys, 1973, p.13]. The resumption of a regular publication of the

White Paper in 1976 illustrates the point [Weinstein, 1983, pp.180-83. Nish, 1980, p.421]. "Defense Agency Director General Michita Sakata wanted to gain public approval and greater legitimacy for the Self Defense Forces" [Weinstein, 1983, p.180]. In effect Sakata wanted to trade a White Paper free of all hawkishness for approval by the public and the opposition parties [Weinstein, 1983, p. 181].

The image that the three branches of the SDF have sought to cultivate is that of a helping hand of the people. The 1964 Tokyo Olympics, for example, offered the GSDF an opportunity of helping to organize the Games in highly visible administrative positions; the recruitment record of the GSDF in the following year was notably better [Brendle, 1975, p.89. Olsen, 1985, p.93]. The SDF seek to project a positive public image especially during natural disasters [Humphreys, 1975, p.39]. In public opinion polls about 10 per cent of the respondents in a 1972 survey expressed the opinion that the SDF should primarily concern itself with public relief, while throughout the 1960s and 1970s about three quarters indicated that emergency relief was in fact the major function of the SDF, with an increasing share of the public, however, also recognizing the defense functions of the SDF in the 1970s [Mendel, 1975, p.163. Marshall, 1981, Charts 7,8]. In the image that the SDF is trying to project among the public, the fight against nature has replaced in many ways the fight against other states. In fact "the greatest degree of public relations success has been achieved through 'selling' the SDF to the public as a disaster relief agency" [Brendle, 1975, p.70]. "Japan's military men and women have in fact been busy clearing up typhoons, giving lessons to schoolchildren in kendo and judo, building snow statues for the Sapporo Festival and generally winning the hearts and minds of the Japanese people, to the point where a majority of Japanese now accept their existence and one occasionally sees uniforms—a rare sight even a decade ago [Sayle, 1983, p.23].

In the late 1970s, according to one public opinion poll, less than 40 percent of the respondents thought that in the future the primary mission of the SDF would be related to national security. "Items such as disaster relief, public welfare, and internal security were viewed collectively as more important tasks for the military to pursue" [Endicott, 1982a, p.450]. Consequently all three branches of the SDF have sophisticated disaster relief organizations which can be mobilized quickly and efficiently on a national scale, but until 1992 not for international relief action. Between 1951 and 1980 the SDF carried out 14,000 relief missions, mobilizing nearly four million personnel [Buck, 1986, p.79]. A recent, prominent instance was the use of the GSDF in August 1985, after an intense intrabureaucratic squabble had wasted precious hours, in searching for survivors of JAL flight 123 which had crashed in a mountainous area of central Japan [McIntosh, 1985, p.36]. The SDF "try to present an image of ready, friendly participation in local community activity offering their facilities for parades and festivals and their men and equipment for certain public works" [Humphreys, 1975, p.39]. In part because of the success of these public relations campaigns "the SDF now have the . . . support of the population" [Vogel, 1989, p.70].

Public opinion toward the SDF reflects these efforts of the SDF. It "presents a picture of public acceptance circumscribed by apathy or distaste" [Brendle, 1975, p.71]. Surveys taken in the 1950s indicate the low prestige and the perceived irrelevance of the SDF to the functioning of contemporary Japan [Mendel, 1954, 1961, 1975. Ishida, 1967. Smith and Ramsey, 1962]. Over time hostility changed to skepticism toward the SDF [Japan Echo, 1981, p.40. Seymour, 1974-75, p.433]. The proportion of the Japanese public which supports a minimal defense posture has increased considerably, in line with the government's reinterpretation of the meaning of Article 9. In the mid-1950s only half of the Japanese public supported such a posture, two decades later that proportion had risen to 80 percent [Mendel, 1975, p.161. Eto, 1983. Nishihara, 1985a, p.135. Endicott, 1982a, pp.447-48. Yamamura, 1989, pp.220-28. Watanuki, 1973, 1974. Marshall, 1981. Getreuer, 1986. Berger, 1992, pp.364-67, 503-08]. But despite these shifts, in 1987 the public ranked questions of national security at the very bottom of its list of priorities, in contrast to questions of law and order which it ranked at the very top [Inoguchi, 1991a, pp.158-60].

Public opinion has also been the target of government policy. The change in norms thus was not only a response to changes in world politics as filtered by Japanese public opinion. Instead the evolution of the normative consensus informing Japan's defense policy was also the result of deliberate efforts by men like Prime Minister Sato (1964-72) and Director-Generals of the JDA such as Yasuhiro Nakasone (1970-71), Michita Sakata (1974-76) and Shin Kanemaru (1977-78). Theirs has been no secret plot for the revival of Japanese militarism but a deliberate attempt of shaping an evolving domestic consensus through incremental changes along the military dimensions of Japan's national security policy.

Prime Minister Nakasone more clearly than any other Prime Minister before or after attempted to use his office in the 1980s to reshape the public climate for Japan's security policy by seeking to influence the normative conceptions of the state held by party officials, bureaucratic leaders and the mass public [Pyle, 1988a, 1988b]. Nakasone's fundamental objection was to break with Japan's role as a subordinate state in the international system and to build a greater sense of self-confidence around the concept of a Japan that was acting as an equal in its relations with the United States as well as other states. He aspired to a presidential style of leadership and showed a much higher profile in foreign affairs than had his predecessors. He used a large number of advisory commissions, staffed by people close to his political vision, which generated policy recommendations that sometimes ran counter to those prevailing in the bureaucracy and the LDP [Pyle, 1988a, p.83. Tamamoto, 1990, pp.498-99].

On the eve of assuming his post Nakasone said, "the first necessity is change in our thinking. Having caught up, we must now expect others to try to catch up with us. We must seek a new path for ourselves and open it up ourselves" [Pyle, 1988a, p.84]. Specifically, Japan was to find a new national consciousness corresponding to its role as a leader in the international system in economic, technological and scientific affairs. The deregulation of the domestic economy and the internationalization of Japanese public and private institutions were for Nakasone essential contemporary aspects of this project of redefining the role of the Japanese state.

However, Nakasone's efforts to instill a new national consciousness extended also to traditional issues like the religious foundations of the Japanese state. This was one reason why he paid so much attention to the Yasukuni Shrine, home of the souls of two and a half million soldiers as well as those convicted as war criminals. Takeo Miki had been the first postwar Prime Minister to visit the Shrine. But he made the visit, in 1975, as a private citizen. Accompanied by his cabinet and 172 LDP Diet members Nakasone was the first postwar Japanese Prime Minister to visit the Shrine in his official capacity. The outrage in China, Korea and other Asian states was so great that Nakasone did not attend in 1986 and left the decision to attend up to each member of his cabinet [Muramatsu, 1987, p.316].

The official Prime Ministerial visit to the Yasukuni Shrine in 1985 was controversial because it represented a serious political attempt to contest an important norm under which the SDF continues to operate. For the SDF remains a purely secular organization and, in contrast to the Imperial Army and Navy, is prohibited from having any relations with Shinto religion [Hardacre, 1989, pp.133-59]. Like the secret enshrinement in October 1978 of fourteen convicted war criminals on the symbolically important 33rd anniversary of their deaths, it was the cause of a bitter public controversy [Olsen, 1985, p.87]. Prime Minister Nakasone declared in 1985 that the visit of government officials to the Shrine had no religious character but was a social act of courtesy to the families of the dead. As long as these visits did not adhere strictly to Shinto rituals they were not deemed unconstitutional. However, in a widely noted decision Judge Tadao Kasuya, presiding over the Sendai High Court in January 1991, drew a firm line when he ruled that official visits of cabinet ministers and the Emperor to religious shrines were in violation of the Constitution's stipulation that state officials refrain from religious education and all other religious activities. The ruling emphasized explicitly that the visit of the Emperor would be unconstitutional. "Such a visit would have an enormous impact—an impact incomparably greater than that from similar conduct by the prime minister—on the society" [Japan Times, 1991]. Since the government won the lawsuit on the narrow issue of not having to return to the taxpayers the small amount of money donated to the shrine after the visit, it could not appeal the verdict. The fact that judge Kasuya retired from the bench a few days after this ruling was interpreted by many as a clear sign that this act of judicial activism fell outside of the bounds of Japan's normal judicial politics.

For Nakasone and his followers "the real underlying issue in Japan's defense debate is security versus security plus honor" [Kataoka, 1980, p.6]. Reflecting on Nakasone's style of governance and his efforts to create a distinctive ideology of the Japanese state, Michio Muramatsu argues that "comprehensive policies . . . usually suggest a combination of individual policies that are, to some extent, interconnected . . . Prime Minister Nakasone was the first to initiate a wide national debate, assembling over 100 intellectuals in nine advisory councils, to formulate 'comprehensive policies'. He thus sidestepped the bureaucracy and relied instead on deliberative councils and advisory commissions whom he could control to push, among others, his policies for a more active security policy . . . There is something in Nakasone's behavior in promoting these comprehensive policies that satisfies Japanese nationalism . . . In my opinion, the several 'comprehensive policies' express the first stage of Nakasone's search for an 'identity of the state'" [Muramatsu, 1987, pp.309,312,319]. Takashi Inoguchi's analysis takes a similar aim. "The Japanese nation, like a weathercock, must have a fixed part, according to Nakasone. That is nothing other than national identity" [Inoguchi, 1991a, p.74].

Most controversially at home, Nakasone wanted to break the military taboo embodied in Article 9 of the Peace Constitution. As a young member of the Diet, at the age of thirty-two, he had sent a 7,000 word petition to General MacArthur in which he asked for constitutional revision and an independent military. "MacArthur is said to have looked briefly at this petition, crumpled it up and thrown it in the wastebasket" [Pyle, 1988a, p.82]. Upon taking office Nakasone pushed for a series of controversial policy initiatives, such as the 1983 transfer of military technology agreement with the United States and the break in the 1 percent rule of the defense budget as a consequence of Japan's defense build-up. And he made a number of startling pronouncements, for example his description of Japan as an "unsinkable aircraft carrier" thwarting the backfire bombers of the Soviet Union. Nakasone's conception of a new role for Japan thus sought to establish a new national consensus on defense.

Yet for all his political boldness, Prime Minister Nakasone was severely restrained in articulating the new norms he favored. In his pronouncements Nakasone normally relied on the established political discourse of "Peace Constitution", "posing no threat to other countries", "the three nonnuclear principles", "exclusively defensive defense", and "never becoming a great military power." As Atsushi Odawara has pointed out "these all express the brakes on military expansion. Nakasone is known both abroad and at home as a prime minister who has been enthusiastic about expanding defensive capabilities. Yet when speaking in public, even he cannot but do so within the framework of the Peace Constitution" [Odawara, 1985, p.249]. Even so Nakasone's political initiatives on defense issues were punished by the electorate. The LDP suffered one of its worst electoral setbacks since 1955 in December 1983. Most informed observers attributed that outcome to Nakasone's "hawkishness." "In effect Nakasone had to choose between his hawkishness and the prime ministership. He chose to remain as prime minister, and his public position on defense became . . . low-key and inoffensive to the Japanese voters" [Weinstein, 1988, p.24]. In the July 1986 elections the LDP more than recouped its losses and won one of its greatest victories since 1955.

It is inherently difficult to determine whether public opinion led to a change in policy or whether a shift in policy occasioned a change in public attitudes. Stephen Vogel, for one, makes a strong case for the decisive influence of government policy in leading public opinion. "The Japanese government did not, after all, suddenly announce a new policy, but introduced relatively small changes incrementally. The government coupled movements toward a more assertive defense posture with publicly announced limits on defense, and consistently made an effort to justify changes to the public . . . It is no accident that Defense White Papers and statements by top political leaders have consistently stressed the 'understanding of the people'. LDP leaders have tried to create this 'understanding', and all in all, they have been quite successful" [Vogel, 1989, p.83].

Deliberate political attempts which have sought to shape the public climate as well as the fading of historical memories and the waxing and waning of international tensions have left their mark on Japan's gradually evolving defense consensus. It is very hard to discern when precisely the "Yoshida consensus" on Japan's national security policy was modified by the greater emphasis on defense that has marked Japan's security policy in recent years. Prime Minister Nakasone's first visit with President Reagan in 1983 was important because it shifted the terms of public debate. A few years earlier Prime Minister Ohira's invocation of Japan as an unsinkable aircraft carrier was used to defend his preferred policy of restraining expansion in the defense budget. Nakasone's widely reported use of the same term was describing his commitment to the defense build-up of the 1980s. Proponents of unarmed neutrality and autonomous defense had always defined the two ends of a spectrum; but the consensus on defense policy was altered because "the weight of the conservative mainstream has shifted" [Vogel, 1989, p.66].

This shift toward a new conservative consensus weakened the traditional elements inside the LDP and the bureaucracy who favored strict limits on defense. The majority of the LDP in the 1980s supported a gradual expansion of Japan's defense. According to one poll published by Nihon Keizai Shimbun, by 1980 almost four-fifths of the LDP Lower House Diet members backed an expansion in the role of the Self Defense Forces with only a handful opposed [Vogel, 1989, p.67]. Forty-six percent opposed arms exports; 37 percent favored a revision of the Constitution.

Among the opposition parties the Japan Communist Party (JCP) has resisted totally the postwar security policy. But the JSP, especially in the 1980s, has gradually moved away from a policy of unarmed neutrality. Over time the polarization in Japanese politics around the issue of military security thus has become less evident. Before 1983 the JSP's official position had viewed the government's defense policy as a blatant violation of the Constitution. But in 1983, the then chairman of the JSP, Masashi Ishibashi, shocked a large number of the party's supporters when he suggested that although the SDF were unconstitutional, they were created legally, that is, by majority vote in the Diet. This idea had originally been propounded by Naoki Kobayashi, a scholar of constitutional law. Ishibashi's move had the purpose of laying the groundwork for a future coalition government with the Komeito and the DSP. The impact of this political move derived at least in part from an expression (goho) which, on the face of it, seemed to imply that the SDF enjoyed a substantive legality in the eyes of the JSP [Asahi Shimbun, January 13 and 31, February 28, 1984, 14th ed. Vogel, 1989, p.85]. According to JSP Diet member Kenji Kawamata the JSP has "to accept the shift in public opinion and recognize the SDF. Otherwise we may still be the party of the constitution, but we will never be the party of the people" [Vogel, 1989, p.85]. Nevertheless the JSP still continues to regard itself as the true keeper of Japan's Peace Constitution and thus Japan's pacifistic and democratic character. In the early 1990s the party mobilized its supporters against the overseas deployment of the SDF. Similarly after an extensive intraparty debate the Komeito, or Clean Government Party, officially recognized the SDF and, to a lesser extent, the U.S.-Japan Mutual Security Treaty for the first time in the early 1980s, a change in policy that was ratified by a party congress in 1981.

But there are real limits to the political flexibility of the opposition parties. The Komeito's basic position is, for example, that the SDF should be strictly limited to the defense of Japan's territory, airspace and waters. Female supporters in particular have constrained the room of maneuver of the Komeito leadership as it has tried to strike a bargain with the LDP leadership on the issue of the SDF's participation in international peacekeeping operations. Such restraints are weaker in the more "hawkish" Democratic Socialist Party (DSP). It first recognized the SDF in 1975, was not committed to the one-percent-ceiling of the defense budget, views the Soviet Union and Russia as a threat to Japanese security interests in East Asia, and favors a tough espionage law [Vogel, 1989, pp.84-86]. But it emphasizes the need for civilian control over the SDF, as illustrated by its recent insistence on giving the Diet an authority to approve the deployment of the SDF on U.N. peacekeeping operations. With the end of the Cold War the debate is shifting away from the traditional issue of the legitimacy of Japanese rearmament toward a concern over the role of the SDF in relation to Japan's growing international responsibilities in areas such as regional security, international peace keeping and disaster relief [Interview Nos. 19, 20, 21, Tokyo, June 18 and 19, 1991]. In sum, in both shaping policy and being shaped by it Japan's social norms have gradually evolved over time while continuing to reflect the lessons learned from the 1930s and 1940s.

2. Legal Norms.

The social norms that are expressed in Japan's changing public opinion interact with the legal norms that help define Japan's military security policy. Japan's "linkage between internal constitutionalism and foreign policy is admittedly unique among the world's democracies" [Beer, 1989, p.69]. And it is equally unique that the opposition to Japan's rearmament has challenged frequently since 1955 the constitutionality of Japan's armed forces in the courts [Sato, 1979. Kasuya, 1985. Kobayashi, 1991. Ito, 1991. Nishi, 1987. Beer, 1984, pp.11-13. Okazaki, 1986, pp.76-80]. The courts have given indirect support to the government's defense policy. But what matters politically is not only the result of litigation but the fact that legal disputes remain unresolved. This signals to all that the normative basis of Japan's security policy remains contested.

Japan's Constitution renounces war as an instrument of national security policy. The core of this distinctive aspect of Japan's policy is the famous Article 9 of the Constitution which has imposed severe restraints on the conduct of Japan's security policy. "Article IX is to the Japanese Constitution what the right to life, liberty, and the pursuit of happiness is to the American constitution: more than mere written words on a piece of document, it has become the very essence of the Japanese regime or polity" [Kataoka, 1980, p.5]. As Chalmers Johnson notes, "Most Japanese equate Article 9 of the Constitution with democracy itself; to alter one is to alter the other" [Johnson, 1992, p.24]. Attempts to revise the Constitution in line with an evolving government policy failed. With the hope of rewording Article 9, Prime Minister Kishi had set up in 1957 the Investigation Committee for the Constitution. But a commission report finally issued in 1967 failed to settle the controversial issue of constitutional revision [McIntosh, 1986, pp.29-30]. Over the years support for a possible revision of the constitution to legalize full-scale rearmament has gradually decreased. Since the early 1960s the opponents of constitutional revision have outnumbered supporters by a margin varying between two- and three-to-one [Asahi Shimbun Yoron Chosa-shitsu, 1988, p.175. Japan Echo, 1981, pp.40-41. Ishida, 1967, pp.32-35. Emmerson and Humphreys, 1973, pp.10-11. Okazaki, 1982b, p.468. McIntosh, 1986, p.30. Bobrow, 1989, pp.598-99]

Japan's postwar Constitution was based on a draft that had been prepared in the Government Section of the Supreme Commander for the Allied Powers (SCAP). This section had based much of its work on the report of the State-War-Navy Coordinating Committee SWNCC-228, "Reform of the Japanese Governmental System" which was adopted in January 1946 [McNelly, 1962, 1987, and 1975, p.99. Berger, 1992, pp.69-76. Ro, 1976]. But the famous clause that prohibited war and arms was inserted by General MacArthur himself. Its wording resembles closely that of the Kellog-Briand Pact of 1928, A General Treaty for the Renunciation of War. Article 9 reads:

Aspiring sincerely to an international peace based on justice and order, the Japanese people forever renounce war as a sovereign right of the nation and the threat or use of force as means of settling international disputes.

In order to accomplish the aim of the preceding paragraph, land, sea and air forces, as well as other war potential, will never be maintained. The right of belligerency of the state will not be recognized.

The political opposition has given a strict reading to Article 9 and has used the courts to challenge the gradual evolution in the government's security policy. The Supreme Court was thus drawn into a political battle between Right and Left that went beyond the constitutionality of the SDF. In the eyes of the opposition at stake was not only the principle of judicial review, but the power and willingness of the Supreme Court to preserve key provisions of the Constitution against the reactionary impulses of a government which in the 1950s had seriously contemplated a wholesale revision of the Constitution. Over the years critics have filed a number of legal cases that have sought to challenge the constitutionality of the government's defense policy (See Table A-1 in the Appendix) [Henderson, 1968. Itoh and Beer, 1978. Maki, 1964. Satoh, 1982. Kasuya, 1985. Seymour, 1974-75. Wada, 1976. McNelly, 1975, 1982. Sato, 1979].

The first challenge to the government's shift in policy occurred soon after the end of the Allied Occupation. Arguing that it contravened Article 9 of the Constitution, the Secretary General of the Left JSP petitioned the Court to declare the National Police Reserve unconstitutional [McNelly, 1975, pp.102-08. Maki, 1964, pp.362-65]. The Court ruled unanimously that judgments in Japanese court cases could be rendered only when concrete legal disputes exist between specific parties. In contrast to Germany, for example, the Court has no power to determine in abstract the constitutionality of particular laws or executive orders. For this reason the government has always taken every precaution not to give rise to any concrete legal disputes that might be challenged in the courts. For example, condemnation of private lands for use by the SDF has been studiously avoided for fear that landowners might bring the issue to the courts. Instead the SDF have taken over military bases that were gradually relinquished by the American military [McNelly, 1975, p.103]. At other times the government has refrained from appealing court decisions involving the SDF, such as the Eniwa case decided by the Sapporo District Court against the government in 1967. For that ruling was based on very narrow grounds that left unaddressed the controversial question of the constitutionality of the SDF [McNelly, 1975, p.105].

The second challenge to the constitutionality of the SDF was brought before the Supreme Court in 1959 [Maki, 1964, pp.298-361. Itoh and Beer, 1978, pp.103-30]. Protestors demonstrating against the enlargement of the base were arrested after illegally entering an American base near Sunakawa. They argued in court that the law they had allegedly violated was unconstitutional. For it implemented the 1951 U.S.-Japan Security Treaty which permitted the stationing of American troops in Japan and, according to the brief of the defense lawyers, thus contravened Article 9. With supporters of the government and the opposition fully mobilized around the issue of the renewal of the U.S.-Japan Security Treaty in 1960, a Tokyo District Court found in favor of the defendants when it ruled that the statute in question was in violation of Article 9 and thus unconstitutional. The government appealed the decision to the Supreme Court. In its decision the Court argued that since the Constitution did not abolish Japan's right to self-defense, it did not prohibit the Japanese government from asking other states for security guarantees. Without ruling on the constitutionality of the SDF directly, the Court concluded that the Constitution did not forbid the stationing of foreign troops in Japan, and that the Security Treaty thus was not obviously unconstitutional [Ishimoto and Hirobe, 1987, pp.121-22]. However, "in the Sunakawa case, the Supreme Court pointed out explicitly that it was not ruling on the constitutionality of the existence of indigenous military forces intended for the self-defense of the nation" [McNelly, 1975, p.105]. Thus the Self-Defense Forces have remained in a constitutional limbo. But the restraint the Supreme Court exercised and its receptivity to the political question principle were undoubtedly a source of comfort to the advocates of the SDF.

While there were two additional court rulings in the 1960s (the Eniwa and Sakane cases outlined in Table A-1), the Naganuma case represented the third major challenge to the constitutionality of the SDF under Article 9 of the Constitution [Seymour, 1974-75. Wada, 1976. McNelly, 1975, pp.106-07]. At issue was the elimination of part of a public forest for the construction of a surface-to-air missile base of the Air Self-Defense Force. In September 1973 the Sapporo District Court found that the laws creating the SDF and the JDA were clearly unconstitutional. Judge Fukushima was very explicit in avoiding the legal pretexts that might have been used to sidestep the issue of the constitutionality of this politically controversial ruling. Instead he argued vigorously for a broad interpretation of the Court's power of judicial review. The ruling challenged the cabinet's interpretation and General MacArthur's own second thoughts, included in the 1951 Japanese Peace Treaty, according to which Article 9 did not commit Japan to "never" maintain any self-defense capability [Mendel, 1975, p.154].

This broad political interpretation of the role of the judiciary in determining the constitutionality of crucial instruments of state power occasioned intense political conflict within the judiciary as well as between the government and the judicial branch. Judge Fukushima was a member of the Young Jurists League (Seihokyo), the center of progressive younger judges who were opposed to the conservative political establishment in Japan. In August 1969 the head of the Sapporo District Court, Judge Kenta Hiraga, had urged Judge Fukushima in writing to exercise restraint in the Naganuma case. Fukushima took strong exception to this attempt at exerting influence and brought the issue to the attention of the judicial conference of the District Court. Judge Hiraga was criticized in a report that the District Court filed with the Supreme Court. The issue was leaked to the press. Eventually the Supreme Court reprimanded both judges and transferred Hiraga to the Tokyo District Court. Attempts to have Judge Fukushima disqualified at one point included deliberations in the Diet's impeachment committee. The indignant resignation of the judge was submitted in protest and subsequently withdrawn [Itoh, 1989, pp.265-69. McNelly, 1975, p.108]. The issue of the constitutionality of the SDF was thus part and parcel of a broader "judicial crisis" in the early 1970s [McNelly, 1975, pp.108-09].

The government appealed Judge Fukushima's decision and in August 1976 the Sapporo High Court reversed the ruling of the District Court. But it again refused to rule on the constitutionality of the SDF which it judged to be a political matter ultimately subject to a decision by the Diet rather than the Court [Okazaki, 1982b, p.470. Sato, 1979, p.17]. One significant aspect of this important case is emphasized by John Haley. Having won in the district court in 1973, "the plaintiffs refused to accept the government's offer to make a special appeal to the Supreme Court, which would have by-passed the high court and prevented further delay in a final determination of the issue. This refusal to allow the special appeal was based on tacit recognition by the plaintiffs and their attorneys that they had no hope of winning on appeal. They knew they would lose but still persisted. Why? The Naganuma case and other lawsuits over the Self-Defense Forces that continue to be brought can be viewed best, I believe, as a form of political action. So long as the issue continues to be litigated in well-publicized cases, a political consensus against the Self-Defense Forces may be forged or at least one favoring their legitimacy remains in doubt" [Haley, 1988, pp.4-5].

The prolonged process of litigation that the opposition has waged in order to keep a firm policy consensus around Japan's enlarged defense role from emerging has thus given the government its share of victories. Some legal cases, such as the Mito District Court ruling in the Hyakuri case of February 1977, have strengthened the position of the SDF. These decisions indicate in essence that Article 9 forbids only armed forces which have the capacity for making war. At what point the strength of the SDF would exceed the capacity for self-defense "is a matter for political decision" [Sato, 1979, p.17]. In effect these court interpretations reinforced the view of successive Japanese cabinets that "legal arguments have . . . reached a point at which the right of self-defense and the existence of the SDF are accepted as constitutional" [Okazaki, 1982b, p.470. Hayashi, 1978].

Besides its contested constitutional basis an additional distinctiveness of Japan's legal norms affecting military security is the lack of specific legislation for times of national emergency [Interview Nos.7 and 8, Tokyo, December 10 and 11, 1991]. The SDF's secretly prepared "Three Arrows Study" dealt with many aspects of preparedness for emergency situations, such as the outbreak of another war on the Korean peninsula [Berger, 1992, pp.340-344]. Leaked in 1965 to the opposition parties it was hotly debated in the Diet. The debate focused largely on the possibility that, as in the 1930s, the SDF might potentially escape civilian control. Japan has thus lacked emergency legislation. In 1972, for example, the mayor of Yokohama and his supporters physically stopped the transfer of tanks by the U.S. military from the Sagamihara Depot to Yokohama harbor. Their action was based on a Cabinet Order, regulating heavy vehicles, which made the transfer illegal. The tanks made it to the harbor only after the Cabinet formally exempted U.S. military vehicles from the regulation. Similarly, the sensational, undetected landing of a Soviet MIG-25 fighter at Hakodate Airport in Hokkaido in 1976 was treated in accordance with domestic law (as a routine case of the illegal entry of a foreign national) rather than international law (as the intrusion by a foreign plane into Japanese airspace) [Johnson and Packard, 1981, pp.154-55].

In fact a state-of-emergency does not appear in any plans for the SDF's full-scale mobilization. At present, in times of crises the SDF would have no legal base for unrestricted movement in Japan. "In theory, troops must get permission from property owners before they cross their property to fend off an invader. Tanks or other vehicles being sent to repel that invasion are supposed to stop at all red traffic lights they encounter, and any defender of Japan must, by law, calculate the risks he faces and can respond only with a level of violence proportionate to that being inflicted on Japan. Any defender who kills an invader under circumstances that are not clearly life-threatening could conceivably be charged with murder" [Olsen, 1985, pp.93-94]. Thus who can sound alarms in the eventuality of an air attack, and who should supervise civil defense measures are issues that are simply not addressed by the existing SDF law [Sassa, 1991c, p.61]. Natural disasters are dealt with on a decentralized and ad hoc basis. Although they are not extensive some prefectures have earthquake disaster training routines. But it is not clear what would be done in a military emergency [Interview No. 8, Tokyo, December 11, 1982]. Finally, there exists no separate system of military law. The SDF lack the authority to court martial members of the SDF in times of war [Auer, 1973a, p.50]. Also, in the eyes of the SDF, the existing legal framework does not allow them to counter surprise attacks effectively. When he chaired the Joint Staff Council in 1978 General Kurisu made publicly the case for the possibility of "supralegal" actions by the military in times of emergency, short-circuiting the process required by the SDF Law. Under the law, an order issued by the Prime Minister is an absolute prerequisite for the SDF's use of force in the defense of Japan. When there is an especially urgent necessity, the Prime Minister may issue an order for a defense operation without the approval of the Diet. However, the Diet's approval still has to be sought immediately after the order has been issued. But, without exception, the use of force in the absence of a Prime Ministerial order is illegal (Article 76, 88). Kurisu argued that the law was deficient in not allowing the SDF to counter surprise attacks which left no time for the issuing of such an order. He stated that the SDF could not but resort to supralegal action under inadequate legislation [Buck, 1986, p.73. Carpenter and Gibert, 1982, p.264. Otake, 1983a, pp.184, 187-89. Nishihara, 1983/84, pp.201-03]. General Kurisu appeared to challenge the principle of civilian supremacy over the military for which he was roundly criticized. Because of other controversial statements that he had made at the time, he was forced to resign.

"The lack of concern by Japanese officials . . . was illustrated by the response to Kurisu's criticism made by the then Defense Vice Minister Maruyama. When asked by reporters what the Japanese armed forces should do if such a situation occurred, his . . . response was, 'flee'" [Carpenter and Gibert, 1982, p.264]. Maruyama's view was widely shared among the Japanese public. A survey conducted by the Prime Minister's Office revealed in 1981 that in the event of a foreign invasion only 6 percent of the respondents said that they would join the SDF and fight; 11 percent favored unarmed resistance; and 35 percent would support the SDF in unspecified ways [Nishihara, 1983/84, p.191].

The belief in the inevitability of peace is thus deeply enshrined in the legal norms governing the use of military force in Japan. Since 1977 the government has tried to address this problem through studies on emergency legislation. It has tried to assuage the kind of public uproar that the "Three Arrows Study" had created in 1965. The government subscribed explicitly to the principle of civilian control and constitutional adherence in times of emergency. But it did not consider sensitive issues such as domestic unrest and internal security. And by ruling out a system of mass conscription or infringements on the freedom of speech in times of emergency, the government's proposal left untouched the power of the media [Berger, 1992, pp.482-90. Otake, 1983a, pp.232-33]. Yet partly for lack of a pressing need the issues have not been laid to rest legally. The JDA's first interim report issued in 1981 on legislation for emergency situations made several proposals concerning laws administered by the JDA. A second interim report of 1984 did the same for laws administered by other organizations of the government. No report has yet been issued on matters which do not fall under jurisdictions of particular government organizations. They include evacuation of citizens, protection of civilian ships and aircraft, use of radio waves, and building of POW camps. These issues have apparently been assigned to the Cabinet Security Office for discussion [Boeicho, 1991a, pp.147, 266-76. Defense Agency, 1990, pp.98, 256-65. Holland, 1988, p.13. Johnson and Packard, 1981, p.155. Nishihara, 1983/84, p.201]. But "in case the threat of hostilities emerged, JDA experts have little doubt that such laws could be speedily pushed through the Diet" [Berger, 1992, p.489].

The ambiguous role of Japan's legal norms is illustrated also by the National Defense Program Outline (NDPO). For the first time since 1945 Japan organized its defense policy in 1976 around an explicit strategic doctrine. It was articulated in the NDPO which sought to galvanize public consensus in support of a modernization of the military [Defense Agency, 1990, pp.247-51. Mochizuki, 1983/84, pp.154-57. Chapman, Drifte and Gow, 1982, pp.64-71. Berger, 1992, pp.357-63. Umemoto, 1985a, pp.40-54; 1988, pp.38-39. Kurokawa, 1985a, pp.2-5. Satoh, 1982, pp.18-21. Levin, 1988, pp.8-12. Weinstein, 1983, pp.180-83. Vogel, 1984, pp.9-10,38. Han, 1983, pp.686-88. Nishihara, 1983/84, pp.180-83. Cheng, 1990, pp.6-9]. The Miki Cabinet (1974-76) introduced the NDPO (boei keikaku no taiko) as Japan's long-term defense policy in October 1976. Based on the concept of threshold deterrence and the mobilization of a "standard defense force" (kibanteki boeiryoku), the NDPO expressed the view that Japan should deploy a peace-time military large enough to repel small aggressions, should aim at a qualitative development of its defense capabilities, and should create an infrastructure permitting a quick and effective mass mobilization in the eventuality that a large-scale attack were to be imminent. According to the NDPO Japan's defense policy goal was to "repel limited and small-scale aggression, in principle without external assistance. In cases where the unassisted repelling of aggression is not feasible . . . Japan will continue an unyielding resistance by mobilizing all available forces until such time as cooperation from the United States is introduced, thus rebuffing such aggression" [Tanaka, 1990, p.6].

The NDPO committed Japan to establish adequate military forces to forestall the creation of a vacuum of power in East Asia. It was sufficiently vague to permit various interpretations and thus gave the government tactical flexibility in conducting its security policy in the 1980s. In this it resembled the Basic Policy for National Defense that was adopted in 1957 and required the creation of a minimum self-defense capability sufficient to ensure Japan's security [Holland, 1988, pp.13-14]. The Basic Policy proposed "to deal with external aggression on the basis of the Japan-U.S.

Security Arrangements, pending more effective functioning of the United Nations . . . to develop progressively the effective defence capabilities necessary for self-defence, with due regard to the nation's resources and the prevailing domestic situation; to support the activities of the United Nations and promote international co-operation, thereby contributing to the realization of world peace; and to stabilize the public welfare and enhance the people's love for country, thereby establishing the sound basis essential to Japan's security" [Satoh, 1982, p.18].

According to this statement the basic mission of the SDF was to defend Japan against direct and indirect aggression from abroad. By most acounts this objective was not met in the first four five-years plans. The Basic Policy of 1957 neither defined what would constitute a minimum defense capability, nor indicated how such a capability could be assured. This ambiguity left the government with great flexibility in the process of policy implementation. To some extent this is also true of the NDPO. Specifically, by defining the limits imposed on the SDF in numerical-quantitative terms, thus excluding all technological-qualitative aspects of defense policy, the NDPO offered an escape hatch for one of the most important issues of Japan's growing military strength. Most participants in the bureaucratic and political process of drafting the NDPO were clearly aware of this [Interview Nos. 7, 10, 14 and 15, Tokyo, December 10, 12, 13 and 14, 1991]. The policy allowed a substantial qualitative upgrading of frontline equipment. The ratio of spending on frontline equipment to the defense budget was about 18 percent in 1976; it increased to about 29 percent in 1985 [Hirose, 1989, p.211]. The procurement of expensive weapon systems widened the gap between the actual force level and that stipulated by the policy [Kurokawa, 1985a, pp.23-24]. In addition to upgrading weapons, the government, in the 1980s, characterized the NDPO as only one part of a larger defense buildup plan [Umemoto, 1985b, pp.327-29].

The NDPO had a double meaning. It set a ceiling to Japan's defense capability. At the same time it stipulated a "standard defense force" which could be interpreted flexibly [Kurokawa, 1985a, p.4]. The need for a ceiling was a response to prevailing domestic political sentiments at the time. The NDPO was "a 'sugar-coated pill' to achieve a form of domestic detente with the opposition on defense matters" [Chapman, Drifte and Gow, 1982, p.67]. The administration limited "the role of the SDF to that of repelling a 'limited and small-scale attack.'" More importantly, the Cabinet made a decision on November 5 limiting defense spending to less than one percent of GNP. "The opposition parties were not to let the LDP rid itself" of this decision for more than ten years [Vogel, 1989, p.67]. In other words, at the very time at which the Miki Cabinet laid the groundwork for a major expansion of Japan's military, it also adopted a new policy designed to limit future expansion of the SDF. This fiscal limit was the subject of intense political debate during the defense build-up of the 1980s. Although the conventions of Japan's fiscal policy kept the official figures below the one percent limit until 1987 the general drift of policy was unmistakable. When the defense budget finally exceeded the one per cent limit in 1987 "the opposition and the newspapers were so worn out from crying 'sheep' that they let out no more than a gentle murmur" [Vogel, 1989, p.80].

The normative conflict over the U.S.-Japan relation as the overarching political framework for Japan's security has continued to exist at a low pitch during the last two decades. The gradual changes under the NDPO illustrate the changing nature of that relationship. "It seems that the government is gradually changing its fundamental defense policy without revising the NDPO, just as it has rearmed the country without revising the 1946 constitution" [Nishihara, 1983/84, p.183]. Mike Mochizuki argues in a similar vein. "Many in Japan interpreted the NDPO as a dovish plan to maintain present force levels, not to justify a significant military build-up . . . the program was, however, particularly successful in getting 60 to 70 percent of the public to support the government's defense policy. Consequently, the NDPO is a watershed in postwar defense policy not because it marked a major departure in military policy, but because it helped to create an environment in which the open discussion of security issues was no longer taboo" [Mochizuki, 1983/84, pp.156-57. Interview No.23, Kyoto, June 24, 1991].

By most accounts the NDPO was successful in creating a political environment which permitted the military buildup of the 1980s. The concept of a "standard defense force" has not prevented a build-up of land defense capabilities in Hokkaido, an increase in the anti-submarine capabilities of the Japanese navy around Japan, as well as an extension of the air- and sea-space around Japan considered essential for purpose of defense [Tanaka, 1990, p.6]. In short, what was not contemplated in 1976 has been achieved in the 1980s. And despite the dramatic changes in world politics in 1989-90, the NDPO remains the authoritative guideline for Japan's defense policy in the early 1990s [Defense Agency, 1990, p.91]. The Defense Agency recommended recently that the NDPO should continue to inform Japanese security policy since no "vacuum of power" should be permitted to appear as long as Russia retains very high levels of offensive naval and air power around Japan. The Cabinet and the Security Council of the Cabinet approved that recommendation in December 1990 for the first three years (1991-1993) of the five-years defense plan. In fact, the force structure recommended for the 1990s, with only a few exceptions, closely resembles the structure of the SDF of the late 1970s and the 1980s. But subsequently, responding to the reduction of threat posed by Russia, the government has placed the revision of the NDPO on its agenda [Asahi Shimbun, January 31 and March 26, 1992, 13th editions]. While the basic strategy informing Japan's security policy, according to most officials, is correct in its fundamentals, it may also need to be amended, or reformulated, to include more explicitly Japan's growing concern over issues of regional security and stability. Security and stability are affected by possible changes in Russian and American deployments as well as political developments on the Korean peninsula and throughout Asia [Interview No.21, Tokyo, June 19, 1991].

Typical of Japan's national security policy is the tendency of Japanese leaders, in shaping their foreign and defense policies, to balance normative goals with the demands of existing conditions. Those arguing that the Constitution permits "purely defensive" forces still must come to grips with the fact that even without aircraft carriers and long-range missiles and bombers, Japan's naval forces and medium-range aircraft have undoubtedly an offensive military capability. Legal norms leave considerable room for political discretion. "The use of the minimum necessary force to defend Japan . . . is not necessarily confined to the geographic scope of Japanese territorial land, sea and airspace. Generally speaking, however, it is difficult to make a wholesale definition of how far this geographic area stretches because it would vary with separate individual situations" [Defense Agency, 1990, p.86]. The result is that the question of whether the SDF should be allowed to possess specific weapon systems depends, in the words of the JDA's White Paper, "on the judgment whether the country's total strength will or will not exceed the constitutional limitations by possessing such armaments . . . the use of armed strength is confined to the minimum necessary" [Defense Agency, 1990, pp.85-86].

James R. Van de Velde captures the inherent flexibility in Japan's security policy which favors incremental adjustments when he writes that "Japanese defense policy remains a function of Diet resolutions and leadership choices . . . the Japanese will continue to reinterpret their Constitution to fit emerging defensive needs . . . The fact that Japan has kept Article 9 but reinterpreted systems to be defensive—evolving from at first only mine-sweepers to fighters and now to submarines—suggests that the Article fails as an expression prohibiting force yet remains sacrosanct with the Japanese public as a perceived obstacle to militarism in Japan . . . As long as a constitutional basis is avoided for the SDF in Japan, public opinion will remain a major determinant in Japanese security policy" [Van de Velde, 1987, pp.26, 41, 42, 43. Vogel, 1989, pp.77-83].

But this is only one half of the story. For there exists a specific political practice that gives some of the legal restrictions imposed on the SDF a quasi-constitutional status. "The government is obliged by opposition parties to express its opinion to the Diet that the particular weapon or activity involved would not be a violation of the Constitution. Some examples are highly charged symbolic issues. For example, the reinstallation in 1982 of bombing sights in the F-4, removed in 1968 because they were then thought to contradict the Peace Constitution's prohibition of offensive military capabilities, was the occasion for the opposition parties to boycott the Diet sessions for five days in February 1982. The arguments advanced by the government in such debates, and repeated in many sessions over a long period of time, with the passing of time tend to become highly salient criteria that must be satisfied [Okazaki, 1982b, p.470]. Several of the most prominent, long-standing policies that have restrained the growth of Japan's military power result not from Japanese law but from policies that have acquired such a "semi-constitutional" status and that can be altered only slowly and at great political cost. A series of taboos have been imposed on the Japanese military designed to curtail its growth. "In a sense these taboos can be viewed as a sort of tacit social contract between the conservative government and a broader spectrum of society that exchanges toleration of the armed forces for promises to contain their growth and activities" [Berger, 1992, p.345].

The normative context of Japan's security policy is defined neither by Article 9 of the Constitution nor by the public mood of the moment, but by the interaction between social and legal norms which condition the definition of the interests that inform Japan's security policy. At bottom, the tug and pull in the normative context of Japan's security policy centers on the threat that an extreme nationalism might pose to Japan's constitutional democracy [Beer, 1987, p.7]. What is at stake politically is not the viability of the Constitution itself but the incremental steps of reinterpreting it and thus gradually altering the norms that inform Japan's security policy. "In Japan, people notice these little incidents, these little events that take place to which there is protest because of their symbolism. Foreign observers usually miss the point that, although none of these things by themselves are really important, the thrust of the whole web of events and incidents and policies is quite important. It is a long, connected, and continuing postwar sequence that concerns them" [Beer, 1987, p.12]. In short at stake in this conflict over norms is the fear of the past, of a "possible creeping ultra-nationalism . . . leading improbably but eventually to adventurous militarism" [Beer, 1987, pp.13-14].

C. Disputed Norms : Political Security and the U.S.-Japan Relationship

Japan's national security policy is also shaped by the social and legal norms that affect Japan's relationship with the United States, specifically the security treaty and the public climate surrounding what is often referred to as Japan's "most important" link with the outside world. Most scholarly and journalistic writings on Japan agree on the fact that Japanese decisionmakers view the world largely through the prism of the U.S.-Japan relationship, a fact that is readily borne out by any number of personal conversations or interviews. But since Japanese public opinion is still deeply shaped by the pacifist norms expressed in Article 9 of the Constitution, the evolution of the U.S.-Japan relationship toward a typical military alliance has been gradual and incomplete. At the same time it is important to remember that Japan remains still fundamentally an isolationist country. This isolationism is a lesson learned from the disastrous loss in World War II. Before 1945 imperial ambition and power politics brought war and poverty. The peaceful pursuit of economic objectives has brought peace and prosperity since 1945. For the Japanese elite it is today a very far-fetched idea that Japan could once again be entangled in a violent international conflict. Weinstein calls this isolationism a "deep-seated, pervasive mind-set" [Weinstein, 1982a, p.30].

With the removal of Japan as an active participant from international power politics, the relationship with the United States became the essential factor in the Japanese interpretation of most international developments. The Security Treaty with the United States of 1951 and the Treaty of Mutual Cooperation and Security of 1960 are essential, politically hotly contested, elements of the normative context for Japan's security policy [Weinstein, 1971. Drifte, 1983. Harries and Harries, 1987. Hopper, 1975b]. The 1951 Treaty was not a mutual defense agreement. And it did not provide for joint consultations or joint military actions in times of crisis or war. Like Article 9 of Japan's Constitution the Security Treaty of 1960 renounced war as an instrument of national policy. From the government's perspective Japan's security continues to be protected by its undiminished willingness to accept the stationing of American troops on Japanese soil. Complicated consultation mechanisms in times of emergency are legally mandated between the United States and Japan. The operative bilateral mechanisms now in force most likely would be used just as would the SDF in Japan in times of crisis [Olsen, 1985, p.94. Nishihara, 1983/84, pp.203-05].

What to an American eye looks largely like a traditional military alliance between two countries, rooted in the initial treaty of 1951, from the Japanese perspective is not a political arrangement for collective self-defense. This is the reason why as late as 1981 the use of the term "alliance" in the final communique signed by Prime Minister Suzuki and President Reagan at the occasion of the Prime Minister's May 1981 visit in Washington, led to a political storm in Japan because of the military connotations of the term. The controversy eventually forced Foreign Minister Ito's resignation [Olsen, 1985, pp.23-24. Weinstein, 1982a, pp.26-29. Tokinoya, 1986, pp.4-9. Umemoto, 1985a, pp.55-57]. The term "alliance" connotes a degree of risk sharing and a mutuality of interest which are prohibited by Articles 5 and 6 of the Security Treaty. In short, Prime Minister Suzuki's statement appeared to contradict the general thrust of Japan's post-war security policy which had aimed at avoiding being drawn into the global affairs of the United States. The security arrangements with the United States were designed to counter attacks only on Japan, in return for assuring the United States of use of bases in Japan, but not for any political or military support in its regional defense of the Western Pacific. In the Japanese view of things the relationship with the United States defines as much a political and economic as a military relationship. The change in the title of the Treaty from "Security Treaty" in 1951 to the "Treaty of Mutual Cooperation and Security" in 1960 may be irrelevant for Americans. For the Japanese, however, it expresses a political perception that continues to this day to separate Japan from the United States.

The huge demonstrations and riots against the 1960 Treaty and the eventual resignation of Prime Minister Kishi revealed the deep divisions in Japan's politically attentive public over the desirability of a close relationship with the United States and the international norms and interests that it embodied [Mendel, 1966, pp.4-5; 1969, pp.626-27; 1971-72, pp.526-29]. The opposition objected to the Treaty and Prime Minister Kishi's high-handed method of pushing ratification by the Diet. Kishi and his followers in the LDP, on the other hand, strongly favored a renegotiation of the 1951 Treaty, the creation of more balanced, bilateral relations with the United States, and Treaty revision as a first step toward eventual changes in Japan's Constitution. The Treaty has remained a source of deep unease among a substantial, though declining, number of Japanese. It has not been a catalyst for the creation of a set of shared norms around the emergence of a Pacific Community constituted by Japan and the United States. But the Treaty has increasingly become accepted politically as furthering the long-term interests of both Japan and the United States. The massive demonstrations in 1960, before the ratification of the U.S.-Japan Mutual Security Treaty as well as before its renewal in 1970, were unsuccessful in severing Japan's link with the United States. Today the majority of the public accepts the Treaty as well as the position of the SDF in Japanese politics [Asahi Shimbun Yoron Chosa-shitsu, 1988, p.181. Sorifu Koho-shitsu, 1991, p.15].

From the very beginning it was clear that the Peace Treaty would not be popular but, at best, would be viewed as an unavoidable evil for a nonpunitive peace settlement [Weinstein, 1971, p.55]. Despite the political controversies of the 1950s and 1960s the United States has basically retained a favorable image among the Japanese population. The Japanese public, however, has viewed American bases persistently in a negative light as a potential threat to Japan's security through America's possible involvement in a war in Asia [Bobrow, 1989, p.593. Mendel, 1966, pp.6-7; 1967, pp.446-47; 1969, pp.626-27; 1970, pp.1062-63; and 1971-72, pp.530-31]. Support for the 1960 Treaty of Mutual Cooperation and Security and the importance of Japan's relationship with the United States, however, has remained strong [Mendel, 1975, pp.172-75. Marshall, 1981, Chart 5, Table 11. Bobrow, 1989, 586-96]. In the eyes of the conservatives "creative" ambiguity and a "flexible" interpretation of Japan's Constitution have made it possible for Japan and the United States to utilize the Treaty to cope with a changing security environment in East Asia. Beyond its military importance the Treaty is, for policymakers, "vital to Japan's interests because of the international respectability it provides Japan . . . Given the commitment of the current Japanese political establishment to this concept, it would take a political cataclysm similar to World War II to provoke formal abrogation" [Immerman, 1990, pp.10, 16, 19]. But there is little evidence in the polls that what is often referred to as a "special" relationship between Japan and the United States has the qualities of the "special" relationship between Britain and the United States [Russett, 1963]. Without a sense of community, a significant part of the Japanese public views the relationship much like its political leaders, as a beneficial arrangement for the pursuit of Japanese interests pursued flexibly in a relationship that must be maintained on a long-term basis.

Because Japan was steadfast in its refusal to rearm and to make an active military contribution to America's plans for a regional defense perimeter in Asia, the 1951 Security Treaty did not provide for mutual consultations [Ishimoto and Hirobe, 1987, pp.117-21]. If the United States was to defend Japan until Japan was able to defend herself, this promise was made on American terms and in light of the general interests of the U.S. in the Far East. Specifically, Article 1 gave the military forces of the United States a very broad assignment. Their scope of action was not restricted to Japan; the terms of their deployment were left solely to the decision of the United States; and lacking the element of mutuality, their status and operation was in no way tied to the United Nations. In short in contrast to NATO and ANZUS, this was not a mutual security treaty but a unilateral U.S. agreement. This fact convinced the Japanese government that the Treaty needed to be revised as soon as it was signed.

In contrast Articles 5, 6 and 10 of the 1960 Treaty embody the "formal, explicit guarantee and the mutuality sought by the Japanese government." They tie the treaty much more clearly to the United Nations [Weinstein, 1971, p.88. Aruga, 1989]. The 1960 Treaty provides for the mutual obligation to act against an attack directed at either party. But this obligation extends only to Japan and American forces stationed in Japan. Because it would have violated the prohibition of collective defense and security arrangements, as stipulated, according to the government, in Article 9 of the Constitution, the Treaty does not provide for military action to meet common dangers other than those directed against territories under the administration of the Japanese state. Dealing with the purpose of stationing foreign military forces on Japanese soil, Article 6 mentions Japanese security ahead of international peace and security in the Far East. And it no longer makes any reference to the potential need for foreign intervention to contain potential threats to Japan's internal security by large domestic protests.

Finally, Articles 4 and 6 of the 1960 Treaty and the accompanying exchange of notes incorporate a system of prior consultation on certain matters dealing with major changes in the deployment of U.S. troops or equipment, and use of bases for the purpose of military combat. Should the United States decide on new deployments of forces involving more than a division of the army, a task force of the navy, or a squadron of the airforce, it must consult with the Japanese government. The same holds for the introduction of nuclear warheads, intermediate- and long-range missiles, and the construction of launching sites for such missiles on American bases in Japan. Finally, the use of Japanese bases during the Vietnam war was a controversial subject. Logistically Okinawa handled about three-quarters of the 400,000 tons of goods that the American forces consumed in Vietnam each month. The Kadena air base averaged a takeoff or landing every three minutes around the clock, for a total of more than a million flights between 1965 and 1973 [Havens, 1987, pp.87-88]. Opposition to the basing of B-52 bombers on Okinawa was voiced in the Diet [Richardson, 1977, pp.257-58]. But since Okinawa was not covered by the Treaty, and since Japanese bases were not staging areas for combat, the issue of the need for "consultation" during the Vietnam war was sidestepped. Prior consultation is not mandatory when logistic operations are being carried out from bases in Japan [Kim, 1972, p.63]. The Treaty's relatively loose provisions for consultation represent, the government has argued on the basis of a joint U.S.-Japanese communique signed in 1960, a convergence of interests between the United States and Japan, rather than, as the opposition maintains, a set of empty procedures leaving Japan without veto power. Reliance on such "flexible" consultative mechanisms represents a Japanese concession in a Treaty that grants Japan, in American eyes, very favorable terms on the key question of Japan's military defense.

Article 6 and the exchange of notes have not interfered with Japan serving as a forward base of the U.S. military in Asia [Emmerson, 1971, pp.89-97. La Feber, 1989, pp.96-116]. Until the end of the 1980s at no time was this clearer than during the Vietnam war. Tokyo's civilian airport at Haneda processed almost 100,000 American service personnel during the first year of major troop commitments as well as over 2,000 military charter flights in 1967 [Havens, 1987, p.159]. A 1966 report for the Military Preparedness Subcommittee of the U.S. Senate noted that "it would be difficult to fight the war in Southeast Asia without Yokosuka and Sasebo" [Havens, 1987, p.87]. The government took the position that the U.S. forces stationed in Japan could, under Article 6 of the Security Treaty, operate in Vietnam, which is not a part of the Far East. Indeed, the Foreign Minister acknowledged that Japan was not neutral in the Vietnam War [Emmerson, 1971, p.84]. The broad interpretation of Article 6 and the exchange of notes was also quite evident in the aftermath of the Gulf War. Japan did not object to the fact that U.S. troops stationed in Japan were sent off to military engagements outside of Asia. The meaning of the concept of "Far East", which U.S. troops stationed in Japan are supposedly defending, was never a central point of discussion [Watanabe, Y., 1991, pp.244-45]. U.S. forces stationed in Japan have also been dispatched to the Indian Ocean and the Middle East at various times in the 1970s and 1980s [Nishihara, 1990, p.4]. The regional security aspects which were controversial during the Vietnam war have now been redefined, as the Security Treaty apparently has acquired a global function. In the government's view, legally speaking U.S. troops are free to leave Japan without consent of the Japanese government, since they are starting their military "operations" only when approaching the area of engagement, in this case the Mideast. This voids the neccessity of having to reach explicit agreements between the U.S. and Japanese government on the objectives of particular troop movements and thus sidesteps the controversial issue of "prior consultations" under the provisions of the Security Treaty, arguably the umbrella under which all of Japan's security policy is now conducted [Interview Nos. 15 and 22, Tokyo, December 14 and 18, 1992].

The Security Treaty and the Treaty of Mutual Cooperation and Security between Japan and the United States have provided umbrellas for political arrangements that have drawn the two countries closely together on questions of national security. Under the auspices of the Security Treaty of 1951 the Japanese and the United States governments negotiated the Mutual

Defense Assistance Agreement of 1954. It created a legal basis for the provision of American military equipment and military technology. And it clarified the terms of Japan's contribution to the stationing of American forces in Japan [Weinstein, 1971, pp.74-75]. The preamble of the Agreement placed Japan's defense policy explicitly within the United Nations framework with language that the Japanese government had tried and failed to have included in the 1951 Security Treaty. But the preamble also stipulated explicitly that Japan's defense effort was to be limited so that it would not exceed Japan's economic capacities and thus endanger its economic and social stability. At the same time the Japanese government formally acknowledged in Article 7 its commitment to a limited rearmament. In return the United States government recognized that Japan's economic and political cooperation "contributed to the common defense and constituted a proper basis for mutuality in the security arrangements. This was a significant shift from Mr. Dulles' position in the 1951 negotiations, which had made large-scale rearmament and military cooperation in regional defense the basis for a mutual security agreement" [Weinstein, 1971, p.75].

D. Conclusion

The variable tension between social and legal norms requires from the Japanese government a flexibility that satisfies both sets of norms. This is not an easy task and often runs counter to the clear-cut logic of international politics. The tensions between legal and social norms facilitates in Japan incremental policy changes less typical in legal cultures which require that a change in policy is codified in law.

For example, the original intent of Article 9 was to prohibit Japan from having a fighting force, including for defensive purposes. But over time this interpretation has gradually shifted. The Police Reserve force that was created in 1950 to defend Japan's internal security, after U.S. troops had moved to Korea, was justified by the government because it was said to be no fighting force. Before 1954, according to the government, this embryonic defense force did not have any military potential. After 1954, however, the government shifted its view and argued that the SDF "did not constitute the kind of war potential forbidden by Article 9" [McNelly, 1975, p.100. Kim, 1972]. War and the threat of force were renounced as an instrument for settling international conflicts, but not as a means of self-defense. An alternative view, at times also articulated, was that since Japan did not renounce the right of self-defense, she did not renounce either the military means for self-defense [McNelly, 1975, pp.100-01]. "Faced with strong pacifist demands to the effect that Article 9 prohibited any rearmament, the government claimed that Article 9 actually allowed Japan to exercise its right of self-defense. It was a new interpretation, based on a new emphasis placed on the first ten words of the second paragraph of the article. In other words the new interpretation was that Japan might have a force as long as it would use it not 'as means of settling international disputes' but simply as a means of self-defense. The new justification was also based on Article 51 of the United Nations Charter, which refers to the right of self-defense as an inherent right of any nation. Hence the euphemism known as the 'Self-Defense Force'" [Nishihara, 1985a, p.135].

The normative consensus which embraces Japanese security policy is shaped by the historical lessons of World War II and the reemergence of Japan as a peaceful and prosperous actor in world politics since 1945. Characteristic of Japan's political culture is the fact that a pacifism deeply ingrained in a substantial segment of the Japanese public has a very complex relation to the constitutional mandate imposed by Article 9. The Constitution has been reinterpreted in the past in interaction with an evolving public consensus on what were judged to be the requirements of Japanese security policy in a changing world. This accounts perhaps for the fact that the overwhelming majority of the Japanese public now has come to accept the SDF while at the same time refusing adamantly to amend Article 9 [Eto, 1983, pp.56-57]. This process of reinterpretation is grounded in a deep public resentment and fear of any experimentation with a policy that might rely on the threat or use of military force. The normative constraints have made it impossible: to revise Article 9 of the Constitution; to build nuclear weapons or to agree to their deployment on Japanese soil; to dispatch Japanese troops abroad in combatant roles even as part of an international peacekeeping force; to sell weapons abroad; and to raise the JDA to ministerial status. For any or all of these measures connote the strengthening of the military and thus raise fears of a return to the political conditions and practices that prevailed before 1945 [Weinstein, 1971, p.125].

That the complex interplay between social and legal norms that helps define Japan's national security policy is likely to persist is indicated by the striking difference between public opinion and legal opinion on the issue of military security. A 1981 poll, for example, indicated that 61 percent of the public favored the SDF at its present level of strength and 22 percent wanted to see the SDF grow stronger. By contrast at the same time a survey of legal scholars showed 45 percent wanted to see the SDF abolished and another 15 percent wanted it weakened. "Thus 83 percent of the public favored preserving or increasing the SDF while 60 percent of legal experts favored abolition or reduction of the forces. The two polls also showed that while 17 percent of the public felt the SDF were unconstitutional 47 percent felt that they were not unconstitutional. By contrast, 71 percent of the legal experts believed that the forces were unconstitutional and only 27 percent found they were not unconstitutional" [McNelly, 1982, p.357].

The relationship between social and legal norms has been uncontested on the issue of economic security; it has been deeply divisive on questions of military security; and it has been the subject of political controversy on the issue of political security. These differences, Part 5 will show, correspond to patterns of policy change which vary between a far-reaching flexiblity in policies dealing with economic security, a remarkable "rigidity" on questions of military security, and a variable adaptability on issues of political security.

V

Japan's National Security Policy

Japan's national security policy has two distinguishing features. It is comprehensive. Besides military issues it also includes economic and political security concerns. And it is characterized by a variable mix of policy flexibility and rigidity or "strategic pragmatism" [Schmiegelow and Schmiegelow, 1990] which, to one observer, at best "is characterized by a shrewd pragmatism and, at worst, by an irresponsible immobilism" [Sato, 1977, p.389]. The comprehensiveness of policy is shaped by the structures of Japanese politics. The domestic structure of the Japanese state strengthens the economic and political dimensions of security policy. Its transnational structure has reinforced the military dimension of security policy. The normative context in which Japan's security policy is defined helps explain the mix of flexibility and rigidity in policy (terms which are defined here analytically, not politically). On economic issues uncontested norms of security facilitate policy flexibility. On military issues deeply contested security norms lead to policy rigidity. Finally, on political security issues the normative context has sometimes favored policy adjustment and at other times worked against it. In short, structures and norms interact in explaining the comprehensive definition of security as well as the pattern of policy adjustment.

Responding to the political constraints on Japan's military power both from the conservatives (the Yoshida foreign policy line of stressing economic over military means of statecraft) and from the progressives (a determined opposition to any possible sign of a reappearing militarism) Japan's security policy has stressed economic and political elements as well as military ones. Since the early 1950s, Japan has emphasized the separation of economic from security policy, keeping as low a political profile as circumstances would permit, a policy seen by some as spectacularly successful until the Gulf War of 1991 [Olsen, 1985, pp.10-11]. To date virtually all of the major aspects of Japan's security policy remain linked to the Yoshida line that was articulated by the third Prime Minster of postwar Japan and continued by two of his most ardent and successful disciples, Prime Ministers Ikeda (1960-64) and Sato (1964-72). And Prime Minister Fukuda often spoke of Japan's omnidirectional and peaceful foreign policy in the mid-1970s (zenhoi heiwa gaiko). Like the Yoshida line it, too, revealed Japan's extreme caution even if, according to one American critic, it presumed "to do something diplomatically by not doing anything" [Olsen, 1985, p.11].

But since the mid-1970s a new "realism" in foreign policy, both on diplomatic and military issues, has moved center stage [Scalapino, 1977. Hellmann, 1977. Momoi, 1977. Mochizuki, 1983/84. Okimoto, 1978a, p.59. Vogel, 1984. Umemoto, 1985a, pp.93-148. Berger, 1992, pp.141-59,187-197. Pyle, 1982. Langdon, 1985. Drohan, 1990, pp.30-35. Carpenter, 1982]. But "realism" meant different things to different people. To the pacifist Left it meant, first and foremost, to maintain a policy that observed the letter and the spirit of Japan's Peace Constitution. To the nationalist Right it meant a reassertion of Japan's national role in world politics, symbolized to a small fringe by the acquisition of nuclear weapons. Most importantly the new "realism" has spread in Japan's political center, between the gradually waning position of the Left and the lack of mass appeal of the nationalist Right. "Political realists are the inheritors of the Yoshida strategy and now form the mainstream of Japanese strategic thought. These strategists are called 'political' realists because their primary concern is with the political and diplomatic implications of Japan's security policy. Domestically they are sensitive to the persistence of pacifist sentiments and fears" [Mochizuki, 1983/84, pp.158-59]. In contrast "military realists" put the military balance in Asia at the center of their analysis and derive from it the need for close political cooperation with the United States; but compared to political realists they show less concern for public sensibilities on the issue of national defense in domestic politics.

Exposed to the new global pulls and constantly threatened by a strong domestic opposition, both from the Left and from the nationalist Right, successive LDP governments have adhered to a security policy that has been flexible on economic issues, rigid on military issues and tried to adapt so as to defend Japan's political security, specifically its relationship with the United States. In other words, Japan's ruling policy consensus is the result of a convergence of views that differ in their analysis of the primary causes of security policy. In the emerging discussion about Japan's security policy after the Cold War the "realists" continue to maintain their predominance, between outspoken nationalists on the Right and the advocates of drastic arms reduction on the Left [Mochizuki, 1992a, 1992b].

A. Economic Dimensions of Security

The history of Japan's policy of economic security shows that the structures and the normative context have favored flexible policy adjustment to changing international conditions. The incentives which Japan's domestic and transnational structures create for policymakers have all favored adjustment. And policy adjustment was facilitated by the fact that the normative context of policy choice was uncontested: in the area of energy imports and in the quest for enhancing its technological autonomy Japan must reduce its vulnerability.

1. Reducing Economic Vulnerability.

The oil crisis of 1973 was a dramatic event for most industrial countries. In their response each of them revealed starkly different visions of how to manage their affairs in a world of high-price energy. The United States, for example, responded to the energy crisis of 1973 with "Project Independence" and the creation of a rapid deployment force for times of crisis. The gut reaction of American policymakers and the American public was to restore a situation of energy independence and self-reliance. This was not the reaction of Japan. Central to the conception informing the energy policy of the Japanese government was the notion that Japan's dependence on foreign energy supplies was inescapable [Akao, 1983. Chapman, Drife and Gow, 1982. Momoi, 1977. Saxonhouse, 1977. Ilgen and Pempel, 1987, pp.122-42. Tanaka, 1986. Samuels, 1987. Ellingworth, 1972. Journal of Japanese Trade and Industry, 1983. Bobrow and Kudrle, 1987. Sato, 1991.]. If nuclear energy generated by imported uranium is counted under the foreign category, Japan's dependence on foreign energy resources was still an astounding 91 percent in 1985 [Fukami, 1988, p.157]. MITI's concept of energy security takes into account five factors: dependence on imports in primary energy suppply, dependence on oil in primary energy supply, dependence on oil imports, dependence on the Strait of Hormuz for importing oil, and dependence on the Middle East as a source for primary energy supply. By any of these measures, compared to other states, Japan remains remarkably dependent on foreign energy supplies [Agency of Natural Resources and Energy, 1990, p.16. Nihon Kogyo Shinbun, 1989, p.35]. Vulnerablity is a fact of life that Japan had no choice but to accept [Cowhey, 1985, p.201]. Within that general context "the policies that have been selected have followed a coherent line and have been more or less responsive to the country's need . . . Japan succeeded in implementing its plans to a degree that other governments found difficult to achieve" [Vernon, 1983, pp.82,97].

Japan has ameliorated its vulnerability with an active resource and aid diplomacy of the government. But that diplomacy was coupled with the technological innovativeness of Japanese industry responding to the cues of market prices. An adaptable private sector response has led to greater national security. What could be ameliorated through the government's policy was not international vulnerability but an excessive dependence on Mideast oil as the primary source of energy. Put differently, the government's role did not eliminate dependence but sought to provide stable energy supplies in an unstable world. On the other hand, in lowering its dependence on foreign sources of energy, private business enhanced Japan's national security over time through the application of energy-efficient technologies.

Japan has made persistent efforts to diversify its dependence on foreign sources of energy through a reliance on markets [Morse, 1981. Murakami, 1982]. This policy predates the oil crisis of 1973 [Tanaka, 1986, pp.2, 113]. In 1961 the Japanese government served notice to the foreign companies, then dominating the Japanese oil industry, that it intended to play a more active role in shaping the future evolution of Japan's energy markets. MITI introduced a number of measures to limit the acquisition of new equity by foreign firms and also used its allocative powers to constrain further growth of international oil corporations in the Japanese market [Vernon, 1983, p.92].

The 1960s saw also the beginning of small scale foreign investment in resource intensive industries which aimed at the same objective. In transferring production to resource-rich areas and in establishing ownership of or control over overseas enterprises, Japanese firms, it was hoped, would be able to reduce their vulnerability to possible disruptions in supply. Since many of Japan's foreign investments in extractive industries operated at a deficit, profitability was often only a secondary objective [Ozawa, 1979, p.185]. Besides coal, bauxite, and uranium, overseas investment in oil became a particular area of government and business attention. In 1967 MITI reorganized the Japan Resource Development Corporation to form the Petroleum Development Public Corporation (PDPC). It provided financing to encourage Japanese oil companies to undertake new exploration overseas while also seeking to attract other Japanese corporations not active in the oil industry [Tanaka, 1986, p.50]. Foreign investment in overseas petroleum projects tripled during the 1960s.

In cooperation with Japanese business by the early 1970s the Japanese government thus was in the process of countering its vulnerable dependence on the import of raw materials, including oil, through a variety of measures: shifting the economy away from resource-intensive industries, gaining a greater degree of national control over the oil industry, restructuring foreign purchasing agreements, and stepping up overseas investment. But these efforts were small and had not been able to make much of a dent on Japan's growing dependence on foreign sources of energy supply. Between 1946 and 1973 Japanese energy consumption, spurred by high economic growth, increased seven-fold, twice as fast as in the other major industrialized countries [Fukami, 1988]. And the dependence and vulnerablility of Japan's economy did not become a paramount policy issue, until the oil shock of 1973 moved this issue to the forefront of Japan's political agenda. After 1973 Japan's raw materials policy became tightly integrated with a general economic policy that had recognized the rise of high-technology industries as the most promising avenue for reducing Japan's dependence on resource-intensive industries in the long-term [Hein, 1990]. The government adopted a two-pronged policy of reducing dependence on oil and increasing the efforts of private industry to develop new energy-saving technologies. In the words of Prime Minister Fukuda: "There is no question that we would take the long-term view. Now it is understood that world resources are limited, it is unavoidable for a resource-poor country like Japan to adopt cooperation attitudes and promote international exchange. This is the only way for Japan to survive . . . Basically we will try to find alternative resources and sources of energy. But this will take time. In the meantime, Japan will have to make efficient use of scarce resources and economize" [Far Eastern Economic Review, July 25, 1975, p.30. Onitsuka, 1990].

Japan's policy did not change after the second energy crisis of 1979. The government trusted the country's general economic strength and flexibility to cope with adjustments and to maintain or forge additional links with oil producing countries in the Third World. In the words of one high-ranking MITI official it was clear that Japan "has the technology, the capital and human resources to make us increasingly indispensable to developing countries who need our help" [Far Eastern Economic Review, September 28, 1979, p.64]. But besides foreign aid and resource diplomacy, the Japanese government trusted in the adaptability of Japanese business. The Japanese government made this point explicitly when it released, soon after the second oil shock, a MITI report which showed that in the 1970s Japan had been more flexible in adjusting to energy constraints in part through greater gains in labor productivity and overall economic growth [Far Eastern Economic Review, December 14, 1979, pp.47-48].

Japan's bilateral and multilateral oil diplomacy took on a much more active character after 1973. First and foremost, Japan tried to diversify further its sources of supplies to reduce its dependence on unstable Middle

East states [Cowhey, 1985, pp.201-213. Quo, 1986. Caldwell, 1981a and 1981b]. Southeast Asia, China, and Mexico in particular became additional, important suppliers for Japan in the 1970s without, however, measurably reducing Japan's dependence on Mideast oil by the time the second oil shock hit. Japan also relied on its growing aid budget to cultivate good relations with potential suppliers of raw materials, including oil. In the Mideast, in particular, Japan tried to build up good relations with stable Arab regimes [Caldwell, 1981a, 1981b. Nester and Ampiah, 1989]. This bilateral approach was more important than the intensification of multilateral energy policies, for example, through the International Energy Agency (IEA) or the coordination among the major oil purchasers in international energy markets [Cowhey, 1985, pp.201-213. Quo, 1986. Morse, 1981. Yoshitsu, 1984].

In addition, the government assisted and occasionally participated in foreign investments designed to develop reliable sources of energy overseas [Ozawa, 1979, pp.33-37]. It made aggressive use of aid and tax concessions. Parastatal bodies such as the Export-Import Bank increased the availability of loans to Japanese firms investing in raw materials abroad. This assistance was designed to help finance equity ownership in overseas ventures, to provide debt capital for such ventures, and to finance the purchase of plants and equipment from Japan to be installed overseas [Ozawa, 1979, p.35]. Similarly the Japanese Overseas Investment Corporation also assisted developing countries interested in hosting joint ventures with Japanese firms. The Corporation conducted preliminary surveys on the practicality of proposed ventures in these countries and provided interest-free loans to smaller Japanese firms participating in approved ventures [Ozawa, 1979, p.36]. As was true of mining, food processing and other critical raw materials, the facilitation of foreign investment in overseas oil processing became a critical ingredient for close government-business relations in seeking to mitigate the enormous vulnerabilty that Japan appeared to face in international energy markets [Ozawa, 1979. Vernon, 1983, pp.83-98. McKean, 1983]. Specifically, the National Oil Corporation was set up to provide loans for such a venture [Yager, 1984]. This foreign investment strategy was risky as Japan's largest resource investment project with Iran illustrated. A multi-billion dollar joint project negotiated with the Shah of Iran eventually was stopped because of the Iranian revolution and the Iran-Iraq war [Curtis, 1977. Caldwell, 1981b. Yoshitsu, 1984, pp.83-103]. In addition, more recently the Japanese government also has sought to encourage Japanese and foreign firms to participate in oil explorations on the continental shelf off the Japanese archipelago. In January 1992 Russia granted a U.S.-Japan consortium the right to begin exploration of what is considered to be enormous reserves of oil and gas just off the Sakhalin Island. The decision to involve the Mitsui Corporation was interpreted as a Japanese signal that this 10 billion dollars contract might have significant implications for resolving the conflict between Russia and Japan about the Northern territories [Sanger, 1992].

But Japan's energy policy was also intimately linked to its evolving industrial policy. The oil shock of 1973 reinforced a position that the Japanese government had embraced already in the early 1970s [Murakami, 1982]. In its view Japan's greatest future advantage was the rapid development of energy-saving high-technology industries. The shut-down of Japan's aluminum industry in the 1970s and 1980s was indicative of the general policy Japan followed [Samuels, 1983. Bang-Jensen, 1987]. The nuclear industry, on the other hand, was supported actively, against growing domestic opposition, with the intent of both reducing Japan's dependence on foreign energy supplies and of strengthening Japan's position in an important high-technology sector. Before 1973 Japan had virtually no nuclear power industry. By 1990 the industry provided 9 percent of the energy needs of the Japanese economy, and the government hoped to double that figure by the end of the century [Chandler and Brauchli, 1990, p.A4]. Furthermore, energy research is the largest single item in MITI's budget. In 1987 MITI funneled almost 1 billion dollars into energy research, more than into all other projects combined [Chandler and Brauchli, 1990, p.A4]. The development of knowledge-intensive, clean industries promised numerous advantages since markets for high technology products were expanding rapidly and could be serviced well by Japan's trained labor force and innovative management. In other words, just as in the evolving relationships between civilian and military technologies, market developments played into the hands of Japanese policymakers. And as was true of Japan's discovery of the "spin-on" phenomenon from civilian to military technologies, applications and products, the Japanese government read correctly early signs of how Japan should position itself in future markets. Its evolving industrial policy was not a reaction to the oil shock of 1973. But the oil shock made more compelling the implementation of a policy that it had settled on before.

Compared to other industrial states Japan's consumption structure has been disproportionately skewed towards industrial manufacturing, the economic sector with the greatest potential for adjusting to changing energy prices. In 1985 industry accounted for about one half of Japan's total energy consumption; corresponding German and American data are about one-third [Nihon Kogyo Shimbun, 1989, pp. 674,682. Agency of Natural Resources and Energy, 1990, p.4]. The government's first task thus was to assure a stable supply of energy for Japanese industry, while trusting in the industry's ability in the longer-term to adjust flexibly to higher prices and thus to maintain its competitiveness in international markets. The overall reduction of energy consumption or the development of indigenous energy sources simply were not viable policy options, and they were never considered seriously. Japan's vulnerability could be altered; it could not be eliminated. The improvement of energy efficiency was achieved largely through the competitive behavior of firms. But it was spurred also, as in many other fields, by public funds which were allocated by semi-public agencies [Suzuki, 1985].

Evolving market trends were as important in changing Japan's energy policy as was direct government intervention in energy markets [Morse, 1982, p.255]. This is an element of Japan's search for "comprehensive security" that is frequently overlooked. The government expected that the private sector, heeding market signals, would rationalize its energy costs and thus remain, at a minimum, on par with Japan's major industrial competitors. While the energy policy of the government was undoubtedly important, it was often marked by "caution, hesitation, and lack of determination" [Shibata, 1983, p.143. Belgrave, Ebinger and Okino, 1987]. Declarations of intent, unenforceable guidelines and suggestions for alternative sources of energy mattered less than a successful macroeconomic policy which reduced inflation and an acquiescent labor force that was willing to adapt to changing conditions on world markets. The government's policy did not succeed in reducing Japan's reliance on foreign energy sources. It did, however, manage to switch the line-up of foreign energy suppliers. The share of the major international oil corporations declined while direct purchasing through bilateral resource dipomacy increased. Japan's growing energy efficiency thus resulted most substantially from the adjustment of firms in markets, specifically the technologcial change in manufacturing industry [Miyata, 1987. Shibata, 1983, p.153]. The average elasticity of energy consumption to economic growth for the ten-year period before 1973 was 1.2; it dropped during the next decade to 0.1. Change in the elasticity of oil consumption was even greater with the figures recorded, respectively, at 1.6 and -0.3 [Sakisaka, 1985]. In comparative terms Japan had succeeded in reducing its vulnerability to an astonishing degree. By 1990, The Economist concluded, "Japan, it seems, is no longer more vulnerable to higher oil prices than France or West Germany" [The Economist, 1990, p.61]. This was the result of a policy that Ronald Morse has characterized as an "adaptive process to new situations; a tactic that is pragmatic and not overly reactive" [Morse, 1982, p.255].

The 1980s was also a decade of deregulation in Japanese energy markets. The government relied on markets to redirect its domestic energy policy, particularly in the oil distribution sector. Production quotas were repealed in 1989 and restrictions imposed on the building of gas stations was lifted in the same year. A total of eleven domestic petroleum wholesalers lowered the profitablity of the energy industry further. MITI is advocating mergers among several firms to create greater efficiencies and higher profit rates [Nihon Keizai Shimbun, 1991].

The result of these policies has been striking. By the mid-1980s about one-tenth of Japan's oil came from reserves developed by Japanese firms with government assistance. Government-secured oil accounted for more than 40 percent of oil imports [Akaha, 1986, p.258]. The policy was spectacularly successful in decreasing Japan's dependence on oil. In sharp contrast to the other industrialized states, in 1973 oil accounted for more than three-quarters of Japan's total energy consumption. Through substitution of nuclear power and gas, this share had dropped by more than 20 percentage points by the mid-1980s and was within range of the figures for the other industrialized states [Lesbirel, 1988, p.287. MacDonald, 1986, p.148. Imai, 1992, p.3. Agency of Natural Resources and Energy, 1990, p.4]. Between 1973 and the end of the 1980s Japan's economic output more than doubled; yet oil imports fell by 25 percent [Chandler and Brauchli, 1990, p.A4].

Compared to the U.S. and Germany Japan's overall energy efficiency has made moderate gains [Agency of Natural Resources and Energy, 1990, pp.11, 42. Organization for Economic Co-operation and Development, 1987, pp.3, 237, 327, 525]. But the historical record of the last two decades shows that Japan has achieved a very important measure of energy security. Two facts stand out. Japan's economic growth no longer depends on the availability of additional sources of oil. Furthermore, in relative terms, Japan exceeds its competitors in energy efficiency [Agency of Natural Resources and Energy, 1990, p.11]. Thus the government's policy of lessening Japan's dependence on oil without interrupting economic growth has been largely successful. And while government policy has not led to any appreciable increases in Japan's relative energy efficiency after 1973, the inherent energy efficiency of the Japanese economy that predated the oil shocks of the 1970s have left business in a strong position to compete in world markets. This is particularly striking in the relative energy efficiency of Japan's manufacturing industries which exceeds the macro-economic levels of Japan's energy efficiency.

In sum, the government's approach to dealing with Japan's energy vulnerability sought to achieve gains in comprehensive security through maintaining sustainable economic growth at a rate that would neutralize the economy's overall dependence on foreign sources of energy while relying on the private sector to maintain competitiveness in world markets. There is no evidence that on questions of energy vulnerability any government agency thought in terms of relative gains. By 1973 Japan was already more energy efficient than its major industrial competitors, and it has been a trend setter in energy research and rationalization since. Yet Japanese officials do not evaluate the effect of supply disruptions in terms of the relative competitive position of Japan, even though that competitiveness would probably increase with increasing oil prices [Interview Nos. 6 and 17, Tokyo, June 12 and 17, 1991. Interview Nos. 7 and 21, Tokyo, December 10 and 18, 1991]. In the words of one authoritative MITI publication:

"The optimum structure of the supply and demand of energy (the best mix of energy), in which security, cost and adaptability to needs are well-balanced, will be a flexible structure matching the requirements of supply and demand. It will also suit the 'multiple energy era', in that it will be highly technology-intensive, efficient and beneficial to users, and capable of filling single energy demand with multiple resources of energy. This best mix of energy will be attained only under the following conditions—the promotion of energy related technology, the provision of a proper competitive environment based on a strengthened energy supply system, and the development of an international policy on natural resources. These three conditions are, so to speak, the three keys to attaining the best mix" [MITI, 1986, p.14].

2. The Economic Logic of Military Procurement.

The reduction of Japan's economic vulnerability intersects with the rapid push of Japanese industry toward technological frontiers. In the words of the Financial Times after the second oil shock "Japan's need to pay its way in a world of scarce and costly oil constitutes the main reason why the country will be placing more emphasis than ever during the next ten years on upgrading its industries and obtaining a global 'technological supremacy' at least in some chosen areas" [Financial Times, July 21, 1980, p.1]. The military implications of Japan's technological eminence have so far not impeded an unrestrained push towards a position of international leadership that is likely to have profound effects on Japan's national security policy.

Japan's growing economic and technological strength is pushing the country inexorably into the role of a leading producer of weapon components. The boundary between military and nonmilitary products and production processes has become less clear in the 1980s. This is true in particular in cutting-edge technologies where Japan is strong, such as new materials, avionics, artificial intelligence and optical data storage. These technologies are distinguished by the concurrence of both "spin-on" and "spin-off" processes between military and civilian technologies [Pempel, 1990a, pp.5-6. U.S. Congress, Office for Technology Assessment, 1988,1989, 1990. Morse, 1987. Samuels, 1991, pp.55-56. Friedman and Samuels, 1992. Vogel, 1989, pp. 13-14, 30-41, 73. Borrus and Zysman, forthcoming, pp.23-29. Vogel, 1991. Drifte, 1985a, p.76. Nagata, 1987]. This poses both a serious challenge and a great opportunity to government and business who, in the process of defense production, traditionally have emphasized "the economic gains of military production at least as much as their military benefits" [U.S. Congress, 1990, p.61].

Attuned to the role of technology for economic prosperity at home and export competitiveness abroad, Japanese manufacturers have traditionally looked to military technologies for their potential commercial applications. "Arms production" writes Reinhard Drifte, "is used for the maximum benefit to the civilian economy" [Drifte, 1986a, p.55]. For example, the braking system of Japan's bullet trains was adapted from the F-104 fighter jet. The oil hydraulic technology of the F-86F was adapted to the needs of fire truck hoses. And American gyroscope technology was adapted for the use in bowling alleys, horse-racing starting gates and seismographic equipment. Nissan Motors used parts of the F-86F engine for testing shock resistance in automobiles as well as for resistance measurements of skyscrapers. And Japanese manufacturers have begun to turn the composite and ceramic materials that the Pentagon has developed for armor plates, rocket nozzles and structural parts of warplanes into commercially successful products such as fishing rods, sailboat masts and tennis racquets [Pempel, 1990a, pp.13-14,21].

But that process is now also working in the opposite direction. In the 1980s "Japan's electronics companies see in the military application of their technologies a broadening of their technological base" [Drifte, 1985a, p.64]. More importantly, Japan's rapid advances in commercial technologies have significant military implications. "Thanks to the'electronics-ization' of defense," says Mitsubishi Electric Managing Director Takeshi Abe, "the stage is finally set for Japan to build weapons even better than those made in the United States" [Vogel, 1989, p.30]. In the area of semiconductors, for example, a study of the U.S. Defense Department reported Japanese firms to lead American firms in 12 of 24 major areas of semiconductor technology while the United States firms led in only four, with eight areas being too close to call [Fong, 1990, p.6]. For example, integrated circuits produced with gallium arsenide were originally developed in the civilian sector but are now driving the development and production of Japan's phased-array radar for the FSX plane. Military orders can push, as in this case, Japan's technology lead in the civilian sector [Chinworth, 1990b, p.9]. The 1990 DoD list of critical technologies has Japan leading the United

States in five of twenty critical technologies (semiconductor materials and microelectronic circuits, simulation and modeling, photonics, superconductivity and biotechnology); and it judges Japan to be in a position of parity in three others (parallel computing, high-energy density materials and composite materials). Based on the strength of its electronics industry Japan has made great strides in developing a national capability for missile production. It produces currently four missiles under U.S. license: the Sparrow, Sidewinder, Hawk and Patriot. It produces four tactical missiles itself and is in the process of developing a follow-on generation of missiles such as the XAAM-3, XSSM-1 and Keiko. Deploying a limited Anti-Ballistic Missile (ABM) system against missiles fired from the Chinese mainland or Korea will probably be within Japan's technological reach in the next decade, as will the successful firing of medium-range or long-range missiles.

An informal consensus exists among policymakers concerned that the objective of Japan's defense related industrial policy does not differ in any significant way from the general principles informing Japan's industrial policy. Japan should develop Japanese technologies as far and as fast as possible, and it should be able to maintain the weapons it builds as efficiently as possible [Interview Nos. 1 and 21, Tokyo, December 9 and 18, 1991]. This policy requires a willingness to pay a high premium for the elusive goal of enhancing Japan's future technological autonomy. Coproduction programs with the United States, for example, have doubled the price of important weapon systems for Japan. But they also have helped transform Japan's leading defense contractor, MHI, in the words of Daniel Todd, from a simple "licenser producer" to a "lead prime" in the area of missile technology [Todd, 1988, pp.258-259]. Japan's policy thus is often designed "to enhance domestic industrial capabilities and reduce dependency on the United States for future weapons programs . . . Rather than looking for 'spinoffs' from defense production, the policy thrust is directed toward finding 'spin-ons'. By utilizing new or existing commercial technologies for other applications, military production can thus become a means of recouping research and development expenditures as well as a means of reducing unit costs in civilian sectors" [Chinworth, 1990a, p.219]. Recent shifts in Japan's military posture in the 1980s, T.J. Pempel argues similarly, are as congruent with technological as with military considerations. Since MITI as the primary advocate of technological advance, did not play a significant role in the defense spending increases of the 1980s [Otake, 1983a, p.303], this evolution was not the result of conscious policy planning. But it is congruent with one important assumption informing Japan's policy. Security flows not only from the acquisition of military hardware but also from the development of advanced equipment that can be adapted to civilian or military purposes. Security policy is deeply rooted in economic considerations [Pempel, 1990a].

Japanese policymakers have been forced to think about a new technology policy just as the traditional distinction between civilian and military technologies has eroded, and while the United States has made increasing demands for a more balanced sharing of technology between American and Japanese corporations. MITI for one has been very explicit that old distinctions are eroding quickly between domestic and international affairs on the one hand and between civilian and military technologies on the other. "Patterns of technology diffusion related to dual-use technologies are changing . . . there are not a few cases of the effective diffusion of'key technologies' from military to civilian sectors. In order not to lag behind the West in international competitiveness in the future, it is undoubtedly necessary to participate as appropriate in the military sector through close contact with top rank Western firms. Most advanced technologies are already dual-use" [Tsushosangyosho Daijin Kanbo, 1988, p. 116]. The TRDI supports this position when it writes that "our view is that there is no black v. white, military v. civilian technology. All technology is just different shades of gray" [U.S. Congress, Office of Technology Assessment, 1990, p. 106].

TRDI is committed to building weapons that are based on national technologies. Considering the narrowness of Japan's present base of militarily relevant technologies, this project may not become a viable policy for another decade or two, especially if the United States chooses to oppose this policy. But the general direction of Japan's technology-based procurement policy is unmistakeable [Interview No.6, Tokyo, December 10, 1991]. According to a senior Japanese official, the increasing competition from the Newly Industrializing Countries (NICs) is forcing the Japanese into high-value added industries. "We have to go value-added, and all that is left is space and defense" [Vogel, 1989, p.73]. Other government agencies such as MOF and the Economic Planning Agency concur and jointly proposed in 1983 a "stimulation of investments and both internal and external development by increasing the involvement of private investors even in those sectors which are traditionally reserved for the State or which are at present limited or hampered by . . . laws passed in the peculiar atmosphere of the first years after the war" [Drifte, 1986a, p.53].

As is true of many of the modern weapon systems that it is building under license from the United States, Japan's broader technological push enjoys American support. In the area of C3I, for example, Japan's technological advances have led to both a closer integration with the United States while at the same time creating as well a technological capacity for Japan's greater autonomy in the future. In the 1960s and 1970s Japan's SDF had moved much more cautiously in this direction than had other government agencies, such as the NPA or large corporations [Yomiuri Shimbun, March 23, 1983]. Bobrow, for example writes that earthquake-disaster management moved Japan "to develop survivable systems of communications, command and control. These measures are by and large regarded, even by many on the left of Japanese politics, as in a different category from rearmament . . . because they use technologies attractive for civil purposes . . . At the same time they can be presented to the United States as signs of a trend in favor of more formidable military defense capability" [Bobrow, 1984, p.43]. These efforts remained fairly rudimentary, however. But since a defecting Soviet pilot landed a MIG-23 undetected in Hokkaido in 1976, Japan's policy has gradually improved its C3I capabilities.

Traditionally Japan has had a very extensive intelligence exchange with the United States. Signal intelligence and satellite photographs are apparently quite frequently swapped. And it is likely that the JDA receives regularly either satellite photographs or satellite photograph-derived information concerning Soviet and Russian naval and air activity and capability in the vicinity of Japan, as well as the deployment of troops and weapons like the SS-20. In the Intelligence Exchange Conference between the U.S. Commander-in-Chief Pacific Fleet and the MSDF "the most extensive exchange undoubtedly occurs with respect to ocean surveillance information, particularly regarding Soviet naval movements" [Richelson, 1988, p.266]. In the 1980s a report prepared by the Crisis Control Affairs Group, headed by a Cabinet minister and dealing with measures to counter national emergencies, recommended that the JDA should operate its own reconnaissance satellite rather than just relying only on U.S. intelligence [Mainichi Shimbun, November 22, 1984]. Thus it comes as no surprise that the C3I system of the SDF may be more closely linked with the U.S. Forces than with Japan's civilian government. "When the SDF submarine Nadashio collided with a fishing boat in July 1988, which resulted in 30 civilian deaths, the U.S. Seventh Fleet knew of the incident in two or three minutes, but it took some 20 minutes for the Japanese Coast Guard to receive information on the incident from the SDF" [Takahara, 1992a, p.18].

The SDF is currently in the middle of building an Integrated Defense Digital Network (IDDN) which will serve as a technologically advanced information grid for integrating defense capabilites all over Japan. Although the SDF are prohibited by Diet resolutions passed in 1969, from using outerspace for military purposes, in the 1980s the MSDF began to transmit information through communications satellites. One of them was the Fleetsat satellite used by the U.S. Navy. By 1993 the MSDF and the GSDF are scheduled to activate a transponder on the American "superbird" satellite, launched by the Mitsubishi-affiliated Space Communications Corporation. According to a government interpretation advanced in 1985, it is permissible for the SDF to use dual-purpose satellites. The use of surveillance satellites will be controversial, but may get on the agenda in the future [Asahi Shimbun, May 31, 1992, 13th edition. Davis, 1984a. Drifte, 1990b, pp.18-21. Fujishima, 1992, pp.176-78. Interview Nos. 15, 16, 20, and 21, Tokyo, June 17, 18, and 19, 1991. Daily Yomiuri, March 23, 1983]. By 1995, an intelligence organization integrating the operations of the SDF with those of civilians in the JDA is scheduled to be in place. It may be put under the authority of the JSC. About 20 years ago the SDF blocked a proposal by JDA chief Nakasone to integrate the intelligence operations of JDA civilians and the three branches of the SDF for fear of losing control over intelligence to the civilians. Now, in contrast, an integration of intelligence gathering is viewed more favorably by the SDF as an useful way for bringing civilians and military professionals into closer contact [Interview No.21, Tokyo, June 19, 1991].

The United States is fully supportive of this growing Japanese capability which, it hopes, will add to American sources of intelligence in Asia. In the 1980s the exchange of intelligence between the two countries became more extensive. However, the United States does not share all important information with Japan. Although the U.S. appears to have been generous in providing the Japanese military with the information it requested, the asymmetry in the relation was a source of unease for the Japanese [Interview No.8, Tokyo, December 11, 1991]. The United States and Japan reportedly completed in 1989 a two-years, classified study of the improvement of mutual communication, with a specific focus on C3I. Simply for reasons of topography and geography the U.S. Navy in particular has supported the free flow of information and intelligence between the two countries [Interview No.8, Tokyo, June 13, 1991. Richelson, 1988]. The additional Japanese capabilities would simply intensify the extensive flow of intelligence between the two countries.

The Gulf War has driven home the same point in Japan as all over the world. A first-rate C3I capablility is the essential, first requirement for succeeding in future conventional wars. Japan's technological leadership in areas such as the manufacturing of sensors and computergraphics will make it, together with the human intelligence of interpreting especially Asian data, an important source of high-quality intelligence. For example, Japanese not American intelligence officials established in the spring of 1991 that North Korea was perhaps operating a nuclear facility not serving civilian purposes. An enhanced national command capability may be supportive of and supported by governments of the United States and Japan as a further strengthening of the security arrangements between the two countries. But such capability contributes also to the creation of a national option.

The growing dependence of the United States on Japan in some defense-related areas reflects a shifting balance of technological strength between the two countries. Traditionally much of the defense technology that Japanese firms relied upon was American. Technology transfers have been a fundamental aspect of Japan's defense procurement policy with the added benefit that they "offered the greatest technological benefits to domestic industry" [Chinworth, 1990a, p.197]. But the growth of a new form of technological nationalism has made this form of technology import policy increasingly problematic. With Japan making deep inroads into some of the traditional strongholds of American industry, especially in high-tech areas, Congress has been increasingly hesitant to permit Japanese corporations to share in the defense technologies in which the U.S. has invested enormous resources—the United States spends currently 140 times more on military R and D than does Japan [Pempel, 1990a, p.19. Interview No.2, Tokyo, June 11,1991]. Trade protection in Congress has been strong throughout the 1980s; but that protectionism has acquired an ominous undertone particularly when it touches on defense-related companies or industries, as evidenced by Fujitsu's attempted take-over of Fairchild, the Toshiba sales to the Soviet Union and the application of clause 2332 of the Trade Enhancement Act, which aims at defending domestic industries for national security reasons [Inoguchi, 1991a, pp.93-99].

With its rapid move to the frontiers of civilian high-technology industries Japan has become, in a non-traditional sense, a major military power, mostly without a conscious plan. The U.S. Critical Technologies Plan for 1990 argues that the United States lags the Soviet Union in only one out of twenty technologies crucial to the long-term technological superiority of American weapons systems. Japan, however, leads in five areas: semiconductors, robotics, superconductivity, certain areas of biotechnology, and photonics [Vogel, 1990, p.3. Vogel, 1991, pp.6-9]. Informed American observers predict that several key technologies are likely to leave a major impact on the weapons of the future: very high speed integrated circuits, digital gallium arsenide circuits, microwave monolithic integrated circuits, fiber optic communications, image and speech recognition, ceramics, flat displays and mercury cadmium telluride for infrared detectors. Japanese firms are very strongly positioned in the development of these technologies [Vogel, 1990, pp.3-4. Keddell, 1990, p.249. Vogel, 1991, p.56]. Controlling important segments of the global semiconductor market will give Japanese firms the power to cut off American defense contractors from a vital raw material for their production. Furthermore establishing a lead in civilian product cycles becomes a major military asset because civilian product cycles are only two or three years long while military product cycles evolve over five to fifteen years [Vogel, 1990, p.4]. And while Japan is becoming less dependent on American military technology, America is evidently becoming more dependent on Japanese commercial technology. The export of dual-use components is likely to be a mainstay of Japan's militarily relevant exports—without a change in the existing policy prohibiting military sales [U.S. Congress, 1991, pp. 108-09]. Clyde Prestowitz for one concludes that "while the United States has sought security by giving away technology, Japan has sought it by hoarding technology, even from the United States, its primary source" [Prestowitz, 1988, p.140].

Japan's policies for reducing its vulnerability in international energy markets and increasing its technological autonomy have been as flexible in adjusting to changing conditions as they have been persistent. The reason lies in the structures and normative context in which the government debated and implemented policies dealing with the economic aspects of Japan's security.

B. Military Dimensions of Security

In sharp contrast to Japan's flexible policy of adjustment on issues of economic security, on military questions Japan's security policy has been very rigid in adjusting to change. The transnational pressure from the United States for an enlarged defense role has clashed with the political restraints under which the military operates in Japan's domestic politics. And it has been counteracted as well by the normative context in which Japan's security policy is considered and acted upon.

1. The One Percent Ceiling.

Japan's defense policy is probably known best for its commitment to keep defense spending below or close to one per cent of GNP. Like all political symbols this one has ambiguous meanings. According to the way NATO member states calculate military expenditures, that is including pensions and annuities, Japan's defense expenditures amount to about 1.6 percent of GNP. But for a variety of reasons in Japan these annuities and pensions are included in the budget of the Ministry for Health and Welfare. Japan's one percent policy did not result from a sudden conversion to pacifism after losing a long and bloody war. The ceiling resulted instead from the high economic growth after the mid-1950s and conscious policy choices since the mid-1970s [Sakanaka, 1990, p.61]. The comparison with the United States and the Soviet Union is striking. With defense spending of about 5 to 7 percent of GNP throughout most of the postwar period according to Seymour Melman between 1947 and 1989, the U.S. Department of Defense spent 8.2 trillion in 1982 dollars, about 10 percent more than the combined value of America's industry and infrastructure investment in 1982 [New York Times, June 3, 1990 p.F12]. And arguably one of the important causes of the demise of Communism and the break-up of the Soviet Union were enormous defense outlays that were totally out of line with the underlying weakness of the Soviet economy.

Japanese defense expenditures declined from a high of about 1.8 percent in 1955 to around 0.8 percent by the mid-1960s. This decline was a result of the Yoshida foreign policy line which stressed economic reconstruction over security issues, of a self-conscious policy after 1954 to eschew Japan's traditional emphasis on military production, and of the strong performance of the Japanese economy since the mid-1950s. The one percent ceiling was announced as a formal commitment of the government by the Miki Cabinet in 1976 [Calder, 1988, pp.411-39. Holland, 1988, pp.49-52. Chuma, 1987. Hook, 1988, pp.389-90. Drifte, 1985b, pp.154-55. Drifte 1985a, pp.20-26. Vogel, 1989, p.68. Kurokawa, 1985. Masuoka, 1989. Nanto, 1981. Sakanaka, 1990, p.61]. In a period of political weakness for the LDP at home and detente abroad, the public mood favored reigning in defense spending. In response, the government gave up formulating a five-years defense buildup plan starting from 1977, which was projected to involve expenditures twice as large as those under the fourth plan. It adopted the NDPO instead and packaged it with the one percent ceiling [Otake, 1983a, pp.133-37]. The NDPO, which set quantitative limits to Japan's overall defense force, and the ceiling, which imposed a limit on annual defense spending, were designed to assure the public and the opposition parties that defense spending would be kept under control. The creation of the NDPO did not arouse domestic political opposition. Rather criticism came from the SDF which viewed its concept of "basic defense force" as belittling the need to counter existing threats [Hirose, 1989, pp.176-84, 200-01]. As a package the one percent ceiling and the NDPO focused also on a streamlining of military spending and a general change in the process of formulating defense policy [Interview No.23, Kyoto, June 24, 1991. Umemoto, 1985a, pp.49-50. L'Estrange, 1990, pp.16-17. Endicott, 1982a, pp.452-54. Tanaka, 1990, p.6]. With the adoption of the NDPO the government ceased to formulate defense plans for a fixed time period [Han, 1983, pp.688-95]. Instead under the pressure of fiscal uncertainty caused by the inflation of the mid-1970s, the government adopted what it called the "single fiscal-year formula." But for political reasons this formula did not work. Because of the inconvenience of preparing budget requests annually in the absence of a five-year plan, the JDA began to draw up the Mid-Term Defense Program Estimate (MTDPE) in 1978. Reformulated every three years, these estimates listed the number of major weapon systems which were to be bought in a given five-years period. These estimates, however, expressed only the plans of the JDA and were not approved by the MOF, not to speak of the NDC or the Cabinet. But they began to acquire political importance when the U.S. government pressed strongly in the 1980s for a quickening of the pace at which they were to be realized, and when they were utilized in the formulation of the defense budget inside the Japanese government [Hirose, 1989, pp.209-10, 228].

The one percent ceiling promised moderate growth in defense spending and thus was an acceptable compromise among the MOF, the JDA and the defense specialists inside the LDP. Originally this limit helped the JDA in procuring funds from the MOF. But when the economy turned sluggish in the late 1970s and early 1980s the MOF imposed strict controls in the name of fiscal prudence and thus made it very difficult for the JDA to meet the goals of the defense build-up as articulated in the NDPO and the Mid-Term Defense Program Estimate [Keddell, 1990, pp.41-94. Otake, 1982. Holland, 1988, pp.53-57. Auer, 1988]. Japan's defense spending was a major item on the agenda at the U.S.-Japan summit in May 1980. President Carter suggested at the meeting an early attainment of the MTDPE goals. But Prime Minister Ohira, while calling Japan an ally of the U.S., avoided making any specific commitment. It was after Ohira's unexpected death that year that the Japanese government's resistance to defense budget increases weakened [Keddell, 1990, pp.151-52. Otake, 1983a, pp.348-50].

Even though defense spending increased sharply in the 1980s, relative to other budgetary items, because of fiscal constraints the government was forced to announce in 1984 that it would have to push back the target date for Japan's defense build-up from 1988 to 1991 [Keddell, 1990, pp.110-28]. The one percent ceiling was evidently prevailing over American pressure for an acceleration of Japan's defense build-up. Nakasone failed in his attempt in 1985 to formally rescind the ceiling. But the path to the scrapping of the ceiling was carefully paved by a Cabinet decision in September of that year. It elevated the MTDPE to an official government plan, which would be much more authoritative, and approved the spending of 18.4 trillion yen between 1986 and 1990. The Cabinet's commitment to the spending of such a sum and the projected GNP growth made it certain that sooner or later defense expenditure would exceed the one percent limit [Maswood, 1990, p.56. Shiota, 1987, pp.144-45]. Subsequently, in proposing a defense budget for FY 1987 that amounted to 1.004 percent of GNP, the Nakasone government dismantled the symbolic figure [Berger, 1992, pp.490-501. Johnson, 1986, pp.567-70. Holland, 1988, p.52]. In a decision in January 1987, the Cabinet formally abolished the ceiling. But at the same time, it declared that the total outlays authorized by the government for the period between 1986 and 1990 (18.4 trillion yen) would be the limit replacing the one percent ceiling [Asagumo Shimbun-sha, 1991, p.25]. That is, as in 1976, for reasons of assuaging domestic opposition, the government sought to package the breaking of the one percent barrier with some official limit on defense expenditures. Furthermore, the Cabinet decision stated that the "spirit" of the 1976 decision on the one percent ceiling would continue to be respected [Asagumo Shimbun-sha, 1991, p.25]. And Nakasone, pointing to the fact that the planned outlays of 18.4 trillion yen would amount to 1.02 percent of GNP on a yearly basis, emphasized that the decision involved no significant departure from previous policy [Maswood, 1990, p.61]. It needs to be noted, however, that according to the Cabinet decision in January 1987 defense budgets after 1990 would be determined upon consideration of the "international situation, economic and fiscal circumstances, etc." [Asagumo Shimbun-sha, 1991, p.25]. There was left open "the possibility that over the long term the ceiling may not exist" [Maswood, 1990, p.61]. The idea of the NDPO to discard five-years plans thus has not survived bureaucratic, domestic and international political pressures. However, the figure for Japan's defense spending has hovered around the one percent mark (1.013 percent in 1988, 1.006 in 1989, 0.997 in 1990, and 0.954 in 1991) [Asagumo Shimbun-sha, 1991, p.239. Defense Agency, 1990, pp.163,291]. The three percent increase currently planned for 1991-95 will bring defense spending probably below one percent of GNP.

Throughout the 1980s the United States pressured Japan to increase its defense budget. Considering Japan's growing wealth American policymakers and politicians have often pointed to what they called an American "defense subsidy" for Japan. According to one estimate between 1952 and 1974 the cumulative costs for Japan of having to pay national defense expenditures that were average for the industrial states might have been as high as 30 percent of Japan's GNP [Okimoto, 1982a, p.251]. In that case annual economic growth might have been lowered by as much as 2 percent annually [Patrick and Rosovsky, 1976, pp.44-45]. Another study estimates that if Japan had a defense budget of 5 percent, the value of America's security guarantee amounted to about 300 billion dollars for the 1970s and to about 50 billion dollars a year in the early 1980s [Cordesman, 1983a, p.28. Lockwood, 1985]. These figures contrast to some extent with the conclusions of a simulation suggesting that "economic growth in Japan is not dependent on keeping defense expenditures below 1 percent of GNP . . . Japan's economy is clearly capable today of sustaining substantially larger defense outlays without suffering serious setbacks in either the rate of growth or the size of the economy" [Okimoto, 1982a, pp.263-64]. Another study confirms these calculations for the high-growth decade of the 1960s. Had Japan's defense/GNP ratio been 6.5 percent, or approximately the U.S. level, the effect on Japan's growth rate would have been a modest decline from 9.29 to 8.76 percent [Dekle, 1989, p.127].

The reasons for a continued increase in Japan's defense budget include the inconclusive end of the Cold War in Asia; the delayed payment practices of the JDA; and, most importantly, the political pressure from the United States for burdensharing, coupled with a further thinning of the military presence of the United States in the Pacific. In addition the substantial research outlays of private industry in military technologies, in anticipation of future decisions in favor of development and profits far healthier than in commercial products, also push total defense outlays upward. Even though Japan is increasing real defense expenditures while virtually all other industrial states are cutting defense expenditures sharply, Japan's relative defense spending remains by far the lowest among all of America's major allies [Interview No.1, Tokyo, June 11, 1991]. The one percent limit has raised over the years deep concern and resentment in the United States, especially in Congress, about the issue of equitable burdensharing between the two countries [Holland, 1988, pp.26,16-17,51]. But in sharp contrast to other security issues directly related to the Japanese military, American pressure has not been able to shift Japanese policy significantly.

One important reason lies in the fact that the Japanese Left both inside and outside the Diet, despite its increasing acceptance of the SDF, has continued to hold the government as close as possible to the one percent figure, in full knowledge that on the issue of limited defense spending it enjoys substantial public support. Furthermore, the JSP's outlook is shared to some extent by some segments in Japan's conservative political coalition that regard defense spending as economically wasteful and politically useless. The politics of defense spending illustrate the rigidity of policy adaptation when the normative context is politically deeply contested. Once uttered in the Diet political restrictions quickly consolidate into an official government position that adds to the numerous built-in brakes imposed on Japan's security policy. "The policy of abandoning the 1% ceiling is characteristic of the step-by-step approach to change that often seems inconsequential to many foreigners. Yet it falls within a familiar pattern that can eventually lead to significant shifts in policy" [Holland, 1988, p.52]. Japan's economic growth also has to some extent vitiated the effect of a limitation on the relative share of Japan's defense expenditures. By the early

1990s the MSDF, for example, had over 50 destroyers, about twice as many as the Seventh Fleet of the United States. And the ASDF also commands a significant force, although still considerably smaller than the 850 fighter and attack aircrafts that the United States deploy in Asia. Nevertheless, the limitations imposed on defense spending since 1976 have been a reassurance for the Japanese public and opposition parties that the government's restrained military policy would continue. And these limitations sought to convince members of the conservative camp that macroeconomic considerations remained a vital aspect of Japan's security [Bobrow and Hill, 1986].

2. Sending the SDF Overseas.

Policy rigidity has also marked a second issue, Japan's steadfast refusal to send members of the SDF abroad in combat roles, even as members of U.N. peacekeeping missions. This policy resulted from a deliberate policy of caution and restraint rooted in the traumatic experience of losing a disastrous war. During the Korean War Japan was much more fully involved on the Korean peninsula than was being publicly revealed at the time [McNelly, 1987, p.9]. Although no Japanese soldiers fought in Korea, Japanese shipping and railroad experts and crews worked in Korea under American or U.N. command. Their number ran into the thousands. Between October and December 1950 Japan deployed 46 minesweepers manned by 1,200 men; two boats were sunk, one man was killed and eight men were injured [Auer, 1973a, p.49. 1973b, pp.64-66]. Almost one-third of the support ships of the Inchon amphibious landing were manned by Japanese crews [Olsen, 1985, pp.75-76]. But this involvement occurred under the Occupation.

Although the issue of Japan's possible participation in U.N. peacekeeping operations had been an issue of discussion and analysis inside MOFA, throughout the postwar era strong public opposition always had lent such bureaucratic discussions an air of unreality. The U.N. requested the Japanese government to send SDF officers to Lebanon in 1958, but the request was denied. In response to the U.N. Security Council's passing of a resolution to impose economic sanctions against Rhodesia the MOFA drafted the U.N. Resolutions Cooperation Bill in 1965. But with the opposition parties and parts of the government firmly resisting, the bill was not submitted to the Diet. In 1969 Prime Minister Sato stated that Japan would participate in "any international peacekeeping machinery" which might be set up in Vietnam after a ceasefire had been negotiated [Emmerson, 1971, p.130]. In 1983 a MOFA advisory group suggested

Japanese participation in peacekeeping operations, but again because of stiff domestic opposition, the government decided against making such a commitment to the U.N. [Asahi Shimbun, September 26, 1991, 13th ed.]. When the U.S.-Japan Advisory Commission recommended in 1984 that the SDF participate in U.N. peacekeeping operations public sentiment backed, at most, Japan's participation in international disaster relief operations [Mainichi Shimbun, October 6, 1984].

In mid-1987 the United States asked its NATO allies as well as Japan to assist the U.S. navy by sending destroyers and minesweepers for the protection of international shipping in the Gulf against potential attacks from Iran and Iraq. While the Security Division of the Foreign Ministry as well as the Prime Minister were leaning toward complying with the request, Cabinet Chief Secretary Gotoda was adamantly opposed. Gotoda argued that compliance with the U.S. request would violate Japan's postwar policy of not allowing Japanese military personnel to be part of an exercise of force overseas. Such a move might endanger Japanese ships and involve Japan in hostilities [Keddell, 1990, p.230].

In response to the crisis following Iraq's invasion of Kuwait, the United States again suggested in August 1990 that Japan send minesweepers and tankers to the Gulf [Ministry of Foreign Affairs, 1991b. Purrington and A.K., 1991. Pohl, 1991. Buruma, 1991. Tamamoto, 1990-91. Inoguchi, 1991b. Katahara, 1991]. The Japanese government refused to comply again on the grounds that minesweepers might get drawn into hostilities. SDF ships were finally sent to the Gulf in April 1991—after the end of the war. The MSDF had carefully prepared for this eventuality since August 1990. And after the end of the war MOFA's Security Division also had begun to consider seriously this policy option. Various factors worked in favor of deployment. Germany's decision to send minesweepers prodded the MOFA into a stronger advocacy role for Japan taking a similar stance. MITI recognized the need for sending minesweepers so that the Japanese-owned Arabian Oil Company could again begin exporting oil from Saudi Arabian ports. Yet MITI apparently refrained from taking a public stance, preferring instead business organizations to press for the dispatch of SDF ships. Public opinion supported this move. According to one poll conducted in March 1991, 63 percent of the respondents backed the policy while 29 percent were opposed. Some of the opposition parties were not strongly opposed either. Komeito did not formally approve the dispatch of the minesweepers. But the government's decision enjoyed the support of a substantial number of Komeito's Diet members [Asahi Shimbun, May 4, 6, 9, 10 ,15, 16, and 18, 1991, 13th ed.]. This episode clearly indicated that the categorical opposition to the overseas deployment of the SDF had lost some of its persuasiveness in Japanese domestic politics [Interview Nos. 1, 4, 5 and 18,

Tokyo, June 11, 12 and 18, 1991. Ogata, 1987]. It is unlikely, however, that Japan will quickly move to extend its participation in multinational military action authorized by the U.N., despite the dramatic changes in the international system that appear to many observers, especially in the United States, to suggest such a change in policy as a necessary adjustment in the post-Cold War era.

The United Nations Peace Cooperation Bill that Prime Minister Kaifu introduced in the Diet in October 1990 revealed the political constraints under which the government was operating. The U.N. Peace Cooperation Corps that the government was proposing to institute was to be composed of volunteers on loan from government agencies including the SDF and the Maritime Safety Agency which is part of the Ministry of Transportation. Its task was to include a variety of noncombatant functions including the monitoring of a truce, administrative consultations with governments after the cessation of hostilities, the monitoring of elections, the provision of medical, transportation and communication services, and the rendering of assistance to refugees and reconstruction activities. Under no circumstances was the Corps to be allowed to engage in the "use of force" or the "threat of the use of force." Like a police force members of the Corps would only carry small weapons to be used exclusively for self-protection. But according to the bill the Corps would be permitted to cooperate with nations acting to put U.N. resolutions into effect. Diet deliberations made clear that the government intended to have the SDF operate in the area of logistics and support for multinational forces deployed in the Gulf at the time. Critics contended that cooperation with the multinational forces, even if restricted to logistics and support, would constitute an use of force. Thus only 20 to 30 percent of the public backed the bill [Tanaka, 1990, p.19]. All opposition parties were against it, and even inside the LDP less than half of the Lower House members supported the bill [Asahi Shimbun, November 9 and 10, 1990, 13th ed.]. The bill died in November 1990 in the Diet without having been put to a vote.

In September 1991, the government submitted the United Nations Peacekeeping Operations Cooperation Bill to the Diet. According to one public opinion poll, in June 1991 50 percent of the public were for and 40 percent were against the SDF's participation in peacekeeping operations of the United Nations [Asahi Shimbun, June 19, 1991, 10th ed.]. The writing of the new bill evidently took into account the low level of support the 1990 version had generated. The bill restricted itself to authorizing the SDF's participation in U.N. peacekeeping operations and humanitarian international rescue operations. The 1980 Cabinet decision which interpreted Article 9 of the Constitution as prohibiting sending the SDF overseas with any mission involving the use of force remained a major obstacle for the government in preparing the 1991 bill. Whether the use of arms, in the face of organized attack, by the dispatched SDF personnel constitutes legitimate self-defense or exemplifies a use of force banned by the constitution was a major issue debated inside the government [Interview No.19, Tokyo, June 18, 1991]. The final version of the government bill apparently decided in favor of the latter interpretation. It made overseas deployment of the SDF as part of a peacekeeping operation conditional on the opposing sides' agreement to a ceasefire, their acceptance of the deployment of the peacekeeping force, and the neutrality of that force [Asahi Shimbun, September 19, 1991, 11th ed.]. Furthermore, in order to prevent the use of force by Japanese personnel abroad, the government claimed that the SDF would not be placed under the operational command of the United Nations. SDF personnel would be permitted to use arms only for individual self-defense, not as part of any organized military action [Tanaka, 1991, pp.40-41]. This attenuated version of the original legislation passed the Lower House in 1991 and was sent to the Upper House.

The government's interpretation of Article 9 appears to have made compliance with Japan's Constitution incompatible with United Nations norms on peacekeeping operations. Whether it would be feasible to maintain a national command over SDF personnel deployed abroad on peacekeeping operations was one of the major points of contention in the Diet debates [Sasaki, 1991, p.202]. Placement of SDF personnel under U.N. command would require a major change in the government's interpretation of Article 9. Thus the government faced a difficult dilemma. The bill was amended in the Upper House, and it passed both Houses in June 1992. The final version of the bill did not resolve the dilemma. But it froze, until authorization by a future law, SDF participation in peacekeeping operations that might involve a combat role. Furthermore, the three party coalition supporting the final bill informally agreed not to implement SDF participation in logistical operations such as the transporting of weapons [Asahi Shimbun, June 16, 1992, 13th edition]. SDF units sent abroad under the new law will "stay far from the sound of gunfire" [Sanger, 1992b, p.E4]. The final compromise is consistent with the public's response to the bill. In a public opinion poll taken in November 1991, 33 percent of the respondents were in favor of and 58 percent were against SDF participation in lightly armed peacekeeping forces whose mission it was to separate combatants [Asahi Shimbun, May 1, 1992, 13th edition].

Participation in U.N. peacekeeping operations is not the only option for dispatching the SDF overseas. In the public's perception the most valuable part of the SDF does not lie in the protection it provides for Japan but in its emergency relief operations. This predilection for the fight against nature over the fight against man provides a supportive public climate for

Japan's participation in international relief efforts. After the 1987 earthquake in Mexico, Japan was severely criticized for its refusal to participate in the ensuing international relief effort. Legislation subsequently adopted in 1987 explicitly excluded SDF personnel from participation and provided for the sending of volunteer experts in various fields. When Bangladesh was hit by a typhoon in the summer of 1991 causing more than 100,000 fatalities, Japan dispatched two helicopters and a rescue team of firemen [Interview Nos.1,4 and 16, Tokyo, June 11 and 17, 1991]. In 1991 the government submitted to the Diet a bill amending the disaster relief legislation of 1987 to permit the sending of SDF personnel abroad [Asahi Shimbun, March 16, 1992, 13th edition. Interview No.19, Tokyo, June 18, 1991]. The bill passed the Diet in June 1992 [Asahi Shimbun, June 16, 1992, 13th edition].

With the number of overseas Japanese increasing from 300,000 to 600,000 between 1980 and 1990 an advisory committee to the MOFA recommended in the summer of 1991 that the government should increase its capability, including transport planes and telecommunications, to get in touch with potential crisis points around the globe to protect Japanese living overseas [Interview No.22, Tokyo, June 19, 1991]. In 1992 the government submitted an amendment of the SDF Law to the Diet. It would permit SDF aircrafts to rescue Japanese citizens overseas in case of emergency. Although the government maintained at the same time that the SDF would not be dispatched overseas in cases that might require the use of force, the amendment met strong opposition in the Diet [Asahi Shimbun, March 11, 16, 19, April 5, May 8, 1992, 13th edition]. In the 1990s Japan will confront also the issue of how to secure the shipment of plutonium from France to Japan. While a decision has been taken to have members of the Maritime Safety Agency (MSA) rather than of the MSDF accompany such transports, the fear of a possible "seajacking" by terrorists could reopen the discussion [Sanger, 1989]. Overseas police-style protection operations and the dispatch of relief teams thus are plausible political options for the deployment of Japanese military personnel overseas.

In this entire controversy the JDA has taken a strong interest. But it has been cautious in its attitude towards the possible overseas deployment of the SDF. In June 1991 the JDA announced that it favored sending SDF personnel abroad, but only for the purpose of helping in disaster relief operations and for overseeing elections and ceasefires in U.N. peacekeeping operations. The JDA remained, however, skeptical about having the SDF participate in peacekeeping operations that involve them in a combat role. The reason for this hesitancy was quite clear. The JDA did not want to subject the SDF to political controversy while public suspicion against it still remained quite strong. In contrast, the MOFA, possibly with an eye toward

Japan's involvement in the Cambodian peace process, became a strong advocate of the participation of the SDF in peacekeeping operations [Asahi Shimbun, June 8 and August 16, 1991, 13th ed.]. A second reason for the caution of the JDA was its overriding interest in defining a new role for the SDF in coping with regional conflicts, in cooperation with the United States, as the Russian threat in East Asia declined. Compared to this task Japan's involvement in peacekeeping operations was less important for the JDA. The JDA is not in principle opposed to the SDF's participation in such operations. But in contrast to establishing a new regional mission for the SDF, it deems peacekeeping operations at this time to be of secondary importance [Asahi Shimbun, September 12 and 27, 1991, 13th ed.]. The prospect of committing perhaps several thousand men to peacekeeping at a time of severe personnel shortage has also been a deterrent. And the SDF has been acutely aware of the negative effects that a difficult peacekeeping mission might have on the morale of the SDF as well as the prospects for successful recruitment [Taoka, 1991, p.16].

The issue of sending military personnel abroad illustrates with great clarity the rigidity of Japan's security policy even though the pressure from the United States and rapidly changing conditions in the international system made policy flexibility appear advantageous to some. But the constraints of Japan's domestic structures and the normative context in which its security policy was defined appeared to prevent major changes in Japan's security policy in the early 1990s.

3. The Three Non-Nuclear Principles.

The Japanese public opposes nuclear weapons probably more strongly than the public in any other Western state [Mendel, 1961, pp.151-68. Okimoto, 1982b. Drifte, 1990b, pp.23-29. Emmerson, 1971, pp.339-61. Endicott, 1975, pp.91-101. Sorenson, 1975. Akaha, 1985a, p.83. Hatsuse, 1986, p.77. Toyoda, 1985]. In 1987 1,067 communities, including seven prefectures and 400 cities, had declared themselves as nuclear-free zones as compared with 180 in Britain and 154 in West Germany [Drifte, 1990b, p.26]. Furthermore, the three non-nuclear principles have been an integral part of Japan's national security. In the words of former Prime Minister Sato this means "not to make such [nuclear] weapons, not to possess them, and not to bring them into Japan" [Sigur, 1975, p.187]. Prime Minister Kishi had stated as early as 1959 that "Japan would neither develop nuclear weapons nor permit them to be brought into the country" [Kubo, 1978, p.109]. In the words of Tsuneo Akaha "the nonnuclear principles have been supported by a national consensus from which the government cannot deviate without risking a major political turmoil" [Akaha, 1985a, p.75]. Japan's Prime Ministers and Foreign Ministers typically refer to the principles as the nation's irrevocable policy (kokuze). In contrast to the German military, Japanese defense officials have never participated in any American nuclear war planning. Thus "the Japanese approach is one of total reliance on American strategy" [Van de Velde, 1988b, p.29]. The political sanctity of this non-nuclear norm, and the anticipated public outcry should it be violated, explains perhaps why the number of research institutes dealing with defense issues remains very small [Akaha, 1985a, p.83]; why few party politicians command the relevant technical expertise; and why the policymakers in the JDA and SDF have no particular interest in the issue of Japan's nuclear armament.

The trauma of Hiroshima and Nagasaki, it is sometimes argued, has instilled in Japan, perhaps more than in any other society, a profound commitment to the peaceful resolution of all diplomatic conflicts. The metaphor of "Japan's nuclear allergy" as a disease that needs to be overcome reflects the fact that language is an instrument in the political conflict over the norms that inform Japanese security policy [Hook, 1990, pp.67-85]. The political discourse surrounding Japan's security policy is ambiguous and often lacks strategic rationale. For the different views on national security "are only marginally related to external events" [Tsurutani, 1980, p.176]. But it is also true, as Masataka Kosaka has pointed out, that "Japan should not be too proud of its position on nuclear weapons, for its policies were not created intentionally; Japan's security policy was born out of necessity and has developed through the interaction of opposing points of view. It is, in a word, an accidental product of circumstances and politics" [Kosaka, 1986, p.135].

The fear of the Japanese public of being drawn into an escalating Vietnam war and the great unease in Japan spawned by China's nuclear test explosions as well as by the prospect of the reversion of Okinawa without the removal of U.S. nuclear weapons prompted Prime Minister Sato in 1967 to spell out the three non-nuclear principles as one of the central tenets of Japan's security policy—not to possess nuclear weapons, not to produce them, and not to permit their introduction into Japan [L'Estrange, 1990, p.4. Takahara, 1992b, p.38]. The specific occasion for this announcement was a Diet debate on the reversion of Okinawa to Japan. But as Prime Minister Sato declared before the Diet in the following year, the three non-nuclear principles were only one of four pillars of Japan's nuclear policy. It included as well promotion of worldwide disarmament, reliance on the U.S. nuclear deterrence, and peaceful use of nuclear energy [Hook, 1988, p.387]. Japan's non-nuclear policy was thus neither total, nor unconnected to a pressing political problem of the day, the conclusion of an agreement between the United States and Japan concerning Okinawa. Nonetheless, the principle was soon embraced by both the public and the political elite in the Diet. On November 24, 1971, when the Lower House finally voted on the reversion of Okinawa, it also adopted a formal resolution that, among others, expressed support for the three non-nuclear principles [Akaha, 1984, pp.852-53]. And this policy was reaffirmed when Japan decided in 1976 to ratify the Nonproliferation Treaty (NPT) [Okimoto, 1978a, 1978b. Endicott, 1982a, pp.457-58].

The domestic consensus against the possession and production of nuclear weapons is overwhelmingly strong. When Prime Minister Nakasone refused once to recognize the three non-nuclear principles explicitly as an "irrevocable" policy, and referred to them simply as an "important" policy, he caused a political storm. Subsequently he changed his position in public and apologized for his "lack of understanding" of the government's long-standing policy [Akaha, 1984, p.872]. With the anti-nuclear movement gaining strength in Japan, Prime Minister Nakasone pledged that Japan would not permit U.S. warships carrying Tomahawk nuclear cruise missiles to enter Japanese ports. But six months later he changed his stance and announced that the United States could use nuclear weapons in joint U.S.-Japanese defense operations, should Japan's actual survival be at stake. "The Mutual Security Treaty was again cited as the rationale for applying what, in this case, was regarded as an extremely flexible interpretation of Japan's non-nuclear principles" [Tow, 1986, p.132]. Analogously, the 1989 Defense White Paper dropped the adjective "basic" from its description of Japan's non-nuclear policy. After serious criticisms from the opposition in the Diet, the JDA chose through what it referred to as an "editorial" change, to restore the original wording in the 1990 edition of the White Paper.

A widely-publicized discussion before the Diet in 1978 reconfirmed the impression that the government's non-nuclear policy since the late 1950s had been a matter of policy discretion rather than a constitutional requirement [Kamo, 1982, pp.188-89]. Prime Minister Kishi had stated this very clearly in 1959. The first White Paper on Defense in 1970 claimed that small-size nuclear weapons were defensive and thus legally permissible. In the same year the head of the Cabinet Legislation Bureau, Masami Takatsuji, broadened the scope of defense capabilities by including explicitly "defensive nuclear weapons", a position that Prime Minister Sato supported explicitly [Van de Velde, 1988a, pp.239-40]. The "possession of nuclear weapons, it is widely believed by the Japanese people, would violate Article IX, yet no Japanese government has ever declared the possession of nuclear weapons unconstitutional" [Van de Velde, 1988b, p.19. Endicott, 1975, pp.41-46]. Considering its official policy and the public's deep aversion,

Japan's possible acquisition of nuclear weapons "expresses a latent interest in maintaining a nuclear weapons option" [Van de Velde, 1988b, p.20. Olsen, 1985, p.112]. It remains at present no more than an abstract political possibility. It is thus likely that "neither the Japanese government nor the private sector will call, in the foreseeable future, for overt revision of the Three Principles. However, this argument needs to be complemented by a consideration of the ways in which the government has quietly circumvented the Three Principles and other constraints on military policy" [Corning, 1989, p.284]. Also this strong social norm supporting the three non-nuclear principles is a source of dismay among the few that would like to see the issue of nuclearization on the political agenda. This is so in particular since Japan has acquired the technological capabilities to build medium-range and long-range missiles that could deliver nuclear warheads to Korea, China and the Soviet Union [Interview Nos. 18 and 20, Tokyo, June 18, 1991]. In contrast to the 1970s the restraints that remain are political.

The Japanese government has adhered to the norm of a non-nuclear policy while taking shelter under the nuclear umbrella of the United States, and while supporting the global and theater nuclear strategy of the United States. It has thus adhered to a dual strategy of calling for nuclear disarmament and prohibiting the presence of nuclear weapons on Japanese soil while also acknowledging the utility of the American deterrent for Japan's military security. Norms and interests are thus deeply intertwined. The reasons the Japanese government has "not yet felt the need to build an independent nuclear force," writes James Van de Velde, "may be a function more of the credibility of this American extended deterrent, Japan's geostrategic position in East Asia and the particulars of the defense of Japan, and less a function of the idealistic pronouncements of Japan's commitment to remaining nuclear weapon-free" [Van de Velde, 1988b, p.20].

The policy of the three non-nuclear principles has not been free from contradictions. In particular the government's claim that nuclear weapons were not being introduced into Japan has always had a hollow ring to it. On the very day that former Prime Minister Sato received the Nobel Peace Price for his adoption of a non-nuclear policy, a retired U.S. navy admiral, Gene LaRocque, ridiculed the notion that the U.S. navy would have its ships dispose of nuclear weapons before entering Japanese waters [Söderberg, 1986, p.46. Van de Velde, 1988a, pp.263-67. Olsen, 1985, p.25]. A 1974 report in the New York Times told of a 1960 agreement permitting the introduction of nuclear weapons by ship or aircraft. "The Japanese had deliberately not retained a written text so as to be able to deny the agreement" [Drifte, 1990b, p.25]. As early as mid-1970s Japanese public opinion thus harbored a widespread suspicion that the third of the non-nuclear principles (non-introduction) was regularly violated [Akaha, 1984, p.871; 1985a, p.78. Van de Velde, 1988b, p.23].

The issue remained submerged until former U.S. Ambassador Edwin Reischauer gave two interviews in the spring of 1981 in which he described long-standing arrangements that had permitted American warships carrying nuclear weapons to make port calls in Japan. For American policymakers weapons "in transit" were not being "introduced into" Japan. "Introducing" for American policymakers meant offloading, stationing or storing nuclear weapons on Japanese soil. For the Japanese government, despite public skepticism, the category of "introducing" included weapons in transit. In a second interview Reischauer insisted that American nuclear weapons policy toward Japan was an open secret and should not be a surprise to anyone, despite the traditional policy of the United States navy neither to deny nor to confirm the existence of nuclear weapons on any of its ships [Halloran, 1981. Stokes, 1981a, 1981b. Drifte, 1990, p.25. Hook, 1988, pp.387-88. Akaha, 1984, p.872. Van de Velde, 1988a, pp.257-62]. The uproar over Ambassador Reischauer's statements was very strong not because of what he had said, but because, as a relative insider, he had dared to speak up at all, exposing, perhaps inadvertently, that Japan's security relationship with the United States was inherently in contradiction with the third of its non-nuclear principles. Furthermore, Reischauer reopened a painful discussion about whether nuclear-armed planes of the U.S. airforce were flying in and out of Japan, and whether nuclear weapons were being stored at Okinawa.

Prime Minister Suzuki tried to sidestep the controversy by stating that the Japanese government had always trusted that the United States had lived up to the U.S.-Japan Security Treaty. Since the United States, under the provisions of a prior agreement, was expected to notify the Japanese government if it were to bring nuclear weapons into Japanese waters or territory, and since such notification had not been forthcoming, the Japanese government's position was that such weapons had not been brought into Japan and that it was going to continue to trust U.S. fidelity in the future [Olsen, 1985, p.25. Keddell, 1990, p.155]. To reinforce the impression of the three non-nuclear principles as a basic policy, both Houses of the Diet in May 1982 unanimously adopted resolutions calling for international disarmament which stated, among others, that the three non-nuclear principles were Japan's essential policy. Yet in 1987 the JCP found in the U.S. Library of Congress a declassified telegram from 1966 by Dean Rusk that substantially supported the 1974 New York Times story and the account of Ambassador Reischauer. In the summer of 1987 the Kyodo news agency reported the 1984 instruction by the Commander-in-Chief of the U.S. Pacific Forces that instructed regional military commanders in several countries, including Japan, to work out plans to control nuclear accidents [Drifte, 1990b, pp.25-26].

The frequency with which nuclear-powered American ships or ships likely to carry nuclear weapons have visited Japanese ports, as part of the bilateral security arrangements, makes the apparent breach of the principle of nonintroduction significant for an interpretation of Japan's security policy. Between 1964 and the early 1980s nuclear-powered submarines have paid 180 visits to Japan. In the later phases of the Vietnam war, in 1972, with the United States resuming the bombing of North Vietnam and the Seventh Fleet mining North Vietnamese coastal waters, American nuclear-powered submarines visited Japanese ports as many as thirty times. With the American withdrawal from Southeast Asia and the coming of detente this number declined to about five to ten a year. By 1982 that number had, however, increased again to as many as twenty. And in 1985 at least 32 nuclear submarines called at Yokosuka and Sasebo [Akaha, 1984, pp.873-74; 1985a, pp.79-81. Drifte, 1990b, p.24]. The stationing of the carrier Midway in Yokosuka and of the nuclear-powered Enterprise in Sasebo also has raised suspicion that some of the attack-fighters of the Enterprise may be equipped with nuclear weapons. Furthermore, the refurbished New Jersey which is equipped with 32 intermediate-range Tomahawk cruise missile has been granted visitation rights at Sasebo, as has the carrier Carl Vinson which was reassigned from the Atlantic to the Pacific in order to beef up America's nuclear capacity. As a result the American effort to counter the Soviet naval build-up of the 1970s and 1980s with a strengthened naval deterrence has brought as many as 200 nuclear weapons into the Western Pacific, and presumably also into Japanese territorial waters [Akaha, 1984, p.876]. Japan's non-nuclear policy apparently was subordinated, at least in part, to the facts established by America's policy of nuclear deterrence.   The ambiguity with which the Japanese government has treated the third non-nuclear principle helps bridge the clash between formal statements and underlying truth [Van de Velde, 1988b, p.23]. Whatever the original intent of Japan's Peace Constitution, under the government's interpretation it does not prohibit legally Japan's acquisition of nuclear weapons. Although the Japanese government claims to have adhered firmly to its non-nuclear policy, that policy contains elements of flexibility (defined here in analytical not policy terms) permitting an incremental change in policy. Government policies "are subject to interpretation by public officials in the course of implementation or execution. This interpretation is then scrutinized by the body politic. If reaction is passive enough . . . the interpretation stands" [Endicott, 1975, p.45]. This flexibility has afforded Japan protection, for example, in international negotiations leading to the extension of its territorial limits from three to twelve miles offshore in 1977. The extension excepted the five straits around Japan which are used for international navigation. If coastal waters were totally enclosed by Japan's jurisdiction, Japan's non-nuclear policy would bring the government in conflict with the Soviet and possibly the U.S. navy. "Under domestic pressure to extend the territorial limit to protect coastal fishermen from Soviet competitors but wishing not to produce a domestic legislation contradicting an internationally accepted or acceptable legal principle, the government decided to'shelve' its territorial claim in the straits areas while extending it to twelve miles in other coastal areas" [Akaha, 1985a, pp.81-82; 1985b]. Although the government claimed that this decision was not related to the three nonnuclear principles, critics argued that the restrictive application of the extension of Japan's jurisdiction was directly contravening the intent of those principles.

On nuclear issues, "if the Europeans excel in the game of strategic positive rationalism, the Japanese certainly are not poor players in the arena of political-strategic dialectics—what I call the software (as opposed to the hardware) approach" [Nakanishi, 1977, p.88]. The norm against the acquisition of nuclear hardware is closely intertwined with Japan's long-term interests as officials interpret them in light of domestic and international opposition to Japan's acquisition of nuclear weapons. Monte Bullard argues, perhaps too optimistically, that a major "reason for not developing a nuclear capability is the pragmatic reasoning of . . . leaders in Japan who will see that military nuclearization will cost Japan much more than it gains in its dealings in the international system. In fact, I see Japan breaking historical precedent (coupling of military and economic power) and becoming the vanguard of new methods of conflict resolution between sovereign nations in the international system. Japan will be the leader, by necessity, in skillful diplomatic maneuvers and subtle economic pressures to promote its interest on the world scene" [Bullard, 1974, p.853].

C. Political Dimensions of Security

The gradual redefinition of the primary military purpose of the SDF, in the evolving U.S.-Japan security relationship, and the controversy over Japan's strict export controls over the shipment of weapons and military technologies reveal a variable pattern of policy flexibility and rigidity. This pattern is the result of the different structural and normative influences that operate on Japan's security policy. The shift of the SDF from internal policing to national defense which ended in the 1970s did not receive much attention outside Japan. But the growing importance of Japan's role as a junior partner in its relationship with the United States did. The gradual move toward a de facto regional security role, in conjunction with the United States, directed against the Soviet Union in the 1980s, amounted to a substantial modification of Japan's traditional security policy that has elicited much discussion and analysis on both sides of the Pacific. Among specialists this is increasingly true also of the difficult issue of Japan's export of technologies potentially relevant for military production, one of the most difficult issues the security relationship now confronts [Saito, 1990. Mendl, 1984. Ozaki and Arnold, 1985. Van de Velde, 1988a. Steinert, 1981. Osgood, 1972. Weinstein, 1982. Smith, Vittorelli, and Saeki, 1983. Nishihara, 1985b and 1986. O'Neill, 1984, 1987. Nakada, 1980. Morley, 1986. Weinstein, 1978. Tow, 1986. Leifer, 1986. Kimura, 1986. Kosaka, 1986. Weinstein, 1983. Johnson and Packard, 1981. Tsurutani, 1981. Alagappa, 1988. Iriye and Cohen, 1989]. The change in Japanese policies dealing primarily with the political dimension of security, in particular with the relationship between the United States and Japan, result from structural factors and a normative context that differ from issue to issue and thus have contributed to a more variable pattern of policy adjustment than has been true of issues dealing primarily with military or economic aspects of security. Specifically, increasing defense cooperation was achieved more easily than the sharing of militarily relevant technologies.

1. Growing Military Links with the United States.

Remarkable about the growing military links between Japan and the United States in the 1980s is the relatively uncomplicated pattern of policy adaptation. The gradual loosening of many of the traditional restraints that had been imposed on the SDF was marked by political discussions that have been sharp in contrast to the lack of debate on the issue of economic security but that were mild compared to the intense controversies that have characterized the military aspects of Japan's security policy. As a result, in this instance Japanese policy has evolved rather flexibly to changing international conditions.

The strategy of the GSDF was for many years shaped by an important memorandum that Foreign Minister Ashida had drafted in 1947. Japanese foreign policy was guided by the conviction that in the face of a potentially serious threat from the Soviet Union, and given the deterrent power of the American navy and airforce, Japan's armed forces were to serve primarily a domestic policing purpose against a possible Communist insurrection [Weinstein, 1971, pp.49, 106, 109, 112, 116-19, and 1975, pp.42, 44, 46].

"As a consequence, it seemed perfectly reasonable to Prime Minister Yoshida and Foreign Minister Ashida to propose a'mutual' defense agreement with the United States, while asking the U.S. government to assume virtually the entire burden of Japan's external defense" [Weinstein, 1975, p.57]. The Japanese government hoped to achieve a mutual defense relationship with the United States, in seeking to convince the United States that it was deploying strong paramilitary police forces to defend the country against a Communist-led insurrection at home.

In terms of the SDF's mission as well as equipment, "their primary function was internal security" [Weinstein, 1971, p.109]. In the 1950s Japan's discredited military had only one option of achieving respectability after 1945, through the promise of "victory on the home front . . . many military men have made it clear that they consider the suppression of leftist subversion at home to be one of the main tasks both of the ex-servicemen's leagues and of the defence forces themselves" [Morris, 1958, p.19]. Throughout the first two postwar decades this original domestic mission of the SDF was reflected in the deployment of the SDF. Of the thirteen divisions of the GSDF only four were stationed in Hokkaido, the most likely point of attack by the Soviet Union. The other divisions were deployed quite evenly throughout Japan, close to its major metropolitan areas and industrial complexes [Weinstein, 1971, p.121 and 1975, p.52. Interview Nos.6, 12 and 15, Tokyo, December 10, 12 and 14, 1991].

Japan's deviance from a more traditional mass army relying on the institution of conscription may partially result from "the rather unique mission of her armed forces" [Curry, 1976, pp.73-74]. Throughout the 1950s and 1960s the GSDF were "equipped, deployed and trained to maintain internal security" [Weinstein, 1974, p.368]. In the 1960s the SDF undertook well-publicized, special "public security" exercises. Between September 18 and 22, 1962, for example, some units of the GSDF were reported to have trained in anti-riot exercises at an army post in the outskirts of Tokyo [Mainichi Shimbun, July 23, 1991]. The Vietnam War turned the attention of the GSDF from mass disorders in the streets to possible insurrections in the form of a protracted guerrilla war, aided perhaps by Peking or Moscow. Such a war of "national liberation", it was thought, might accompany a renewal of hostilities on the Korean peninsula [Weinstein, 1974, p.368]. This scenario was the background to the secret "Three Arrows Plan" that was leaked in 1965. And at the height of the Vietnam protest movement, in the fall of 1969, the Japanese press reported that a total of 70,000 members of the SDF could be mobilized for riot duty to contain, if necessary, massive demonstrations [Havens, 1987, p.189]. When the JDA, under its Director Nakasone, issued the first Defense White Paper in 1970, it contained many references to the maintaining of internal security [Berger, 1992, p.358]. Throughout the 1960s, however, both the government and the SDF were very much aware of how explosive it would have been for the military to intervene in domestic politics [Weinstein, 1971, pp.116-21, 1974, pp.368-70, and 1975, pp.49-52. Emmerson, 1971, pp.130-31]. Although the GSDF served as a back-up to the police, riot control was the task assigned to the police [Interview No.12, Tokyo, December 12, 1991]. The best defense of Japan's internal security, in the defense planners' way of thinking, lay in the social stability that economic prosperity promised [Weinstein, 1975, pp.49-52].

Japan's oversized ground forces thus reflect the original mission of the SDF to help secure Japan's internal security. But other factors helped perpetuate the deployment pattern and size of the GSDF. Possible instabilities on the Korean peninsula made advisable a reasonably strong military presence in the Northern part of Kyushu, far removed from the Soviet threat to Hokkaido. Furthermore, GSDF troops bring valuable votes to LDP politicians and desired economic activities and financial assistance to local governments. This favored an even deployment throughout Japan. An army plagued by problems of recruitment and the small number of reserves naturally was not eager to add to its problems by sending a large number of men to the harsh climate of Northern Japan. Finally, the most popular mission of the GSDF remains the protection of the Japanese population against natural disasters which, like internal insurrections, can strike anywhere [Interviews Nos.4,7,8,9 and 16, Tokyo, June 11,13 and 17, 1991. Friedman and Lebard, 1991, pp.355-56].

But gradually in the 1950s and 1960s the SDF began to assume also the more traditional task of defending Japan's external security. After the outbreak of the Korean War General MacArthur authorized the creation of the National Police Reserve, the nucleus of the Self Defense Forces. It became a military force that eventually would participate in Japan's external defense without, however, being strong enough either to muster a national defense on its own or to participate, as the Americans had wished, in regional security measures in Asia. The law establishing the SDF in 1954 authorized them not only to maintain public order when necessary but also "to defend Japan against direct and indirect aggression" [Weinstein, 1971, p. 108]. In times of emergency a total of eight divisions could be shifted to Northern Japan. The deployment of the GSDF changed in response to the weakening of America's Asian position, after the loss of the Vietnam war, and to the growing military presence of the Soviet Union in Asia. About half of the total fire power of the GSDF and much of its heavy equipment were concentrated on the defense of Hokkaido. Instead of preparing against indirect attacks in the interior of Japan, reserves began training in cold climate against an anticipated direct attack in the North. Each division stationed in Hokkaido was reinforced by a tank company which will be equipped in the 1990s with the new M90 tank, a Japanese product hailed to be superior to the U.S. M1 and the German Leopard [Nishihara, 1983/84, p.187. Interview No.4, Tokyo, June 11, 1991].

In a second important shift the GSDF and JDA adopted in 1986 a strategy of "seashore" or "forward" defense which is being implemented in 1991-96. Although it appears to have been developed independently from the forward deployment of the Seventh Fleet under America's "maritime strategy", seashore defense of the home territories against a possible amphibious attack from Soviet naval forces extended the control of the GSDF over the straits surrounding parts of Japan. This poses a direct challenge to the Russian navy which would have to break through the straits to gain access to the Pacific. As an integral part of the operations involving all three military services, it points to a growing role of the GSDF in the maritime strategy of the U.S. in Asia [Interview Nos.12 and 23, Tokyo, December 12 and 19, 1991. Okazaki, Nishimura and Sato, 1991, pp.100-01. Smith, 1990, p.21]. "Seashore" or "forward" defense responded to the increasing capabilites of the Soviet navy. In particular, it was a response to the maritime "bastion" strategy through which the Soviet Union and now Russia have deployed their strategic nuclear submarines in the Sea of Okhotsk. Since the critical supply lines between these submarines and the Sea of Japan and Vladivostok run through the Soya and Tsugaru Straits, neighboring Hokkaido and northern Japan constitute a serious threat to the naval power of Russia and are both likely targets of attack in the eventuality, small as it may be, of war. The GSDF is seeking to neutralize that threat by establishing a credible convential deterrence which would seek to attack and destroy a Russian naval invasion before it could reach the shores of Hokkaido [Defense Agency, 1990, p.111. Nishimura, 1991b, pp.10-11. Interview No.23, Kyoto, June 24, 1991].

"Seashore" or "forward" defense reveals the ambiguity inherent in high-technology weapons—surface-to-ship missiles (SSM) now, multiple-launch rocket systems (MLRS) in the future—that equip Japan's SDF, although deployed for defensive purposes, with important offensive capabilities [O'Connell, 1987, pp.55-56,65. Interviews Nos.4, 7 and 9, Tokyo, June 11 and 13, 1991]. The adoption of this new strategic posture of the GSDF will make possible some reduction in the number and readiness of troops placed in Northern Japan—more than half of the GSDF are concentrated to the North of Tokyo—and accelerate the move to lighter, more mobile units, equipped with technologically sophisticated missiles. Considering these trends and the new security climate after the end of the Cold War as well as the break up of the Soviet Union, the JDA civilians should be able to ally with the innovators in the GSDF against the traditionalists and thus be able to withstand pressure for more troops and heavy equipment [Interviews Nos.4, 8, 9, 15, 21 and 22, Tokyo, June 11, 13, 17 and 19, 1991]. At the same time the deployment pattern of the 1980s completes a very substantial change in policy. The GSDF is no longer a paramilitary force with a primary mission of containing internal subversion. It has become instead a military force that, in the pursuit of "self-defense", is driven by technology and geography to project its power offshore and thus, potentially, to engage Russia's formidable naval forces. This change in policy is particularly noteworthy because it broadens the meaning and practice of the notion of "self-defense", a key concept by which Japanese elites and the mass public interpret the country's position in the international system. The concept of "defensive defense" (senshu boei) was coined in the Diet deliberations in 1972. But the idea had informed Japan's security policy since the mid-1950s [Interview No.16, Tokyo, June 17, 1991. Defense Agency, 1990, pp.83,87].

In contrast to the GSDF the ASDF has not experienced any substantial changes in strategy. New equipment has been added to counter improved Soviet airpower. While its manpower of 45,000 uniformed personnel will probably decrease, the ASDF hopes to adjust for this decline through changes in equipment as well as the privatization of some of its logistical services. But the general framework of close cooperation with the U.S. airforce has not changed. Air surveillance of the three straits and the Sea of Japan is achieved in close cooperation with the United States navy and airforce. Indeed, the force posture of the ASDF is so heavily skewed toward short interceptors—most of its 440 fighter aircrafts fall under that category—that some observers speak of a de facto integration of the Japanese ASDF with its American counter part [Interviews Nos.9, 10, 12, 16 and 22, Tokyo, June 13, 14, 17 and 19, 1991. Interview No.11, Tokyo, December 12, 1991].

The MSDF's growing links to the American navy has resulted in an even more imbalanced force [Auer, 1973b]. The MSDF has a substantial anti-submarine warfighting (ASW) capability; it engages in surveillance and intelligence; and it is prepared to assist the American navy in controlling the three strategic straits surrounding Japan. But the configuration is very imbalanced. The number of its destroyers and aircrafts tracking submarines and supporting U.S. naval forces in the Pacific is too large while the number and sophistication of its submarines is too small for an independent protection of Japan's territorial waters and the sealanes leading to Japan. Among all the three branches of the SDF the demands for a more balanced force structure thus have been strongest in the MSDF. A more balanced naval force is said to require perhaps as much as a 50 percent increase in the current manpower (50,000) of the MSDF. Furthermore the MSDF has, for reasons of status and strategy, never concealed its preference for the acquisition of through-deck cruisers or light helicopter aircraft carriers which would strengthen its ASW and air defense capabilities, thus reinforcing its links with the U.S. navy. Equipped with vertical-take-off-and-landing (VTOL) aircrafts, such as the Harrier jump jets, these ships might also give the MSDF an independent offensive capability in the Sea of Japan in times of crisis or war, should the American navy hesitate to commit one of its carriers to that exposed, forward position, close to the Russian homeland.

In the words of Friedman and Lebard, "the heart of Japan's defense policy has been to allow the United States to take care of it" [Friedman and Lebard, 1991, p.297]. But in Japan's relations with the United States the traditional American definition of security in narrow military terms has often clashed with the Japanese view of comprehensive security [Kajima, 1969. Langdon, 1973. Reed, 1983. Sneider, 1982. Nations, 1984. Smith, 1991. Rubinstein, 1988. International Institute for Global Peace, 1991. Nishimura, 1991a, 1991b. Carter and Nakasone, 1992. Ministry of Foreign Affairs, 1991a. Kishino, 1991. Buckley, 1992. Friedman and Lebard, 1991, pp.259-324]. From the perspective of Washington the security arrangements with Japan are a defense alliance against the Soviet Union and Russia. From the perspective of Tokyo the full title of the treaty that was renegotiated in 1960 remains essential. It is a treaty about mutual security and cooperation. Under the assumption that the nuclear and conventional deterrence was being provided by its American ally, Japan's SDF were prohibited from developing any offensive military capabilities. But in the 1980s the shifting military balance in East Asia and American demands have put strong pressure on Japan to adapt its military stance within the context of the U.S.-Japan relationship [Interview Nos.2, 5, 15 and 22, Tokyo, June 11, 12, 17 and 19, 1991. Endicott, 1984]. Within the political framework that links Japan and the United States, the economic aspects of their security relationship have always figured prominently for Japan [Kosaka, 1973]. The Mutual Defense Assistance Program of 1954, for example, refers explicitly to the fact that "economic stability will be an essential element for consideration in the development of its defense capacities . . . Japan can contribute only to the extent permitted by its general economic conditions and capacities" [Okimoto, 1982a, p.239]. The American nuclear umbrella provided military conditions that were extremely favorable to the economic expansion of Japan.

But from the perspective of the United States "Japan is ideally suited as a base for forward deployment of U.S. forces" [Okazaki, 1982a, p.191]. Japan is a very important link in America's Asian system of nuclear deterrence. And it is an integral part of America's global network of command, control, communication and intelligence. Numerous Japanese facilities are linked with both the North American Air Defense (NORAD) and the Strategic Air Command (SAC), and they are an integral component of the World-Wide Military Command and Control system (WWMCCS) operated by the U.S. Department of Defense [Toyoda, 1985, p.62]. The high frequency radio systems that make possible the work of the Pacific Command and the SAC are stationed at Kadena, Iruma, Owada, and Tokorozawa. The navy's low frequency transmitter is stationed at Yosami, one of six in the world that relays firing orders to the Trident submarines as well as attack submarines equipped with nuclear-tipped cruise missiles. Finally, Japan is fully integrated into the network of supplies for all U.S. forces in the Western Pacific. U.S. bases in Japan currently provide 80 percent of the oil storage facilities West of Hawaii, and American ammunition depots in Japan account for over 50 percent of the total land-based capacity of U.S. armed forces in the Western Pacific [Arkin and Chappell, 1985, p.487]. These facts confirm that "the U.S. military's Japan-based communications, planning, targeting, and refueling infrastructure . . . make Japan an indispensable component of U.S. nuclear war-fighting plans" [Arkin and Chappell, 1985, p.487].

While economic frictions increased, the defense links between the United States and Japan tightened in the 1980s. The Guidelines for Japan-U.S. Defense Cooperation were issued in November 1978. The results of the joint studies conducted subsequently by the U.S. and the Japanese militaries remain classified. The Guidelines deal with three contingencies: deterrence of aggression against Japan, joint action in case of an armed attack on Japan, and the assistance that Japan might offer to the U.S. in situations in the Far East that might affect Japanese security [Takahara, 1992, p.12]. The Guidelines gave operational meaning to the NDPO's view of the role U.S. and Japanese military forces were to play in Japan's defense. The Guidelines spelled out a division of labor between the two militaries and provided for increasing levels of cooperation in operation, logistics and intelligence [Umemoto, 1985a, pp.53-54. Interview No.14, Tokyo, December 13, 1991]. This was the first step toward reaching higher levels of interoperability of the two militaries. Japan's defense build-up during the 1980s has provided the planes and ships supposedly necessary to accomplish new missions [Johnson, 1986, p.570. Defense Agency, 1990, pp.213-316].

Critics of Japanese security have charged that "the intensification of cooperation between the two militaries, pursued under the Guidelines, has in fact led to Japan's further subordination. In this sense, the Guidelines can be regarded as an informal revision of the Security Treaty" the result of which was "to lock Japanese forces into an overarching US strategy"

[Hook, 1988, p.384]. At the same time joint exercises have not only strengthened the military capabilities of the SDF through the study of tactics, strategy and practical experience [Interview No.11, December 12, 1991]. They have also succeeded in preparing the SDF better for times of crisis by specifying rules designed to prevent premature, accidental military engagement of the enemy [Interview No. 3, Tokyo, December 9, 1991]. As a follow-up to the Guidelines a number of top-secret war contingency planning documents have been drawn up [Hook, 1988, pp.390-91]. Joint defense planning and exercises, the possible creation of the Japan-U.S. Defense Coordination Center, intelligence exchange, joint operational preparations, growing interoperability of military equipment, and the promise of Japanese assistance, under certain conditions, to U.S. forces outside of Japan in times of emergency all point to the growing links between the SDF and the U.S. military in the 1980s and significant changes in Japan's defensive military posture [Akaha, 1990, p.17].

Important changes in the security links between Japan and the United States are illustrated by the decision of the Japanese government, taken in full accord with the United States, to extend its sealane defense to 1,000 miles and to deploy Japan's MSDF in the mining or blocking of the straits of Soya, Tsugaru and Tsushima around Japan, with the intent of bottling up hostile fleets, Soviet and Russian, in times of war. In training exercises in the 1980s the MSDF has operated as part of U.S.-Japanese battlegroups accompanying U.S. aircraft carriers. The MSDF is thus developing a capability that is beyond the handling of defensive assignments, even though, in comparison to the ASDF, its force structure is still skewed [Interview No.11, December 12, 1991]. This level of operational cooperation goes far beyond any commitments Japan made in the NDPO or the Guidelines, both of which mandate a strictly defensive posture for the SDF [Mochizuki, 1983/84, p.161. Arkin and Chappell, 1985].

During his visit to Washington in 1981, Prime Minister Suzuki, in a controversial statement, extended Japan's self-defense perimenter to include sealanes up to 1,000 miles from Japan. After some clarifications the government's policy was aimed not at patrolling the South China Sea and the Philippines (as they fall within 1,000 miles from Japan's southernmost islands) but at containing the growing Soviet navy in the Pacific (1,000 miles extended from Tokyo). American policymakers seized on Suzuki's Washington statement and ardently pushed the new policy as a Japanese pledge to support America's overextended air and naval power in the Pacific against a growing Soviet military presence [Sneider, 1986]. Shortly after taking office Prime Minister Nakasone decided to undertake, jointly with the United States, a study of how to make operational the extension of Japan's sealane protection across a 1,000 mile stretch of the Pacific Ocean to the

South and West of Japan. This measure was intended to provide support for the operations of the U.S. Navy in the area as well as to free American naval forces for deployment closer to the Mideast [Interview Nos.8 and 12, Tokyo, June 13 and 14, 1991. Olsen, 1985, pp.96-97. Drifte, 1985b, pp.156-57].

Because it established Japan, in principle if not yet in fact, as a regional naval power in Asia, Friedman and Lebard view the extension of military responsibilities to 1,000 miles beyond the home islands as "the first and most important step of the postwar period for Japan's foreign policy" [Friedman and Lebard, 1991, p.266]. The sealane defense concept was not covered by the NDPO and thus represents a gradual change in the mission of the SDF without an explicit change in Japan's defense policy [Nishihara, 1987, p.186. Nishimura, 1991b]. The growing gap between an unchanging official policy and the reality of a growing regional security role for the Japanese SDF created remarkably little domestic controversy. As was true in the shift in mission and equipment by which the SDF have moved in the 1980s to control the straits surrounding Japan, the protection of the sealanes makes the Japanese government in fact a participant in "collective defense" measures, together with the United States and the Republic of Korea—in apparent violation, in the eyes of the government's critics, of the Japanese Constitution. Japan's growing defense cooperation with the United States thus is evidently weakening the policy constraints under which the SDF had operated before the 1980s.

Looking beyond the Cold War the capability to project military power at least up to the 1,000 mile perimeter around Japan is a strategic option that some Japanese military planners feel is necessary to provide the necessary air defense at the edge of the 1,000 mile zone. This will require eventually either a midair refueling capability or the construction of small aircraft carriers. To date Japan's political leadership has not assented to this controversial demand of the MSDF. For such a military capability could be construed as offensive, especially in times of declining political tension with the successor states of the Soviet Union [Interviews Nos.8, 16 and 22, Tokyo, June 13, 17 and 19, 1991. Auer, 1989]. Japan's "situation illustrates the difficulty of drawing limits around a defense-oriented force." It is very difficult to solve defense problems "without creating at the same time an offensive force that raises concerns among other nationals in the region" [Bergner, 1991, p.185]. In short, Japan is moving toward a strategy of offshore land-, air- and sea-defense. This is a "significant departure from its long-standing orientation of, first, 'internal defense' and then 'defense at the water's edge'" [Levin, 1988, p.17].

In a similar vein Japan also agreed to construct an air-defense screen across Japan to interdict long-range Soviet and Russian bombers, fighter bombers and tactical aircrafts [Johnson, 1986, p.570]. And since 1985 the Japanese government has permitted the deployment of two squadrons of F-16 fighter aircrafts, potentially capable of carrying nuclear weapons, at Misawa in northern Japan, with the cost to be borne equally by Japan and the United States. These bombers can reach the Eastern part of the Soviet Union and thus are inherently "offensive." Similar problems are raised with the stationing of 300 Green Berets at Okinawa in September 1983 and the deployment of SH-3H Sea King helicopters on the Yokosuka-based aircraft carrier Midway; these helicopters can carry nuclear depth charges for antisubmarine warfare. Japan's close integration with the U.S. military and its offensive strategy in Asia as well as the growing interoperability of different weapon systems, such as the AWACS, go far beyond Japan's professed aim of possessing a military capability sufficient to independently counter only small-scale invasions. Japan has instead joined de facto in the sort of collective defense effort that the government claims is part of Japan's right to self-defense while the Socialist opposition maintains it to be unconstitutional even under the government's interpretation.

There has been a longstanding controversy over Japan's participation in collective defense measures. The doctrine of collective defense is itself a relatively recent international norm that the United States, based on the precedent of the Western hemisphere, created to supplant the obligations deriving from the more traditional European system of alliances. The Security Treaty with the United States and the notes which were exchanged at the time of its signing involved, in American eyes, a substantial American concession. For, in the absence of any revision of Article 9, the U.S. obligation to defend Japan was made explicit. Article 9 of Japan's Peace Constitution , under the government's interpretation, has a very narrow conception of "self" when it comes to questions of collective defense. Japan is not bound by the Security Treaty to defend the United States in case of aggression by a third party. The government's position, as has occasionally been noted, is not the only conceivable one. It would, for example, be quite plausible, some argue, that in case of treaty relationships which spell out mutual defense obligations, at the time of attack the identity of the partner state and one's own state must be assumed, as in NATO, thus requiring an identity of response. Proponents of such a view note that Article 9 of the Constitution prohibits only the use of force as a means for settling international disputes, not as a means of self-defense.

In general, the Japanese government is severely constrained in pursuing policies aiming at collective defense measures in bilateral or regional alliances. As long as Japan has not been the target of direct aggression, public opinion appears to support the interpretation that makes it unconstitutional for Japan to come to the assistance of an allied country that has been attacked by a hostile third country [Okazaki, 1982b, p.471]. "The Government believes," writes the Defense Agency, "that the Constitution does not permit it to dispatch armed forces to foreign territorial land, sea and airspace for the purpose of using force, because such a deployment of troops overseas generally goes beyond the minimum limit necessary for self-defense . . . the exercise of the right of collective self-defense exceeds the minimum limit and is constitutionally not permissible" [Defense Agency, 1990, p.86]. Because of Japan's disastrous defeat in World War II, that is, for essentially historical reasons, the domestic norms circumscribing Japan's security policy make formal collective defense arrangements a highly implausible policy option.

The aftermath of the Gulf War generated an intense political discussion in Japan that underlined also the salience of the norm opposing Japan's participation in collective security efforts. The deployment of the SDF as part of an international peacekeeping force raises thorny constitutional issues for Japan. On the one hand it may be considered in conformity with Japan's renunciation of war since the military capacity to be used by a U.N. force has nothing to do with the application of national force which is explicitly banned by the Constitution. However, the Japanese government committed itself in 1980 in writing to a position that if the purpose or mission of an U.N. peacekeeping force were to be "accompanied" by the use of violence, Article 9 of the Constitution would prohibit SDF participation [Interview No.19, Tokyo, June 18, 1991]. On the other hand, if such a U.N. force were not to use force, the deployment of the SDF would not be banned by the Constitution. But even then a special law would have to be passed by the Diet since this provision for the deployment of the SDF is not included in the SDF Law. In the Diet discussions in the fall of 1990 Prime Minister Kaifu indicated that he did not intend to deviate from the 1980 government interpretation [Tanaka, 1990, pp.17-18]. The United Nations Peacekeeping Operations Cooperation Law, passed in 1992, provided for the overseas deployment of the SDF without overturning that interpretation.

The prohibition of the deployment of SDF forces overseas dates back to a resolution adopted by the House of Councillors in 1954. Even though the government argues that the SDF's possible participation in U.N. peacekeeping forces is not covered by this resolution, the domestic compromise embodied in the 1992 law did not authorize the sending of armed Japanese troops overseas. Japan's possible participation in collective security arrangements is thus very strictly circumscribed as sending the SDF abroad remains very controversial. With participation even in lightly armed peacekeeping operations an issue of great controversy, it was a matter of course that intense conflict emerged over the modalities of Japan's possible participation in an international military force in the Mideast in 1990-91

[Sanger, 1990]. The domestic controversy over collective security efforts is thus illustrative of the importance of the norm that constrains Japan's adoption of collective defense measures.

However, Japan's de facto support for the U.S. military role in Asia has been extended in the 1970s and 1980s. The 1978 "Guidelines for Defense Cooperation" stipulated greater cooperation on military matters including the sharing of information and joint planning of military exercises [Van de Velde, 1988a, pp.177-82. McIntosh, 1986, p.33]. This set the stage for more far-reaching agreements that were reached in the 1980s. The established constitutional interpretation of Article 9 permitting individual self-defense thus has eventually been relaxed. Successive conservative governments have broadened the concept of 'individual self-defense'. The Nakasone Cabinet, for example, argued that it would be constitutional for Japanese naval forces to help protect U.S. naval forces outside of Japan's territorial waters in war-time, if those forces were on their way to defend Japan. This new interpretation widens the area of joint operations between American and Japanese naval forces and moves Japan closer to the role of a typical military ally of the United States [Nishihara, 1987, p.8]. It also claimed that, in an emergency, the SDF could counter an attack on foreign ships carrying goods to Japan. Furthermore, the Cabinet did not rule out consenting to a U.S. blockade of the straits, even when an attack on Japan was only imminent [Asagumo Shimbun-sha, 1991, pp.440-42. Ishiguro, 1987, pp.250-51]. These new interpretations became a focal point of the defense debate. A possible future development involves an Acquisition Cross Service Agreement (ACSA). Such an agreement would integrate services such as refueling and transportation for the American and Japanese militaries. In 1991, the DoD began to press the Japanese government to conclude the agreement to support U.S. military action in regional conflicts. U.S. proposals on an ACSA had been made since 1988, but only for joint training purposes [Asahi Shimbun, May 10, July 25, November 29, 1991, 13th editions]. An additional example of how the government has reinterpreted prior practice to meet new demands occurred in June 1991. The JDA approved for the first time the refueling of U.S. ships by Japanese ships in the Gulf. Refueling of U.S. ships by the SDF had previously been permitted only in joint exercises [Asahi Shimbun, June 21, 1991, 13th ed.]. The JDA, however, pointing to the fact that German helicopters were also refueled, maintains that refueling was not part of a security cooperation between the U.S. and Japan [Interview No.4, Tokyo, December 9, 1991].

In sum, the notions of individual and collective self-defense have shifted over time thus permitting incremental policy change. Instead of being confined to a narrowly conceived definition of the Japanese home territories, the SDF have extended their mission, as articulated in the joint communique signed after a meeting of Prime Minister Suzuki and President Reagan in May 1981, to defend the sea and air spaces surrounding Japan [Nishihara, 1983/84, p.183]. The original, narrow conception of defending only the Japanese home territories thus has been replaced, without any explicit change in constitutional interpretation, by a politically restrained defense posture which aims at both a strengthening of the U.S.-Japan "alliance" and a "stabilization" of Asian affairs [Interview No.21, Tokyo, June 19, 1991]. In the words of Masashi Nishihara who welcomes such a change, "the concept of self-defense is basically stretchable. Japan can be a regional power" by coordinating its individual self-defense measures with security measures of other countries [Sneider, 1986. Nishihara, 1983/84, p.197].

This gradual shift of the SDF toward the defense of external security is reinforced by Japan's acquisition of weapons that are increasingly sophisticated and that blur the distinction between offensive and defensive military capabilities. It is important to note that this policy of growing technological sophistication enjoys strong support on both sides of the Pacific. Japanese defense specialists favor this policy partly because they regard the acquisition of sophisticated weapons produced under foreign license as an indispensable stepping stone for an increasingly autonomous Japanese armaments industry [Interview No.2, Tokyo, June 11, 1991]. The American defense industry welcomes additional sales. And policymakers in Washington want to see Japanese defense outlays and capabilities enhanced. As a result Japan's traditional, inward focus on a "defensive defense" has gradually given way to a more "offensive defense" posture that is closely integrated with the United States. The defense plans which the Japanese government has adopted for 1986-90 and 1991-1995 include qualitative jumps in the ability of the SDF to destroy enemy forces before they reach Japan, to fight for a prolonged period of time, and to strengthen its command, control, communication and intelligence capabilities. In response to the build-up of Soviet military capabilities in Asia in the 1980s and developments in weapons technologies, each of the three services of the SDF is acquiring weapon systems that blur the distinction between defense and offense [Inoguchi, 1985, p.28. Auer, 1989].

In the 1990s the GSDF is being equipped with what is widely regarded as one of the world's best, if not the best, tank, Japan's M90. More importantly, its new strategy of seashore defense gives a compelling rationale to the purchase of MLRS and the deployment of sophisticated surface-to-ship missiles that seek to secure Japan's control of the straits and pose a serious potential threat to the Russian navy. The MSDF's close cooperation with the U.S. Navy, especially in anti-submarine warfare, rests heavily on an aircraft, the 104 P-3Cs, which is replacing 100 older P-2Js and PS-1s. Each of the newer aircrafts increases the patrol range by a factor of 10 and thus give Japan a more realistic capacity to defend its sealanes up to 1,000 miles away from the home territories. And the four Aegis destroyers, half of the eventual total that the MSDF hopes to deploy, are in all likelihood too large for Japan's naval forces. The Aegis is the electronic center helping to defend a taskforce of ships, including U.S. carriers, against the possible missile and aircraft attacks of a potential adversary. For Japan's naval forces, heavily skewed toward ASW warfare, such a large number of destroyers is probably excessive [Interviews Nos. 16, 18 and 21, Tokyo, June 17, 18 and 19. Interview No. 11, Tokyo, December 12, 1991]. As a support for the air-defense systems of U.S. carriers these destroyers are plausible weapons systems that will add, however, to the projection of the offensive capabilites of the MSDF in the form of long-range missiles. The MSDF's mission of defending 1,000 miles of sealanes around Japan could probably be met with the addition of these weapon systems [Interview No. 11, Tokyo, December 12, 1991]. But with the acquisition of these weapon systems it is clear that any clear-cut distinction between offense and defense in Japan's security policy evaporates.

The United States has pressed Japan to equip its ASDF with 14 American-built AWACS, rejected in the mid-70s in favor of shorter range systems which had less "offensive" implications [Sneider, 1986]. An important reason for the change in policy was American and Japanese concern about the American trade deficit. In the end Japan decided to acquire four planes, with the MOF vetoing additional purchases. How much of the planes' electronic gear will really be advanced still is undetermined, and a possible source of future friction. The intelligence gathering capacity that Japan thus acquires is inherently ambiguous; it can serve defensive or offensive purposes. As in the case of the MLRS and Aegis destroyers, the primary purpose of the AWACS is to identify an enemy and attack it while it is still far away from the Japanese home territories. For those supportive of procuring the aircraft, better surveillance and intelligence is essential for an adequate air defense of Japan [Interview No. 23, Kyoto, June 24, 1991]. With AWACs planes stationed perhaps as far away as 100 miles, Japan's airspace, like the sea surrounding Japan, needs to be defended "offensively." The replacement of the 210 F-104s by 223 F15-J Eagle fighters, each costing 65 million dollars, serves the same purpose. Whatever unease Japan's politicians may have had, advances in missile technology have made this extension in the definition of what constitutes Japan inevitable in the eyes of the professional military [Interview Nos. 10, 16, 20 and 21, Tokyo, June 13, 17, 18 and 19. Tora, 1991].

Japanese politicans and defense specialists are quick to point to the absence in Japan's military arsenal of the kind of offensive weapons barred by the Constitution as interpreted by the government. Japan's GSDF does not have amphibious assault troops; its MSDF has not deployed aircraft carriers; and the ASDF does not have long-range bombers or a capacity for mid-air refueling. Yet Japan's offensive military capabilities are evidently increasing. For the time being, this increase is occurring in close consultation with the United States (as in the case of the Aegis destroyer) or in reaction to American pressure (as in the case of the AWACS planes). But this increase in capabilities would acquire a totally different meaning should Japan's relationship with the United States change fundamentally. The pressure of the MSDF for a more balanced force structure, including the persistent demand for light helicopter aircraft carriers to strengthen the ASW capabilites of the MSDF, confirms that the Japanese military, like all militaries, is accustomed to thinking about military capabilities rather that political intentions, particularly now that its mission includes the defense of 1,000 miles of sealanes [Interview Nos. 15 and 23, Tokyo and Kyoto, June 17 and 24, 1991. Akaha, 1986]. Similarly, mid-air refueling for Japan's F-15 interceptors would increase Japan's defensive airpower without increasing significantly the number of aircraft [Interview No.22, Tokyo, June 19, 1991]. This issue had come up in the deliberations of the Budget Committee of the Upper House in March 1973 which subsequently prompted the removal of the F-4's air refueling capability. But the successor of the F-4, the F-15, has the same refueling capability without eliciting much public discussion, in apparent violation of Japan's "defensive" defense posture [Chuma and Kanegai, 1985. Sneider, 1986. Interview No.15, Tokyo, June 17, 1991].

To its Asian neighbors Japan's increases in defensive military capabilities are not necessarily reassuring. Many of Japan's weapons could be converted quite easily from a defensive to an offensive posture "following what South Korean President Roh Tae Woo recently described as a mere shift of 'intent'" [Manegold, 1991]. Helicopter aircraft carriers can easily be converted to serve as a base for vertical-take-off-and-landing aircrafts (VTOLs), and mid-air refueling would give Japan's interceptor fighters a range permitting them to fight in the airspace of other Asian states. Within the range of weapons Japan is acquiring, defense and offense are thus not easily distinguished as Japan's technological sophistication in producing weapons increases rapidly and as it has the financial means to buy such weapons from the United States. The partial conceptual and strategic extension of Japan's notion of self-defense to encompass regional security and stability in Asia could evidently be supported by the kind of weapons that Japan has acquired in the 1980s and is expected to purchase in the 1990s [Interview Nos. 18 and 22, Tokyo, June 18 and 19, 1991]. Because of the large size of its defense budget and its strength in high-technology industries, Japan's defensive military capabilities must be counted among the largest and technologically most sophisticated in the world [Samuels, 1991, p.64].

The increasing geographic scope of the notion of "self" defense, rooted in the modern weapon systems that are at the core of Japan's defense build-up, has made for a relatively smooth pattern of policy adaptation. The domestic and the transnational structure of the Japanese state favored adjustment. And the normative context was not prohibitive, especially to the extent that policy change involved the purchase of high-technology weapons that blur the distinction between defense and offense.

In sum, Japan has acquired weapons to fulfill that mission within the U.S.-Japan security arrangement; and within the context of an expanding notion of self-defense Japan is acquiring some offensive capabilities that may be useful in the event, unlikely as it may be, it decides to play a more active part in regional security affairs in Asia [Interview No.12, 15 and 16, Tokyo, June 14 and 17, 1991]. The 1980s have witnessed the growth of a variety of links between the Japanese and the American militaries [Interview No.4, Tokyo, December 9, 1991]. Increases in the physical integration and interoperability of the two military forces has created a system that is essentially of an American making, with Japan playing the role of junior partner. Despite its growth in size and capabilities, especially during the 1980s, in the words of Takashi Inoguchi the SDF remain basically dependent and subordinate to the U.S. military [Inoguchi, 1985, p.27]. The mission of the GSDF to defend Hokkaido is closely linked to broader U.S. operations. The MSDF is specializing in anti-submarine surveillance in the Western Pacific as well as preparing for a potential blockade of the Japanese straits through which the Russian fleet would have to move to gain access to the Pacific. And the ASDF's enhanced role in aerial surveillance and intelligence as well as the interdiction of long-range bombers are auxiliary to those of the U.S. airforce. A critic of Japan's defense policy, Glenn Hook, thus goes as far as to speak of a "'denationalization' of the Japanese military" [Hook, 1988, p.393]. Although opposition has been voiced in Japan, this process of denationalization has occurred without intense domestic controversy even though the defensive mission of the SDF has been affected substantially by the increasing cooperation with the United States. Both in terms of structures and norms the political support at home for policy adjustment was hardly overwhelming. But the opposition against the strong pressure from the United States lacked sufficient force and did not lead to a fundamental challenge to Japan's security policy.

2. The Prohibition of Arms Exports.

Japan's strict control over the export of military technologies has been the most difficult instance of policy adjustment among Japan's political security issues. In the transnational channels linking Japan and the United States American policymakers have pressed hard for an increase in technology flowback during the last decade. But neither Japan's domestic structures nor the normative context of policy have favored this change in policy. Policy adjustment thus has been very difficult and slow.

Japan's strict ban on the export of military products was not the automatic result of the loss of World War II and the subsequent reforms. In the early 1950s about half of Japan's industrial exports were military products. There were deep divisions in industry, in government and even inside MITI about the wisdom of a policy favoring the rebuilding of Japan's defense industries. Yet inside the government, MITI was the major proponent for developing Japan's defense industry for exports. Fearing the eventual emergence of a powerful military-industrial complex, MOF was MITI's main antagonist. The opposition of the MOF derived from its preference for a limited role of the government in the economy as well as its bitter experience in the prewar years with letting military spending get out of hand. In 1952 and 1953 the MOF blocked MITI's proposal to grant Japan's defense contractors preferential tax policies and government subsidies. Because of this opposition the Law on Manufacturing Weapons and Munitions contained only provisions that granted MITI regulatory authority over the defense industry rather than listing specific measures of support as MITI had proposed in the interest of strengthening the industry. The MOF, however, was more forthcoming in the eyes of MITI in the case of the aircraft industry. In 1953 this industry did receive government orders for producing a Japanese aircraft. But in the next year already, with government finances under great pressure, the Security Agency decided in favor of the less costly policy of leasing planes from the United States rather than producing them in Japan. Generally speaking, by 1955 the prospects for Japan's defense industry did not look good.

The MSA funds over which U.S.-Japanese negotiations commenced in July 1953 thus appealed to both MITI and defense contractors as a major opportunity. MITI drew up a funding plan that utilized MSA funds, government allocations, and credits from the city banks. But negotiations inside the Japanese government dragged on throughout 1954. The MOF was opposed to using the government's Fiscal Investment and Loan Program for this purpose; it insisted on using the MSA funds also for civilian industries; and it flatly rejected MITI's proposal to allocate MSA funds for the development of a jet engine that, according to the assessment of the MOF, had little prospect of generating significant sales. The MOF was opposed by a powerful coalition consisting of MITI, the Security Agency, MOFA, DPC, and the U.S. government. The conflict was finally resolved by a cabinet decision taken in August 1955 that basically backed the position that the MOF had advocated. Indeed, by early 1955 a shift in American policy forced MITI to abandon its hope for creating a defense industry geared to produce for world markets. With the end of the wars in Korea and Indochina the American administration no longer perceived a need to make Japan its weapons arsenal in Asia [Otake, 1984a, pp.29-58]. Thus only after the defeat of the proponents of a military-based strategy of industrialization (MITI and DPC) at the hands of the proponents of a commercial strategy (MOF and the city banks) was the stage set for Japan's eventual success in developing commercial products and technologies which was to fuel its export drive on world markets during subsequent decades. The prohibition of arms exports must be seen against this historical background.

Building on bureaucratic regulations adopted in 1960 with the intent of curbing the export of arms, Prime Minister Sato enunciated in 1967 the "Three Principles on Arms Exports" which prohibited arms exports to (1) Communist bloc countries, (2) countries prohibited from receiving arms by United Nations resolutions, and (3) countries involved or likely to be involved in an international conflict [Hummel, 1988 and 1991. Chinworth, 1987, pp 111-15. Söderberg, 1986]. Japanese business made the 1967 ban on the export of military equipment a political issue when it confronted a serious slump in profits in the wake of the first oil price shock of 1973. But business pressure backfired. A change in policy, although viewed favorably by MITI, was strongly resisted by the opposition parties, and the government chose to strengthen the ban instead. In 1976 Prime Minister Miki announced that the ban would be extended to all areas of the world and to the exports of all equipment necessary for arms production [Asagumo Shimbun-sha, 1991, p.474. Kurokawa, 1986, p.216]. In April 1978 MITI Minister Komoto affirmed before the Diet that in addition the export of technologies relevant for weapons production would be prohibited [Hummel, 1988, p.11]. A resolution passed by both Houses of the Diet in March 1981 reaffirmed the ban [Endicott, 1982a, p.454. Pempel, 1990a, p.6. Drifte, 1985b, pp.155-56. Okimoto, 1981, pp.282-85, 302-04. Nau, 1981]. According to data provided by the U.S. Arms Control and Disarmament Agency (ACDA) Japan exported 320 million dollars worth of arms in 1983, 280 million in 1984, 100 million in 1985, 130 million in 1986 and 80 million in 1987, with virtually all of these sales presumably falling under the "dual-use" category [Hummel, 1990, p.3. Hummel 1988, pp.25-36. Tanaka, 1990, p.4. Drifte, 1985a, pp.79-82]. By international standards these are negligible sums.

There exist a number of loopholes that Japanese firms can exploit to escape these strict restrictions. The export of dual-use high-tech electronics products and components is probably the most important of these [Yoshihara, 1988, p.142]. And the growing internationalization of Japanese business is also creating increasing difficulties in monitoring the behavior of Japanese firms [Drifte, 1990b, pp.16-17]. In an effort to develop an airtight monitoring system, since the late 1980s Japan has thus taken a leading role in international efforts to create a number of international regimes governing the exports of products and technologies essential to the building of weapons of mass destruction. The Gulf War of 1991 intensified Japanese interest in reaching international agreements on ABC-relevant weapons technologies [Interview No.24, Tokyo, December 19, 1991]. In the nuclear suppliers group, in the Australia Group dealing with biological and chemical weapons, in the Missile Technology Control negotations, and in the internationalization of a bilateral U.S.-Japan arrangement controlling the export of supercomputers, the Japanese government has been an active participant in creating international agreements dealing in particular with the export of dual-use technologies. Its involvement in these international negotiations is consistent with the fact that Japan has adopted the most restrictive export ban on weapons adopted by any of the industrial states [Interview No.24, Tokyo, December 19, 1991].

This effort is fraught with difficulties at both the international and the domestic level. According to the established government definition "weapons" are "objects that are used by militaries and directly employed in battle" [Asagumo Shimbun-sha, 1991, p.475]. "Japanese firms have been able to export some military items because the Japanese define 'military' in a much narrower sense than Americans do . . . A naval base in Vladivostok, for example, boasts a state-of-the-art floating dock made in Japan ostensibly for commercial use. In addition, Japanese corporations are important suppliers of components to the U.S. Department of Defense and to other NATO allies as well" [Vogel, 1989, p.79]. Dual-use products and components that can be assembled into different products are not covered by Japan's export ban. They are administered by MITI in an informal manner.

During the Gulf War in 1991, for example, domestic political considerations counselling restraints existed. To secure critical supplies of Japanese high-tech components used in a variety of weapons, the American government had to ask for the assistance of the Japanese government to persuade Japanese firms to ship electronic products to American forces in the Gulf on a priority basis. In the words of a senior official of the U.S. government this was "the first time that our growing dependence on certain critical components was spotlighted in a war setting . . . We were lucky we were dealing with allies" [Eckhouse, 1991. Samuels, 1991, p.63]. U.S. pressure overcame domestic doubts about a substantial shipment of Japanese communications equipment. MITI had to ascertain very quickly what stockpiles of material existed in Japan and then help organize rapid shipments. According to one industry source about one-fifth of the chips in weapons like the Patriot missile are made in Japan. "All the electronic components are just spaghetti filled with boards upon boards packed with chips made in Japan" [Asahi Evening News, January 26, 1991]. And all those chips, whether made by Japanese or American suppliers, sit on a small slab of black ceramic produced by Kyocera Corporation of Kyoto which controls the military-grade semiconductor packaging market. In the words of the managing director, Shunji Nosaka, "What we do is sell packages to chip makers. We don't know how they use them . . . Our products may be used for weapons. We have no way of confirming that, so I can't say any more . . . We don't know our involvement. We don't try to find out" [Schlesinger, 1991].

The government has not confirmed press reports that the Japanese government, using civilian ships, moved electronic parts, components and possibly products directly to the Gulf [Interview No.6, December 10, 1991]. Had there been substantial domestic opposition, which there was not, a ready loophole existed under Article 12 of the U.S.-Japan Status of Forces Agreement for supplying the United States with war-related equipment in times of need [Mainichi Shimbun, February 6, 1982]. The article exempts from the export ban American military forces stationed in Japan when it orders equipment for use in Japan. However, the Japanese government has no means for monitoring whether the U.S. Department of Defense is using the material in Japan or is shipping it elsewhere in the world. Weapons containing critically important components, or the components themselves, may have been moved out of Japan along this channel in the past or might be moved in this manner in the future [Interview Nos.3,11,14 and 17, Tokyo, June 11,14 and 17, 1991. Drifte, 1985a, p.82].

In the 1980s the ban on the export of weapons was redefined in some respects, especially as it affected the United States. First, Japan permitted in November 1983 the export of military technology to the United States within the context of the 1954 Mutual Defense Assistance Act [Söderberg, 1986, pp.126-56. Van de Velde, 1988a, pp.331-69. Tow, 1983 and 1987. Kinoshita, 1989. Davis, 1984b. Keddell, 1990, p.163-65. Hummel, 1988, p.17. Drifte, 1985b, pp.155-56. Rubinstein, 1987a. Drifte, 1985a, pp.84-87. Business Week, 1983]. This change in policy was important for several reasons. It broke with Japan's traditional ban of the export of military technologies. It also created a framework for future evolution in the interoperability of Japanese and American weapons systems. In the words of Prime Minister Nakasone the agreement was reached "'consistent with mutuality within the framework of the relevant provisions of the Japan-United States Mutual Defence Assistance Agreement'" [McIntosh, 1986, p.33]. In the words of at least one American businessman the purpose of the 1983 agreement was very clear. "I think the best way to stay ahead of the Japanese is to get access to their technology." With fewer than 20 percent of the 10,000 scientific and technical papers annually published in Japanese, the 1983 agreement appeared to be a good way to overcome high linguistic and technological hurdles [Browning, 1984, p.1]. The policy was not popular with the public. According to one poll more than two-thirds of the Japanese respondents were opposed to the sale of weapons technology to the United States [McIntosh, 1986, p.72].

Japan and the United States set up the Joint Military Technology Commission (JMTC) which was charged to review both the requests of the U.S. government and the response of the Japanese government. The Japanese government committed itself specifically to facilitate the flow not only of military technology but also of the transfer of dual-use technologies, and in particular production technologies of interest to the United States. Technologies such as gallium arsenide, opto electronics, compound materials, ceramics and heat-resistant materials might have application for advanced weapons systems [George, 1988, p.266. Interview No.14, Tokyo, June 15, 1991. U.S. Congress, 1990, pp.61-62. Rubinstein, 1987a, p.46].

The intent of the establishment of the JMTC was to increase the flow of technology from Japan to the United States. In this it did not succeed for a variety of reasons. The agreement was drafted by bureaucrats trained in law rather than engineering and thus was much too general. For different reasons both American and Japanese firms were very hesitant to forge new technology links. The bureaucratic rigidity of the American Defense Department interfered with the implementation of the program. And, most importantly, American firms simply lacked reliable sources of information about which Japanese firms were developing which specific technologies. As a result the United States applied for only three technology transfers in the 1980s. Japan transferred technology related to SAM missiles, the construction of naval vessels and the modification of U.S.naval vessels [Interview No.14, Tokyo, June 17, 1991. U.S. Congress, 1990, p.69].

This is a paltry figure considering the 40,000 separate contracts that Japanese firms signed between 1951 and 1984 to acquire foreign technology, the more than 100 military coproduction agreements in which Japanese manufacturers were using U.S. technologies in the 1980s, and the 10:1 ratio in the flow of Japanese researchers sent to the United States as contrasted with American researchers sent to Japan in the second half of the 1980s [Interview No.11, Tokyo, June 14, 1991. Frost, 1985. Schlesinger and Pasztor, 1990. Samuels, 1991, p.54]. Already prior to 1983 the export of dual-use technologies had been permitted. But the Japanese government hoped to encourage Japanese firms to be more forthcoming by releasing also the restrictions on the export of military technologies. It is standard operating procedure for Japanese firms, coproducing with American firms or producing under American license, to inform the JDA quarterly about the engineering modifications they have made. For the quarter starting on July 1, 1991 the figure was 700. The JDA sends that list to the DoD which in turn circulates it among the relevant American defense contractors. The American firms have the right to ask for the improved technologies under the terms of the original licensing agreement. Certain procedures governing the export of military products and technologies must be satisfied but apparently do not pose a barrier [Interview Nos. 20 and 25, Tokyo, December 18 and 19, 1991].

In the area of dual-use technology private firms typically own the technology and, for obvious reasons, are not eager to share those technologies with potential competitors in the United States [Interview No.25, Tokyo, December 20, 1991]. The fear of a hostile public reaction in Japan, the reluctance to part with technologies in the absence of a possibility to export products, and the anticipation of only minor sales were the most important obstacles that held Japanese firms back from following the government's wish of loosening the restrictions impeding the flow of military technologies to the United States [Asahi Shimbun Keizai-bu, 1989, p.76. Interview No.11, Tokyo, June 14, 1991].

When President Reagan invited Japan to join Britain, Germany and France to participate in searching for what he described as an alternative to the system of nuclear deterrence, Prime Minister Nakasone took considerable time before signing in 1987 an agreement laying out the conditions of Japan's participation in the Strategic Defense Initiative (SDI). While it adds to Japan's technology base, SDI participation is foremost a symbol of the government's political commitment to the U.S.-Japan Mutual Security Treaty [Falkenheim, 1988. Takase, 1985. Pierre, 1987. Hook, 1988, p.388. Rubinstein, 1987a, p.47. Vogel, 1989, pp.37-39]. The delay was due not only to the slow decisionmaking in Tokyo but also to some serious political hesitations about the ambiguity of the technological and strategic implications of the SDI program [Decker, 1987]. Furthermore, the economic incentives that Japanese business initially saw in participating in the development of potentially revolutionary military technologies with direct implications for commercial products was soon tempered. For it became quickly apparent that German businessmen failed to gain substantial research funding from the SDI program. In addition Japanese businessmen worried increasingly over a drain of their technology to the United States

[Decker, 1987, p.169]. In the end the Japanese decision was taken not on military or economic but on political grounds. On this issue, as on many others, Japan simply had to play the role of loyal ally.

Japan's growing technological prowess will make it increasingly important for the United States. Japan is the only major partner of the United States that does not have, or desire to have, reciprocal defense trade. With the exception of the controversial issue of compensation for the costs of stationing U.S. troops in Japan, the United States enjoys a de facto one-way defense trade relationship. If the defense contracts signed between 1986 and 1990 are implemented, annual defense trade between the United States and Japan will rise from 1.0 to 2.5 billion dollars. This imbalanced trade is likely to last. The United States outspends Japan in defense-related R and D by a factor of 15 and in aerospace by a factor of 46. Since the United States spends about twice as much in real terms as do the Japanese on R and D, the imbalance in defense and aerospace R and D in real dollar terms is about 30:1 and 92:1 respectively [Vollmer, 1991, pp.29,31]. Thus, only in areas where Japan could directly rely on civilian investments for its military security objectives would it have a realistic chance to pursue a military-strategic option. And there is no indication that any significant coalition in Japanese politics is forming to press this cause.

Technology sharing and codevelopment with the United States thus remain the most plausible policy for Japan, even though this will increase the strains in U.S.-Japan relations. This is illustrated by the hotly contested and politically controversial decision in favor of the codevelopment of the FSX aircraft [Noble, 1990. Nishihara and Potter, 1990. Vogel, 1990, pp.10-14. Garby, 1989. U.S. Congress, 1990, p.62. U.S. Congress, 1991, pp.22-23. Obata, 1988. Kohno, 1989. Mastanduno, 1990, pp.12-26. Drifte, 1985a, pp.31-36. Samuels and Whipple, 1989, 293-305. Gros, 1989, pp.36-42. Defense Agency, 1990, pp.182-183. Green, 1990. Friedman and Samuels, 1992]. In the United States the FSX issue was defined as pitting alliance politics against technology transfer. Interested in the interoperability of Japanese and American equipment the U.S. Department of Defense in particular was favorably disposed toward the project. For it guaranteed large contracts for the American defense industry and promised some flow-back of technological developments that might result from this project. Many politicians, however, especially in Congress, saw the arrangement as ceding technological secrets to Japanese manufacturers who would use them in order to attack in the near future one of the last bastions of America's preeminence in high-technology industry, the aerospace industry [Pempel, 1990a, p.7]. General Dynamics as the major U.S. contractor for the FSX will provide among others an advanced airframe while Japanese defense contractors will contribute phased-array radar and new lightweight materials for the wings. U.S. firms will receive around 35-45 percent of the development costs of the plane, paid by the Japanese government, and about 40 percent of the total work as well as five billion dollars realized through the eventual sale of the plane to the SDF. In contrast to codevelopment projects in NATO, the United States does not intend to buy any of the FSX planes.

"At the crux of the FSX issue is not the question of whether to'buy American' or'produce Japanese'; rather, it is technology transfer" [Rubinstein, 1987a, p.47]. Indicated already in the mid-1980s by a shift in MITI policy in favor of codevelopment in the commercial aircraft market, the FSX episode confirmed an important change in Japanese policy [Interview No.3, Tokyo, June 11, 1991]. At this stage in the evolution of Japan's defense industry, but not necessarily for the indefinite future, "Japan's technological independence in aerospace can only come through international joint ventures in which Japan plays the role of a co-equal partner. Accordingly, MITI shifted its funding for the aerospace industry from indigenous R&D to support for international joint ventures—an unprecedented change" [Gros, 1989, pp.45-46].

This change in public policy is of fundamental importance for what Japanese officials regard as one of the most important growth industries that Japan needs to master in the next two decades. Because four-fifths of Japan's aerospace production is accounted for by the military market this is particularly true for the area of defense. Throughout the postwar years the U.S. Defense Department had relegated commercial considerations to secondary importance and favored coproduction on military and political grounds. While the Defense Department neglected commercial considerations, American corporations did not. Coproduction became their favored strategy because license fees and a lucrative upgrade business were generating profits far in excess of those that could be made through off-the-shelf sales. This preference was enhanced when the United States ended all military aid to Japan in 1968. By 1975 coproduction had become an established practice. The Japanese government also favored coproduction over direct purchases from American defense contractors. The interests of the Japanese government and American defense contractors thus have converged. Japanese defense officials are very clear about wanting to achieve greater technological autonomy from the United States in important defense technologies. "'It gives me chills to think how much we still depend on U.S. parts,' laments Yasuo Komoda, a former major general in the Ground Self-Defense forces" [Vogel, 1990, p.8]. Off-the-shelf purchases are normally rejected since they do not enhance the level of Japan's indigenous defense capacity [Interview No.11, Tokyo, June 14, 1991]. The success of this strategy during the last several decades has even led Steven

Vogel to claim that "Japan's options are no longer constrained by technology, but openly by politics" [Vogel, 1990, p.10].

The terms of bargaining between Japan and the U.S. have shifted over time. With "technonationalism" rising in both Japan and the United States, "the line between economics and defense has largely vanished in the high-tech fields found in FSX development" [Nishihara and Potter, 1990, p.26]. A 1984 report of the Defense Science Board pointed to Japan's indigenous defense production and underscored the growing links between commercial and military technologies. Japanese policymakers now take as a given the growing importance not only of spin-offs from weapon to civilian products but of spin-ons, that is the relevance of civilian technologies for weapon procurement. Negotiations about the codevelopment and coproduction arrangements for the FSX were contentious in part because of the growing awareness of Japan as a rising producer of high-tech products and components, both civilian and military. For example, Naito Ichiro, former head of the JDA's Technical Research and Development Institute, has argued that "once demand for a fighter aircraft exceeds 300 units it will be possible to establish a mass production system that eventually will enable us to gain sight of the civil aircraft market" [Samuels and Whipple, 1989, p.306]. And many Japanese officials argue that various Japanese civilian projects underway could be linked to a program of indigenous aircraft production: the fighter design effort and T-2 Control Configured Vehicle testing program of Mitsubishi Heavy Industries, the radar work of Mitsubishi Electric Company, the flight computer program of Fujitsu, the avionics research of Nippon Electric Company and Hitachi, as well as various composite material and stealth technology projects [Garby, 1989, p.9. Samuels, 1991, pp.59-64].

But these are visions of the future. At this stage coproduction and codevelopment help to secure for Japanese industries technologies that will create a stronger base from which eventually to produce major weapons systems solely with Japanese resources. Technological self-sufficiency is a general, long-term objective of important bureaus of ministries such as MITI as well as the JDA. This goal enjoys wide political and social support [U.S. Congress, 1990, p.67. Interview No.25, Tokyo, December 19, 1991]. The FSX episode is not the only recent example, in the area of defense, that touches this objective. When in 1991 it was discovered that Japan Aviation Electronics Industry (JAEI) had shipped illegally missile components to Iran, the U.S. State Department imposed an export embargo on the firm thus threatening the supply of components and spare parts for which JAEI is the sole source to the ASDF. A prolonged embargo would have made it impossible for all three branches of the SDF to operate at normal strength [Fujishima, 1992, pp.216-17. Interview No.23, Tokyo,

December 19, 1991]. Like the FSX debacle this episode strengthens resolve on the part of some elements of the Japanese government to attain technological self-sufficiency in important weapons systems. But Japan's government is internally split on issues involving that objective. In the debate over the FSX in the early 1980s, for example, JDA's TRDI and Air Staff Office, and MITI's Aircraft and Ordnance Division favored domestic development while MITI's Trade Bureau, JDA's budget officials, the MOF and MOFA were cautious or opposed [Samuels and Whipple, 1989, p.294. U.S. Congress, 1990, p.67. Interview Nos.8 and 16, Tokyo, June 13 and 17, 1991]. MITI's Aircraft and Ordnance Division switched its position, to the dismay of SDF officers, around 1986 [Asahi Shimbun Keizai-bu, 1989, pp.237-40].

The FSX coproduction as well as other recent decisions—among them the MSDF's decision to buy Aegis destroyers through the Foreign Military Sales program of the United States as well as the probable purchase of a number of AWACS planes—involve, to those holding the objective of reaching eventually the stage of technological self-reliance, the adjusting of such objective to the political requirements of forging a consensus inside the Japanese government and placating a nervous American ally without undercutting it [U.S. Congress, 1990, p.68]. The deployment of Aegis and AWACS would be a "quantum leap" in Japan's postwar defense policy [U.S. Congress, 1990, p.68]. In a carefully researched report the Office of Technology Assessment concludes that "for the JDA, the important thing is the precedent of deploying state-of-the-art military systems that will give the Self-Defense Forces greater technological leverage. Once these foreign-supplied systems are deployed," however, domestic upgrades may be substituted for foreign components in deployed systems. "This may lead to further pressures for the development of totally domestic replacements . . . Focusing excessively on the aircraft industry risks missing the point of a diversified Japanese long-term industrial strategy of using technological inputs from military production for everything from fishing rods to high performance aircraft" [U.S. Congress, 1990, pp.68, 71]. The estimated 40,000 separate contracts that Japanese firms signed between 1951 and 1984 to acquire foreign technologies are evidence of the breadth of the Japanese technology acquisition [Samuels, 1991, p.54]. T.J. Pempel argues similarly that Japan's companies seek "to position themselves well for future commercial competition in production involving higher technology." Much of the recent shift in Japanese military and defense policy, while representing a change in external security policy, also serves in effect "to ensure the external conditions needed to guarantee an economically motivated technology base" [Pempel, 1990a, p.6].

The controversy over the FSX was very public and has overshadowed other unsuccessful attempts to deal with the problem of technology sharing. The 1983 technology agreement and Japan's participation in SDI, for example, did precious little to accelerate the flowback of Japanese technology to the United States [Interview No.6, December 10, 1991]. Considering repeated failures in policy the 12th Meeting of the Japan-U.S. Systems and Technology Forum agreed in September 1990, therefore, on five areas of technology in which flow-back from Japan to the United States would be strongly encouraged: rocket engines, infrared sensors, magnetic technology, ceramics, and advanced material replacing traditional steel. On the Japanese side the agreement represents, however, a delicate political coalition, with MOFA playing the role of strong proponent and MITI that of reluctant ally. For MITI has first-hand experience in dealing with private firms which are extremely reluctant to share proprietary technologies, especially since the intended recipient is the American Department of Defense. It might subject business to detailed regulations and expose it to the risk of bad publicity in Japan [U.S. Congress 1991, pp.115-120]. And in contrast to MOFA, MITI does not see its mission in the sharing of Japanese technology with the U.S. producers but in creating a more autonomous technology base for Japan's civilian and defense industrial base.

Since American pressures for technology transfer have grown in the 1980s, and are likely to grow further in the future, in the interest of securing the political relationship with the United States MITI will probably make partial concessions. It will do so in particular if it can use American pressure, together with the JDA, to seek greater leverage over private corporations. This, however, may require relaxing existing restrictions on the export of military technologies and products and, perhaps, granting the permission to export the products of joint ventures with American firms [Interview Nos.3, 6, 8 and 11, Tokyo, June 11, 12, 13 and 14, 1991]. But this is a controversial option that would probably be entertained seriously only if the anticipated cutbacks in military spending were to force the closure of major defense production lines. More likely is an expansion in the sharing of militarily relevant technology with the United States without any change in the policies affecting the production or exports of weapons. Over time Japan's unilateral export restrictions have become diluted for a number of reasons, including "the demands resulting from a military alliance with a nuclear superpower" [Drifte, 1990b, p.84].

In sum, the adjustment of Japan's security policy to facilitate the flow of militarily relevant technology from Japan to the United States has been fraught with difficulties. The United States has pressed hard for a change in Japanese policy. But neither Japan's domestic structure nor the normative context in which security policy is debated and resolved has favored policy change on an issue of increasing importance for Japan's relationship with the United States. Steven Vogel concludes that "given its technological and economic strength, Japan has the capability to become a major military power within the not-too-distant future (10-25 years)." Japan's choice will be constrained increasingly by politics, not technology [Vogel, 1991, p.3].

D. Conclusion

One of the core tenets in the realist study of international relations holds that rational state actors seek to maximize relative gains in the international system and in doing so adjust their behavior to the dictates of a changing international situation. But Japanese policymakers, rather than following the logic of realist doctrine, have responded to the domestic and transnational structures in which security policy is formulated and implemented. Since the mid-1970s Japan has experienced great changes in the international system which affect its security. The weakening of the American position in East Asia and the growth of a Soviet military presence in the late 1970s, the second Cold War in Europe in the early 1980s, dramatic changes in Soviet defense and foreign policy since the mid-1980s, and the break-up of the Soviet Union in 1991, however, have elicited no sharp changes in Japan's security policy. In short, there exists no close relation between the great changes that have affected the international system during the past two decades and the evolution of Japan's security policy along its economic, military and political dimensions.

The organization of power in the Japanese government, in the relations between state and society, and in Japan's transnational relations with the United States has balanced an emphasis on the economic and political dimensions of security in Japan's domestic structure against the military dimension of security in the transnational structure of the U.S.-Japan relationship. Politically the pressure from the domestic opposition of the LDP on the one hand and pressure from Washington on the other were the two key factors. Japanese security policy attempted to reconcile the contradictory pressures from these two sources even if it appeared to be "irrational" from the perspective of systemic theories of international relations.

The normative context which has informed Japan's security policy has been of equal importance. As discussed in Chapter 4, that context was consensual on issues of economic security; it was deeply contested on questions of military security; and it was disputed on the political aspects of Japan's security. On questions of economic security both structures and norms encouraged the adaptability of Japan's energy and technology policy.

It is thus impossible to isolate the effects the normative context had on policy adaptation. On military issues such as defense spending, the dispatch of the SDF for peacekeeping operations overseas, and the three non-nuclear principles the structural effects on policy are indeterminate. While domestic structures have worked against an expansion in Japan's military role, the transnational structures of the Japanese state have supported such an expansion. Policy rigidity resulted from the normative context more than the indeterminate effect of state structure. The political dimension of Japanese security, finally, reveals a variable pattern of policy change. While norms were not particularly favorable, structures and norms facilitated a relatively flexible policy, for example, in the acquisition of modern weapons blurring the distinction between offense and defense, in the growing defense cooperation between the two countries, and in the expansion of the notion of individual self-defense. On the issue of technology transfer, by contrast, domestic and transnational structures created clashing incentives and thus were indeterminate in their effects on policy. The normative context of policy, on the other hand, was clearly unfavorable. Japan's security policy thus has been marked by policy rigidity. We can conclude that it is the normative context rather than the military or economic content of policy that is important in shaping the pattern of policy adjustment.

The intimate links between Japan's evolving defense policy and the changing character of military technology also illustrates the economic dimension of Japan's security policy. For a variety of political and technological reasons security issues are becoming more submerged and hidden in market relations [Borrus and Zysman, forthcoming]. Perhaps no one is more attuned to this shift than are the economic leaders of Japan. American calls for free trade in defense to combat a growing "military protectionism" and the establishment of a "Defense GATT" [Burt, 1991] on the one hand and American technonationalism on the other have left only a small impression on Japan's business leaders, civil servants and politicians. Japanese leaders are seeking to reconcile the tension inherent in their long-term move toward technological autonomy which may rupture Japan's dependency on U.S. military technologies on the one hand and their recognition of the political desirability of future cooperation and reciprocal technology exchanges with the United States on the other[Chinworth, 1990a, pp.229-30].

Many Japanese officials are imbued deeply by the traditional notion that national self-reliance is an unquestioned good. In this view, according to a JDA official, it is best "if all the equipment is produced from a local base without any hindrance, and its quality is superb" [Carrel, 1983]. On the other hand, Japanese firms have never been reluctant to link up with foreign firms. Similarly, gaining access to the knowledge base of other societies and forging long-term relationships for mutual gains, based on a relationship of mututal vulnerability, is not a frightening prospect for Japan's economic policymakers. It is in fact the condition under which big business and government have lived during the last forty years. Exclusively national responses to technological change are in this perspective increasingly anachronistic. Corporate strategies of joint production, foreign investment, cross-licensing and codevelopment are a strong indication of the eagerness of Japan's business leaders to work in situations of mutual vulnerability. Willingness to integrate with other corporations and societies, based on the notion of long-term interest, is an acceptable prospect for Japanese economic elites because they expect to do relatively better in such relationships than most foreign firms and governments. For MITI and business leaders Japanese defense policy is an effective strategy for serving a central element of Japan's definition of national security, growing technological autonomy and industrial competitiveness [Samuels and Whipple, 1989, pp.305-08]. In their perspective defense policy thus becomes one instrument among several to ease Japan into the next century and a new, more international phase of its national evolution. Japan's search for a new, political role in the world, will remain inextricably linked to the same old, economic base. National defense is one important tool for preserving the basic mission of Japan's economic statecraft [Pempel, 1990a, p.22].

Changes in Japan's security policy are gradually creating new options for Japan's military. By 1984 the SDF had over 50 destroyers, twice as many as the U.S. Seventh Fleet. Japan had as many ASW aircraft as was under the entire Pacific Command of the United States Armed Forces. And Japan's 400 fighter aircraft exceeded the combined total that the United States had stationed in Japan, the Republic of Korea and the Philippines [Keddell, 1990, pp. 169-70]. Japan's military options are not explicitly national. If Japan would want to create a national military capability it would have to acquire the offensive systems it now shuns for political reasons or, at a minimum, a broad range of stealth technologies [Interview No.23, Kyoto, June 24, 1991]. The political consensus in Japan is wide and deep that military issues cannot be separated from political considerations. But the high-tech nature of the weapons Japan is acquiring create a base from which such a national military option could be pursued in the event, unlikely as it appears now, that political perspectives should no longer be viewed as dominating military perspectives.

Imperceptible policy change, concealed by the variable tensions betweeen social and legal norms, may still lead to significant new options for Japan's security policy. As Steven Vogel wrote in 1984 "in the long run . . . incremental decisions could lead Japanese defense policy in any one of several very different directions . . . After ten years of slightly accelerated incremental build-up the Japanese people, the media, and the politicians may be much more accustomed to the idea of a postwar Japanese military" [Vogel, 1984, pp.46,54]. A few years later Vogel appeared to have shifted his position somewhat: "whether it is a military superpower or not, Japan at the end of the century will wield considerable influence in global power politics. Japan will be a'great power' in the international system, although it may be a great power of a new and different kind" [Vogel, 1991, p.35]

Closer defense cooperation with the United States in the 1980s has created a broader range of policy choice for Japan. Part of the difficulty in evaluating this change derives from the fact that a semblance of policy continuity has been cautiously maintained. During a decade of significant military buildup, the NDPO, the three non-nuclear principles, and the principles of defensive defense and individual self-defense all have officially remained intact. The national option that is being created now may not be exercised. But in Japan the French saying "plus ca change, plus c'est la meme chose" is inapplicable. In the words of Takashi Inoguchi "change comes with the disguise of constancy" [Inoguchi, 1985, p.32].

VI
Conclusion

Since the Meiji Restoration a wealthy nation and a strong military (fukoku kyohei) have been the traditional objectives of Japanese security policy. With the end of the Pacific War this traditional maxim has been modified rather than abandoned. Military security is now embedded in a broader definition of national security. By traditional measures of military strength Japan ranks far behind its major industrial competitors. In 1985, before the break-up of the Soviet Union, Japan's ground forces ranked 28th, its airforce 23rd and its navy ranked seventh in terms of total tonnage and eleventh in the number of hulls [Hatsuse, 1986, pp.88-89. Asahi Shimbun Japan Access, December 2, 1991]. Relying on a formula that takes account of personnel strength, firepower, training and other measures of military power, the U.S. Department of Defense has compared Japan with the member states of NATO. In military manpower Japan ranks eighth, between Spain and Greece. It ranks ninth in ground forces, between Spain and the Netherlands. The strength of the Japanese airforce ranks eighth, between Turkey and Spain. And in naval power Japan ranks fourth, between France and Germany. However, the MSDF is less than one-tenth of the size of the U.S. navy [Halloran, 1991, p.8. Hatsuse, 1986, pp.88-89].

A rough estimate of the costs Japan would incur if it were to build a conventional military force commensurate with its economic strength and the size of its population suggests annual expenditures of 150 to 200 billion dollars for a decade, considerably more, that is, than current estimates of the economic costs of German unification in the 1990s [Halloran, 1991, pp.18-19]. These are very large sums even for an economy of Japan's size. They are congruent with the fact that questions of national security continue to be viewed not so much in military as in economic and political terms. In recent decades Japan's security policy has eschewed the traditional trappings of military status and power. On this point Herman Kahn was clearly mistaken when he projected in 1981 that Japan was likely to build nuclear

203

weapons by the late 1980s, and that West Germany would immediately follow suit [Asahi Evening News, April 7, 1981]. Only a small fringe in Japanese society currently views the possession of nuclear weapons as a symbol of international stature that Japan should aspire to. Most Japanese view nuclear weapons and a strong military as generating neither wealth nor strength but immense political and military risks instead.

The pursuit of civilian high-technology products does not, even though it is making Japan into one of the world's leading producers of technologies and components with direct military relevance. In his recent book Shintaro Ishihara minces few words in discussing the Gulf war. "Computers were placed on most major weapons America used in the Gulf War, and the high-capacity semiconductors that constitute the brains of these computers were mostly made in Japan. Of the semiconductors used in the modern weapons which are indispensable for the American strategy, 93 types are foreign-made. Only one is British. The remaining 92 are all produced in Japan" [Ishihara and Eto, 1991, p.123]. According to this view the status of the United States as a superpower is illusory because it no longer rests on a secure foundation of technological leadership in areas central to national security. The 1988 Defense Science Board of the United States concluded similarly that "we are, and will remain, dependent on foreign resources for critical components of our weapons systems. We cannot eliminate foreign dependency in this era of a globalized defense industry. We can and must eliminate the apparent loss of leadership in key defense technologies" [Noble, 1990, p.34]. Ishihara thus merely says openly what many Japanese and the U.S. Department of Defense acknowledge obliquely [U.S. Congress, 1990,1991].

Neither outright confrontation nor political acquiescence in U.S.-Japanese relations, is the likely political background for the future evolution of Japan's security policy. For Japanese leaders "autonomy and alliance need not be and are not currently antithetical" [Curtis, 1981, p.873]. In the 1970s the SDF and the Security Treaty were increasingly accepted by the Japanese public. During the 1980s the domestic impetus for incremental changes in favor of an increased defense posture were unmistakable. In the 1990s defense spending is likely to grow at a lower rate while the political pressure for the participation of the SDF in international peacekeeping operations will increase. How Japan's neighbors and allies, including the United States, will react to these gradual changes remains to be seen. But according to Susan Pharr Japanese foreign policy continues to be built around a "low-cost, low-risk, benefit-maximizing strategy" that, in the eyes of the conservatives, "has served Japan's national self-interest extraordinarily well in the past, and that continues to do so today" [Pharr, 1992, p.2].

The structures and norms that define Japanese security interests make it likely that within the established framework for interpreting Japanese security in international political and economic terms Japan will pursue a more activist policy in Asia, supported by a continued alliance with the United States. This would conform to the emergence of a new regionalism in Europe centering around EC92 and a united Germany but involving as well the United States as a participant in a regional collective security agreement and as a partner and competitor in the European single market. Compared to Germany the structural integration of Japan with its neighbors is smaller. But as is true of the German case the domestic, transnational and normative determinants of Japan's security policy point to a continuation of a policy that favors international cooperation with the United States and the Western Alliance [Berger, 1992].

This world of regions may, however, reflect what James Kurth has called a shift from the Atlantic to the Pacific Basin paradigm [Kurth, 1989]. International economic liberalization acquires a radically new meaning when it is not a general precept informing economic policy but is practiced instead by mercantilist states only at specific stages of their industrial development. And the break-up of the Soviet Union and the diminution of the Russian threat in the Far East eliminates the practice of extended deterrence while leaving in place the finite deterrence that has characterized Asian security arrangement since World War II. The United States, Japan, China and the other Asian states will give shape to Asia's regionalism in the coming decades. In its first detailed analysis of the world after the Cold War the Pentagon concluded that a combination of Japanese economic and technological prowess with American military power is likely to continue to shape Japan's approach to its national security [New York Times, 1992. Tyler, 1992].

Both as a complement and as a possible alternative Japanese security policy is likely to emphasize Asian regional security structures in the coming years. Since the demise of the Southeast Asia Treaty Organization (SEATO) there exists no regional security organization in Asia. Asian security is organized by a set of bilateral security pacts revolving around the United States. But since the early 1980s the Association of Southeast Asian Nations (ASEAN) member states has begun to consider some regional security issues at its meetings [Nakagawa, 1984, pp.829-30]. In the 1970s and 1980s the Japanese government was adamantly opposed to engaging the Soviet Union in regional arms control talks. But with the demise of the Soviet Union and a growing fear of a serious deterioration of U.S.-Japanese relations Japan's interest in a sustained security dialogue in Asia is bound to grow, as illustrated at the 1991 ASEAN Post-Ministerial Conference. With American military presence in Asia weakening Japan is likely to become a more vocal advocate of cooperative regional security regimes. A key issue for Japanese foreign policy will be not only to guarantee the continued involvement of the United States and China in Asia but to decide also whether ASEAN should gradually develop some security functions or whether Indonesia should become Southeast Asia's regional hegemon, tied closely to Japan and loosely to the United States.

What is at stake is the future political definition of Japan's international context. In contrast to the United States and Europe the rationale for Japan's SDF was not limited only to the Soviet threat. American pressure and the importance of Japan's political relationship with the United States, that is, political factors, created the main rationale for the substantial increase in Japan's military capabilities during the last two decades. The clash between America's global-military interests and Japan's national-economic concerns partly explains why Japan's most important "ally", the United States, in the 1980s has been "the occasion of more foreign policy, and foreign economic policy, controversies than all of Japan's potential enemies combined" [Pempel, 1990b, p.28]. In the future, countering Russia may continue to be important in the minds of some defense planners [Interview No.6, December 10, 1991]. Furthermore, possible instabilities in Asia, on the Korean peninsula and in China have convinced important segments of the LDP and the bureaucracy of Japan's need for a minimum defensive capability even without a clear enemy [Interview No.13, Tokyo, December 13, 1991]. However, the strategy and equipment which the SDF has adopted during the past fifteen years may not be adequate to deal with less defined security threats in Asia in the future. But even without a Soviet threat Japan's ties with the United States are likely to remain an essential ingredient of its security policy.

Structures, we have argued, account for the comprehensive character of Japan's security policy. The organization of power in Japanese politics, specifically within the government's bureaucracy as well as the party system, and more broadly in state-society relations, tends to suppress the military concerns and interests that the transnational dimension of Japan's state activates. In 1970 former Ambassador Edwin Reischauer remarked "that there is a deep distrust of militarism in Japan, but a growing feeling that the country can't avoid the international responsibilities that require a strong military force" [Mendel, 1970, p.1049]. This has proved to overestimate Japan's willingness to accept an expansive role for its military.

But it is important to understand the reason for Japan's evident reluctance to acquire the traditional military trappings of a great power. Japanese pacifism has very little resemblance to Western-style pacifism. For many in Japan peace is unsettling to the extent that it connotes balance in a symmetrical bipolar or multipolar setting [Galtung, 1974, p.357]. Japan's yearning for peace is based "on a profound, collective reaction against World War II and a lot that has happened as a result of the war" [Beer, 1987]. It is impossible to sort out the effect of World War II or Japan's broader historical evolution from the effects of social structure and norms. Kazuo Ogura, for example, sees an interactive relationship between the two when he writes that "due to the defeat in World War II, and the collapse of a code of previously held ethics, the Japanese have shied away from projecting their beliefs and ideals internationally. Indeed, even now, almost 50 years after defeat, they still appear to be apprehensive of even expressing one" [Ogura, 1991]. Johan Galtung sees a fundamental cause buried more deeply in Japan's history as it has shaped social structures and norms. For him Japan is a country "which has a technology without a message" [Galtung, 1974, p.356]. Finally, an even broader view of history points to the absence of deep bonds of interdependence between Japan and the outside world. These and other historical interpretations remain open for further discussion. But Japan's passive stance toward affairs affecting international peace has been noted by many observers.

While their interaction with various political structures requires careful examination, Japan's social and legal norms appear to account for the flexibility and rigidity with which Japan's security policy adapts to a changing world. Normative agreement on the issue of economic security makes for flexible policy adjustment while contested norms on military issues makes Japan's security policy rigid in coping with change. Political security issues, dealing with different facets of the U.S.-Japan relationship, show a variable pattern that underlines the political importance of normative consensus rather than the inherent character of policy issues. The evolving role of the SDF in the U.S.-Japan security relationship was relatively unproblematic even though it had a substantial military aspect to it. The issue of transferring technologies of interest to American defense contractors, on the other hand, has proven very difficult, even though it has a large economic element to it. Norms are less contested in the first, political-military case than they are in the second, political-economic case.

The tension between legal and social norms has been a central feature of the normative context of Japanese security policy. Article 9 of the Constitution has been contested politically between Right and Left for more than three decades. But its very existence is as central to the self-definition of Japan's position in the modern world as is the First Amendment for the United States. However, Japan subscribes to the widely held view that the international system still remains a society of states, governed by interests, not a community of nations held together by norms. Japan sees itself surviving in this society of states through constant redefinition of the interests that inform its security policy. Japan's domestic law does not grant precedent to international law, as is increasingly true in Europe and the European Court of Justice, and thus does not ground Japan's security policy in an international community. Japanese law does, however, provide support for political actors who contest the legitimacy of a course of action made possible by domestic and international structures and the evolution of social norms. Legal norms thus help constrain the changes in policy that are also forced by a situational logic.

The growing importance of the military aspects of Japanese security in the 1980s, for example, was brought about incrementally and flexibly without affecting any dramatic changes in either state structures or social and legal norms. As Steven Vogel observes even advocates of a military build-up "realize that the constraints against rearmament still carry force, and that above all, expansion must be incremental . . . Even the hawks realize that the push for military expansion will be most successful if it is implemented gradually" [Vogel, 1984, p.46]. Neither the Constitution nor the Mutual Security Treaty were changed to accommodate the defense build-up of the 1980s. "A move to revise the Constitution would entail too many political costs. A revision of the Security Treaty is also unnecessary" because, in the eyes of the conservatives, the current treaty benefits Japan and can be interpreted flexibly to permit bilateral defense cooperation [Mochizuki, 1983/84, p.160]. An informal reinterpretation of legal norms has permitted a broadening in the definition of Japan's right to self-defense [Vogel, 1984, p.52]. In short, the normative context of policy choice embodies a political contest involving the interplay of social and legal norms which maintains, by and large, the legitimacy of the policy changes that it permits. The normative context of Japan's security policy is thus defined by a political discourse that approximates neither the tenets of political realism nor of political idealism. In the words of Henry Nau "the realist view does not go far enough when it defines interest (i.e., wealth and power) and ignores identity (i.e. whose wealth and power), and the Wilsonian view goes too far when it assumes a common political identity (i.e. all nations express similar political values) and considers relative power and wealth to be irrelevant" [Nau, 1990b, p.8. Nau, 1990a]. Japan is an example of a country that defies description in terms of the categories of realism and idealism. The tension between legal and social norms that help shape Japan's evolving security policy raises a question: "Is it better for Japan to plan to fight a war for which it is prepared or to prepare for a war it may have to fight" [Levin, 1988, p.25].

In an effort to create stronger bonds, Japan's government may seek to intensify the mutual vulnerabilities between Japan and the United States. A European comparison may be helpful here. The unexpected turn of French foreign policy on questions of European integration since the mid-1980s appears to be motivated primarily by the objective of tying down in a European framework a Germany that otherwise might be too strong and threatening to French interests. Tying down a potentially volatile and unpredictable ally is a daunting task not only for the French but also the Japanese. American reaction to Japanese security policy has been unpredictable. In the words of Yasuhiro Nakasone, former head of the JDA and former Prime Minister, "some Americans argue that Japan is not doing enough for its own defense. Other Americans argue that a step-up in Japanese defense capabilities would lead to a revival of militarism. Japanese are at a loss to know what to do. One side says get off the bus, the other side says get on" [Olsen, 1985, p. 12]. Important sectors in Japanese politics will be considering, especially in the sphere of military security, a structural integration of defense and defense related high-technology industries across the Pacific.

Such integration would not only cut against the relentless push of Japanese corporations for a position of leadership in world markets but, more importantly, also against the American preference for national autonomy and political unilateralism, especially on questions of national defense. Acceptance of a condition of mutual vulnerability does not disagree with the Japanese interpretation of sovereignty as the juridical equality of actors who remain differentiated by status and cultural legacies. But since it would vitiate the existence of any one decisive source of political power and influence, such an international system of asymmetric vulnerabilities may not agree with American notions of autonomy. It would acknowledge instead the existence of multiple nodes of power that require playing a skillful game of politics. It is the kind of politics that the Japanese have cultivated at home in the last 40 years.

We have argued here that these changes will not translate into sharp breaks in Japan's security policy. For it is only the external balance of power as mediated by domestic and transnational structures and norms that drives Japan's security policy. Both its domestic structures and the normative context in which security interests are defined appear to be evolving only very gradually.

A comparison with Japan's policy of internal security offers some additional insights into why its external security policy is likely to evolve only gradually in a time of dramatic international change [Katzenstein and Tsujinaka, 1991]. The penetration of the Japanese military by other bureaucratic and political organizations is markedly greater than that of the powerful police. Unlike the police the military is not closely linked to Japanese society; but Japan's defense economy, although small in absolute size is carried by the dynamism of Japan's civilian technologies. Transnational military ties, especially with the United States, are probably stronger on questions of external security than are the international links of the Japanese police on questions of internal security. And the low degree of vulnerability of Japan to any serious threat to its internal security has favored an autonomous policy stance in contrast to Japan's reliance on the American political guarantee of its external security. Structural constraints and opportunities thus make an independent policy more likely for questions of internal than external security. On this score Karel Von Wolferen is mistaken when he applies his general argument about the lack of political control by anyone over the Japanese state to both the military and the police. "The police, like the military, are essentially in charge of themselves" [Von Wolferen, 1990, p.A23; 1991, pp.34-35]. The data point rather to much greater political restraints on the military than the police.

Since Japan's SDF have their origin as a police force, internal and external security are clearly related. This is reflected specifically, for example, in the SDF's restrained outlook on the use of arms which is more typical of a police force than of an army [Interview No.8, Tokyo, December 11, 1991]. More generally, both the Japanese military and police subscribe to a comprehensive view which sees security at home and abroad intimately linked to, respectively, socio-political and economic-political conditions. On both internal and external security issues the interplay of social with legal norms help define the interests that inform Japanese policy. In the case of internal security this has facilitated the gradual expansion of police power in state and society while impeding international policies by underlining, until very recently, the importance of the notion of Japanese "uniqueness." On questions of external security, in contrast, the interplay of social with legal norms has been more complex. In some instances it has facilitated a gradual redefinition of Japan's international role by providing the political space necessary for making some important adjustments in security policy. On other issues, by contrast, the normative context in which the interests of Japanese security policy are defined has resulted in stalemate.

In contrast to the position advanced in this monograph other analysts articulate a more pessimistic view. Hisahiko Okazaki, for example, draws a sobering historical analogy between the Japan-U.S. relationship and the 17th century naval rivalry between the Netherlands and England, to sound a note of warning about Japan and the United States [Okazaki, 1990b]. At the root of that conflict was England's jealousy of Dutch prosperity. "England may not have had the economic and technical prowess needed to outtrade the Dutch, but it could use its geographical and strategic advantages to control their trade routes and fishing grounds and so cut them off from the source of their wealth and power" [Okazaki, 1990b, p.14]. A pacifist trading nation, the Dutch believed that a common enemy (Spain), a shared ideology (Protestantism), and similar political institution (republicanism), would make war between the two countries impossible. They were wrong. With the vanishing of the Spanish threat England, and in particular Parliament, increasingly came to view Dutch economic power as England's most serious threat. English protectionism in the form of the Navigation Act of 1651 was so ruinous to foreign competition that the Dutch were drawn reluctantly into a war which, without friends, they could not win. Okazaki argues, however, that Japan's interests are best served not by confrontation with the Americans or a turn to Asia but by strong links to the Anglo-American world [Okazaki, 1990b, p.16]. "Was there some way," he asks, "for the Netherlands to avoid conflict with England even while preserving its own security and maintaining its status as a major economic power? If so, where did the Dutch go wrong?" [Okazaki, 1990b, p.16].

Answers to these questions require an analysis of the evolving structures and norms shaping Japan's security policy as well as of the effects that policy has on other states. The structures and norms that help shape the policies of Japan's political leadership suggest at the end of the Cold War a simultaneous choice of Japan's growing economic involvement with Asia on the one hand and its continued, close if altered, security relationship with the United States on the other. The future role of Japan in the international system is likely to be shaped by the intersection of these two spheres of policy and politics.

References

Agency of Natural Resources and Energy, Ministry of International Trade and Industry. 1990. Energy in Japan: Facts and Figures. Tokyo: Agency of Natural Resources and Energy.

Akaha, Tsuneo. 1984. "Japan's Nonnuclear Policy," Asian Survey 24,8 (August): 852-77.

Akaha, Tsuneo. 1985a. "Japan's Three Nonnuclear Principles: A Coming Demise?" Peace and Change 11,1 (Spring): 75-89.

Akaha, Tsuneo. 1985b. Japan in Global Ocean Politics. Honolulu: University of Hawaii Press.

Akaha, Tsuneo. 1986. "Japan's Response to Threats of Shipping Disruptions in Southeast Asia and the Middle East," Pacific Affairs 59,2 (Summer): 255-77.

Akaha, Tsueno. 1987. "The Political Economy of Japanese Security Policy," paper prepared for delivery at the Conference on the Role of Small and Medium Powers in the International Alliance System, Acadia University, Wolfville, Nova Scotia, October 18-21.

Akaha, Tsuneo. 1990. "Comprehensive Security as an Alternative to Military Security in the Post-Hegemonic World: The Japanese Model and its Applicability in East Asia," paper prepared for delivery at the 1990 International Studies Association Convention, Washington D.C., April 10-14.

Akaha, Tsuneo. 1991. "Japan's Comprehensive Security Policy: A New East Asian Environment," Asian Survey 31,4 (April): 324-40.

Akaha, Tsuneo. n.d. "U.S. Hegemonic Decline and Its Implications for U.S.-Japan and Other Alliances in Asia-Pacific," unpublished paper, Department of Political Science, Bowling Green State University, Bowling Green, Ohio.

Akao, Nobutoshi, ed. 1983. Japan's Economic Security. New York: St. Martin's.

Akita, George. 1967. Foundations of Constitutional Government in Modern Japan, 1868-1900. Cambridge, Mass.: Harvard University Press.

Alagappa, Muthiah. 1988. "Japan's Political and Security Role in the Asia-Pacific Region," Contemporary Southeast Asia 10,1 (June): 17-54.

Angel, Robert C. 1988-89. "Prime Ministerial Leadership in Japan: Recent Changes in Personal Style and Administrative Organization," Pacific Affairs 61,4 (Winter): 583-602.

Arase, Yutaka. 1957. "Nihon Gunkoku-shugi to Masu Media" ("Japan's Militarism and Mass Media"), Shiso 399 (September): 33-47.

Arkin, William M. and Chappell, David. 1985. "Forward Offensive Strategy: Raising the Stakes in the Pacific," World Policy Journal 2,3 (Summer): 481-500.

Aruga, Tadashi. 1989. "The Security Treaty Revision of 1960," in Akira Iriye and Warren I. Cohen, eds., The United States and Japan in the Postwar World, pp.61-79. Lexington: University of Kentucky Press.

Asada, Sadao. 1973. "The Japanese Navy and the United States," in Dorothy Borg and Shumpei Okamoto, eds., Pearl Harbor as History: Japanese-American Relations, 1931-1941, pp.225-59. New York: Columbia University Press.

Asagumo Shimbun-sha. 1991. Boei Hando Bukku (Defense Handbook). Tokyo: Asagumo Shimbun-sha.

Asahi Shimbun Keizai-bu. 1989. Mili-tech Power: Kyukyoku no Nichibei Masatsu (Mili-tech Power: The Ultimate Japan-U.S. Conflict). Tokyo: Asahi Shimbun-sha.

Asahi Shimbun Keizai-bu. 1991. Rupo--Gunji Sangyo (Reportage: Arms Industry). Tokyo: Asahi Shimbun-sha.

Asahi Shimbun Yoron Chosa-shitsu. 1988. Za Nippon-jin: Rittai Chosa (The Japanese: A Three-dimensional Research). Tokyo: Asahi Shimbun-sha.

Auer, James E. 1973a. "Japanese Militarism," U.S. Naval Institute Proceedings, (September): 47-55.

Auer, James E. 1973b. The Postwar Rearmament of Japanese Maritime Forces, 1945-71. New York: Praeger.

Auer, James E. 1988. "Japan's Defense Policy," Current History 87,528 (April): 145-48,180-82.

Bamba, Nobuya. 1972. Japanese Diplomacy in a Dilemma: New Light on Japan's China Policy, 1824-1929. Kyoto: Minerva Press.

Bang-Jensen, Lars. 1987. "State, Industry, and the Character of Consensus: Government Intervention in the Primary Aluminum Industry in the United States and Japan," Ph.d. dissertation, Cornell University.

Banno, Junji. 1989. Kindai Nihon no Shuppatsu (The Embarking of Modern Japan). Tokyo: Shogakukan.

Banno, Junji. 1992. The Establishment of the Japanese Constitutional System. London, New York: Routledge.

Barnett, Robert W. 1984. Beyond War: Japan's Concept of Comprehensive National Security. New York: Pergamon-Brassey.

Barnhart, Michael A. 1987. Japan Prepares for Total War: The Search for Economic Security, 1919-1941. Ithaca: Cornell University Press.

216

Beasley, William G. 1963. The Modern History of Japan. New York: Praeger.

Beasley, William G. 1987. Japanese Imperialism, 1894-1945. Oxford: Oxford University Press.

Beasley, William G. 1990. The Rise of Modern Japan. London: Weidenfeld.

Beckmann, George. 1957. The Making of the Meiji Constitution. Lawrence, Kansas: University of Kansas.

Beer, Lawrence W. 1984. "Japan's Constitutional System and Its Judicial Interpretation," Law in Japan 17: 7-41.

Beer, Lawrence W. 1987. "The Domestic Constraints on Japanese Security Policies," in Ronald A. Morse, ed., Option 2000: Politics and High Technology in Japan's Defense and Strategic Future, pp.5-14. Washington D.C.: Woodrow Wilson International Center for Scholars, Asia Program.

Beer, Lawrence W. 1989. "Law and Liberty," in Takeshi Ishida and Ellis Krauss, eds., Democracy in Japan, pp.67-88. Pittsburgh: University of Pittsburgh Press.

Belgrave, Robert, Ebinger, Charles, and Okino, Hideaki. 1987. Energy Security to 2000. Boulder: Westview.

Berger, Gordon M. 1974. "Ajia Shinchitsujo no Yume: Daitoa Kyoei Ken Koso no Shoso" ("Dreams of a New Order in Asia: Various Aspects of Conceptions of Greater East Asia Co-Prosperity Sphere"), translated by Junji Banno, in Seizaburo Sato and Roger Dingman, eds., Kindai Nihon no Taigai Taido (Modern Japan's Attitudes Towards the Outside World), pp.187-224. Tokyo: Tokyo Daigaku Shuppankai.

Berger, Gordon M. 1977. Parties Out of Power in Japan, 1931-1941. Princeton: Princeton University Press.

Berger, Thomas U. 1992. "America's Reluctant Allies: The Genesis of the Political-Military Cultures of Japan and West Germany," Ph.D. dissertation, Massachusetts Institute of Technology.

Bergner, Jeffrey T. 1991. The New Superpowers: Germany, Japan, the U.S. and the New World Order. New York: St. Martin's.

Bix, Herbert P. 1970. "The Security Treaty System and the Japanese Military-Industrial Complex," Bulletin of Concerned Asian Scholars 2,2 (January): 30-53.

Bix, Herbert P. 1972. "Japanese Imperialism and Manchuria, 1890-1931," Ph.d. dissertation, Harvard University.

Blair, David J. and Summerville, Paul A. 1983. Oil Import Security: The Cases of Japan and Great Britain. Programme for Strategic and International Security Studies, PSIS Occasional Papers, Number 4 (May).

Bobrow, Davis B. 1984. "Playing for Safety," Japan Quarterly 31,1 (January-March): 33-43.

Bobrow, Davis B. 1989. "Japan in the World: Opinion from Defeat to Success," Journal of Conflict Resolution 33,4 (December): 571-604.

Bobrow, Davis B. and Hill, Stephen R. 1986. "Managing Your Protector: Japan's Use of Military Budgets," paper prepared for delivery at the Annual Meeting of the American Political Science Association, Washington, D.C., August 28-31.

Bobrow, Davis B., Kim, Duc, and Hill, Stephen R. 1985. "Putting Up, Not Speaking Up: Japanese Government Resource Allocations to Comprehensive Security," paper presented at the Annual Meeting of the International Studies Association, Washington, D.C.

Bobrow, Davis B. and Kudrle, Robert T. 1987. "How Middle Powers Can Manage Resource Weakness: Japan and Energy," World Politics 39,4 (July): 536-65.

218

Boei Kenkyukai. 1990. Boeicho, Jieitai (Defense Agency, Self Defense Forces). Revised edition. Tokyo: Kaya Shobo.

Boei Nenkan Kankokai. 1991. Boei Nenkan. Tokyo: Boei Nenkan Kankokai.

Boeicho. 1991a. Boei Hakusho (Defense White Paper). Tokyo: Okurasho Insatsu-kyoku.

Boeicho. 1991b. "Kichi Taisaku Keihi no Suii" ("Changes in Expenditure for Base Countermeasures"). Tokyo: Unpublished memo.

Boeicho. 1991c. "Anzen Hosho Mondai ni Kansuru Nichibei-kan no Omo na Kyogi no Ba (Kaisai Jokyo)" ("Major Forums for Japan-U.S. Consultations on Security (Meetings)"). Tokyo: Unpublished memo.

Boeicho Koho-shitsu. 1988. "Bugai Dantai no Genkyo" ("The Present State of Outside Associations"). Tokyo: Unpublished memo.

Borrus, Michael and Zysman, John. Forthcoming. "The Highest Stakes: Industrial Competitiveness and National Security," in Wayne Sandholtz, Michael Borrus, Jay Stowsky, Steven Vogel, and John Zysman, The Highest Stakes: Technology, Economy and Security Policy. New York: Oxford University Press.

Brendle, Thomas M. 1975. "Recruitment and Training in the SDF," in James H. Buck, ed., The Modern Japanese Military System, pp.67-96. Beverly Hills: Sage.

Browning, E.S. 1984. "Japan to Share Arms Know-How with U.S.," Asian Wall Street Journal (August 16).

Buck, James H., ed. 1975. The Modern Japanese Military System. Beverly Hills: Sage Publications.

Buck, James H. 1986. "Japan's Self-Defense Forces," in Edward A. Olsen and Stephen Jurika, Jr., eds., The Armed Forces in Contemporary Asian Societies, pp.70-86. Boulder: Westview Press.

Buckley, Roger. 1992. U.S.-Japan Alliance Diplomacy, 1945-1990. Cambridge: Cambridge University Press.

Bullard, Monte R. 1974. "Japan's Nuclear Choice," Asian Survey 14,9 (September): 845-53.

Burt, Richard. 1991. "Drop Barriers to Defense Trade in the West," The Wall Street Journal (May 22): A14.

Buruma, Ian. 1991. "The Pax Axis," New York Review of Books 38,8 (April 25): 25-28, 38-39.

Butow, Robert J.C. 1961. Tojo and the Coming of the War. Princeton: Princeton University Press.

Calder, Kent E. 1988. Crisis and Compensation: Public Policy and Political Stability in Japan, 1949-1986. Princeton: Princeton University Press.

Caldwell, Martha. 1981a. "Petroleum Politics in Japan," Ph.d. dissertation, University of Wisconsin.

Caldwell, Martha. 1981b. "The Dilemmas of Japan's Oil Dependency," in Ronald A. Morse, ed., The Politics of Japan's Energy Strategy: Resources--Diplomacy--Security, pp.65-84. Berkeley: University of California, Research Papers and Policy Studies No.3, Institute of East Asian Studies.

Calvocoressi, Peter, Wint, Guy, and Pritchard, John. 1989. Total War: The Causes and Courses of the Second World War, revised second edition. New York: Pantheon Books.

Campbell, John Creighton. 1975. "Japanese Budget Baransu," in Ezra F. Vogel, ed., Modern Japanese Organization and Decision-Making, pp.71-100. Berkeley: University of California Press.

Campbell, John Creighton. 1977. Contemporary Japanese Budget Politics. Berkeley: University of California Press.

Carpenter, William M. and Gibert, Stephen P. 1982. "Japanese Views on Defense Burden-sharing," Comparative Strategy 3,3: 261-78.

Carrell, Todd. 1983. "Arms from a Local Base," The Japan Times Weekly, October 8.

Carter, Jimmy and Nakasone, Yasuhiro. 1992. "Ensuring Alliance in an Unsure World: The Strengthening of U.S.-Japan Partnership in the 1990s," The Washington Quarterly (Winter): 43-56.

Chandler, Clay and Brauchli, Marcus. 1990. "How Japan Became so Energy Efficient: It Leaned on Industry," Wall Street Journal (September 10): A1,A4.

Chapman, J.W.M., Drifte, Reinhard, and Gow, I.T.M. 1982. Japan's Quest for Comprehensive Security. New York: St. Martin's.

Cheng, Dean. 1990. The Sun also Rises: Expansion of the Maritime Self-Defense Forces. Cambridge, Ma.: The M.I.T. Japan Program, Science, Technology, Management, MITJP 90-108.

Chinworth, Michael W. 1987. "The Private Sector: Japan's Defense Industry," in Ronald A. Morse, ed., Option 2000: Politics and High Technology in Japan's Defense and Strategic Future, pp.99-121. Washington D.C.: Woodrow Wilson International Center for Scholars, Asia Program.

Chinworth, Michael W. 1990a. "Industry and Government in Japanese Defense Procurement: The Case of the Patriot Missile System," Comparative Strategy 9: 195-243.

Chinworth, Michael W. 1990b. "Japan's Dilemma: Rising Defense Budgets in an Era of Global Cuts," Breakthrough 1,1 (Fall): 7-11.

Chuma, Kiyofuku. 1985. Saigunbi no Seijigaku (The Politics of Rearmament). Tokyo: Chishiki-sha.

Chuma, Kiyofuku. 1987. "What Price the Defense of Japan?" Japan Quarterly 34,3 (July-September): 251-58.

Chuma, Kiyofuku and Kanegae, Kenji. 1985. "When Does a Defensive Weapon Become an Offensive Weapon?" Asahi Evening News (November 5).

Comprehensive National Security Study Group. 1980. Report on Comprehensive National Security. Tokyo: Office of the Prime Minister.

Conroy, Hilary. 1960. The Japanese Seizure of Korea, 1868-1910: A Study of Realism and Idealism in International Relations. Philadelphia: University of Pennsylvania Press.

Conroy, Hilary. 1984. Japan in Transition: Thought and Action in the Meiji Era, 1868-1912. London: Associated University Presses.

Coox, Alvin D. 1973-1974. "Evidences of Antimilitarism in Prewar and Wartime Japan," Pacific Affairs 46,4 (Winter): 502-14.

Cordesman, Anthony H. 1983a. "The Military Balance in Northeast Asia: The Challenge to Japan and Korea," Armed Forces Journal International (December): 27-37.

Cordesman, Anthony H. 1983b. "Japanese Defense: The Strategy of Econometrics," Armed Forces Journal International (February): 20,56.

Corning, Gregory P. 1989. "U.S.-Japan Security Cooperation in the 1990s," Asian Survey 29,3 (March): 268-86.

Costello, John. 1981. The Pacific War: 1941-1945. New York: Rauson, Wade.

Cowhey, Peter F. 1985. The Problems of Plenty: Energy Policy and International Politics. Berkeley: University of California Press.

Crowley, James B. 1962. "Japanese Army Factionalism in the Early 1930s," Journal of Asian Studies 21,3 (May): 309-26.

Crowley, James B. 1963. "A Reconsideration of the Marco Polo Bridge Incident," Jounal of Asian Studies 22, 3 (May): 277-91.

Crowley, James B. 1966a. "From Closed Door to Empire: The Formation of the Meiji Military Establishment," in Bernard S. Silberman and Harry D. Harootunian, eds., Modern Japanese Leadership: Transition and Change, pp.261-87. Tucson: Arizona University Press.

Crowley, James B. 1966b. Japan's Quest for Autonomy: National Security and Foreign Policy 1930-1938. Princeton: Princeton University Press.

Crowley, James B. 1970. "A New Deal for Japan and Asia: One Road to Pearl Harbor," in James B. Crowley, ed., Modern East Asia: Essays in Interpretation, pp.235-64. New York: Harcourt, Brace and World.

Crowley, James B. 1974a. "Japan's Military Foreign Policies," in James W. Morley, ed., Japan's Foreign Policy, 1868-1941: A Research Guide, pp.3-117. New York: Columbia University Press.

Crowley, James B. 1974b. "A New Asian Order: Some Notes on Prewar Japanese Nationalism," in Bernard S. Silberman and Harry D. Harootunian, eds., Japan in Crisis: Essays on Taisho Democracy, pp.270-98. Princeton: Princeton University Press.

Crowley, James B. 1976. "Imperial Japan and Its Modern Discontents: The State and the Military in Pre-War Japan," in Harold Z. Schiffrin, ed., Military and State in Modern Asia, pp.31-59. Jerusalem: Jerusalem Academic Press.

Curry, David. 1976. "A Comparative Analysis of Military Institutions in Developed Nations," Ph.d. dissertation, University of Chicago.

Curtis, Gerald L. 1977. "The Tyumen Oil Development Project and Japanese Foreign Policy Decision-Making," in Robert A. Scalapino, ed., The Foreign Policy of Modern Japan, pp.147-74. Berkeley: University of California Press.

Curtis, Gerald L. 1981. "Japanese Security Policies and the United States," Foreign Affairs 59,4 (Spring): 852-74.

Curtis, Gerald L. 1988. The Japanese Way of Politics. New York: Columbia University Press.

Davis, Neil. 1984a. "SDF Call for Reconnaissance Satellites Eroding'Purely Defensive' Restrictions," The Japan Times (July 4).

Davis, Neil. 1984b. "A Look at the Future of Japan's Military Industrial Complex," The Japan Times (January 4): 11.

Decker, Wayne. 1987. "Japanese Decision Criteria on the Strategic Defense Initiative," in Richard B.Finn, ed., U.S.-Japan Relations: A Surprising Relationship, pp.163-73. New Brunswick, N.J.: Transaction Books.

Defense Agency. 1990. Defense of Japan 1990. Tokyo: The Japan Times.

Defense Production Committee. 1991. "Defense Production in Japan," Tokyo, Keidanren, October.

Dekle, Robert. 1989. "The Relationship between Defense Spending and Economic Performance in Japan," in John H. Makin and Donald C. Hellmann, eds., Sharing World Leadership? A New Era for America and Japan, pp.127-49. Washington D.C.: American Enterprise Institute.

Destler, I. M. 1976. Managing an Alliance: The Politics of U.S.-Japanese Relations. Washington D.C.: Brookings Institution.

Destler, I. M., Fukui, Haruhiro, and Sato, Hideo. 1979. The Textile Wrangle: Conflict in Japanese-American Relations, 1969-1971. Ithaca: Cornell University Press.

Dingman, Roger. 1974. "Nihon to Wilson-teki Sekai Chitsujo" ("Japan and Wilsonian World Order"), translated by Taichiro Mitani, in Seizaburo Sato and Roger Dingman, eds., Kindai Nihon no Taigai Taido (Modern Japan's Attitudes Towards the Outside World), pp.93-122. Tokyo: Tokyo Daigaku Shuppankai.

Dingman, Roger. 1976. Power in the Pacific: The Origins of Naval Arms Limitation, 1914-1922. Chicago: University of Chicago Press.

Dorn, Frank. 1974. The Sino-Japanese War, 1937-41: From Marco Polo Bridge to Pearl Harbor. New York: Macmillan.

Drifte, Reinhard. 1983. The Security Factor in Japan's Foreign Policy, 1945-1952. Ripe, East Sussex: Saltire Press.

Drifte, Reinhard. 1985a. Japan's Growing Arms Industry. Programme for Strategic and International Security Studies, Lausanne, PSIS Occasional Papers, Number 1/85 (July).

Drifte, Reinhard. 1985b. "Japan's Defense Policy: How Far will the Changes Go?" International Defense Review 2: 153-58.

Drifte, Reinhard. 1986a. "Japan's Growing Arms Production and the American Connection," Atlantic Community Quarterly 24,1 (Spring): 50-56.

Drifte, Reinhard. 1986b. Arms Production in Japan: The Military Applications of Civilian Technology. Boulder, Colorado: Westview Press.

Drifte, Reinhard. 1990a. Japan's Foreign Policy. London: Routledge.

Drifte, Reinhard. 1990b. Japan's Rise to International Responsibilities: The Case of Arms Control. London: Athlone Press.

Drohan, Thomas A. 1990. "Politics of US-Japan Security Relations: Origins and Implications of a Security Bargain," paper prepared for delivery at the 1990 Annual Meeting of the American Political Science Association, San Francisco Hilton, August 30-September 2.

Duus, Peter. 1970. "The Era of Party Rule: Japan, 1905-1932," in James B. Crowley, ed., Modern East Asia: Essays in Interpretation, pp.180-206. New York: Harcourt, Brace and World.

Duus, Peter. 1976. The Rise of Modern Japan. Boston: Houghton Mifflin.

Duus, Peter. 1980. Economic Aspects of Meiji Imperialism. Berlin: Ostasiatisches Seminar, FU Berlin.

Duus, Peter. 1984. "Economic Dimensions of Meiji Imperialism: The Case of Korea, 1895-1910," in Ramon H. Myers and Mark R. Peattie, eds., The

Japanese Colonial Empire, 1895-1945, pp.128-71. Princeton: Princeton University Press.

Eckelmann, Robert and Davis, Lester A. 1983. Japanese Industrial Politics and the Development of High Technology Industries: Computers and Aircraft. Report prepared for the Office of Trade and Investment Anaylsis, International Trade Administration, U.S. Department of Commerce. Washington, D.C.: U.S. Government Printing Office.

Eckhouse, John. 1991. "Japan Firms Reportedly Stalled U.S. War Supplies," San Francisco Chronicle (April 30): A1.

The Economist. 1990. "Who dares wins . . . and loses," (September 1), p.61.

Ellingworth, Richard. 1972. Japanese Economic Policies and Security. Adelphi Paper, No.90. London: The International Institute for Strategic Studies.

Emmerson, John K. 1971. Arms, Yen and Power: The Japanese Dilemma. New York: Dunellen.

Emmerson, John K and Humphreys, Leonard A. 1973. Will Japan Rearm? A Study in Attitudes. Washington, D.C.: American Enterprise Institute.

Endicott, John E. 1975. Japan's Nuclear Option: Political, Technical and Strategic Factors. New York: Praeger.

Endicott, John E. 1982a. "The Defense Policy of Japan," in Douglas J. Murray and Paul R. Viotti, eds., The Defense Policies of Nations: A Comparative Study, pp.446-66. Baltimore: The Johns Hopkins University Press.

Endicott, John E. 1982b. "Presentation," in Government Decisionmaking in Japan: Implications for the United States, pp.38-41. Washington, D.C.: U.S. Government Printing Office.

Endicott, John E. 1984. "U.S.-Japan Defense Cooperation in the 1990s," Journal of Northeast Asian Studies 3,3 (Fall): 48-58.

Eto, Shinkichi. 1983. "Japanese Perceptions of National Threats," in Charles E. Morrison, ed., Threats to Security in East Asia-Pacific: National and Regional Perspectives, pp.53-64. Lexington, Mass.: D.C. Heath.

Eto, Shinkichi and Yamamoto, Yoshinobu. 1991. Sogo Anpo to Mirai no Sentaku (Comprehensive Security and Choice for the Future). Tokyo: Kodan-sha.

Fairbank, John K., Reischauer, Edwin O., and Craig, Albert M. 1989. East Asia: Tradition and Transformation, revised edition. Boston: Houghton Mifflin.

Falkenheim, Peggy. L. 1988. Japan and Arms Control: Tokyo's Response to SDI and INF. Aurora Papers No.6. Ottawa: The Canadian Centre for Arms Control and Disarmament.

Farnsworth, Clyde H. 1989. "Japan's Loud Voice in Washington," The New York Times (December 10): F1,6.

Feis, Herbert. 1950. The Road to Pearl Harbor. Princeton: Princeton University Press.

Fong, Glenn R. 1990. "Catching Up and Fighting Back: International Competition and National Research Collaboration in America and Japan," unpublished manuscript.

Fridell, Wilbur M. 1970. "Government Ethics Textbooks in Late Meiji Japan," Journal of Asian Studies 29,4 (August): 823-33.

Friedman, David and Samuels, Richard J. 1992. How to Succeed without Really Flying: The Japanese Aircraft Industry and Japan's Technology Ideology. Cambridge, Ma. The M.I.T. Japan Program, Center for International Affairs, Massachusetts Institute of Technology.

Friedman, George and LeBard, Meredith. 1991. The Coming War with Japan. New York: St. Martin's.

Frost, Ellen. 1985. "Realizing U.S.-Japan Defense Cooperation," The Asian Wall Street Journal (September 1).

Fujishima, Udai. 1992. Gunji-ka suru Nichibei Gijutsu Kyoryoku (The Militarizing Technology Cooperation between Japan and the U.S.). Tokyo: Mirai-sha.

Fujiwara, Akira. 1957. "Soryoku-sen Dankai ni okeru Nihon Guntai no Mujun" ("Contradictions of the Japanese Military at the Stage of Total War"), Shiso 399 (September): 22-32.

Fujiwara, Akira. 1973. "The Role of the Japanese Army," translated by Shumpei Okamoto, in Dorothy Borg and Shumpei Okamoto, eds., Pearl Harbor as History: Japanese-American Relations, 1931-1941, pp.189-95. New York: Columbia University Press.

Fukai, Shigeko. 1988. "Japan's Energy Policy," Current History 87, 528 (April): 169-72.

Fukami, Hiroaki. 1988. Shigen Enerugi Korekara Konaru (Predicting the Future of Natural Resources and Energy). Tokyo: PHP Kenkyujo.

Fukui, Haruhiro. 1970. Party in Power: The Japanese Liberal-Democrats and Policy-Making. Canberra: Australian National University Press.

Fukui, Haruhiro. 1975. "Japan's Security Posture Before and After the Nixon Shocks," in Bernard K. Gordon and Kenneth J. Rothwell, eds., The New Political Economy of the Pacific, pp.143-64. Cambridge, Ma.: Ballinger.

Fukui, Haruhiro. 1977. "Policy-Making in the Japanese Foreign Ministry," in Robert A. Scalapino, ed., The Foreign Policy of Modern Japan, pp.3-35. Berkeley: University of California Press.

Fukui, Haruhiro. 1978. "The GATT Tokyo Round: The Bureaucratic Politics of Multilateral Diplomacy," in Michael Blaker, ed., The Politics of Trade: US and Japanese Policymaking for the GATT Negotiations, pp. 75-169. New York: Occasional Papers of the East Asia Institute, Columbia University.

Fukui, Haruhiro. 1981. "Bureaucratic Power in Japan," in Peter Drysdale and Hironobu Kitaoji, eds., Japan and Australia: Two Societies and Their Interaction, pp. 275-303. Canberra: Australian National University Press.

Galtung, Johan. 1974. "Japan and Future World Politics," Journal of Peace Research 10,4: 355-85.

Gann, Lewis H. 1984. "Western and Japanese Colonialism: Some Preliminary Comparisons," in Ramon H. Myers and Mark R. Peattie, eds., The Japanese Colonial Empire, 1895-1945, pp.497-525. Princeton: Princeton University Press.

Garby, Craig. 1989. "The Case of the FSX," unpublished paper, Ithaca, Cornell University.

George, Aurelia. 1988. "Japan and the United States: Dependent Ally or Equal Partner," in J.A.A. Stockwin, Alan Rix, Aurelia George, James Horne, Daiichi Ito, and Martin Collick, Dynamic and Immobilist Politics in Japan, pp. 237-96. London: Macmillan.

Getreuer, Peter. 1986. Der verbale Pazifismus: Die Verteidigung Japan's 1972-1983 in demoskopischen Befunden. Vienna: Institut für Japanologie, Universitat Wien.

Ginn, William H., Jr. 1982. "Presentation," in Government Decisionmaking in Japan: Implications for the United States, pp.48-77. Washington, D.C.: U.S. Government Printing Office.

Goda, Yutaka. 1991. "Zivilverteidigung und Notstandsgesetzgebung in Japan--unerfullbare innenpolitische Forderungen?" in Heinz Eberhard Maul, ed., Militarmacht Japan? Sicherheitspolitik und Streitkrafte, pp.306-37. Munich: Iudicium.

Gotoda, Masaharu. 1989. Naikaku Kanbo Chokan (Cabinet Chief Secretary). Tokyo: Kodan-sha.

Green, Michael J. 1990. Kokusanka: FSX and Japan's Search for Autonomous Defense Production. Cambridge, Ma.: The M.I.T. Japan

Program, Center for International Studies, Massachusetts Institute of Technology.

Gros, Thomas Dean. 1989. The Japanese Aircraft Industry: Strategy and Implications for Global Markets. Cambridge, Ma.: The MIT Japan Program: Science, Technology, Management, MITJP 89-06.

Habara, Kiyomasa. 1985. "'Kokubo Zoku' to wa Dare ka--sono Seitai to Ronri" ("Who Are the Members of the'Defense Tribe'?: Their Mode of Life and Rationale"), Sekai (November): 81-85.

Hackett, Roger F. 1964. "The Military: Japan" in Robert E. Ward and Dankwart A. Rustow, eds., Political Modernization in Japan and Turkey, pp.328-51. Princeton: Princeton University Press.

Hackett, Roger F. 1965. "The Meiji Leaders and Modernization: The Case of Yamagata Aritomo," in Marius B. Jansen, ed., Changing Japanese Attitudes Toward Modernization, pp.243-73. Princeton: Princeton University Press.

Hackett, Roger F. 1968. "Political Modernization and the Meiji Genro," in Robert E. Ward, ed., Political Development in Modern Japan, pp.65-97. Princeton: Princeton University Press.

Haley, John H. 1988. "Introduction: Legal vs. Social Controls," in John O. Haley, ed., Law and Society in Contemporary Japan, pp. 1-6. Dubuque, Iowa: Kendall/Hunt.

Hall, John Whitney. 1968. "A Monarch for Modern Japan," in Robert E. Ward, ed., Political Development in Modern Japan, pp.11-64. Princeton: Princeton University Press.

Halloran, Richard. 1981. "Nuclear Agreement on Japan Reported," The New York Times (May 19): A5.

Halloran, Richard. 1991. Chrysanthemum and Sword Revisited: Is Japanese Militarism Resurgent? Honolulu, Hawaii: The East-West Center.

Han, Sang-Il. 1983. "Japan's Defense Capability and Defense Policy," Korea and World Affairs 7,4 (Winter): 677-708.

Harada, Akira. 1991. Jieitai Keizaigaku Nyumon: Sokensho: Nippon no Gunjihi (Introduction to the Economics of the Self-Defense Forces: Overall Appraisal: Japan's Military Spending). Tokyo: Kojin-sha.

Hardacre, Helen. 1989. Shinto and the State, 1868-1988. Princeton: Princeton University Press.

Harries, Meirion and Harries, Susie. 1987. Sheathing the Sword: Demilitarisation of Japan. New York: Macmillan.

Harries, Meirion and Harries, Susie. 1991. Soldiers of the Sun: The Rise and Fall of the Imperial Japanese Army. New York: Random House.

Hata, Ikuhiko. 1983. "The Marco Polo Bridge Incident in 1937," in James W. Morley, ed., The China Quagmire: Japan's Expansion on the Asian Continent 1933-41, pp.243-86. New York: Columbia University Press.

Hatakeyama, Hirobumi and Shinkawa, Toshimitsu. 1984. "Kankyo Gyosei ni miru Gendai Nihon Seiji (Contemporary Japanese Politics Viewed from the Case of Environmental Administration), " in Hideo Otake, ed., Nihon Seiji no Soten--Jirei Kenkyu ni yoru Seiji Taisei no Bunseki (Issues in Japanese Politics: Analysis of the Political System Using Case Studies), pp. 233-80. Tokyo: Sanichi Shobo.

Hatsuse, Ryuhei. 1986., "Indices of Japanese Militarization," Kobe University Law Review 20: 61-96.

Havens, Thomas R.H. 1987. Fire Across the Sea: The Vietnam War and Japan, 1965-1975. Princeton: Princeton University Press.

Hayashi, Shuzo. 1978. "Supreme Court Rulings on Constitutional Issues," Japan Echo 5,3: 17-30.

Hein, Laura. 1990. Fueling Growth: The Energy Revolution and Economic Policy in Postwar Japan. Cambridge, Mass.: Council on East Asian Studies, Harvard University and Harvard University Press.

Hellmann, Donald C. 1977. "Japanese Security and Postwar Japanese Foreign Policy," in Robert A. Scalapino, ed., The Foreign Policy of Modern Japan, pp.321-40. Berkeley: University of California Press.

Henderson, Dan F., ed. 1968. The Constitution of Japan: Its First Twenty Years, 1947-67. Seattle: University of Washington Press.

Higashi, Chikara. 1983. Japanese Trade Policy Formulation. New York: Praeger.

Hill, Rear Admiral J.R. 1986. Maritime Strategy for Medium Powers. Annapolis, Md.: Naval Institute Press.

Hirose, Katsuya. 1989. Kanryo to Gunjin: Bunmin Tosei no Genkai (Bureaucrats and Soldiers: The Limits of Civilian Control). Tokyo: Iwanami Shoten.

Hirose, Katsuya. 1990. "Sengo 'Boei Seisaku Sisutemu' ni okeru Seiji to Gunji" ("Politics and Military Affairs in the Postwar 'Defense Policy System'"), in Nihon Seiji Gakkai, ed., Kindaika Katei ni okeru Seigun Kankei (Political-Military Relations in the Modernization Process) (Nempo Seijigaku, 1989), pp.25-46. Tokyo: Iwanami Shoten.

Holland, Harrison M. 1988. Managing Defense: Japan's Dilemma. Lanham, Maryland: University Press of America.

Hook, Glenn. D. 1988. "The Erosion of Anti-Militaristic Principles in Contemporary Japan," Journal of Peace Research 25,4 (December): 381-94.

Hook, Glenn D. 1990. Language and Politics: The Security Discourse in Japan and the United States. Tokyo: Kuroshio Shuppan.

Hopper, David R. 1975a. "Defense Policy and the Business Community: The Keidanren Defense Production Committee," in James H. Buck, ed., The Modern Japanese Military System, pp.113-48. Berverly Hills: Sage.

Hopper, David R. 1975b. "The Politics of Security Policy Formation in Contemporary Japan: The Decision to Extend Automatically the Mutual Security Treaty," paper prepared for delivery at the 1975 Annual Meeting of the American Political Science Association, San Francisco, California, September 2-5.

Hosoya, Chihiro. 1971. "Retrogression in Japan's Foreign Policy Decision-Making Process," in James W. Morley, ed., Dilemmas of Growth in Prewar Japan, pp.81-105. Princeton: Princeton University Press.

Hosoya, Chihiro. 1974. "Characteristics of the Foreign Policy Decision-Making System in Japan," World Politics 26,3 (April): 353-69.

Hosoya, Chihiro. 1976. "The Pre-War Japanese Military in Political Decision-Making," in Harold Z. Schiffrin, ed., Military and State in Modern Asia, pp.19-29. Jerusalem: Jerusalem Academic Press.

Hosoya, Chihiro. 1977. "Taigai Seisaku Kettei Katei ni okeru Nichibei no Tokushitsu" ("Characteristics of Japan and the U.S. in the Foreign Policy Decisionmaking Process"), in Chihiro Hosoya and Joji Watanuki, eds., Taigai Seisaku Kettei Katei no Nichibei Hikaku (A Comparison of Japanese and U.S. Foreign Policy Decision Processes), pp. 1-20. Tokyo: Tokyo Daigaku Shuppankai.

Hosoya, Chirhiro. 1978. "Washington Taisei no Tokushitsu to Henyo" ("The Characteristics and Transformation of the Washington Order") in Chihiro Hosoya and Makoto Saito, eds., Washington Taisei to Nichi-Bei Kankei (The Washington Order and Japan-U.S. Relations), pp.3-39. Tokyo: Tokyo Daigaku Shuppankai.

Hosoya, Chihiro. 1988. Ryotaisen-kan no Nihon Gaiko: 1914-1945 (Japanese Diplomacy Between the Two World Wars: 1914-1945). Tokyo: Iwanami Shoten.

Hoyt, Edwin P. 1985. The Militarists: The Rise of Japanese Militarism since WWII. New York: Fine.

Hummel, Hartwig. 1988. The Policy of Arms Export Restrictions in Japan. International Peace Research Institute Meigaku (PRIME), Occasional Papers Series Number 4, Meiji Gakuin University, Yokohama.

Hummel, Hartwig. 1990. Sayonara Rüstungsexporte : Die Beschränkung des Rüstungsexports in Japan als friedenspolitisches Modell. Tübinger Arbeitspapiere zur Internationalen Politik und Friedensforschung, No. 12, University of Tübingen, Tübingen.

Hummel, Hartwig. 1991. "Rüstungsbeschränkungen in Japan und der Bundesrepublik Deutschland. Die Bedingungen für eine nationale Friedenspolitik," University of Tubingen, Ph.d. dissertation.

Humphreys, Leonard A. 1974. "The Imperial Japanese Army, 1918-1929," Ph.d. dissertation, Stanford University.

Humphreys, Leonard A. 1975. "The Japanese Military Tradition," in James H. Buck, ed., The Modern Japanese Military System, pp. 21-40. Beverly Hills: Sage.

Humphreys, Leonard A. 1978. "Crisis and Reaction: The Japanese Army in the 'Liberal' Twenties," Armed Forces and Society 5,1: 73-92.

Huntington, Samuel P. 1957. The Soldier and the State: the Theory and Politics of Civil-Military Relations. Cambridge, Mass.: Harvard University Press.

Ienaga, Saburo. 1978. The Pacific War, 1931-1945. New York: Pantheon.

Ienaga, Saburo. 1979. Japan's Last War: World War II and the Japanese, 1931-45. Oxford: Blackwell.

Ike, Nobutaka. 1968. "War and Modernization," in Robert E. Ward, ed., Political Development in Modern Japan, pp. 189-211. Princeton: Princeton University Press.

Ilgen, Thomas L. and Pempel, T.J. 1987. Trading Technology: Europe and Japan in the Middle East. New York: Praeger.

Imai, Ryukichi. 1992. The Middle East in the Coming Decade: A Japanese Perspective. Tokyo: International Institute for Global Peace (April).

Imai, Seiichi. 1957a. "Taisho-ki ni okeru Gunbu no Seijiteki Chii (Jo)" ("Political Status of the Military in the Taisho Period: Part 1"), Shiso 399 (September): 3-21.

Imai, Seiichi. 1957b. "Taisho-ki ni okeru Gunbu no Seijiteki Chii (Ge)" ("Political Status of the Military in the Taisho Period: Part 2"), Shiso 402 (December): 106-22.

Imai, Seiichi. 1973. "Cabinet, Emperor, and Senior Statesmen," translated by H. Paul Varley, in Dorothy Borg and Shumpei Okamoto, eds., Pearl Harbor as History: Japanese-American Relations, 1931-1941, pp.53-79. New York: Columbia University Press.

Immerman, Robert. 1990. "The US-Japan Security Relationship: Past, Present and the Future," unpublished paper, New York, Columbia University, East Asian Institute.

Inoguchi, Takashi. 1985. "Japan in Context," paper prepared for presentation at the Japan Political Economy Research Conference, Tokyo, July 23-28, 1985.

Inoguchi, Takashi. 1986. "Japan's Images and Options: Not a Challenger but a Supporter," Journal of Japanese Studies 12,1 (Winter): 95-119.

Inoguchi, Takashi. 1988. "Gendai Nihon ni okeru Kokusai Kankei Kenkyu" ("The Study of International Relations in Contemporary Japan"), Leviathan 2 (Spring): 152-62.

Inoguchi, Takashi. 1991a. Japan's International Relations. London: Pinter.

Inoguchi, Takashi. 1991b. "Japan's Response to the Gulf Crisis: An Analytic Overview," Journal of Japanese Studies 17,2: 257-73.

Inoguchi, Takashi. 1991c. "Japan's Global Responsibilities and Its Role in the New World Order," paper presented at the JIIA-IISS Joint Symposium on Japan's Strategic Priorities in the 1990s, Keidanren Guest House, November 18-20, 1991.

Inoguchi, Takashi and Iwai, Tomoaki. 1987. "Zoku Giin" no Kenkyu (The Study of "Tribe Diet Members"). Tokyo: Nihon Keizai Shimbun-sha.

Inoki, Masamichi. 1991. "Seijika wa Gunji o, Jieitai wa Seiji o" ("Military Affairs for Politicians, and Political Affairs for SDF"), Asteion 21 (Summer): 60-69.

International Institute for Global Peace. 1991. Containing Frictions: Creating a Common Economic Foundation. Tokyo: International Institute for Global Peace, June.

International Institute for Strategic Studies. 1987. East Asia, the West and International Security: Prospects for Peace. Parts I-III. Adelphi Papers Nos. 216-218 (Spring). London: The International Institute for Strategic Studies.

Iriye, Akira. 1965. After Imperialism: The Search for a New Order in the Far East, 1921-31. Cambridge, Mass.: Harvard University Press.

Iriye, Akira. 1966. Nihon no Gaiko: Meiji Ishin kara Gendai made (Japan's Diplomacy: From the Meiji Restoration to the Present). Tokyo: Chuo Koron-sha.

Iriye, Akira. 1970. "Imperialism in East Asia," in James B. Crowley, ed., Modern East Asia: Essays in Interpretation, pp.122-50. New York: Harcourt, Brace and World.

Iriye, Akira. 1971. "The Failure of Military Expansionism," in James W. Morley, ed., Dilemmas of Growth in Prewar Japan, pp.107-38. Princeton: Princeton University Press.

Iriye, Akira. 1972. Pacific Estrangement: Japanese and American Expansion, 1897-1911. Cambridge, Mass.: Harvard University Press.

Iriye, Akira. 1974. "The Failure of Economic Expansion, 1918-1931," in Bernard S. Silberman and H.D. Harootunian, eds., Japan in Crisis: Essays on Taisho Democracy, pp.237-69. Princeton: Princeton University Press.

Iriye, Akira. 1978. The Origins of the Second World War in Asia and the Pacific. London, New York: Longman.

Iriye, Akira. 1981. Power and Culture: The Japanese-American War, 1941-1945. Cambridge: Harvard University Press.

Iriye, Akira. 1984. Senkanki no Nihon Gaiko (Japanese Diplomacy in the Inter-war Period). Tokyo: Tokyo Daigaku Shuppankai.

Iriye, Akira. 1986. Nijuseiki no Senso to Heiwa (War and Peace in the Twentieth Century). Tokyo: Tokyo Daigaku Shuppankai.

Iriye, Akira. 1991. "Japan's Defense Strategy," in Solomon B. Levine and Koji Taira, eds., Japan's External Economic Relations: Japanese Perspectives, pp.38-47. The Annals of the American Academy of Political and Social Science, 513 (January).

Iriye, Akira and Cohen, Warren I., eds. 1989. The United States and Japan in the Postwar World. Lexington: University of Kentucky Press.

Ishida, Takeshi. 1967. "Japanese Public Opinion and Foreign Policy," Peace Research in Japan: 11-40.

Ishiguro, Takeo. 1978. "Jieitai Sosoki no Sibilian Contorolu: Kokkai Rongi o Chushin ni" ("Civilian Control in the Early Years of the Self-Defense Forces: A Focus on Debates in the Diet"), in Eiichi Sato, ed., Seiji to Gunji: Sono Hikakushiteki Kenkyu (Politics and Military Affairs: A Comparative Historical Study), pp.259-95. Tokyo: Nihon Kokusai Mondai Kenkyujo.

Ishiguro, Takeo. 1987. "90 Nendai no Anpo e no Kiseki: Seifu Toben no Hensen ni Miru Guideline Taisei" ("The Path to the Security System of the '90s: The Guideline Regime as Seen from the Changes in Government Replies"), in Korekara no Nichibei Anpo (Japan-U.S. Security Regime in the Future), Hogaku Seminar Sogo Tokushu 38: 240-51.

Ishihara, Shintaro and Eto, Jun. 1991. Danko "NO" to Ieru Nihon-Sengo Nichibeikankei no Sokatsu (Japan That Can Firmly Say'NO': A Summary of Postwar Japan-U.S. Relations). Tokyo: Kobun-sha Press.

Ishimoto, Yasuo and Hirobe, Kazuya. 1987. "Development of Post-War Japanese Studies in Public International Law: Part I, 1945-1964," The Japanese Annual of International Law 30: 89-129.

Itagaki, Hidenori. 1987. "Zoku" no Kenkyu (The Study of "Zoku"). Tokyo: Keizaikai.

Ito, Kobun. 1991. "Die japanische Selbstverteidigung und das Volk-- Sicherheit versus Pazifismus," in Heinz Eberhard Maul, ed., Militärmacht Japan? Sicherheitspolitik und Streitkräfte, pp.259-88. Munich: Iudicium.

Ito, Takashi. 1983. Showaki no Seiji (Politics in the Showa Period). Tokyo: Yamakawa Shuppan-sha.

Ito, Takashi and Momose, Takashi. 1990. Jiten Showa Senzen no Nihon: Seido to Jittai (Glossary: Japan in the Prewar Showa Era: Institutions and Reality). Tokyo: Yoshikawa Kobunkan.

Itoh, Hiroshi. 1989. The Japanese Supreme Court: Constitutional Policies. New York: Markus Wiener.

Itoh, Hiroshi and Beer, Lawrence W. 1978. The Constitutional Case Law of Japan: Selected Supreme Court Decisions, 1961 70. Seattle: University of Washington Press.

Itoh, Mayumi. 1988. "Japanese Perceptions of the Soviet Union: Japanese Foreign Policy Elites' Perceptions of the Soviet Union and Japanese Foreign Policy towards the Soviet Union," Ph.d dissertation, The City University of New York.

Jacob, Jo Dee Catlin, ed. 1991. Beyond the Hoppo Ryodo: Japanese-Soviet-American Relations in the 1990s. Washington D.C.: The AEI Press.

Jansen, Marius B. 1968. "Modernization and Foreign Policy in Meiji Japan," in Robert E. Ward, ed., Political Development in Modern Japan, pp.149-88. Princeton: Princeton University Press.

Jansen, Marius B. 1970. "The Meiji State: 1868-1912," in James B. Crowley, ed., Modern East Asia: Essays in Interpretation, pp.95-121. New York: Harcourt, Brace and World.

Jansen, Marius B. 1975. Japan and China: From War to Peace, 1894-1972. Chicago: Rand McNally.

Jansen, Marius B. 1984. "Japanese Imperialism: Late Meiji Perspectives," in Ramon H. Myers and Mark R. Peattie, eds., The Japanese Colonial Empire, 1895-1945, pp.61-79. Princeton: Princeton University Press.

Japan Defense Agency. 1961. Ethical Principles for Personnel of the Self Defense Forces. Tokyo: Japan Defense Agency.

Johnson, Chalmers. 1977. "MITI and Japanese International Economic Policy," in Robert A. Scalapino, ed., The Foreign Policy of Modern Japan, pp.227-79. Berkeley: University of California Press.

Johnson, Chalmers. 1978. Japan's Public Policy Companies. Washington D.C.: American Enterprise Institute.

Johnson, Chalmers. 1986. "Reflections on the Dilemma of Japanese Defense," Asian Survey 26,5 (May): 557-72.

Johnson, Chalmers. 1989. "MITI, MPT, and the Telecom Wars: How Japan Makes Policy for High Technology," in Chalmers Johnson, Laura D'Andrea Tyson, and John Zysman, eds., Politics and Productivity: The Real Story of Why Japan Works, pp. 170-240. Cambridge, Mass.: Ballinger.

Johnson, Chalmers. 1992. Japan in Search of a "Normal" Role. Institute on Global Conflict and Cooperation, University of California, Policy Paper #3 (July).

Johnson, U. Alexis and Packard, George R. 1981. The Common Security Interests of Japan, the United States and NATO. Cambridge, Mass.: Ballinger.

Jones, F. C. 1954. Japan's New Order in East Asia, 1937-45. London: Oxford University Press.

Journal of Japanese Trade and Industry, 1983. "Ensuring Japan's Econmic Security," (January/February).

Kahn, Herman. 1970. The Emerging Japanese Superstate: Challenge and Response. Englewood Cliffs, N.J.: Prentice-Hall.

Kajima, Morinosuke. 1969. Modern Japan's Foreign Policy. Rutland, Vt.: Charles E. Tuttle.

Kakegawa, Tomiko. 1973. "The Press and Public Opinions in Japan, 1931-1941," translated by Shumpei Okamoto, in Dorothy Borg and Shumpei Okamoto, eds., Pearl Harbor as History: Japanese-American Relations, 1931-1941, pp. 533-49. New York: Columbia University Press.

Kamo, Takehiko. 1982. "The Risk of Nuclear War and Japanese Militarization," Japan Quarterly 29,2 (April-June): 183-96.

Kanesashi, Masao. 1984. "Jiminto Seichokai to'Zoku' Giin" ("LDP Policy Affairs Research Council and'Tribe' Diet Members"), Nihon no Seito (Japanese Political Parties), Jurisuto Zokan Sogo Tokushu 35: 173-78.

Kaplan, J.J. 1975. "Raw Materials Policy: Japan and the United States," in Isaiah Frank, ed., The Japanese Economy in International Perspective, pp.231-47. Baltimore: Johns Hopkins University Press.

Karita, Toru. 1989. Showa Shoki Seiji Gaiko Shi Kenkyu (A Study of Political and Diplomatic History of the Early Showa Period), enlarged and revised edition. Tokyo: Ningen no Kagaku-sha.

Kasuya, Tomosuke. 1985. "Constitutional Transformation and the Ninth Article of the Japanese Constitution," Law in Japan 18: 1-26.

Katahara, Eiichi. 1991. Japan's Changing Political and Security Role. Singapore: Institute of Southeast Asian Studies.

Kataoka, Hiromitsu. 1982. Naikaku no Kino to Hosakiko--Daitoryosei to Giin Naikakusei no Hikaku Kenkyu (Cabinet's Functions and Staff System: Comparative Study of Presidential and Parliamentary Systems). Tokyo: Seibundo.

Kataoka, Hiromitsu. 1987. "Naikaku to Gyosei: 'Koshiki Seifu' to 'Hikoshiki Seifu' no Yakuwari" ("Cabinet and Administration: Roles of 'Formal Government' and 'Informal Government'"), in Nihon Gyosei Gakkai, ed., Naikaku Seido no Kenkyu (A Study of the Cabinet System) (Nempo Gyosei Kenkyu, vol. 21), pp.1-31. Tokyo: Gyosei.

Kataoka, Hiromitsu. 1990. "Naikaku Kanbo (Cabinet Secretariat)," Gyosei Kanri Kenkyu 51 (September): 3-16.

Kataoka, Tetsuya. 1980. Waiting for a'Pearl Harbor': Japan Debates Defense. Stanford: Hoover Institution Press.

Kataoka, Tetsuya and Myers, Ramon H. 1989. Defending an Economic Superpower: Reassessing the U.S.-Japan Security Alliance. Boulder: Westview Press.

Kato, Shuichi. 1964. "The Mass Media: Japan" in Robert E. Ward and Dankwart A. Rustow, eds., Political Modernization in Japan and Turkey, pp.236-54. Princeton: Princeton University Press.

Kato, Shuichi. 1974. "Taisho Democracy as the Pre-Stage for Japanese Militarism," in Bernard S. Silberman and Harry D. Harootunian, eds., Japan in Crisis: Essays on Taisho Democracy, pp.217-36. Princeton: Princeton University Press.

Kato, Yozo. 1991. "Die japanischen Selbstverteidigungsstreitkräfte von der Gründung bis zur Gegenwart," in Heinz Eberhard Maul, ed., Militärmacht Japan? Sicherheitspolitik und Streitkräfte, pp. 66-99. Munich: Iudicuim.

Katzenstein, Peter J. 1989. "West Germany's National Security Policy: Political and International Imperatives since the 1950s," unpublished manuscript, Cornell University, Ithaca, N.Y., July.

Katzenstein, Peter J. 1990. West Germany's Internal Security Policy: State and Violence in the 1970s and 1980s. Western Societies Program, Occasional Paper 28, Center for International Studies, Cornell University, Ithaca N.Y.

Katzenstein, Peter J. and Tsujinaka, Yutaka. 1991. Defending the Japanese State: Structures, Norms and the Political Responses to Terrorism and Violent Social Protest in the 1970s and 1980s. Ithaca, Cornell University, East Asia Program, Occasional Paper No. 53.

Keddell, Joseph, Jr. 1990. "Defense as a Budgetary Problem: The Minimization of Conflict in Japanese Defense Policymaking, 1976-1987," Ph.d. dissertation, Political Science, University of Wisconsin.

Keehn, Edward B. 1990. "Managing Interests in the Japanese Bureaucracy: Informality and Discretion," Asian Survey 30,11 (November): 1021-37.

Kennedy, Malcolm D. 1969. The Estrangement of Great Britain and Japan, 1917-1935. Berkeley: University of California Press.

Kihara, Masao. 1977. "Production of Weapons in Postwar Japan and its Characteristics," The Kyoto University Economic Review 47,1-2 (April-October): 1-26.

Kim, Jai-Hyup. 1978. The Garrion State in Pre-War Japan and Post-War Korea: A Comparative Analysis of Military Politics. Tucson: Arizona University Press.

Kim, Paul S. 1988. Japan's Civil Service System: Its Structure, Personnel, and Politics. New York: Greenwood Press.

Kim, Young C. 1972. "Japan's Security Policy Debate," in Young C. Kim, ed., Japan in World Politics, pp.51-82. Washington D.C.: Institute for Asian Studies.

Kimura, Hiroshi. 1986. "The Soviet Military Buildup: Its Impact on Japan and Its Aims," in Richard H. Solomon and Masataka Kosaka, eds., The Soviet Far East Military Buildup: Nuclear Dilemmas and Asian Security, pp.106-22. Dover, Mass.: Auburn House Publishing.

Kinoshita, Hiroo. 1989. "Mutual Security and Dual-Use Technology: A Consideration of Japanese-U.S. Cooperation," Speaking of Japan 10, 104: 20-24.

Kishino, Hiroyuki. 1991. Managing the Japan-U.S. Alliance in a Rapidly Changing World. Tokyo: International Institute for Global Peace (November).

Kitaoka, Shinichi. 1978. Nihon Rikugun to Tairiku Seisaku (The Japanese Army and Japan's Continental Policy). Tokyo: Tokyo Daigaku Shuppankai.

Klapp, Merri G. 1987. The Sovereign Entrepreneur: Oil Policies in Advanced and Less Developed Capitalist Countries. Ithaca: Cornell University Press.

Kobayashi, Hiroaki. 1991. "Die japanische Verfassungsproblematik-Kriegsverzichtsklausel im Zerrbild der Diskussion," in Heinz Eberhard Maul, ed., Militärmacht Japan? Sicherheitspolitik und Streitkräfte, pp.226-58. Munich, Indicium.

Koh, B.C. 1989. Japan's Administrative Elite. Berkeley: University of California Press.

Kohno, Masaru. 1989. "Japanese Defense Policy Making: The FSX Selection, 1985-1987," Asian Survey 29,5 (May): 457-79.

Kondo, Shigekatsu. 1991. "Japan's Security Interests and Role in the Pacific Rim Cooperation," paper delivered at the International Conference on Pacific Security, "Pacific Rim Security Cooperation," sponsored by the Institute of Foreign Affairs and National Security, Seoul, Korea, November 26-27.

Kosaka, Masataka. 1973. Options for Japan's Foreign Policy, Adelphi Papers, no. 97. London: International Institute for Strategic Studies.

Kosaka, Masataka. 1977. "The International Economic Policy of Japan," in Robert A. Scalapino, ed., The Foreign Policy of Modern Japan, pp.207-26. Berkeley: University of California Press.

Kosaka, Masataka. 1986. "Theater Nuclear Weapons and Japan's Defense Policy," in Richard H. Solomon and Masataka Kosaka, eds., The Soviet Far East Military Buildup: Nuclear Dilemmas and Asian Security, pp. 123-40. London: Croom Helm.

Kosaka, Masataka. 1989. Japan's Choices: New Globalism and Cultural Orientations in an Industrial State. London: Pinter.

Krebs, Gerhard. 1991. "Das Kaiserliche Militär-Aufstieg und Ende," in Heinz Eberhard Maul, ed., Militärmacht Japan? Sicherheitspolitik und Streitkräfte, pp.22-65. Munich: Iudicium.

Kubo, Takuya. 1978a. "Kokubo Kaigi ni Tsuite" ("On the National Defense Council"), Boeiho Kenkyu 2 (May): 107-14.

Kubo, Takuya. 1978b. "The Meaning of the U.S. Nuclear Umbrella for Japan" in Franklin B. Weinstein, ed., U.S.-Japan Relations and the Security of East Asia: The Next Decade, pp.107-25. Boulder: Westview Press.

Kumon, Shumpei. 1982. "Some Principles Governing the Thoughts and Behavior of Japanists (Contextualists)," Journal of Japanese Studies 8,1: 5-28.

Kuranari, Chikara and Mochizuki, Mike M. 1983. "The Prospects for Cooperation in the Defense Industries," in U.S.-Japan Relations: Towards a New Equilibrium, pp.107-16. Cambridge, Mass.: Center for International Affairs of Harvard University, Program on U.S.-Japan Relations.

Kurisu, Hiroomi. 1991. "Koredewa Nihon wa Mamorenai" ("Japan Cannot Be Defended Under the Present System"), Seiron (October): 50-59.

Kuroda, Makoto. 1989. Nichibei Kankei no Kangaekata--Boei Masatsu o Ikite (How to Think About Japan-U.S. Relations: From the Experiences of Trade Frictions). Tokyo: Yuhikaku.

Kurokawa, Shuji. 1983. Nihon no Boeihi o Kangaeru--Gunkaku Rosen no Mekanizumu (Thoughts on Japan's Defense Spending: The Mechanism of Arms Buildup Policy). Tokyo: Daiyamondo-sha.

Kurokawa, Shuji. 1985a. "Japan Stands at the Crossroads: Decision-making Process of the Japanese Defense Budget, 1976-85," paper prepared for delivery at the Twentieth European Conference, Peace Society (International), University of Kent at Canterbury, the United Kingdom, September 1-2, 1985.

Kurokawa, Shuji. 1985b. "Kibanteki Boeiryoku Koso no Seiritsu to Boei Keikaku no Taiko no Kettei: 1976 Nen" ("The Forming of the Basic Defense Force Concept and the Decision on the National Defense Program Outline"), Heiwa Kenkyu 10: 17-27.

Kurokawa, Shuji. 1986. "Keidanren Boei Seisan Iinkai no Seiji Kodo" ("Political Behavior of Keidanren's Defense Production Committee"), in Minoru Nakano, ed., Nihon-gata Seisaku Kettei no Henyo (Transformation of Japanese-style Policymaking), pp.210-36. Tokyo: Toyo Keizai Shimposha.

Kurth, James R. 1989. "The Pacific Basin versus the Atlantic Alliance: Two Paradigms of International Relations," Annals of the American Academy of Political Science 505 (September): 34-45.

Kusano, Atsushi. 1989. "Taigai Seisaku Kettei no Kiko to Katei" ("Structure and Process in Foreign Policy Making"), in Tadashi Aruga, et al., eds., Nihon no Gaiko: Koza Kokusai Seiji, vol. 4 (Japanese Diplomacy: Handbook of International Politics, vol.4), pp. 53-92. Tokyo: Tokyo Daigaku Shuppankai.

Kusaoi, Akiko. 1990. "Silver Screen as Key to Improved SDF Image," Japan Times (November 25).

LaFeber, Walter. 1989. "Decline of Relations during the Vietnam War," in Akira Iriye and Warren I. Cohen, eds., The United States and Japan in the Postwar World, pp.96-113. Lexington: University of Kentucky Press.

Langer, William L. and Gleason, S. Everett. 1952. The Challenge to Isolation, 1937-1940. New York: Harper.

Langer, William L. and Gleason, S. Everett. 1953. The Undeclared War, 1940-1941. New York: Harper.

Langdon, Frank C. 1973. Japan's Foreign Policy. Vancouver: University of British Columbia Press.

Langdon, Frank C. 1985. "The Security Debate in Japan," Pacific Affairs 58,3: 397-410.

Leifer, Michael, ed. 1986. The Balance of Power in East Asia. New York: St. Martin's.

Lesbirel, S. Hayden. 1988. "The Political Economy of Substitution Policy: Japan's Response to Lower Oil Prices," Pacific Affairs, 61,2 (Summer): 285-302.

L'Estrange, Michael G. 1990. The Internationalization of Japan's Security Policy: Challenges and Dilemmas for a Reluctant Power. Berkeley, University of California, Institute of International Studies.

Levin, Norman D. 1988. Japan's Changing Defense Posture. Santa Monica: The Rand Corporation, N-2739-OSD.

Li, Lincoln. 1975. The Imperial Japanese Army in North China, July 1937-December 1941: Problems of Political and Economic Control. Oxford: Oxford University Press.

Lockwood, Robert. 1985. "Equity in Burdensharing between the U.S. and Its Allies with an Application to Japan," Asian Perspective 9,1 (Spring-Summer): 95-116.

Lohmann, David P. 1980. "Process and Substance in Evolution," in James M. Roherty, ed., Defense Policy Formation: Towards Comparative Analysis, pp.227-46. Durham N.C.: Carolina Academic Press.

Lu, David J. 1961. From the Marco Polo Bridge to Pearl Harbor: Japan's Entry into World War II. Washington: Public Affairs Press.

MacDonald, Paul. 1986. "Japan's Oil: Coping with Insecurity," The World Today 42,8-9 (August-September): 147-49.

Magami, Hiroshi. 1991. "Perushia Wan Sokaitei Nisshi" ("Journal of Minesweepers in the Persian Gulf"), Bungei Shunju 69,8 (July): 176-89.

Mainichi Shimbun-sha. 1974. Mainichi Nenkan (Mainichi Yearbook). Tokyo: Mainichi Shimbun-sha.

Maki, John M. ed. 1964. Court and Constitution in Japan: Selected Supreme Court Decisions, 1948-60. Seattle: University of Washington Press.

Makin, John H. and Hellmann, Donald C., eds. 1989. Sharing World Leadership: A New Era for America and Japan. Washington D.C.: American Enterprise Institute.

Manegold, Catherine S. 1991. "The Military Question: Is It Time for Japan to Have a Bigger Army?" Newsweek (November 25): 45.

Marshall, Jim. 1981. "Japanese Public Opinion on Defense and Security Issues," unpublished paper, Washington D.C., USICA, Office of Research.

Mastanduno, Michael. 1990. "America's Response to Japanese Industrial Policy: Do Relative Gains Matter?", paper prepared for the panel on 'Realism and the Exercise of Power', Annual Meeting of the American Political Science Association, San Francisco, August 29-September 2.

Masuoka, Kaname. 1989. "Misunderstanding about the Japanese Self Defense Forces," Survival 5,4 (April): 24-27.

Maswood, S. Javed. 1990. Japanese Defence: The Search for Political Power. Singapore: Institute of Southeast Asian Studies.

Matoba, Toshihiro. 1986. "Jiminto no Seisaku Kettei Katei" ("The Policymaking Process in the LDP"), in Minoru Nakano, ed., Nihongata Seisakukettei no Henyo (Transformation of Japanese-style Policymaking), pp.156-80. Tokyo: Toyo Keizai Shimpo-sha.

Matsuo, Takashi. 1987. "Gekika suru Nichibei Kyodo Enshu" ("Intensifying Japan-U.S. Joint Exercises"), in Korekara no Nichibei Anpo (Japan-U.S.

Security Regime in the Future), Hogaku Seminar Sogo Tokushu 38: 196-213.

Matsushita, Yoshio. 1987. Meiji Gunsei Shi Ron (History of the Military System in Meiji Era), vol.1, revised edition. Tokyo: Kokusho Kankokai.

Matsuzaki, Tetsuhisa. 1991. Nihongata Demokurashii no Gyakusetsu - Nisei Giin wa Naze Umarerunoka (The Paradox of Japanese Democracy: Why Are Second-generation Diet Members Born?). Tokyo: Toju-sha.

Maul, Heinz Eberhard. 1991. Militärmacht Japan? Sicherheitspolitik und Streitkräfte. Munich: Iudicium.

Maxon, Yale Candee. 1957. Control of Japanese Foreign Policy: A Study of Civil-Military Rivalry, 1930-1945. Berkeley: University of California Press.

McIntosh, Malcolm. 1986. Japan Re-armed. New York: St. Martin's Press.

McKean, Margaret. 1983. "Japan's Energy Policies," Current History 82,487: 385-89.

McMichael, Philip. 1991. "Agro-Food Restructuring in the Pacific Rim: A Food Regime Perspective on Agricultural Transformation in Japan/S.Korea, the United States and Thailand," paper presented to the PEWS Conference: "Pacific-Asia and the Future of the World-System," University of Hawaii at Manoa, Honolulu, March 28-30, 1991.

McNelly, Theodore. 1962. "The Renunciation of War in the Japanese Constitution," Political Science Quarterly 77,3 (September): 350-78.

McNelly, Theodore. 1975. "The Constitutionality of Japan's Defense Establishment," in James H. Buck, ed., The Modern Japanese Military System, pp.99-112. Beverly Hills: Sage.

McNelly, Theodore. 1982. "Disarmament and Civilian Control in Japan: A Constitutional Dilemma," Bulletin of Peace Proposals 13,4 (December): 351-64.

McNelly, Theodore. 1987. "The Economic Consequences of Japan's'Peace Constitution'," paper prepared for delivery at the 1987 Annual Meeting of the American Political Science Association, the Palmer House, September 3-6.

Mendel, Douglas H., Jr. 1954. "Revisionist Opinion in Post-Treaty Japan," American Political Science Review 48,3 (September): 766-74.

Mendel, Douglas H., Jr. 1959. "Japanese Views of the American Alliance," Public Opinion Quarterly 23 (Fall): 326-42.

Mendel, Douglas H., Jr. 1961. The Japanese People and Foreign Policy. Berkeley: University of California Press.

Mendel, Douglas H., Jr. 1966. "Japan Reviews Her American Alliance," Public Opinion Quarterly 30(Spring): 1-18.

Mendel, Douglas H., Jr. 1967. "Japanese Views of Sato's Foreign Policy: The Credibility Gap," Asian Survey 7 (July): 444-56.

Mendel, Douglas H., Jr. 1969. "Japanese Opinion on Key Foreign Policy Issues," Asian Survey 9 (August): 625-39.

Mendel, Douglas H., Jr. 1970. "Japanese Defense in the 1970s: The Public View," Asian Survey 10 (December): 1046-69.

Mendel, Douglas H., Jr. 1971-72. "Japanese Views of the American Alliance in the Seventies," Public Opinion Quarterly 35(Winter): 521-38.

Mendel, Douglas H., Jr. 1975. "Public Views of the Japanese Defense System," in James H. Buck, ed., The Modern Japanese Military System, pp.149-80. Beverly Hills: Sage.

Mendl, Wolf. 1984. Western Europe and Japan between the Superpowers. London: Croom Helm.

Milward, Alan S. 1977. War, Economy and Society, 1939-1945. Berkeley: University of California Press.

Ministry of Foreign Affairs. 1991a. Working for the World: The Japan-U.S. Global Partnership in Action. Tokyo: Ministry of Foreign Affairs.

Ministry of Foreign Affairs. 1991b. Japan's Post Gulf International Initiatives. Tokyo: Ministry of Foreign Affairs, August.

Ministry of Foreign Affairs. 1991c. "Nichibei Anpo Jimu Lebelu Kyogi (SSC) Jisshi Jokyo" ("Meetings of Japan-U.S. Security Subcommittee (SSC)"). Tokyo: Unpublished memo.

Misawa, Shigeo and Ninomiya, Saburo. 1973. "The Role of the Diet and Political Parties," translated by Michael K. Blaker, in Dorothy Borg and Shumpei Okamoto, eds., Pearl Harbor as History: Japanese-American Relations, 1931-1941, pp.321-40. New York: Columbia Unviersity Press.

Mitani, Taichiro. 1973. "Changes in Japan's International Position and the Response of Japanese Intellectuals: Trends in Japanese Studies of Japan's Foreign Relations, 1931-1941," translated by G. Cameron Hurst, in Dorothy Borg and Shumpei Okamoto, eds., Pearl Harbor as History: Japanese-American Relations, 1931-1941, pp.575-94. New York: Columbia University Press.

Mitani, Taichiro. 1974. Taisho Demokurashii (Taisho Democracy). Tokyo: Chuo Koron-sha.

MITI, 1986. The Twenty-First Century Energy Vision: Entering the Multiple Energy Era (Summary). Background Information BI-63. Tokyo: MITI.

Miwa, Kimitada. 1986. Nihon Sen Kyuhyaku Yonjugo-nen no Shiten (A Perspective from the Japan of 1945). Tokyo: Tokyo Daigaku Shuppan-kai.

Miyake, Ichiro, Yamaguchi, Yasushi, Muramatsu, Michio, and Shindo, Eiichi. 1985. Nihon Seiji no Zahyo: Sengo 40 Nen no Ayumi (The Coordinates of Japanese Politics: The Course of Forty Postwar Years). Tokyo: Yuhikaku.

Miyata, Mitsuru. 1987. "Change in Oil and Gas Demand and Interfuel Competition since the Oil Crisis in Japan," OPEC Review (Winter): 413-29.

Miyawaki, Mineo. 1980. "Nihon no Boei Seisaku Kettei Kiko to Kettei Katei" ("Structures and Processes in Japanese Defense Policymaking"), Kokusai Mondai 247 (October): 34-62.

Mochizuki, Mike M. 1983/84. "Japan's Search for Strategy," International Security 8,3 (Winter): 152-79.

Mochizuki, Mike M. 1987. "The United States and Japan: Conflict and Cooperation Under Mr. Reagan," in Kenneth A. Oye, Robert J. Lieber, and Donald Rothchild, eds., Eagle Resurgent? The Reagan Era in American Foreign Policy, pp.335-58. Boston: Little, Brown and Company.

Mochizuki, Mike M. 1990. "Japan after the Cold War," SAIS Review 10 (Summer-Fall): 121-37.

Mochizuki, Mike M. 1991a. "U.S.-Japan Security Relations in a New Era," in Chae-Jin Lee, ed., U.S.-Japan Relations in the Post-Cold War Era (in press).

Mochizuki, Mike M. 1991b. "Japanese Security Policy beyond the Cold War: Domestic Politics and International Change," in Miles Kahler, ed., Beyond the Cold War in the Pacific, pp.57-70. La Jolla: University of California, Institute on Global Conflict and Cooperation, IGCC Studies in Conflict and Cooperation, Volume 2.

Mochizuki, Mike M. 1992a. "To Change or To Contain: Dilemmas of American Policy toward Japan," in Kenneth A. Oye, Robert J. Lieber and Donald Rothchild, eds., Eagle in a New World: American Grand Strategy in the Post-Cold War Era, pp.335-59. New York: Harper Collins.

Mochizuki, Mike M. 1992b. "The Soviet Factor in Japanese Security Policy," in Tsuyoshi Hasegawa, Jonathan Haslam, and Andrew C. Kuchins, eds., Soviet-Japanese Relations: Domestic and Foreign Policy Linkages. Berkeley: University of California, Institute of International Studies (in press).

Momoi, Makoto. 1977. "Basic Trends in Japanese Security Policies," in Robert A. Scalapino, ed., The Foreign Policy of Modern Japan, pp.341-64. Berkeley, University of California Press.

Moriya Fumio. 1979. Tenno-sei Kenkyu (A Study of the Emperor System). Tokyo: Aoki Shoten.

Morley, James W. 1957. The Japanese Thrust into Siberia, 1918. New York: Columbia University Press.

Morley, James W. 1986. Security Interdependence in the Asia Pacific Region. Lexington, Mass.: D.C. Heath.

Morris I.I. 1958. "Significance of the Military in Post-War Japan," Pacific Affairs 31,1 (March): 3-21.

Morris, I.I. 1960. Nationalism and the Right Wing in Japan: A Study of Post-War Trends. London: Oxford University Press.

Morse, Ronald A., ed. 1981. The Politics of Japan's Energy Strategy: Resources-Diplomacy-Security. Berkeley: Institute of East Asian Studies, Research Papers and Policy Studies No.3, University of California.

Morse, Ronald A. 1982. "Japanese Energy Policy," in Wilfred Kohl, ed., After the Second Oil Crisis, pp.255-70. Lexington, Mass.: Lexington Books.

Morse, Ronald A., ed. 1987. Option 2000: Politics and High Technology in Japan's Defense and Strategic Future. Washington D.C.: Woodrow Wilson International Center for Scholars, Asia Program.

Muakami, Hyoe. 1983. Japan, the Years of Trial 1919-52. Tokyo: Kodansha International.

Murakami, Teruyasu. 1982. "The Remarkable Adaptation of Japan's Economy," in Daniel Yergin and Martin Hillenbrand, eds., Global Insecurity: A Strategy for Energy and Economic Renewal, pp.138-67. Boston: Houghton Mifflin.

Muramatsu, Michio. 1987. "In Search of National Identity: The Politics and Policies of the Nakasone Administration," Journal of Japanese Studies 13,2: 307-42.

Muramatsu, Michio and Krauss, Ellis S. 1987. "The Conservative Policy Line and the Development of Patterned Pluralism," in Kozo Yamamura and Yasukichi Yasuba, eds., The Political Economy of Japan, vol.1, The Domestic Transformation, pp.516-54. Stanford: Stanford University Press.

Murray, Alan and Lehner, Urban C. 1990. "Strained Alliance," The Wall Street Journal (June 13, 15, 19, 25 and July 2).

Nagata, Minoru. 1987. "The Impact of High Technology on Japanese Security Concepts," in Economics and Pacific Security: The 1986 Pacific Symposium, pp.225-36. Washington D.C.: National Defense University Press.

Nakada, Yasuhisa. 1980. "Japan's Security Perception and Military Needs," in Onkar Marwah and Jonathan D. Pollak, eds., Military Power and Policy in Asian States: China, India, Japan, pp.147-80. Boulder: Westview Press.

Nakagawa, Yatsuhiro. 1984. "The WEPT0 Option,: Japan's New Role in East Asia/Pacific Collective Security," Asian Survey 26,8 (August): 828-39.

Nakajo, Isao. 1987. "Shiryo Kosei: Shinka suru Nichibei Anpo," ("Data: Deepening of Japan-U.S. Security Relations"), in Korekara no Nichibei Anpo (Japan-U.S. Security Regime in the Future), Hogaku Seminar Sogo Tokushu 38: 377-447.

Nakamura, Akira. 1984. "Jiyuminshuto no Yottsu no Kao - Jiminto o meguru Seisaku Kettei Katei no Shironteki Kosatsu," ("The Four Faces of the Liberal Democratic Party: A Tentative Analysis of the Policymaking Process centering on the LDP"), in Akira Nakamura and Yuzuru Takeshita, eds., Nihon no Seisaku Katei--Jiminto, Yato, Kanryo (The Policy Process in Japan: LDP, Opposition Parties, and Bureaucracy). Matsudo: Azusa Shuppan-sha.

Nakamura, Yoshihisa and Tobe, Ryoichi. 1988. "The Imperial Japanese Army and Politics," Armed Forces and Society 14,4 (Summer): 511-25.

Nakanishi, Terumasa. 1977. "U.S. Nuclear Policy and Japan," Washington Quarterly 10,1 (Winter): 81-97.

Nakayama, Shippuu. 1991. "Boeicho to Gunji Sangyo" ("Defense Agency and Arms Industry"), Zaikai Tenbo (January): 234-39.

Nanto, Dick K. 1981. Japan's Defense Expenditures and Policy: Recent Trends and Comparisons with the United States. Washington D.C.: Congressional Research Service, Report No. 81-214 E (September 16).

Nations, Richard. 1984. "Japan's'Omni-Direction' is Now Dead and Gone," Far Eastern Economic Review 126,51 (20 December): 26-29.

Nations, Richard. 1986. "Moscow Upsets Tokyo's Increased Defence Role," Far Eastern Economic Review 131,4 (30 January): 28-29.

Nau, Henry R. 1981. "Economics, National Security and Arms Control," in John H. Barton and Ryukichi Imai, eds., Arms Control II: A New Approach to International Security, pp.113-58. Cambridge, Mass.: Oelgeschlager, Gunn and Hain.

Nau, Henry R. 1990a. The Myth of America's Decline: Leading the World Economy into the 1990s. New York: Oxford University Press.

Nau, Henry R. 1990b. "Rethinking Economics and Security in Europe," prepared for a Conference on Europe, American Enterprise Institute for Public Policy Research, March.

Nemetz, P.N., Vertinsky, I., and Vertinsky, P. 1984-85. "Japan's Energy Strategy at Crossroad," Pacific Affairs 57,4 (Winter): 553-76.

Nester, William and Ampiah, Kweku. 1989. "Japan's Oil Diplomacy: Tatemae and Honne," Third World Quarterly 11,1: 72-88.

Nihon Boei Sobi Kogyokai. n.d. "Shadan Hojin Nihon Boei Sobi Kogyokai no Enkaku to Genkyo" ("History and Present State of the Japan Defense Industry Association (Incorporated)"). Tokyo: Nihon Boei Sobi Kogyokai.

Nihon Keizai Shimbun, Inc. 1991. Japan Economic Almanac 1991. Tokyo: Nihon Keizai Shimbun, Inc.

Nihon Keizai Shimbun-sha. 1983. Jiminto Seichokai (The LDP's Political Affairs Research Council). Tokyo: Nihon Keizai Shimbun-sha.

Nihon Kindai Shiryo Kenkyukai. 1971. Nihon Riku-Kaigun no Seido, Soshiki, Jinji (The System, Organization, and Personnel Administration of the Japanese Army and Navy). Tokyo: Tokyo Daigaku Shuppankai.

Nihon Kogyo Shimbun. 1989. 87-88 Enerugi Sogo Binran (General Directory for Energy 87-88). Tokyo: Nihon Kogyo Shimbun-sha.

Nish, Ian. 1972. Alliance in Decline: A Study in Anglo-Japanese Relations, 1908-1923. London: Athlone Press.

Nish, Ian. 1977. Japanese Foreign Policy 1869-1942: Kasumigaseki to Miyakezaka. London: Routledge.

Nish, Ian. 1980. "Japan's Security Preoccupations," The World Today 36,11 (November): 421-27.

Nish, Ian. 1985. The Anglo-Japanese Alliance: The Diplomacy of Two Island Empires, 1894-1907, second edition. London: Dover.

Nish, Ian, Sugiyama, Chuhei, and Large, Stephen S. 1989. The Japanese Constitution of 1889. London: Suntory Toyota International Centre for Economics and Related Disciplines, London School of Economics and Political Science.

Nishi, Osamu. 1987. The Constitution and the National Defense Law System in Japan. Tokyo: Seibundo.

Nishihara, Masashi. 1983/84. "Expanding Japan's Credible Defense Role," International Security 8,3: 180-205.

Nishihara, Masashi. 1985a. "The Japanese Central Organization of Defense," in Martin Edmonds, ed., Central Organizations of Defense, pp.132-44. Boulder: Westview Press.

Nishihara, Masashi. 1985b. East Asian Security and the Trilateral Countries. The Triangle Papers No.30. New York: New York University Press.

Nishihara, Masashi. 1986. "Japan: Regional Stability," in James W. Morley, ed., Security Interdependence in the Asia Pacific Region, pp.65-92. Lexington, Mass: D.C. Heath.

Nishihara, Masashi. 1987. "The Security of East Asia: Part I," in Robert O'Neill, ed., East Asia, The West and International Security: Prospects for Peace, Adelphi Paper 218, pp.3-13. London: International Institute for Strategic Studies.

Nishihara, Masashi. 1990. "Nichibei Kankei ni okeru Anzen Hosho Joyaku no Igi" ("The Significance of the Security Treaty in the Japan-U.S. Relationship"), Kokusai Mondai 369 (December): 2-14.

Nishihara, Masashi and Potter, David M. 1990. "The Politics of Technonationalism: The FSX Case, 1975-89," paper prepared for delivery at the 1990 Annual Meeting of the Association for Asian Studies, The Palmer House, Chicago, Illinois, April 5-8.

Nishimura, Shigeki. 1991a. Military Balance in Northeast Asia. Tokyo: International Institute for Global Peace (February).

Nishimura, Shigeki. 1991b. Transformation of the U.S.-Japan Defense Posture: The New Soviet Challenge. Tokyo: International Institute for Global Peace (October).

Nishioka, Akira. 1988. Gendai no Sibilian Contorolu (Modern Civilian Control). Tokyo: Chishiki-sha.

Noble, Gregory W. 1990. "Japan, America and the FSX Jet Fighter Plane: Structural Asymmetries in Bilateral Negotiations," paper prepared for delivery at the 1990 Meeting of the Association for Asian Studies, The Palmer House, Chicago, Illinois, April 5-8, 1990.

Obata, Takashi. 1988. Japanese Defense Technology and the FS-X Controversy. Stanford: Center for International Security and Arms Control, July.

O'Connell, John. 1987. "Strategic Implications of the Japanese SSM-1 Cruise Missile," Journal of Northeast Asian Studies 6,2 (Summer): 53-66.

Odawara, Atsushi. 1985. "No Tampering with the Brakes on Military Expansion," Japan Quarterly 32,3 (July-September): 248-54.

Ogata, Sadako. 1954. Defiance in Manchuria: The Making of Japanese Foreign Policy, 1931-2. Berkeley: University of California Press.

Ogata, Sadako. 1966. Manshu Jihen to Seisaku no Keisei Katei (The Manchurian Incident and the Process of Policy Formation). Tokyo: Hara Shobo.

Ogata, Sadako. 1987. "Japan's United Nations Policy in the 1980s," Asian Survey 27,9 (September): 957-72.

Ogura, Kazuo. 1991. "Japan and America: Pride and Prejudice," The New York Times (November 24): 17.

Ohara, Yasuo. 1982. Teikoku Riku Gun no Hikari to Kage (The Bright and Dark Sides of the Imperial Army). Tokyo: Nihon Kyobun-sha.

Oishi, Nobuyuki. 1991. "Defense Industry Establishes Watchdog Association," Japan Economic Journal (August 31).

Okazaki, Hisahiko. 1982a. "Japanese Security Policy: A Time for Strategy," International Security 7,2: 188-97.

Okazaki, Hisahiko. 1982b. "The Political Framework of Japan's Defense," in Douglas J. Murray and Paul R. Viotti, eds., The Defense Policies of Nations: A Comparative Study, pp.468-73. Baltimore: The Johns Hopkins University Press.

Okazaki, Hisahiko. 1986. A Grand Strategy for Japanese Defense. Lanham, Md.: University Press of America.

Okazaki, Hisahiko. 1990a. Joho Senryakuron Noto, Part 2: Rekishi to Senryaku ni tsuite (Intelligence and Strategic Thinking, Part 2: On History and Strategy). Tokyo and Kyoto: PHP Kenkyujo.

Okazaki, Hisahiko. 1990b. "The Anglo-Dutch Conflict: A Lesson for Japan," Japan Echo 17,1 (Spring): 13-16.

Okazaki, Hisahiko, Nishimura, Shigeki, and Sato, Seizaburo. 1991. Nichibei Domei to Nihon no Senryaku (Japan-U.S. Alliance and Japan's Strategy). Tokyo and Kyoto: PHP Kenkyujo.

Okimoto, Daniel I. 1978a. "Ideas, Intellectuals, and Institutions: National Security and the Question of Nuclear Armament in Japan," 2 vols., Ph.d. dissertation, The University of Michigan.

Okimoto, Daniel I. 1978b. "Security Policies in the United States and Japan: Institutions, Experts, and Mutual Understanding," in Franklin B. Weinstein, ed., U.S.-Japan Relations and the Security of East Asia: The Next Decade, pp.9-36. Boulder: Westview Press.

Okimoto, Daniel I. 1981. "Arms Transfers: The Japanese Calculus," in John H. Barton and Ryukichi Imai, eds., Arms Control II: A New Approach to International Security, pp.273-317. Cambridge, Mass.: Oelgeschlager, Gunn and Hain.

Okimoto, Daniel I. 1982a. "The Economics of National Defense," in Daniel I. Okimoto, ed., Japan's Economy: Coping with Change in the International Environment, pp.231-83. Boulder, Colorado: Westview.

Okimoto, Daniel I. 1982b. "Chrysanthemum without the Sword: Japan's Nonnuclear Policy," in Martin E. Weinstein, ed., Northeast Asian Security after Vietnam, pp.128-56. Urbana: University of Illinois Press.

Okimoto, Daniel I. 1989. Between MITI and the Market: Japanese Industrial Policy for High Technology. Stanford: Stanford University Press.

Okimoto, Daniel I., Rowen, Henry S., and Dahl, Michael J. 1987. The Semiconductor Competition and National Security. Stanford: Stanford

Unversity, Northeast Asia-United States Forum on International Policy (December).

Okina, Hisajiro. 1987. "Naikaku Kanbo no Sogo Chosei Kino ni tsuite (On the Comprehensive Coordination Function of the Cabinet Secretariat)," in Nihon Gyosei Gakkai, ed., Naikaku Seido no Kenkyu (A Study of the Cabinet System) (Nempo Gyosei Kenkyu, Vol.21), pp.89-106. Tokyo: Gyosei.

Olsen, Edward A. 1985. U.S.-Japan Strategic Reciprocity: A Neo-Internationalist View. Stanford: Hoover Institution.

Omori, Wataru. 1986. "Nihon Kanryosei no Jian Kettei Tetsuzuki" ("Decision-making Procedures in the Japanese Bureaucracy"), in Nihon Seiji Gakkai, ed., Gendai nihon no Seiji Tetsuzuki (Political Procedures in Contemporary Japan) (Nempo Seijigaku, 1985), pp.87-116. Tokyo: Iwanami Shoten.

O'Neill, Robert, ed. 1984. Security in East Asia. London: St. Martin's Press for The International Institute for Strategic Studies.

O'Neill, Robert, ed. 1987. East Asia, the West and International Security. London: Macmillan Press and The International Institute for Strategic Studies.

Onitsuka, Yusuke. 1990. "The Oil Crises and Japan's Internal-External Adjustment," Working Paper No.15, Department of Social and International Relations, University of Tokyo, Komaba.

Organization for Economic Co-operation and Development. 1987. OECD Energy Balances--1987. Paris : OECD.

Osgood, Robert E. 1972. The Weary and the Wary: U.S. and Japanese Security Poicies in Transition. Baltimore: The Johns Hopkins University Press, The Washington Center of Foreign Policy Research, School of Advanced Studies, Studies in International Affairs, No.16.

Otake, Hideo. 1980. "Boei Futan o meguru Nichibei Masatsu: Sono Keika to Haikei" ("Japan-U.S. Conflict over Defese Burden: Its Development and Background"), Keizai Hyoron (July): 14-25.

Otake, Hideo. 1981. "Gunsan Fukugotai Riron kara mita Nihon no Seiji," ("Japanese Politics seen from the Theory of the Military-Industrial Complex"), Hogaku (Tohoku University), 45,4: 465-502.

Otake, Hideo. 1982. "The Politics of Defense Spending in Conservative Japan," Peace Studies Program Occasional Paper No. 15, Cornell University, Ithaca, New York (February).

Otake, Hideo. 1983a. Nihon no Boei to Kokunai Seiji: Detanto kara Gunkaku e (Japan's Defense and Domestic Politics: From Detente to Military Buildup). Tokyo: Sanichi Shobo.

Otake, Hideo. 1983b. "Hatoyama, Kishi Jidai no Boei Seisaku" ("Defense Policy in the Hatoyama and Kishi Periods"), in Masaki Miyake, et al., eds., Sengo Sekai to Nihon Saigunbi (The Postwar World and Japanese Rearmament), pp.75-111. Tokyo: Daiichi Hoki.

Otake, Hideo. 1984a. "Nihon ni okeru'Gunsankan Fukugotai' Keisei no Zasetsu" ("The Failure of the Attempt at Forming a'Military-Industrial-Bureaucratic Complex' in Japan"), in Hideo Otake, ed., Nihon Seiji no soten--Jirei Kenkyu ni yoru Seiji Taisei no Bunseki (Issues in Japanese Politics: Analysis of the Political System Using Case Studies), pp.13-69. Tokyo: Sanichi Shobo.

Otake, Hideo. 1984b. "Boeihi Zogaku o meguru Jiminto no Tonai Rikigaku-1981 Nendo Boei Yosan" ("Intra-party Dynamics of the LDP over Defense Expenditure Increases: The Defense Budget for FY 1981"), in Hideo Otake, ed., Nihon Seiji no Soten--Jirei Kenkyu ni yoru Seiji Taisei no Bunseki (Issues in Japanese Politics: Analysis of the Political System Using Case Studies), pp.281-96. Tokyo: Sanichi Shobo.

Otake, Hideo. 1990. "Defense Controversies and One-Party Dominance: The Opposition in Japan and West Germany," in T.J. Pempel, ed., Uncommon Democracies: The One-Party Dominant Regimes, pp.128-61. Ithaca: Cornell University Press.

Otsuki, Shinji and Honda, Masaru. 1991. Nichibei FSX Senso: Nichibei Domei o Yurugasu Gijutsu Masatsu (The Japan-U.S. War over the FSX: Technology Conflict that Rocks the Japan-U.S. Alliance). Tokyo: Ronso-sha.

Ozaki, Robert S. and Arnold, Walter. 1985. Japan's Foreign Relations: A Global Search for Economic Security. Boulder: Westview Press.

Ozawa, Terutomo. 1979. Multilateralism Japanese Style: The Political Economy of Outward Dependence. Princeton: Princeton University Press.

Patrick, Hugh and Rosovsky, Henry. 1976. "Japan's Economic Performance: An Overview," in Hugh Patrick and Henry Rosovsky, eds., Asia's New Giant: How the Japanese Economy Works, pp.1-62. Washington D.C: Brookings.

"Peace and Security in Statistics: Public Opinion Poll by the Asahi Shimbun." 1982. Japan Quarterly 29,2 (April-June): 197-99.

Peattie, Mark R. 1975. Ishiwara Kanji and Japan's Confrontation with the West. Princeton: Princeton University Press.

Peattie, Mark R. 1984. "Japanese Attitudes Toward Colonialism, 1895-1945," in Ramon H. Myers and Mark R. Peattie, eds., The Japanese Colonial Empire, 1895-1945, pp.80-127. Princeton: Princeton University Press.

Pelz, Stephen. 1974a. Race to Pearl Harbor: The Failure of the Second London Naval Conference and the Onset of World War II. Cambridge: Harvard University Press.

Pelz, Stephen. 1974b. "Riso no Teikoku: Shin Chitsujo Kensetsu e no Nihon Gunjin no Yume (1928-1940)" ("The Ideal Empire: Japanese Military Men's Dreams for Constructing a New Order (1928-1940)"), translated by Akio Watanabe, in Seizaburo Sato and Roger Dingman, eds., Kindai Nihon no Taigai Taido (Modern Japan's Attitudes towards the Outside World), pp.155-86. Tokyo: Tokyo Daigaku Shuppankai.

Pempel, T.J. 1990a. "From Trade to Technology: Japan's Reassessment of Military Policies," The Jerusalem Journal of International Relations 12,4: 1-28.

Pempel, T.J. 1990b. "From Exporter to Investor: Japanese Foreign Economic Policy," paper prepared for a conference on Japanese Foreign Policy, Grand Cayman, B.W.I., January 16-20.

Pharr, Susan J. 1992. "Japan's Defensive Foreign Policy and the Politics of Burden Sharing," in Gerald L. Curtis, ed., Japanese Foreign Policy (forthcoming).

Pierre, Andrew. 1987. "Japan, Europe, and the Strategic Defense Initiative: The Background," in Ronald A. Morse, ed., Option 2000: Politics and High Technology in Japan's Defense and Strategic Future, pp.15-21. Washington, D.C.: Woodrow Wilson International Center for Scholars, Asia Program.

Powell, Bill and Takayama, Hideko. 1991. "A Japan that Can Take Credit; A New Round of America-Bashing," Newsweek (July 15): 27.

Pohl, Manfred. 1991. "Die japanischen Streitkräfte in die Golfregion? Diskussion um den 'japanischen Ernstfall'" in Heinz Eberhard Maul, ed., Militärmacht Japan? Sicherheitspolitik und Streitkräfte, pp.338-62. Munich: Iudicium.

Prange, Gordon W. 1986. Pearl Harbor: The Verdict of History. New York: McGraw-Hill.

Presseisen, Ernest L. 1958. Germany and Japan: A Study in Totalitarian Diplomacy, 1933-1941. The Hague: Martinus Nijhoff.

Prestowitz, Clyde V., Jr. 1988. Trading Places: How America Allowed Japan to Take the Lead. Tokyo: Tuttle.

Puckett, Robert H. 1990. "Comprehensive Security in Northeast Asia," paper prepared for delivery at the International Studies Association Annual Convention, Washington D.C., April 13.

Purrington, Courtney and K., A. 1991. "Tokyo's Policy Responses during the Gulf Crisis," Asian Survey 31,4 (April): 307-23.

Pyle, Kenneth B. 1988a. "Japan's World Role in the 21st Century," in Cedric L. Suzman and Peter C. White, eds., Japan in the 1980s, VI & VII, pp.76-90. Atlanta, Georgia: The Southern Center for International Studies, Papers on International Issues No.10 (May).

Pyle, Kenneth B. 1988b. "Japan, the World, and the Twenty-first Century," in Takashi Inoguchi and Daniel I. Okimoto, eds., The Political Economy of Japan: The Changing International Context, vol. 2, pp. 446-86. Stanford: Stanford University Press.

Pyle, Kenneth B. 1992. The Japanese Question: Power and Purpose in a New Era. Washington, D.C.: The AEI Press.

Quo, F. Quei. 1986. "Japan's Resource Diplomacy," in Ronald C. Keith, ed., Energy, Security and Economic Development in East Asia, pp.167-84. New York: St. Martin's.

Rapkin, David P. 1990. "Japan and World Leadership?", in David P. Rapkin, ed., World Leadership and Hegemony, pp.191-212. Boulder: Lynne Rienner.

Reed, Robert. 1983. The US-Japan Alliance: Sharing the Burden of Defense. Washington, D.C.: National Defense University Press.

Reischauer, Edwin O. 1971. "What Went Wrong?" in James W. Morley, ed., Dilemmas of Growth in Prewar Japan, pp.489-510. Princeton: Princeton University Press.

Rice, Richard. 1979. "Economic Mobilization in Wartime Japan: Business, Bureaucracy, and Military in Conflict," Journal of Asian Studies 38,4 (August): 689-706.

Richardson, Bradley M. 1977. "Policymaking in Japan: An Organizing Perspective," in T.J. Pempel, ed., Policymaking in Contemporary Japan, pp.239-68. Ithaca: Cornell University Press.

Richelson, Jeffrey T. 1988. Foreign Intelligence Organizations. Cambridge: Ballinger.

Risse-Kappen, Thomas. 1991. "Public Opinion, Domestic Structure, and Foreign Policy in Liberal Democracies," World Politics 43,4 (July): 479-512.

Rix, Alan. 1987. "Japan's Comprehensive Security and Australia," Australian Outlook 41,2 (August): 79-86.

Ro, Chun Whang. 1976. "The Origin and Interpretation of the 1951 U.S.-Japanese Security Treaty," Ph.d. dissertation, Southern Illinois University.

Roberts, John G. 1969. "To Arms, Dear Friends," Far Eastern Economic Review (July 27-August 2): 286-89.

Rubinstein, Gregg A. 1987a. "Emerging Bonds of U.S.-Japanese Defense Technology Cooperation," Strategic Review 15,1 (Winter): 43-51.

Rubinstein, Gregg A. 1987b. "Facing the Challenge: Defense Technology Cooperation Between the United States and Japan," in Ronald A. Morse, ed., Option 2000: Politics and High Technology in Japan's Defense and Strategic Future, pp.47-97. Washington, D.C.: Asia Program, Woodrow Wilson International Center for Scholars.

Rubinstein, Gregg A. 1988. "U.S.-Japan Security Relations: A Maturing Partnership?" Fletcher Forum: 41-54.

Russett, Bruce M. 1963. Community and Contention: Britain and America in the Twentieth Century. Cambridge Mass.: M.I.T. Press.

Saikawa, Takasumi. 1990. "Reisen-go no Beikoku no Anzen Hosho Seisaku to Nihon: Maruta kara CSCE made" ("The American Security Policy after the Cold War and Japan: From Marta to CSCE"), Kokusai Mondai 369 (December): 29-43.

Saito, Shiro. 1990. Japan at the Summit: Its Role in the Western Alliance and in Asian Pacific Co-operation. London: Routledge.

264

Sakai, Akio. 1986. "Nihon Gunji Sangyo no Tenkan" ("The Transformation of Japan's Defense Industry"), Sekai (February): 130-43.

Sakanaka, Tomohisa. 1990. "Boei Yosan Kettei Katei no Mondaiten" ("Problems in the Defense Budget Decision Process"), Aoyama Kokusai Seikei Ronshu 18 (October): 59-88.

Sakanaka, Tomohisa. 1991. "Hosei Totonotte Jittai Nashi" ("Statutory Framework Established, But Substance Lacking"), Asteion 21 (Summer): 70-78.

Sakisaka, Masao. 1985. "Japan's Energy Supply/Demand Structure and Its Trade Relationship with the United States and the Middle East," The Journal of Energy Development 10,1: 1-11.

Sakurai, Hiroyuki. 1990. "Konnichi no Nichibei Kyodo Sakusen: FM 100-5 kara no Kosatsu" ("Contemporary Japan-U.S. Joint Operations: An Examination based on FM 100-5"), Gunji Minron 62 (October): 65-73.

Samuels, Richard J. 1983. "The Industrial Restructuring of the Japanese Aluminum Industry," Pacific Affairs 56,3: 495-509.

Samuels, Richard J. 1987. The Business of the Japanese State: Energy Markets in Comparative and Historical Perspective. Ithaca: Cornell University Press.

Samuels, Richard J. 1989. "Consuming for Production: Japanese National Security, Nuclear Fuel Procurement, and the Domestic Economy," International Organization 43,4 (Autumn): 625-46.

Samuels, Richard J. 1991. "Reinventing Security: Japan since Meiji," Daedalus (Fall): 47-68.

Samuels, Richard J. and Whipple, Benjamin C. 1989. "Defense Production and Industrial Development: The Case of Japanese Aircraft," in Chalmers Johnson, Laura D'Andrea Tyson, and John Zysman, eds., Politics and Productivity: The Real Story of Why Japan Works, pp.275-318. Camnbridge, Mass: Ballinger.

Sanger, David E. 1989. "Plutonium Shipment after 1992," The New York Times (October 12).

Sanger, David E. 1990a. "Japan's Oil Safety Net: Will It Hold?" The New York Times (August 9): D1,D18.

Sanger, David E. 1990b. "After Silence, Japan's Army Pushes for Armed Gulf Role," The New York Times (September 24): A1,A13.

Sanger, David E. 1992a. "U.S.-Japan Group to Explore Big Energy Field Off Siberia," The New York Times (January 29): D1,D5.

Sanger, David E. 1992b. "Japan's Troops May Sail, and the Fear is Mutual," The New York Times (June 21): E4.

Sasaki, Yoshitaka. 1991. "Abunai Garasu Zaiku" ("Dangerous Glass Artifact"), Sekai (November): 197-210.

Sase, Masamori. 1991. "Das japanische Militär-Streitkräfte unter ziviler Kontrolle," in Heinz Eberhard Maul, ed., Militärmacht Japan? Sicherheitspolitik und Streitkräfte, pp.127-62. Munich: Iudicium.

Sassa, Atsuyuki. 1991a. "Posto-Maruta ni okeru Nihon no Chii" ("Japan's Status in the Post-Malta Era"),Chuo Koron (March): 48-59.

Sassa, Atsuyuki. 1991b. "Nihon wa Wangan Senso e no Taio kara Nani o Manabu beki ka," ("What Should Japan Learn from Its Response to the Gulf War"), Shin Boei Ronshu 19,2 (September): 14-22.

Sassa, Atsuyuki. 1991c. "Shin no Anzen Hosho Taisei no Kakuritsu o Mezashite" ("Aiming at the Establishment of a Real Security Regime"), in Haruo Shimada, Yukio Okamoto, Kazuo Ijiri, and Masato Kimura, eds., Sekinin aru Heiwa-shugi o Kangaeru: Kokusai Shakai to Kyozon suru tame ni (Thoughts on Responsible Pacifism: To Co-exist with the International Society), pp. 54-65. Tokyo, Kyoto: PHP Kenkyujo.

Sato, Hideo. 1989. Taigai Seisaku (Foreign Policy). Tokyo: Tokyo Daigaku Shuppankai.

Sato, Isao. 1979. "Debate on Constitutional Amendment: Origins and Status," Law in Japan 12: 1-22.

Sato, Kazuo. 1991. "Japan's Resource Imports," in Solomon B. Levine and Koji Taira, eds., Japan's External Economic Relations: Japanese Perspectives, pp.76-89. The Annals of the American Academy of Political and Social Science, 513 (January).

Sato, Seizaburo. 1977. "The Foundations of Modern Japanese Foreign Policy," in Robert A. Scalapino, ed., The Foreign Policy of Modern Japan, pp.367-90. Berkeley: University of California Press.

Sato, Seizaburo. 1986. "Japan and Pacific-Asian Security," in Robert A. Scalapino, Seizaburo Sato, and Jusuf Wanandi, eds., Internal and External Security in Asia, pp.80-91. Berkeley, Institute of East Asian Studies, University of California, Research Papers and Policy Studies No.16.

Sato, Seizaburo. 1988. "The U.S.-Japan Political and Security Cooperation," Working Paper No.3. Tokyo: University of Tokyo, Komaba.

Sato, Seizaburo and Matsuzaki, Tetsuhisa. 1986. Jiminto Seiken (LDP Government). Tokyo: Chuo Koron-sha.

Satoh, Yukio. 1982. The Evolution of Japanese Security Policy, Adelphi Paper, no. 178. London: International Institute for Strategic Studies.

Saxonhouse, Gary R. 1977. "The World Economy and Japanese Foreign Economic Policy," in Robert A. Scalapino, ed., The Foreign Policy of Modern Japan, pp.281-318. Berkeley: University of California Press.

Sayle, Murray. 1983. "Sowing the Seeds of Suspicion," Far Eastern Economic Review 119,12 (March 24): 22-24.

Scalapino, Robert A., ed. 1977. The Foreign Policy of Modern Japan. Berkeley: University of California Press.

Schlesinger, Jacob M. 1991. "Kyocera Shows Japan's Key Military Role: Dominance in Ceramic Chip-Packaging Exemplifies Hi-Tech Trend," Asahi Evening News (February 5).

Schlesinger, Jacob M. and Pasztor, Andy. 1990. "U.S., Japan Neglect Defence-Trade Issue," The Asian Wall Street Journal (August 7).

Schmiegelow, Henrik and Schmiegelow, Michele. 1990. "How Japan Affects the International System," International Organization 44,4 (Autumn): 553-90.

Sekai Henshu-bu. 1987. "Gunji Taikou" Nihon: Doko made Gunji-ka saretaka (Japan the "Major Military Power": The Extent of Militarization). Tokyo: Iwanimi Shoten.

Sentaku. 1991. "Hajimaru 'Nichibei Gunji Gijutsu Domei' e no Taido" ("A Quickening of Moves toward a Japan-U.S. Military Technology Alliance"), (April): 96-99.

Seymour, Robert L. 1974-75. "Japan's Self-Defense: The Naganuma Case and Its Implications," Pacific Affairs 47,4 (Winter): 421-36.

Shibata, Hirofumi. 1983. "The Energy Crises and Japanese Response," Resources and Energy 5 (June): 129-54.

Shibusawa, Masahide. 1984. Japan and the Asian Pacific Region: Profile of Change. London: Croom Helm.

Shillony, Ben-Ami. 1981. Politics and Culture in Wartime Japan. Oxford: Clarendon Press.

Shimada, Toshihiko. 1983. "Designs on North China, 1933-1937," in James W. Morley, ed., The China Quagmire, pp.11-230. New York: Columbia University Press.

Shinobu, Seizaburo. 1988. "Taiheiyo Senso" to "Mo Hitotsu no Taiheiyo Senso": Dainiji Taisen ni okeru Nihon to Tonan Ajia ("The Pacific War" and "The Other Pacific War": Japan and Southeast Asia in the Second World War). Tokyo: Keiso Shobo.

Shiota, Ushio. 1987. " '1% Waku' Kekkai no 500 Nichi" ("500 Days of the Collapse of the '1% Ceiling'"), Chuo Koron (March): 140-55.

268

Shukan Yomiuri. 1990. "Kore ga Jiminto'Zoku' Giin da," ("These are the LDP'Zoku' Diet Members"), (August 26): 23.

Sigur, Gaston J. 1975. "Power, Politics and Defense," in James H. Buck, ed., The Modern Japanese Military System, pp.181-95. Beverly Hills: Sage.

Simon, Sheldon W. 1986. "Is There a Japanese Regional Security Model," Journal of Northeast Asian Studies 5,2 (Summer): 30-52.

Smethurst, Richard J. 1974. A Social Basis for Prewar Japanese Militarism: The Army and the Rural Community. Berkeley: University of California Press.

Smith, Gerard C., Vittorelli, Paolo, and Saeki, Kiichi. 1983. Trilateral Security: Defense and Arms Control Policies in the 1980s. The Triangle Papers No.26. New York: The Trilateral Commission.

Smith, Robert J. and Ramsey, Charles E. 1962. "Attitudes of Japanese High School Seniors Toward the Military," Public Opinion Quarterly 26 (Summer): 249-53.

Smith, Sheila. 1990. "Henyo suru Nichibei Anpo: Mittsu no Contekusuto no Kento" ("The Changing Security Arrangement between Japan and the U.S.: A Consideration of Three Contexts"), translated by Hideki Uemura, Kokusai Mondai 369 (December): 15-29.

Smith, Sheila. 1991. "The U.S.-Japan Alliance in 1991: Cold-War Dynamics and Postwar Legacies," Japan Review of International Affairs 5 (special issue): 63-81.

Sneider, Daniel. 1986. "In the Name of'Self-Defence'," The Daily Yomiuri (July 13): 5.

Sneider, Richard L. 1982. U.S.-Japanese Security Relations: A Historical Perspective. New York: Columbia University, Occasional Papers of the East Asian Institute, Toyota Research Program.

Söderberg, Marie. 1986. Japan's Military Export Policy. Stockholm: Institute of Oriental Languages, Department of Japanese and Korean Studies.

Sorenson, Jay B. 1975. Japanese Policy and Nuclear Arms. n.p. American-Asian Educational Exchange.

Sorifu Koho-shitsu. 1991. "Jieitai Boei Mondai" ("The Issues Concerning SDF and Defense"), in Sorifu Koho-shitsu, ed., Gekkan Yoron Chosa 23,8 (August): 2-32.

Spaulding, Robert M., Jr. 1970. "Japan's 'New Bureaucrats,' 1932-45," in George M. Wilson, ed., Crisis Politics in Prewar Japan, pp.51-70. Tokyo: Sophia University Press.

Spaulding, Robert M., Jr. 1971. "The Bureaucracy as a Political Force, 1920-45," in James W. Morley, ed., Dilemmas of Growth in Prewar Japan, pp.33-80. Princeton: Princeton University Press.

Steinert, Marlis G. 1981. Le Japon en quete d'une politique etrangere. Geneva: Institut Universitaire de Hautes Etudes Internationales, Centre Asiatique.

Stockwin, J.A.A. 1982. Japan: Divided Politics in a Growth Economy, second edition. London: Weidenfeld and Nicolson.

Stockwin, J.A.A. 1988. "Parties, Politicians and the Political System," in J.A.A. Stockwin, et al., eds., Dynamic and Immobilist Politics in Japan, pp.22-53. Honolulu: University of Hawaii Press.

Stokes, Henry Scott. 1981a. "Tokyo Tries to Divert Nuclear Arms Uproar," The New York Times (May 20): A12.

Stokes, Henry Scott. 1981b. "Japan's Nuclear Furor," The New York Times (June 6): A2.

Storry, Richard. 1957. The Double Patriots: A Study of Japanese Nationalism. Boston: Houghton Mifflin.

Storry, Richard. 1979. Japan and the Decline of the West in Asia 1894-1943. New York: Macmillan.

Storry, Richard. 1985. A History of Modern Japan. London: Penguin.

Sutter, Robert G. 1982. Dealing with Japan: Policy Approaches for a Troubled Alliance. Washington, D.C.: Congressional Research Service, Report No. 82-97F (May 28).

Suzuki, Shigeru. 1985. Nihon no Enerugi Kaihatsu Seisaku (Japan's Energy Development Policy). Kyoto: Mineruva Shobo.

Takahara, Takao. 1992a. "U.S.-Japanese Postwar Military Relations: Towards a Security Community via Asymmetrical Integration," paper originally prepared for the Symposium "The New Europe and the World", Western Michigan University, March 23-24, 1992.

Takahara, Takao. 1992b. "Nihon no'Hikaku Seisaku' to Okinawa Henkan, Josetsu" ("Japan's'Non-nuclear Policy' and Okinawa Reversion: An Introduction"), Kokusaigaku Kenkyu (Meiji Gakuin University) 9 (March): 35-49.

Takamine, Iwao. 1991. "Kokuren Heiwa Kyoryoku Hoan de Ugomeku Zoku Giin," ("Tribe Diet Members Maneuvering over the U.N. Peace Cooperation Bill"), Zaikai Tenbo (January): 240-43.

Takamiya, Tahei. 1971. Jungyaku no Showa-shi (History of Obedience and Disobedience in Showa Era), enlarged edition. Tokyo: Hara Shobo.

Takase, Shoji. 1985. "What'Star Wars' Means to Japan," Japan Quarterly (July-September): 240-47.

Takeda, Kiyoko. 1988. The Dual-Image of the Japanese Emperor. New York: New York University Press.

Tamamoto, Masaru. 1990. "Japan's Search for a World Role," World Policy Journal 7,3 (Summer): 493-520.

Tamamoto, Masaru. 1990-91. "Trial of an Ideal: Japan's Debate over the Gulf Crisis," World Policy Journal 8,1 (Winter): 89-106.

Tanaka, Akihiko. 1990. "Japan's Security Policy in the 1990s," paper prepared for delivery at the Eighth Shimoda Conference, November 16-17.

Tanaka, Shoko. 1986. Post-War Japanese Resource Policies and Strategies: The Case of Southeast Asia. Ithaca, Cornell University, China-Japan Program, East Asian Papers Series, No.43.

Tanaka, Shunichi. 1975. Nihon Senso Keizai Hishi (Secret History of Japan's War Economy). Tokyo: Computer Eiji-sha.

Tanaka, Tadashi. 1991. "Kokuren Heiwa Iji Katsudo to Nihon no Sanka-Kyoryoku" ("U.N. Peacekeeping Operations and Japan's Participation and Cooperation"), Hogaku Seminar 443 (November): 36-41.

Tanin, O. and Yohan, E. 1934. Militarism and Fascism in Japan. New York: International Publishers.

Taoka, Shunji. 1991. "Igai ni Ooi Yuutsunaru Hyojo" ("Unexpectedly Many Gloomy Faces"), AERA (December 3): 16-17.

Taoka, Shunji and Hanochi, Sakae. 1991. " 'Nomiso' Kawaruka Pinchi no Gaimusho" ("Will the 'Brain' Change at MOFA in a Pinch?"), AERA (June 11): 24-26.

Titus, David Anson. 1974. Palace and Politics in Prewar Japan. New York: Columbia University Press.

Todd, Daniel. 1988. Defense Industries: A Global Perspective. London: Routledge.

Tokinoya, Atsushi. 1986. The Japan-US Alliance: A Japanese Perspective. London: International Institute for Strategic Studies.

Toland, John. 1970. The Rising Sun: The Decline and Fall of the Japanese Empire 1936-1945. New York: Random House.

Tora, Shunji. 1991. "SDF Faces Double Crisis," Asahi Evening News (December 8).

Tow, William T. 1982. "U.S. Alliance Policies and Asian-Pacific Security: A Transregional Approach," in William T. Tow and William R. Feeney, eds., U.S. Foreign Policy and Asian-Pacific Security: A Transregional Approach, pp.17-67. Boulder: Westview Press.

Tow, William T. 1983. "U.S.-Japan Military Technology Transfers: Collaboration or Conflict?" Journal of Northeast Asian Studies 2,4 (December): 3-23.

Tow, William T. 1986. "Japan: Security Role and Continuing Policy Debates," in Young Whan Kihl and Lawrence E. Grinter, eds., Asian-Pacific Security: Emerging Challenges and Responses, pp.125-49. Boulder: Lynne Rienner.

Tow, William T. 1987. "Japan, China, and the United States: Strategic Concepts and High Technology," in Ronald A. Morse, ed., Option 2000: Politics and High Technology in Japan's Defense and Strategic Future, pp.23-46. Washington D.C.: Woodrow Wilson International Center for Scholars, Asia Program.

Toyoda, Toshiyuki. 1985. "Japan's Policies since 1945," Bulletin of the Atomic Scientists, 41,7 (August): 57-62.

Trimberger, Ellen Kay. 1978. Revolutions from Above: Military Bureaucrats and Modernization in Japan, Turkey, Egypt, and Peru. New Brunswick, N.J.: Transaction Books.

Tsuneishi, Keiichi. 1990. "Seijika no Dokuso de Sutato shita Genshiryoku Kaihatsu: Genshiryoku Taisei no Kakuritsu" ("Atomic Energy Development Started under the Initiative of Politicians: The Forming of the Atomic Energy Regime"), Ekonomisuto (July 10): 108-09.

Tsunoda, Jun. 1987. Seiji to Gunji: Meiji, Taisho, Showa Shoki no Nihon (Politics and Military Affairs: Japan in the Meiji, Taisho, and Early Showa Periods), and Early Showa Periods). Tokyo: Kofusha Shuppan.

Tsurumi, Kazuko. 1970. Social Change and the Individual: Japan Before and After Defeat in World War II. Princeton: Princeton University Press.

Tsurutani, Taketsugu. 1980. "The Security Debate," in James M. Roherty, ed., Defense Policy Formation: Towards Comparative Analysis, pp.175-94. Durham, N.C.: Carolina Academic Press.

Tsurutani, Taketsugu. 1981. "Japan's Security, Defense Responsibilitites, and Capabilities," Orbis 25,1 (Spring): 89-106.

Tsushosangyosho Daijin Kanbo. 1988. Nippon no Sentaku (Japan's Choices). Tokyo, June.

Tsutsui, Kiyotada. 1984. Showa-ki Nihon no Kozo (The Structure of Japan in the Showa Period). Tokyo: Yuhikaku.

Tyler, Patrick E. 1992. "Pentagon Drops Goal of Blocking New Superpowers," The New York Times (May 24): A1,A14.

Umegaki, Michio. 1988. "The Politics of Japanese Defense," in Stephen P. Gibert, ed., Security in Northeast Asia: Approaching the Pacific Century, pp.53-74. Boulder: Westview Press.

Umemoto, Tetsuya. 1985a. "Arms and Alliance in Japanese Public Opinion," Ph.d. dissertation, Princeton University.

Umemoto, Tetsuya. 1985b. "Boei Seisaku no Henka to Keizokusei" ("Changes and Continuity in Defense Policy") in Akio Watanabe, ed., Sengo Nihon no Taigai Seisaku: Kokusai Kankei no Henyo to Nihon no Yakuwari (Foreign Policy of Postwar Japan: The Transformation of International Relations and the Role of Japan), pp.315-38. Tokyo: Yuhikaku.

Umemoto, Tetsuya. 1988. "Comprehensive Security and the Evolution of the Japanese Security Posture," in Robert A. Scalapino, Seizaburo Sato, Jusuf Wanandi, and Sung-joo Han, eds., Asian Security Issues: Regional and Global, pp.28-49. Berkeley: University of California, Institute of East Asian Studies, Research Papers and Policy Studies No.26.

Umemoto, Tetsuya. 1989. "Anzen Hosho" ("Security"), in Tadashi Aruga, et al., eds., Nihon no Gaiko: Koza Kokusai Seiji, Vol.4 (Japanese Diplomacy: Handbook of International Politics, Vol.4), pp.127-54. Tokyo: Tokyo Daigaku Shuppankai.

Upham, Frank K. 1987. Law and Social Change in Postwar Japan. Cambridge, Mass.: Harvard University Press.

U.S. Congress, Office of Technology Assessment. 1988. The Defense Technology Base: Introduction and Overview--A Special Report. OTA-ISC 374. Washington D.C.: U.S. Government Printing Office (March).

U.S. Congress, Office of Technology Assessment. 1989. Holding the Edge: Maintaining the Defense Technology Base. OTA-ISC-420. Washington D.C.: Government Printing Office (April).

U.S. Congress, Office of Technology Assessment. 1990. Arming our Allies: Cooperation and Competition in Defense Technology. OTA-ISC-449. Washington D.C.: Government Printing Office (May).

U.S. Congress, Office of Technology Assessment. 1991. Global Arms Trade, OTA-ISC-460. Washington D.C.: U.S. Government Printing Office (June).

Usui, Katsumi. 1973. "The Role of the Foreign Ministry," in Dorothy Borg and Shumpei Okamoto, eds., Pearl Harbor as History: Japanese-American Relations, 1931-1941, pp.127-48. New York: Columbia University Press.

Usui, Katsumi. 1983. "The Politics of War, 1937-1941," in James W. Morley, ed., The China Quagmire, pp. 309-435. New York: Columbia University Press.

Van de Velde, James R. 1987. "Article Nine of the Postwar Japanese Constitution: Codified Ambiguity," Journal of Northeast Asian Studies 6,1: 26-45.

Van de Velde, James R. 1988a. "Japan's Emergence into Western Security Doctrine: U.S.-Japan Defense Cooperation 1976-1986," Ph.D. dissertation, Fletcher School of Law and Diplomacy, Tufts University.

Van de Velde, James R. 1988b. "Japan's Nuclear Umbrella: U.S. Extended Nuclear Deterrence for Japan," Journal of Northeast Asian Studies 7,1 (Winter): 16-46.

Vernon, Raymond. 1983. Two Hungry Giants: The United States and Japan in the Quest for Oil and Ores. Cambridge, Mass.: Harvard University Press.

Vogel, Steven K. 1984. A New Direction in Japanese Defense Policy: Views from the LDP Diet Members. Occasional Papers/ Reprint Series in Contemporary Asian Studies, University of Maryland School of Law.

Vogel, Steven K. 1989. Japanese High Technology, Politics, and Power. Berkeley Roundtable on the International Economy, Research Paper #2 (March).

Vogel, Steven K. 1990. "The United States and Japan: Technological Rivalry and Military Alliance," paper prepared for presentation for the Institute for Global Conflict and Cooperation (IGCC) Conference, "Beyond the Cold War in the Pacific," San Diego, CA, June 7-9, 1990.

Vogel, Steven K. 1991. "The Power Behind 'Spin-Ons': The Military Implications of Japan's Commercial Technology," University of California Berkeley, Institute of International Studies, The Berkeley Roundtable on the International Economy, Working Paper 41 (April).

Vollmer, Charles D. 1991. "US Defense Trade and the Global Industrial Base: Japan Case Study." Unpublished manuscript.

Von Wolferen, Karel. 1990. "Why Militarism Still Haunts Japan," The New York Times (December 12): A23.

Von Wolferen, Karel. 1991. "No Brakes, No Compass." The National Interest 25 (Fall): 26-35.

Wada, Hideo. 1976. "Decisions under Article 9 of the Constitution--the Sunakawa, Eniwa and Naganuma Decisions," Law in Japan 9: 117-28.

Watanabe, Akio. 1977a. "Nihon no Taigai Seisaku Keisei no Kiko to Katei" ("Structures and Processes in Japanese Foreign Policymaking"), in Chihiro Hosoya and Joji Watanuki, eds., Taigai Seisaku Kettei Katei no Nichibei Hikaku (A Comparison of Japanese and U.S. Foreign Policy Decision Processes), pp.23-58. Tokyo: Tokyo Daigaku Shuppankai.

Watanabe, Akio. 1977b. "Japanese Public Opinion and Foreign Affairs: 1964-1973," in Robert A. Scalapino, ed., The Foreign Policy of Modern Japan, pp.105-46. Berkeley: University of California Press.

Watanabe, Akio. 1989a. "Nihon no Gaiko" ("Japanese Diplomacy"), in Tadashi Aruga, et al., eds., Nihon no Gaiko: Koza Kokusai Seiji, Vol.4 (Japanese Diplomacy: Handbook of International Politics, Vol.4), pp.1-15. Tokyo: Tokyo Daigaku Shuppankai.

Watanabe, Akio. 1989b. "Southeast Asia in U.S.-Japanese Relations," in Akira Iriye and Warren I. Cohen, eds., The United States and Japan in the Postwar World, pp. 80-95. Lexington, University of Kentucky Press.

Watanabe, Akio. 1991. "Japan's Foreign Policy-Making Process," paper deliverd at the IISA/JIIA Conference on Japan's Strategic Priorities in the 1990s, Keidanren Gotenba House, November 18-20.

Watanabe, Yozo. 1991. Nichibei Anpo Taisei to Nihon-koku Kenpo (The Japan-U.S. Security Regime and the Constitution of Japan). Tokyo: Rodo Junpo-sha.

Watanuki, Joji. 1973. "Contemporary Japanese Perceptions of International Society," Tokyo, Sophia University, Institute of International Relations, Series A-13.

Watanuki, Joji. 1974. "Contemporary Japanese Perceptions of International Society," Tokyo, Sophia University, Institute of International Relations, Series A-19.

Watts, Anthony J. and Gordon, Brian G. 1971. The Imperial Japanese Navy. Garden City: Doubleday.

Webb, Herschel. 1965. "The Development of an Orthodox Attitude Toward the Imperial Institution in the Ninteenth Century," in Marius B. Jansen, ed., Changing Japanese Attitudes Toward Modernization, pp.167-91. Princeton, N.J.: Princeton University Press.

Weinstein, Franklin B. 1978. U.S.-Japan Relations and the Security of East Asia: The Next Decade. Boulder: Westview Press.

Weinstein, Martin E. 1971. Japan's Postwar Defense Policy, 1947-1968. New York: Columbia University.

Weinstein, Martin E. 1974. "Japan's Defense Policy and the Self-Defense Forces," in Frank B. Horton, Anthony C. Rogerson, and Edward L. Warner, eds., Comparative Defense Policy, pp.363-75. Baltimore: Johns Hopkins University Press.

Weinstein, Martin E. 1975. "The Evolution of the Japan Self-Defense Forces," in James H. Buck, ed., The Modern Japanese Military System, pp.41-63. Beverly Hills: Sage.

Weinstein, Martin E. 1979. "Trends in Japanese Foreign and Defense Politics," in William J. Barnds, ed., Japan and the United States: Challenges and Opportunities, pp.155-89. New York: New York University Press.

Weinstein, Martin E. 1982a. "Japan's Defense Policy and the May 1981 Summit," Journal of Northeast Asian Studies 1,1 (March): 23-33.

Weinstein, Martin E., ed. 1982b. Northeast Asian Security after Vietnam. Urbana: University of Illinois Press.

Weinstein, Martin E. 1983. "Japan: External Security Guarantees and the Rearmament Questions," in Raju G.C. Thomas, ed., The Great Power Triangle and Asian Security, pp.173-87. Lexington, Mass.: D.C. Heath.

Weinstein, Martin E. 1988. "Trade Problems and U.S.-Japanese Security Cooperation," The Washington Quarterly 11,1: 19-33.

Whiting, Allen S. 1982. "Prospects for Japanese Defense Policy," Asian Survey 22 (November): 1135-45.

Wilson, George M. 1968. "A New Look at the Problem of Japanese Fascism," Comparative Studies in Society and History 10,4 (July): 401-13.

Wray, Harold J. 1973. "A Study of Contrasts: Japanese School Textbooks of 1903 and 1941-5," Monumenta Nipponica 28,1 (Spring): 68-86.

Wu, Yuan-Li. 1977. Japan's Search for Oil: A Case Study on Economic Nationalism and International Security. Stanford: Hoover Institution Press.

Yager, Joseph. 1984. The Energy Balance in Northeast Asia. Washington, D.C.: The Brookings Institution.

Yamamura, Katsuro. 1973. "The Role of the Finance Ministry," translated by Mitsuko Iriye, in Dorothy Borg and Shumpei Okamoto, eds., Pearl Harbor as History: Japanese-American Relations, 1931-1941, pp.287-302. New York: Columbia University Press.

Yamamura, Kozo. 1989. "Shedding History's Inertia: The U.S.-Japanese Alliance in a Changed World," in John H. Makin and Donald C. Hellmann, eds., Sharing World Leadership? A New Era for America and Japan, pp.203-36. Washington, D.C.: American Enterprise Institute.

Yamauchi, Saburo. 1991. "Keikicho Jinji de Kudeta" ("A Coup in the EPA Personnel Decision"), Gekkan Asahi (July): 100.

Yanaga, Chitoshi. 1968. Big Business in Japanese Politics. New Haven: Yale University Press.

Yoshihara, Koichiro. 1988. Nihon no Heiki Sangyo (Japan's Arms Industry). Tokyo: Shakai Shiso-sha.

Yoshioka, Hitoshi. 1990. "Nihon no Uchu Kaihatsushi no Ichi Danmen" ("An Aspect of the History of Space Development in Japan"), Rekishi-gaku Chiri-gaku Nempo (Kyushu University) 14: 105-45.

Yoshitsu, Michael M. 1984. Caught in the Middle East. Lexington, Mass.: D.C. Heath.

Yui, Masaomi. 1989. Guntai Heishi (Military, Soldiers). Tokyo: Iwanami Shoten.

Ziegler, J. Nicholas. 1992. "Cross-National Comparisons," in John Alic, Lewis Branscomb, Harvey Brooks, Ashton Carter, and Gerald Epstein, eds., Beyond Spin-Off: Military and Commercial Technologies in a Changing World, pp.209-47. Boston: Harvard Business School Press.

Appendix
Table A-1: Important Court Rulings Concerning the SDF and Article 9 of the Constitution

1. The Suzuki Case

On October 8, 1952 the Secretary-General of the Left Socialist Party, Mosaburo Suzuki, appealed to the Supreme Court to declare unconstitutional the establishment of the National Police Reserve. The Court held that Japanese courts have the power only to rule on cases claiming a specific violation of rights, but not on cases presented in abstract.

2. The Sunakawa Case

Japanese and American authorities agreed to construct an extended runway at the U.S. Tachikawa air base. The Japanese government was responsible for surveying the additional land required for the expansion. Demonstrators were arrested and charged with illegally trespassing on the US base. The Tokyo District Court, presided over by Judge Akio Date, tried the case and on March 30, 1959 acquitted the defendants on the grounds that the Special Criminal Law under which they had been charged was "illegally enacted in the implementation of the Japan-U.S. Security Treaty of 1951, which is unconstitutional because it provides for the stationing of U.S. forces in Japan, and the said forces constituted war potential which is forbidden by Article 9." The court held that to find the accused guilty would contravene Article 31 of the Constitution which provides that "no person shall suffer a criminal penalty except according to procedure established by law." The court's reasoning focused on the following points:

(a) Although Article 9 does not deny the right to self-defense, it does not permit the maintenance of war potential for the purposes of self-defense.

(b) The first paragraph of Article 9 regards war as a criminal act and states that Japan will depend on military peace-keeping measures and an international police force under the Security Council as a last resort to maintain the security and survival of Japan.

281

(c) The stationing of American troops in Japan under the Security Treaty, however, is different from the stationing of troops under the command of the United Nations to defend Japan against military attack. American troops will be utilized when in the judgment of the U.S. government they are necessary to maintain the peace and security in the Far East. Thus, there is the risk that Japan could be drawn into a military conflict in which Japan has no direct connection. This is contrary to the spirit of the Constitution.

(d) Although Japan has no control or command over American troops stationed in Japan and although the United States has no obligation to defend Japan, considering the practical utility of the treaty, it is likely that American troops will be used to defend Japan. Therefore, the consent of the Japanese government to the stationing of American troops in Japan violates Article 9's prohibition of the maintenance of war potential. The stationing of US forces in Japan cannot be allowed under the Constitution.

On December 16, 1959, the Supreme Court reversed the judgement of the Tokyo Court. The Supreme Court argued that:

(a) The Constitution renounces neither the inherent right of a sovereign nation to self-defense nor demands defenselessness and non-resistance.

(b) As long as the collective security function of the UN is insufficient for Japan's protection, a security agreement concluded with another country does not contradict the preamble's pacifism.

(c) Permitting US forces to be based in Japan does not contradict the provision of Article 9, paragraph 2 that war potential will never be maintained inside Japan, since Japan cannot be considered as maintaining a foreign military force over which it exercises no right of command or control.

(d) Highly political questions involving a treaty with a foreign power are not a proper subject for judicial review unless they are obviously unconstitutional. Such unconstitutionality is not obvious in the case of the Japan-U.S. Security Treaty.

3. The Eniwa Case

In December 1962 the Nozaki brothers, who managed a farm in the vicinity of the SDF training grounds of Eniwa, Hokkaido, cut a telephone wire used to signal firing instructions to the training ground. They were charged under Article 121 of the SDF Law for damaging articles used in connection with military defense. On March 29, 1967 the Sapporo District Court acquitted the defendants. The court ruled that the telephone wire in question did not fall within the category of implements used for military defense as stated in Article 121 of the SDF Law.

4. The Sakane Case

In 1960 large-scale demonstrations opposed the manner in which Prime Minister Nobusuke Kishi handled the ratification of the Japan-U.S. Security Treaty. As part of this series of demonstrations, court employees held a political meeting at the Sendai courthouse on June 4, 1960. The accused were officials of both the court workers union and other unions. They were charged with incitement of public employees to illegal political acts. At issue was the constitutionality of certain restrictions imposed on the political activities of public employees under the National Public Employee Law, the legal propriety of penalties for engaging in such activities, and the constitutionality of the 1960 Mutual Security Treaty under the Constitution's Article 9.

In ruling on April 2, 1969 on the appeal related to Article 9 of the Constitution and the constitutionality of the Japan-U.S. Security Treaty, the Supreme Court stated that in "rendering legal judgment as to the unconstitutionality of such matters as the new Security Treaty, which are of a highly political nature with an important relationship to the basis of Japan's existence as a sovereign nation, the judicial courts have need of circumspection; so long as that Treaty is not deemed to be clearly contrary to provisions of the Constitution, it should not unnecessarily be held unconstitutional and invalid. Furthermore, it is clear in light of the intent of precedent of the Grand Bench of the present Court that the new Security Treaty is not deemed to be clearly unconstitutional as violating the intent of Article 9, Article 98, paragraph 2, and the Preamble of the Constitution."

5. The Naganuma Case

On June 12, 1969 the Chief of the Sapporo Defense Facilities Office presented to the Governor of Hokkaido a petition directed at the Ministry of Agriculture and Forestry requesting the cancellation of the Forest Preserve Designation of a section located in the Township of Naganuma of the Mt. Umaoi National Forest in Hokkaido. The purpose of the request was to permit construction of an Air SDF Nike-Zeus missile base and connecting roads. Since 1897, extensive areas of the forest had been protected as a forest preserve for the purpose of water resource conservation.

On July 7, 1969 the Ministry of Agriculture and Forestry announced cancellation of the designation pursuant to article 26(2) of the Forest Law which allows the Ministry of Agriculture and Forestry to cancel the Forest Preserve Designation for reasons of public interests. 271 local residents who opposed the base filed suit in Sapporo District Court to seek an injunction against the government's attempts to change the status of the forest. The plaintiffs claimed that the establishment of a missile site in the national forest preserve violates the Forestry Law, which specifies that such a reclassification could only be made in the public interest. The plaintiffs also contended that construction of a missile base would enhance erosion and destroy flood controls now provided by the forest. At the initial hearing on August 22, 1969, the government responded that the reclassification of the forest was in the public interest. The government would establish dams and other facilities to protect the areas against floods. A delay in the construction of the missile base would impair the defense capabilities of the nation. On August 22, 1969 the Sapporo District Court, presided over by Judge Shigeo Fukushima, issued an injunction to stop the construction of the site. The government filed an appeal with the Sapporo High Court.

On January 23, 1970 the Sapporo High Court overruled the District Court's injunction. The court allowed the government to reclassify the forest and begin with the construction of the base. The court held that the government's proposed flood control measures were adequate to cope with dangerous and serious flooding.

On September 7, 1973 the Sapporo District Court revoked the disposition cancelling the Forest Preserve Designation on the grounds that the construction of the missile base did not constitute the required "public interest." The Japanese SDF as presently constituted and the laws under which they exist, violate Article 9 of the Constitution. The court argued:

(a) Whether a law conforms with the principles of the Peace Constitution must be examined and decided from the point of view of the criterion the Minister of Forestry and Agriculture uses to determine whether to revoke the status of the forest preserve, the public good. The court defined "war potential" in Article 9 to mean "an organization of men and material organized for the purpose of engaging by force in military operations against an enemy."

(b) The court held that the Constitution's "three fundamental principles" of pacifism, democracy, and respect for fundamental human rights "must be treated as an integrated whole." Looking at the "the right to live in peace" in the second paragraph of the Preamble, the court argued that it refers not simply to the indirect consequential benefit of the people living in peace as a result of the government's service but also to the maintenance of the concept of pacifism.

(c) The court held that Japan possesses a right to self-defense. This right, however, is not necessarily exercised through military might. Other channels for self-defense include (1) the police, whose duty it is to maintain domestic order and who can, in an emergency, prevent an invasion; (2) mass insurrection of an armed populace opposing an invasion; (3) non-military self-defense channelled through intelligence and efforts of the people; and (4) the United Nations, which has undertaken timely police action in many international conflicts.

On August 5, 1976 the Sapporo High Court decided the Naganuma Case. It held that under the Court Organization Law and the Administrative Case Litigation Law, the plaintiffs could bring an administrative suit against the government only if they have the requisite legal standing to sue. This requirement is met only when the challenged action by the government actually infringes or can be expected to infringe a right under substantive law or an interest protected by law. Although the interest of the plaintiffs in preserving the watershed protected by the cancelled forest designation for farming, crops and flood control is sufficiently concrete and individual, this interest is cancelled by new water conservation facilities that the government has built. Thus the plaintiffs no longer have standing to sue. The court also held that under the "political question" doctrine, the issue of the constitutionality of the SDF is not justiciable unless the SDF are in apparent violation of Article 9.

On September 9, 1982 the Supreme Court stated that the appellants do not possess a legal interest (standing) to sue.

6. The Konishi Case

An SDF warrant officer, Makoto Konishi, was charged under the SDF Law for inciting sabotage of training. On February 22, 1975 the Niigata District Court found him not guilty. According to the sentence, the proof of the crime remained incomplete due to the unwillingness of the JDA to provide the court with necessary evidence. The court did not touch on the claim by the defense that the SDF were unconstitutional. The case was referred back to the district court by the Tokyo High Court on January 31, 1977. It stated that the lower court failed to exhaust the available means for gathering evidence in the case. On March 27, 1981 the Niigata District Court, reasoning that Konishi's actions did not constitute inciting of sabotage, again found him not guilty. It did not judge on the constitutionality of the SDF. The prosecution decided not to appeal the case.

7. The Hyakuri Base Case

Ruling on a suit questioning the constitutionality of the Hyakuri Base, on February 17, 1977 the Mito District Court handed down a ruling that in the event of foreign military attack, the right to self-defense and the preparation for defensive self-defense were not unconstitutional. The plaintiff appealed the decision to the High Court.

On July 7, 1981 the Tokyo High Court stated that it can rule on the appeal without addressing the constitutional issues raised. Since there was no evidence that a basic human right of the plaintiff has been or will be violated, the court would not rule on the question related to Article 9 of the Constitution.

On June 21, 1989 the Supreme Court ruled against the plaintiff without judging on the constitutionality of the SDF.

8. The Enshrinement of a Deceased SDF Officer Case

An SDF officer died while on active duty, and upon request by a prefectural veterans association, he was enshrined over the protest of his Christian widow. She filed a suit, maintaining that the SDF were involved in making the request, and that the SDF's action violated the constitutional ban on religious activities by the state. She asked the court to revoke the request and to award her compensation for damages caused by the state's unconstitutional act. On March 22, 1979 the Yamaguchi District Court ruled that the SDF violated the constitution and the widow's right to freedom of religion and awarded her compensation. On June 1, 1982 the Hiroshima High Court upheld the lower court's judgment that the SDF's act of requesting the enshrinement of the officer was unconstitutional. But on June 1, 1988 the Supreme Court ruled that the SDF were not substantively involved in making the request to the shrine. It also claimed that, in general, a state request for enshrinement does not constitute state involvement in religious activities. Furthermore, according to the court's decision, even if the state engages in religious activities, affected citizens do not necessarily have a right to redress under the principles of private law.

9. The Niijima Missile Firing Range Case

Local residents claimed that a site on which missile test firing facilities were constructed by the JDA was not town property but a traditional commonage of local residents. On March 22, 1978 the Tokyo District Court found in favor of the residents. But the Tokyo High Court rejected the right of commonage, and ruled that whether or not development and possession of modern weapons violated Article 9 was a "political question" on which the courts had no authority to rule. On January 22, 1982 the Supreme Court did not touch on the constitutionality of Article 9 since it was not raised in the appeal of the residents and it rejected the claim that a right of commonage existed in this case.

10. The Yokota Base Case

Residents living in the vicinity of Yokota air base filed a suit against the noise of American aircraft, including night flights, demanding compensation for past and future damages. On July 13, 1981, the Tokyo District Court at Hachioji ruled that the management and operation of the base was a matter of the U.S. military and that filing a suit against the Japanese government was unreasonable. The prohibition of night flights was a matter of diplomatic negotiations between the US and Japanese governments and thus a political matter on which the court could not rule. But the court ruled also that the government must pay to 114 local residents 22.715 million yen for past damages. The Tokyo High Court on July 15, 1987 upheld the District Court decision, while increasing the compensation for past damages.

11. The Atsugi Base Case

Atsugi base is operated jointly by the MSDF and the U.S. Navy. The Yokohama District Court ruled on October 20, 1982 on a suit demanding a flight ban as well as compensation. Arguing that SDF flights were a part of public administration and that U.S. flights were implementing the Security Treaty, the court dismissed the suit as not appropriate for a civil case. But the court awarded 80 residents a total of 36.24 million yen compensation for past damages. On April 9, 1986 the Tokyo High Court ruled that a flight ban was not within its purview, and also denied the residents compensation for past damages.

12. The Komatsu Base Case

Residents living in the vicinity of Komatsu air base filed a suit asking for a ban on night flights by U.S. and Japanese military aircraft as well as compensation for damages. The residents claimed the SDF to be unconstitutional. On March 13, 1991 the Kanazawa District Court ruled against the flight ban, while awarding compensation to 270 residents for past damages. But it did not touch on the issue of the constitutionality of the SDF.

CORNELL EAST ASIA SERIES

For ordering information, please contact the *Cornell East Asia Series*,
East Asia Program, Cornell University, 140 Uris Hall, Ithaca, NY
14853-7601 USA, (607) 255-6222.